The Papacy,
the Jews,
and the
Holocaust

Frank J. Coppa

The Papacy, the Jews, and the Holocaust

The Catholic University of
America Press · Washington, D.C.

LIBRARY OF CONGRESS CATALOGING-IN-PUBLICATION DATA
Coppa, Frank J.
    The papacy, the Jews, and the Holocaust / Frank J. Coppa.
        p. cm.
    Includes bibliographical references and index.
    ISBN-13: 978-0-8132-1449-8 (cloth : alk. paper)
    ISBN-10: 0-8132-1449-1 (cloth : alk. paper)
        1. Catholic Church—Relations—Judaism.   2. Judaism—
Relations—Catholic Church.   3. Christianity and antisemitism—
History.   4. Papacy—History.   I. Title.
BM535.C636 2006
262´.13—dc22   2005018125

CONTENTS

INTRODUCTION

The Papacy and the Jews between History and Polemic

When the first Pope set foot in Rome, the Jews were

already there. *

THE PAPACY, OR OFFICE OF THE BISHOP OF ROME, has long played a crucial role in Western civilization, exercising a unique role in Catholicism and generating widespread interest.[1] Some writers, linking the cross and the swastika, have seen its history and theology as steeped in hostility toward the Jews and as influencing what one writer has called "the longest hatred," anti-Semitism.[2] In the post–World War II era, and increasingly since 1963, there has been renewed scrutiny of Rome's alleged "pathological" aversion to Jews, which forms part of the literature on Jewish-Christian relations.[3] My inquiry focused initially on Pius XII's stance during the Holocaust, but it

---

* Sam Waagenaar, *The Pope's Jews* (La Salle, Ill.: Open Court, 1974), 11.

1. Some studies of the papacy are scholarly, others more journalistic. A few, such as Luigi Marinelli's *Via col vento in Vaticano* (1999), which has delved into the dark side of the Vatican, supposedly exposing the intrigues and plots therein, has seen its author summoned before the Roman rota. Likewise critical is the recent study by Garry Wills, whose title *Papal Sin: Structures of Deceit* (2000), reveals its message. Others, such as Richard P. McBrien's *Lives of the Popes: The Pontiffs from St. Peter to John Paul II* (1997), Eamon Duffy's *Saints and Sinners: A History of the Popes* (1997), P. G. Maxwell-Stuart's *Chronicle of the Popes: A Reign-by-Reign Record of the Papacy from St. Peter to the Present* (1997), and Frank J. Coppa's *Encyclopedia of the Vatican and Papacy* (1999) have not caused as much controversy. While these latter studies have concentrated more on the popes than on the papacy, the work of Thomas J. Reese, S.J., *Inside the Vatican: The Politics and Organization of the Catholic Church* (1996), focuses on the politics and organization of the Catholic Church, as its subtitle indicates.

2. Robert S. Wistrich, *Antisemitism: The Longest Hatred* (New York: Schocken Books, 1991), 3–42.

3. A good, though dated, review of this historiography is found in James E. Wood Jr., "A Selective and Annotated Bibliography on Jewish-Christian Relations," *JCS* 13 (spring 1971): 317–40. A more recent survey of Jewish-Christian relations will be found in the thirty-two essays tracing this relationship from the ancient world to the present found in *Christianity and Judaism: Papers Read at the 1991 Summer Meeting and the 1992 Winter Meeting of the Ecclesiastical History Society* (Cambridge, Mass: Blackwell, 1992).

has expanded to encompass the broader question of the papacy and the Jews. Indeed, the troubled relationship between the two has provoked much controversy over the last four decades. On the one hand, controversy has been generated by the attempt to trace the roots of the Holocaust and to assign responsibility. On the other hand, it has been fueled by the conflict within the Church between liberals and conservatives, who diverge on John XXIII's *aggiornamento* and the innovations produced by the Second Vatican Council (1962–65). As early as the nineteenth century Johann von Döllinger noted that Jews and liberal Catholics had a common enemy in papal autocracy. Some Catholics, deeming the papacy essential, reject all criticism of the institution, while others, acknowledging its centrality, insist that it be purged of errors and excesses.[4]

These developments reinforced each other in the early 1960s, when the discussions of the Second Vatican Council coincided with the publication of Rolf Hochhuth's sensational play, which criticized the "silence" of Pius XII during the mass murder of European Jews during World War II. Others chimed in that the papacy was guilty of sins of commission as well as those of omission. It has even been suggested that the Vatican has countered Hochhuth's and others' critique of Pius XII by seeking to elevate Pius to sainthood.[5] In this atmosphere, polemical attacks and defensive discourse have prevailed over historical inquiry. The present work seeks neither to prosecute the papacy nor to provide an apologia for its policies on Jews, neither to denigrate nor to defend its response to the anti-Semitism of the fascist regimes of the twentieth century. It aims to transcend the thicket of controversy and provide a historical account of the relationship between the papacy and the Jews in the modern age, and to explore the interaction between clerical anti-Judaism and secular anti-Semitism. In light of the polemical debate this subject has aroused in the past sixty years, this is easier said than done.

Hochhuth's play *Der Stellvertreter* (The Deputy), first performed in Germany in 1963, was almost immediately translated into a dozen other languages, sparking a controversy about Pius XII's role during the geno-

---

4. James Carroll, *Constantine's Sword: The Church and the Jews* (Boston: Houghton Mifflin, 2001), 484. For a critical evaluation by a Catholic, see Garry Wills, *Why I Am a Catholic* (Boston: Houghton Mifflin, 2002).

5. Carroll, *Constantine's Sword*, 531.

cide and the general responsibility of previous popes and the Catholic Church for bringing it about. The projected beatification of Pius XII in 2000 and the release in 2002 of the Costa Gavras film *Amen,* based on Hochhuth's drama, unleashed a new storm of controversy. Some writers have argued that Pius XII's "silence" can be understood only within the context of centuries of Christian "disparagement" of Jews, and have postulated that the difference between Christian anti-Judaism and Nazi anti-Semitism was one of degree, not of kind, and that both contributed to the Holocaust. Indeed, some have concluded that Christian anti-Judaism provided much of the basis for modern anti-Semitism, and have traced its sources to the anti-Judaic bias of the New Testament and the teachings of the Church Fathers.[6] Christian authors who have traced modern anti-Semitism to Christian anti-Judaism include Rosemary Ruether, Malcom Hay, Edward H. Flannery, James Parkes, Friedrich Heer, Roy Eckart, and more recently James Carroll and William Nicholls. Nicholls sees anti-Semitism as flowing from the accumulated Christian hatred of the Jews going as far back as the Gospels.[7] Malcolm Hay perceived a "chain of error" fostering the unjustified papal response to the Jews stemming from St. Bernard, St. John Chrysostom, St. Ambrose, and St. John the Evangelist.[8]

Others have denied the Christian roots of anti-Semitism, noting the difference between clerical anti-Judaism, motivated by religious considerations, and modern anti-Semitism, based on a racial ideology.[9] Opponents of this view find the distinction between anti-Judaism and anti-Semitism illusory, denouncing it as an unconvincing attempt to separate the papacy and the Church from the anti-Semitism that culminated in the Holocaust. These critics claim that the border between the two was fluid and that they merged into a broader movement. Indeed, some have divided anti-Semitism into two major components: racial and ideological, the for-

6. See Jules Isaac, *The Teaching of Contempt: Christian Roots of Anti-Semitism,* trans. H. Weaver (New York: Holt, Rinehart and Winston, 1964). See also Fred Gladstone Bratton, *The Crime of Christendom: The Theological Sources of Christian Anti-Semitism* (Boston: Beacon Press, 1969)

7. See Hyam Maccoby, "Origins of Antisemitism," *Midstream* (Dec. 1998): 38; William Nicholls, *Christian Antisemitism: A History of Hate* (Northvale, N.J.: Jason Arson, 1997).

8. Hay quoted in Carroll, *Constantine's Sword,* 423.

9. See Gregory Baum, *Is the New Testament Anti-Semitic?* (Glen Rock, N.J.: Paulist Press, 1965).

mer referring primarily to the racist movement that emerged at the end of
the nineteenth century and the latter roughly corresponding to the age-
old anti-Judaism of the Church.[10] I think this classification confuses rather
than clarifies the issue, and I use the term anti-Judaism to describe religiously inspired movements against the Jews and anti-Semitism to describe racially motivated ones. I do so cautiously.

The twofold division here employed is based on motive rather than
act, for during the course of the nineteenth and twentieth centuries both
anti-Judaism and anti-Semitism often had recourse to similar rhetoric
and shared some policies. In 1998 the Vatican admitted as much, acknowledging the existence of an anti-Judaism "that was essentially more socio-
logical and political than religious." However, it hastened to add, this
"racist element . . . was foreign to Christian teaching."[11] Granting that
racism violates the basic tenets of the faith, one might ask why the Church
leadership often failed to "clearly" and "publicly" denounce it. The record
reveals that the papacy and the Catholic press, from time to time, presented not only negative religious images of Jews but hostile assessments of
Jewish social, cultural, and political life closely identified with modern
anti-Semitism—the term concocted by the journalist Wilhelm Marr in his
volume *The Victory of Judaism over Germanism,* published in 1879. Very
probably the anti-Jewish pronouncements of part of the Catholic press
did more to influence the attitude of Catholics toward Jews than papal decrees or pronouncements ever did. Both contributed to the degradation,
segregation, and persecution of Jews. In fact, until the end of the nineteenth century, the Jesuit-run *Civiltà Cattolica* decried the abolition of the
ghettoes that had provided protection for both Christians and Jews. Raul
Hilberg has outlined five incremental steps leading to the destruction of
the European Jews: definition, expropriation, concentration, deportation,
and finally elimination.[12] If the papacy was a precursor in expropriation,
concentration, and even deportation, it had a religious rather than a racial
basis, and finally favored conversion rather than extermination. Whatever

10. Gene Bernardini, "The Origins and Development of Racial Anti-Semitism in Fascist
Italy," *JMH* 49 (Sept. 1977): 432–34.

11. See Owen Chadwick's review of David I. Kertzer, *The Popes Against the Jews: The Vatican's Role in the Rise of Anti-Semitism,* in the *New York Review of Books,* 28 March 2002, 14.

12. See Raul Hilberg, *The Destruction of the European Jews,* 3 vols. (New York: Holmes
and Meier, 1985).

the basis of ecclesiastical degradation of Jews, clerical condemnations and stereotypical images persisted into the twentieth century, with some still advocating the segregation of Jews. These negative assessments even appeared in the semiofficial *Osservatore Romano* and the *Civiltà Cattolica*, which preserved close ties to the Vatican.

My differentiation of anti-Judaism and anti-Semitism intends neither to excuse ecclesiastical or papal action or inaction toward the Jews, nor to imply that Christian hostility toward Jews over the centuries had no impact on the development of secular anti-Semitism. The usage is explanatory rather than apologetic, aiming to clarify rather than exonerate. Many recognize that the religious motive behind Christian persecution aimed at eventual conversion and religious unity, while the Nazi racial program sought Jewish extinction as a means of preserving Aryan purity. Consequences are not the same thing as intentions, however, and both merit study.

To complicate the picture, many of the most influential works on the Church and the Holocaust have been produced not by historians and theologians but by dramatists, novelists, journalists, and lawyers, some of whom question whether the Holocaust can be understood or represented by a rational historical approach. From Hochhuth's controversial play in 1963 to Cornwell's 1999 study, with the inflammatory title *Hitler's Pope: The Secret History of Pope Pius XII*, nonhistorians have driven much of the discourse, widening the divide between "denigrators" and "defenders" of Pius XII, the Catholic Church, and the papacy. This literature has unleashed a torrent of sweeping generalizations whose cumulative effect has clouded rather than clarified important questions.

The novelist James Carroll has explored the long-range hostile attitude of the papacy and the Church toward the Jews in *Constantine's Sword: The Church and the Jews* (2001). This volume provides a broad survey of Christian hostility toward Jews from the age of Constantine and the Council of Nicea (325) to the horrors of Hitler's Holocaust during World War II. Anthropologist David I. Kertzer's *The Popes against the Jews: The Vatican's Role in the Rise of Modern Anti-Semitism*, published the same year, focuses, as the subtitle indicates, on the more recent period, as does Garry Wills's *Papal Sin: Structures of Deceit* (2000), which likewise concentrates on the Church and modern anti-Semitism. Daniel Goldhagen, author of *Hitler's*

Willing Executioners: Ordinary Germans and the Holocaust (1996), recently published a long article stressing the relationship between the Church's anti-Judaism, Nazi anti-Semitism, and the Holocaust, in which he presents in capsule form many of the conclusions of his book *A Moral Reckoning: The Catholic Church during the Holocaust and Today* (2002).[13]

A number of Christian and Jewish writers have assumed the Church's complicity in the Holocaust. One has claimed that Christianity sowed hostility and that Judaism reaped the whirlwind.[14] Among other things, James Carroll claims that the popes who supported the Roman ghetto were keepers of the keys of the last and most squalid "concentration camp" before those of the Nazis. He thus perceives the Roman ghetto as "the antechamber" of the death camps. Pinchas Lapide writes that only centuries of anti-Jewish preaching can account for the fact that the anti-Semitic absurdities of Houston Stewart Chamberlain were accepted in the 1890s. Many of Lapide's contentions are supported by David Kertzer, who notes "that forcing Jews to wear yellow badges and keeping them locked in ghettoes were not the inventions of the Nazis in the twentieth century, but a policy the popes had championed for hundreds of years."[15]

The Christian theologian Hans Küng says much the same thing. "None of the anti-Jewish measures of the Nazis—distinctive clothing, exclusion from professions, the Nuremberg 'laws' forbidding mixed marriages, expulsions, the concentration camps, massacres, gruesome funeral pyres—was new," he notes. "All that already existed in the so-called Christian Middle Ages . . . and in the period of the 'Christian' Reformation."[16] William Nicholls reached a similar conclusion, convinced that the Holocaust flowed from Christian hatred of the Jews over the centuries. These and other critics imply that Christianity's leadership in general, and the pope in particular, provided inspiration, justification, and concrete policies for the persecution of Jews, and thus were responsible for many of the

13. Daniel Jonah Goldhagen, "What Would Jesus Have Done? Pope Pius XII, the Catholic Church, and the Holocaust," *New Republic*, 21 Jan. 2002, 22.

14. Pinchas E. Lapide, *Three Popes and the Jews* (New York: Hawthorn Books, 1967), 116.

15. Carroll, *Constantine's Sword*, 449, 465; Lapide, *Three Popes and the Jews*, 87; David I. Kertzer, *The Popes against the Jews: The Vatican's Role in the Rise of Modern Anti-Semitism* (New York: Knopf, 2001), 5.

16. Hans Küng, "Introduction: From Anti-Semitism to Theological Dialogue," in *Christians and Jews*, ed. Hans Küng and Walter Kasper and trans. John Maxwell (New York: Seabury Press, 1975), 11–12.

enormities of modern anti-Semitism, culminating in the Holocaust.[17] Were they?

In examining the papacy's attitude toward the Jews, and the relationship between Christian anti-Judaism and Nazi racism, one must keep in mind the difference between advocacy and historical scholarship. While advocacy is selective and emotional, scholarship seeks a certain detachment from present constraints and personal biases. Unfortunately, in recent years those who have explored the role of the Church during the Holocaust increasingly assume a partisan stance as either accusers or defenders of Pius XII, the papacy, and the Catholic Church during this troubled time. In fact, much of the literature on the papacy and the Jews seems to reflect a process of selection that bolsters a preconceived interpretative bias. Writers often see their preconceptions not as prejudices to be questioned and transcended but as beliefs to be bolstered and affirmed. Not surprisingly, the resulting historiography of denunciation and exculpation has generated more heat than light. The search for truth has been often subordinated to the desire to indict or exonerate, leaving many questions unanswered. Was there a common papal policy during these years, or did Pius XI and Pius XII vary in their responses? What factors shaped their positions? Did papal policy change over time? How, if at all, did papal anti-Judaism differ from Nazi anti-Semitism? Did the prevailing anti-Judaism of the Church play a crucial role in its "half-hearted response" to the Nazi genocide? Did the Christian policy of Jewish "disparagement" and teaching of contempt facilitate the Holocaust? Was anti-Judaism a precursor to, or precondition for, anti-Semitism? Did the former necessitate the latter? These and other questions need to be explored dispassionately, even if they cannot always be fully answered.

The present volume explores the Vatican's response to modern anti-Semitism. It both examines Rome's reaction during the fascist period and delves into the historical development and impact of theological anti-Judaism. Although we necessarily look at the past through the lens of the present, we pay a price for interpreting past events in terms of contemporary concerns. My research has led me to conclude that developments are seldom if ever driven by a single force but flow from a multiplicity of fac-

17. Jacob Katz, *From Prejudice to Destruction: Anti-Semitism, 1700–1933* (Cambridge: Harvard University Press, 1980), 319.

tors. To be sure, some considerations are more important than others, but this is to be determined by historical inquiry rather than imposed by preconception. I have sought to untangle these matters in the chapters which follow.

A Note on Sources

A study of the papacy and the Jews in the modern age must not only transcend ideological preconceptions and preestablished mindsets but must consider the availability of sources. For developments up to 1922, the Secret Vatican Archive (ASV), an intrinsic component of the Holy See, is not only the oldest but the most important archive for a work like this one. Containing more than twenty-five miles of shelves stacked with documents, it contains sources crucial to the history of the papacy and its relationship to Western institutions, the modern state, other religious groups, including the Jews, and considerably more. The Vatican, Lateran, and Avignon registers of this repository contain more than three thousand bulls and briefs dealing with Jews in the Middle Ages. Originally organized to assist the curia and the Roman pontiff in the governance of the Church, it sheds considerable light on historical developments since the ninth century. Designated "secret" because it originally formed part of the secret library of Sixtus IV (1471–84), the term persisted because these archives were deemed private until Leo XIII (1878–1903) opened them in 1881. Generally, a "seventy-five-year rule" pertains—and today these papers are open through the pontificate of Benedict XV (1914–22). For developments through the mid-nineteenth century, the Archivio di Stato di Roma (ASR), which contains some of the papers of Cardinals Ercole Consalvi and Giacomo Antonelli, is helpful. There are important texts on sixteenth-century papal fiscal policy and the imposition of taxes on Jews in the Papal States in the ASV, the ASR, and the Archivio Storico Capitolino (ASC). The complete texts of all Venetian Inquisition trials dealing with Jews and accused Judaizers from 1548 through 1681 have been printed in eleven volumes, the last of which appeared in 1993.[18]

At the opening of the twenty-first century, the ASV remained closed

18. *Processi del S. Uffizio contro ebrei e giudaizzanti (1642–1681)*, vol. 11, ed. Pier Cesare Ioly Zorratini (Florence: Olschiki Editore, 1993).

for the crucial pontificates of Pius XI (1922–39) and Pius XII (1939–58) as well as their successors, despite the pleas of individuals, organizations, and various governments that they be opened. This led some to suggest that our understanding of papal history after 1922 had to await the complete opening of this repository. I disagree, because the subject is too important for historians to neglect. To do so would allow others to form judgments and conclusions, often on the basis of biased accounts, unreliable sources, and tainted narratives. Furthermore, in mid-February 2002 the Vatican relented and revealed that it would make available some of the papers of Pius XI and Pius XII. In fact, early in 2003 the papers of the pontificate of Pius XI were partially opened, with the promise that those of Pius XII would soon follow.

Cardinal Jorge Maria Jejia, the Vatican librarian, announced that some 3.5 million files on prisoners of World War II would be made available on CD-ROM on the Vatican's website in January 2003. In 2004 the Vatican Archives published in two volumes (Inventory and Documents) the record cards of millions of prisoners about whom the Vatican had gathered information, including the reports of apostolic nuncios and delegates who visited the prison camps.[19] Concomitantly, the Church partially opened the archives, revealing its activities and role in prewar Germany from 1922 to 1939. Actually, some of the documents of the Vatican Archives for the crucial years of World War II have been published in the eleven volumes of the *Actes et documents du Saint Siège relatifs à la seconde guerre mondiale* (*ADSS*), edited by a group of Jesuits who were allowed access. While the documents published to date tell us something about what the Church did and did not do to combat Nazi racism and genocide, they reveal far less about papal motivation. Often inner sentiments are not revealed in public correspondence and documentation, although access to these papers would prove helpful. Specialists in the field do not expect startling revelations to flow from these papers, but they do expect that they will provide a broader factual base for the existing scholarly historiography.[20]

19. *"Inter Arma Caritas": The Vatican Office of Information for Prisoners of War, Instituted by Pius XII (1939–1947)* (Vatican City: Vatican Archives, 2004).

20. In this regard see Michael Feldkamp, *Goldhagens unwillige Kirche* (Munich: Olzog, 2003).

Other sources help to compensate for the partial availability of the Vatican Archives since 1922. Among these are the papers catalogued in the Istituto Paolo VI in Brescia, the archives of the other powers, and the printed correspondence of their representatives to the Holy See. Particularly useful in this regard are the Archives du Ministere des affaires Etrangeres (Paris), the Archivio Storico del Ministero degli Affari Esteri (AMAE) (Rome) and the Public Record Office in London, which contains a wealth of information about developments since 1922. Part of the diplomatic correspondence has been published in *Documents on German Foreign Policy, 1918–1945* (from the archives of the Germany Foreign Ministry, Series D, 1937–1945) (London: H. M. Stationery Office, 1949–83).

In addition, the printed acts of the Holy See appear in the *Acta Apostolicae Sedis* (*AAS*), Rome's equivalent of an official gazette or organ for Vatican documents. It publishes (most often in Latin) the official texts of encyclical letters, apostolic constitutions and exhortations, as well as some of the more solemn allocutions of the popes. These printed acts, like the encyclical letters of the papacy, are available down to the present. In September 1908, during the pontificate of Pius X (1903–14), the promulgandi (the apostolic constitution on the promulgation and publication of laws and official acts of the Holy See) provided that these would be published in the *AAS* by the Vatican Press.[21] *The Pope Speaks: American Quarterly of Papal Documents* publishes a selection of papal addresses and documents in English translation. The official website of the Holy See (http://www.vatican.va/holy_father/) offers a virtual treasure trove of Vatican documents not readily available elsewhere. Among other things it provides papal addresses, allocutions, speeches, encyclicals, letters, and telegrams. It publishes pertinent papal documents, reports of the Commission for Religious Relations with Jews, as well as the reports and documents of various Jewish leaders and organizations.

For background material one can now consult what some have denounced as the "archives of repression." At the end of the twentieth century, perhaps to mark the opening of Christianity's third millennium, Joseph Cardinal Ratzinger, prefect of the Congregation of the Faith, announced the opening of the Roman Inquisition's central archive. The

---

21. Promulgandi, 29 Sept. 1908, *PP* 1:74.

Archivio della Congregazione per la Dottrina della Fede (ACDF) contains the records of the Congregation of the Index for its entire existence, 1571–1917.[22]

One can also glean much about the various pontificates since Benedict XV from the pages of the *Osservatore Romano: Giornale quotidiano politico-religioso* (*OR*), the daily authoritative voice of the Vatican, first issued in Rome on 1 July 1861. This semiofficial daily newspaper reproduces most papal talks as well as official documents in the original Latin text as well as in Italian. From 1890 on, the Vatican published a daily edition of the journal, with weekly editions in English, French, Spanish, Portuguese, German, Polish, and Italian. Some consider it the closest thing to the official voice of the Vatican, because it is owned by the Holy See and submits all editorial material to a department of the Vatican's secretariat of state. Vatican opinion on issues can often be ascertained from reading the columns of the Jesuit-run *Civiltà Cattolica* (*CC*), which was founded in Naples in 1850 and has been published in Rome since 1888. Although the *Civiltà Cattolica* remains under the direction of the Jesuits, it has long displayed an intense loyalty to the papacy, to the point that some have deemed it a virtual mouthpiece of the pope.

Likewise useful are the printed speeches and discourses of Popes Pius XI, Pius XII, John XXIII, Paul VI, and John Paul II. For the Second Vatican Council, a vast official printed documentary base is available, as is the published correspondence of many of its participants. Claudia Carlen has published the papal encyclicals (*PE*) from 1740 to 1981 in five volumes. Volumes 3 (1903–39), 4 (1939–58), and 5 (1958–81) are particularly useful for the pontificates following Benedict XV. The material collected in the *Annuario Pontificio* or *Annual Papal Directory* provides valuable historical as well as ecclesiastical information on the modern and contemporary papacy. The encyclical Pius XI commissioned against racism and anti-Semitism, *Humani Generis Unitas* (*HGU*), has finally been uncovered, and its juxtaposition of the traditional clerical anti-Judaism and condemnation of Nazi and fascist anti-Semitism is revealing.[23] The "secret encycli-

---

22. Anne Jacobson Schutte, "Palazzo del Sant'Uffizio: The Opening of the Roman Inquisition's Central Archive," *Perspectives* (May 1999): 25–28.

23. See Georges Passelecq and Bernard Suchecky, *The Hidden Encyclical of Pius XI*, trans. Steven Rendall (New York: Harcourt, Brace, 1997). See also Frank J. Coppa, "The Hidden

cal" sheds considerable light on the Church's traditional anti-Judaism, on the thought of Pius XI, who commissioned it, and on the policy of Pius XII, who decided to shelve it. Finally, there is a vast secondary literature on the papacy and the Jews. Since much of this is ideologically driven, it must be used with caution. The debate it has provoked on Pius XII is documented in José Sanchez's *Pius XII and the Holocaust: Understanding the Controversy,* and in *The Pius War: Responses to the Critics of Pius XII,* edited by Joseph Bottum and David G. Dalin.[24]

Encyclical of Pius XI against Racism and Anti-Semitism Uncovered—Once Again!" *CHR* 84 (Jan. 1998): 63–72.

24. José M. Sanchez, *Pius XII and the Holocaust: Understanding the Controversy* (Washington, D.C.: Catholic University of America Press, 2002); Joseph Bottum and David G. Dalin, eds., *The Pius War: Responses to the Critics of Pius XII* (Lanham, Md.: Lexington Books, 2004).

ABBREVIATIONS

AAES	Archivio della Sacra Congregazione per gli Affari Ecclesiastici Straordinari
AAS	*Acta Apostolicae Sedis,* published by Vatican Press, Vatican City
ACDF	Archivio della Congregazione per la Dottrina della Fede
ADSS	*Actes et documents du Saint Siège relatifs à la seconde guerre mondiale,* ed. Pierre Blet et al. (Rome: Libreria Editrice Vaticana, 1965–81).
AHR	*American Historical Review*
AS	Archivio Storico
ASR	Archivio di Stato di Roma
ASS	*Acta Sanctae Sedis* (*AAS* after 1908), published by Vatican Press, Vatican City
ASV	Archivio Segreto Vaticano
CC	*La Civiltà Cattolica*
CHR	*Catholic Historical Review*
DBFP	*Documents on British Foreign Policy, 1919–1939,* 2d series, vol. 5. London: H. M. Stationery Office, 1956.
DDI	*I Documenti Diplomatici Italiani, published by the* Commissione per la pubblicazione dei Documenti diplomatici, 8th series, 1935–39, vol. 13; 9th series, 1939–43, vol. 3. Rome: Libreria dello Stato, 1953, 1959.
DGFP	*Documents on German Foreign Policy, 1918–1945* (Series D, 1937–1945, vols. 1–5), ed. Paul R. Sweet. London: H. M. Stationery Office, 1957.
HGU	*Humani Generis Unitas,* Pius XI's encyclical against racism and anti-Semitism.
JCS	*Journal of Church and State*
JMH	*Journal of Modern History*
OR	*L'Osservatore Romano*
PE	*The Papal Encyclicals,* 5 vols., ed. Claudia Carlen. Raleigh, N.C.: McGrath Publishing, 1981.

PP   *Papal Pronouncements: A Guide, 1740–1978.* Vol. 1, *Benedict
            XIV to Paul VI;* vol. 2, *Paul VI to John Paul I,* ed. Claudia
            Carlen. Ann Arbor: Pierian Press, 1990.

RDHSWW   *Records and Documents of the Holy See Relating to the
            Second World War,* vol. 1, *The Holy See and the War in
            Europe, March 1939–August 1940,* ed. Piere Blet et al., trans.
            Gerard Noel (Washington, D.C.: Corpus Books, 1968).

SS   Segreteria di Stato

SSE   Segreteria di Stato Esteri

The Papacy,
the Jews,
and the
Holocaust

1

PAPAL ANTI-JUDAISM IN THEORY AND
PRACTICE OVER THE MILLENNIA

---

*The whole crowd answered, "Let the responsibility for his
[Jesus'] death fall on us and on our children!" (Matthew
27:25)*

*Inasmuch as they [the Jews] have made an appeal for
our protection and help, we therefore admit their petition
and offer them the shield of our protection through the
clemency of Christian Piety.**

DEFENDERS AND DENIGRATORS of the papacy have explored its policies and
practices toward Jews over the centuries in order to commend or condemn the institution. Since Rome's position toward the Israelites was di-
alectical, oscillating between paternal protection and overt persecution,
both camps have found evidence for their preconceived conclusions and
stereotypical prejudices. Focusing on one aspect of the relationship while
virtually ignoring the other makes for interesting polemic but not for
good history. "Since it is so important to reject an inhuman anti-Semitism
and to encourage formation of a truly human relationship between Chris-

---

* Letter of Pope Gregory X (1271–76) in Brian Tierney, ed., *The Middle Ages* (New York:
Knopf, 1970), 1:230.

tians and Jews," in the words of one observer, "it is indispensable to investigate the history of their mutual relationship as precisely as possible."[1] This chapter traces the emergence and development of anti-Judaism from early Christianity to the eve of the French Revolution.

Both Judaism and Christianity have long shared an aversion to openly accepting Jesus as a Jew. Over the centuries they often agreed on little else.[2] Relations between the two faiths have been influenced by the authority of the Bible and the Church Fathers, on the one hand, and by popular contempt and prejudice, on the other. The two, of course, are not mutually exclusive. Jesus, his disciples, his parables and prophecies all emerged from the Jewish faith, sharing monotheism, Jewish history, the Mosaic laws, and other sacred writings of the Judaism of the Old Testament. Although Jesus proclaims in the Gospel of John that salvation comes from the Jews and that his parables are unmistakably Jewish, anti-Judaism soon emerged among some of his followers. The Gospels themselves show Jesus chiding and correcting the scribes, Pharisees, and other Jewish leaders.[3] Biblical scholars believe that Paul's writings (50–60 C.E.) had an influential impact on the Gospels written from 70 to 110 C.E., which sought to show that the Jewish Scripture foreshadowed Jesus' life, death, and resurrection.[4] Early Christians were convinced that the mission of Judaism had been fulfilled in the teachings of Christ but learned to their dismay that a majority of Jews did not concur.[5] This proved disconcerting to the disciples of Jesus,

1. Hans Conzelmann, *Gentiles, Jews, Christians: Polemics and Apologetics in the Greco-Roman Era*, trans. M. Eugene Boring (Minneapolis: Fortress Press, 1992), xxvii.

2. Joseph Sivers, "Jesus of Nazareth as Seen by Jewish Writers of the XX Century," http://www.vatican.va/jubilee_2000...zine/ju_mag_01111997, accessed 20 April 1998.

3. James E. Wood Jr., "Editorial: Jewish Christian Relations in Historical Perspective," *JCS* 13, no. 2 (spring 1971): 194–95; Michael Cook, "The New Testament: Confronting Its Impact on Jewish-Christian Relations," in *Introduction to Jewish-Christian Relations,* ed. Michael Shermis and Arthur E. Zannoni (New York: Paulist Press, 1991), 34.

4. Within the past several decades many works have addressed the question of the relationship between the New Testament and the Jews, among them John G. Gager, *The Origins of Anti-Semitism: Attitudes toward Judaism in Pagan and Christian Antiquity* (New York: Oxford University Press, 1985); E. P. Sanders, *Paul and Palestinian Judaism* (Philadelphia: Fortress Press, 1977); Conzelmann, *Gentiles, Jews, Christians;* and John Rousmaniere, *A Bridge to Dialogue: The Story of Jewish-Christian Relations,* ed. James A. Carpenter and Leon Klenicki (New York: Paulist Press, 1991).

5. Wolfgang S. Seiferth, *Synagogue and Church in the Middle Ages: Two Symbols in Art and Literature,* trans. Lee Chadeayne and Paul Gottwald (New York: Frederick Ungar, 1970), 14–15.

who did not envision founding a new faith but believed they were following the mission of Israel to its logical and inexorable conclusion.

Paul above all was determined to stress the continuity between Judaism and early Christianity, which called for the acceptance of Jesus as the Jewish messiah. He was distressed to learn that most Jews rejected this depiction, seeing it as a radical departure from, rather than the fulfillment of, Judaism. The hostility between the two was mutual as Christian devotion to Jesus became prominent. It led to a bitter polemic between Jewish synagogues and "Jewish Christians," as the "old Jews" condemned the proclamation of Jesus as son of God a violation of the Torah, or first five books of the Old Testament.[6] Nor would Jews accept the notion that Christ rather than the Torah represented the way and the life, adamantly denying the deity of Christ proclaimed by Paul and Matthew.

The early Church Fathers, in turn, perceived the messiah still invoked by the Jews as an "anti-Christ" and "emanation of Satan." To make matters worse, from the perspective of the emerging faith, the Jews who rejected Jesus insisted that they alone were in possession of the revealed truth.[7] They took steps to silence their increasingly outspoken rivals by resorting to a vigorous persecution, even before the revolt of 70 C.E. The Jewish historian Josephus reports that James, brother of Jesus and head of the Church in Jerusalem, was executed as a heretic in 62 C.E. at the behest of the temple's high priest.

Paul, the Greek-speaking Jew of Tarsus, met Jesus only in a vision. A persecutor of Christians before his conversion in about 35 C.E., he later complained of Jewish persecution, becoming one of the founders of the Christian faith. In 2 Corinthians 11:24 Paul complained of the persecution of the Jews as well as of the pagans. Some fifteen years later he wrote to the Thessalonians that "The Jews drove us out, and displease God and oppose all men by hindering us from speaking to the Gentiles that they may be saved."[8] Paul was thus one of the first to contrast Christian universalism

6. Hyam Maccoby, *The Mythmaker: Paul and the Invention of Christianity* (New York: Harper Collins, 1987), 4–5, 11–13; L. W. Hurtado, "Pre–70 CE Jewish Opposition to Christ-Devotion," *Journal of Theological Studies* 50 (April 1999): 35–39.

7. Joel Carmichael, *The Satanizing of the Jews: Origin and Development of Mystical Anti-Semitism* (New York: Fromm, 1992), 34; Jacob Katz, *Exclusiveness and Tolerance: Studies in Jewish-Gentile Relations in Medieval and Modern Times* (Oxford: Oxford University Press, 1961), 3.

8. Conzelmann, *Gentiles, Jews, Christians,* 250; Rousmaniere, *Bridge to Dialogue,* 12.

with Jewish particularism, which he increasingly opposed. He believed that the "blindness" of the Jews led them to reject the Incarnation, but since he was convinced that Israel remained integral to the divine design, he believed that Jewish eyes would eventually be opened and that the Jews would be saved. Others, however, condemned the Jewish obstinacy as a repudiation of their own.[9]

From almost the very beginning, practical questions, political considerations, and religious reorganization influenced the relationship between Jews and Christians. For one thing, the disciples of Christ, following Paul's mandate, soon reached out to the Gentiles, while most Jews did not, provoking the Gentile accusation that Jews were "haters of humanity." In the eyes of some Jews, God's law enjoined their separation from other peoples, "in order that we might not mingle at all with any of the other nations."[10] Paul, among others, considered this notion obsolete. Furthermore, Christians eventually abandoned Jewish ceremonial law, upholding the conviction that the saving act of the one God had universal application. Christian-Jewish relations were also affected by the two revolts of the Jews against the Romans in 66–70 C.E. and 132–35 C.E. Following these conflicts Judaism was reorganized, its teaching office regulated, its canon tightened, and the distinction between itself and fringe groups such as Christians sharpened. Rejection of heresy was incorporated into Jewish liturgy, and Christians increasingly were perceived as heretics with whom no compromise was permissible or possible.[11] Various scholars acknowledge Talmudic hostility toward first-century Christians, Jews perceiving Jesus as a "deceiver of Israel" whose teachings were denounced as evil. By the end of the first century, at the Council of Jamnia (90 C.E.), official Judaism pronounced Christianity an apostasy and a disavowal of Israel and God's law.[12] Tolerance was scorned by both sides.

Following the restrictions imposed on Jews in Rome during the reign of Claudius (49 C.E.), the revolt of the Jews in Judea in 66 C.E., and the destruction of Jerusalem four years later, the new "Christians" sought to differentiate themselves from Jews, whom the Romans saw as rebellious sub-

---

9. Küng, "From Anti-Semitism to Theological Dialogue," 10.
10. Conzelmann, *Gentiles, Jews, Christians*, 20.
11. Ibid., 37, 232, 252.
12. Wood, "Editorial," 200.

jects and persistent troublemakers. Ample evidence suggests that the Romans perceived the Christians as essentially Jews and believed they were implicated in Jews' seditious activities. They also apparently believed that the movement of Jesus formed part of the agitation that culminated in the Jewish revolt, a theory bolstered by the fact that Jesus was crucified by the Romans for sedition as a rebel.[13] Perhaps the desire to distance themselves from their fellow Jews, who were driven out of Palestine in 70 C.E., explains why the developing Christian sect sought to exculpate the Romans for the death of Jesus, placing the onus upon the shoulders of the Jews, who outnumbered them and were officially recognized by the Romans as a nation.[14]

Both the destruction of the temple and the Jewish dispersion that followed were interpreted by the early Church as divine retribution for the Jews' rejection and "slaying" of Jesus. Such an interpretation flowed in part from Jewish theological formulations that had long perceived the disasters burdening Israel as punishment for the transgressions of its people. As a consequence, the Roman-Jewish war provoked a rift between Jewish messianists in Palestine and the followers of Jesus in the Diaspora, who desperately sought to dissociate themselves from Jewish revolutionaries and activists.[15] There were now distinct Christians and Jews, as Judeo-Christianity disappeared.

The French historian Jules Isaac, in his book *Jesus et Israel*, notes that even though Jesus had been condemned to a Roman punishment (crucifixion), by a Roman procurator (Pontius Pilate), responsibility was shifted to the Jews. "That the Roman pronounced the death sentence under pressure from the Jews all four Gospel writers to be sure earnestly bear witness with one voice," Isaac writes, immediately adding, however, that "as their testimony is an indictment which is prejudiced and impassioned, circumstantial and belated, frankly speaking, we find it impossible to accept without reservation."[16] On the other hand, the Talmudic reconstruction of the events leading to the death of Jesus assumes some Jewish responsibility. It

---

13. Carmichael, *Satanizing of the Jews*, 11, 38.
14. Conzelmann, *Gentiles, Jews, Christians*, 249.
15. Wood, "Editorial," 201; Carmichael, *Satanizing of the Jews*, 19.
16. Quoted in Leon de Poncins, *Judaism and the Vatican: An Attempt at Spiritual Subversion*, trans. Timothy Tindal-Robertson (London: Britons, 1967), 15–16.

reads: "On the eve of Passover Yeshu was hanged. For forty days prior to the execution, a herald went forth and cried, 'Yeshu of Nazareth is going to be stoned because he has produced sorcery and beguiled Israel, leading her astray. Let everyone who knows something in his favor come forward in his defense.' He was therefore hanged on Passover."[17]

The anti-Judaism of the New Testament reflects more than simple retaliation for the Jewish "persecution"; it appears motivated by the need for the new religion to differentiate itself from its parent.[18] Those who divided over the identity of Jesus interpreted the Hebrew Scriptures as bolstering their divergent claims. "Christianity made a sharp distinction between the Old and the New Testament, and interpreted the former only in terms of its fulfillment of the latter," one observer has noted, adding, "The main interest in the Old Testament of the church fathers was as a quarry of proof texts that Jesus was the Christ foretold by the prophets."[19] According to Paulinus of Nola (c. 400 C.E.), "The Old Covenant establishes the New, the New fulfills the Old: in the Old is hope, in the New faith. But the Old and New are wedded by the grace of Christ." In the words of St. Augustine, "In the Old Testament the New is concealed, in the New Testament the Old is revealed."[20] The fathers of the Church in the first centuries in both the East and the West agreed that the Jewish people had been repudiated and replaced by the Church, which was designated to bring salvation to all of humanity. Christianity was no longer perceived as a Jewish sect but as a separate faith.

Whatever the motivation, a degree of anti-Judaism has been perceived at the core of Christian theology since the fourth Gospel, attributed to John, which makes more than seventy references to the Jews, many of them negative. The Church in John's Gospel is estranged from Israel, while the Old Testament is presented as a witness to Jesus and the unbelief of the Jews who refused to recognize him. In this fourth Gospel the Church does not perceive the Jews in a social, political, or national sense but as enemies

---

17. John M. Oesterreicher, *The New Encounter between Christians and Jews* (New York: Philosophical Library, 1985), 74.

18. Cook, "New Testament," 48–49; Lapide, *Three Popes and the Jews*, 39.

19. James William Parkes, *Prelude to Dialogue: Jewish-Christian Relations* (New York: Schocken Books, 1969), 25.

20. Paulinus of Nola quoted in Seiferth, *Synagogue and Church in the Middle Ages*, 14; Augustine quoted in Rousmaniere, *Bridge to Dialogue*, 37.

of Jesus, as "children of the devil" and the "synagogue of Satan."[21] In fact, the notion that the Jews killed Jesus originates in John's Gospel. John deemed the Jews deicides and held them collectively responsible. This argument was repeated in the apocryphal writings of the second century, including the Gospel of Peter, which exonerated Pilate but blamed the Jews for Christ's crucifixion.[22]

Some writers contend that Mark and Matthew, by contrast, place the blame on the chief priest and his close followers. Furthermore, the Gospels of Matthew and Luke make far fewer references to "the Jews"—some five or six—and more often than not the reference is to only those Jews who confront and combat Jesus, rather than to all Jews. There is controversy here, too, with some branding Matthew not only the most Jewish but also the most biased of the evangelists. Jules Isaac writes that Matthew alone notes that Pilate washed his hands to absolve himself of innocent blood and that his Gospel alone has the Jewish crowd cry out, "His blood be upon us and upon our children."[23] Unquestionably, the New Testament—which sought to differentiate the new religious beliefs from the traditional—spawned negative stereotypes of Jews that persisted for centuries and had unfortunate consequences. In fact, many Catholic and Jewish scholars concur on the anti-Jewish bias of the New Testament. After World War II, Isaac revealed the close relationship between the vilification of the Jewish people and Christian preaching and practice, which flowed from the New Testament.[24] Some of his contentions were disputed by Catholic theologians, but eventually most of his conclusions were accepted.[25]

The new faith moved away from its parent incrementally, and some of its adherents even accepted the Roman charge that the Jews engaged in ritual murder. In the first half of the second century, the letter of Barnabas

---

21. Conzelmann, *Gentiles, Jews, Christians*, 257.

22. Wood, "Editorial," 201.

23. Isaac quoted in Poncins, *Judaism and the Vatican*, 16.

24. Cook, "New Testament," 36. See also Rosemary Radford Ruether, *Faith and Fratricide: The Theological Roots of Anti-Semitism* (New York: Seabury Press, 1974), esp. the chapters "The Greek and Jewish Roots of the Negative Myth of the Jews," "The Growing Estrangement: The Rejection of the Jews in the New Testament," "The Negation of the Jews in the Church Fathers," and "The Social Incorporation of the Negative Myth of the Jews in Christendom"; and Jules Isaac, *Jesus and Israel* (New York: Holt, Rinehart and Winston, 1971)

25. See Gregory Baum, *The Jews and the Gospels* (New York: Newman Press, 1961).

not only claimed that the old covenant had been replaced by the new but, adding insult to injury, charged that Israel had never understood the Old Testament and had been attacked by the Gentile nations for its sinfulness. Cyprian of Carthage (d. 258 C.E.) claimed that Christ's new law abrogated the law of Moses and "the era of the old temple." To his mind "the destruction of Jerusalem was a judgment on the Jews." At the same time, the notion evolved that the Jewish people as a whole were guilty of Christ's crucifixion.[26] Subsequently, other beliefs, developments, and actions deepened the estrangement.

At the Council of Elvira of 306, the Spanish bishops prohibited Christians from exchanging hospitality or intermarrying with unconverted Jews. During the reign of Constantine (306–37), there was a total separation between Judaism and Christianity as well as the Christian abrogation of the ritual practices proscribed by the law of Moses.[27] In 325, at the Council of Nicea, it was determined that henceforth Easter would be celebrated on a different date from the Jewish Passover, while prohibiting Christians from participating in Passover seders and Jews from attending Easter services. In 380 the Council of Lucca abolished the seventh day of the week as the Sabbath, insisting that Christians should sanctify Sunday, the first day of the week.[28] In 387 St. John Chrysostom (c. 349–407), patriarch of Constantinople, preached a series of anti-Jewish sermons at Antioch, charging the Jews with deicide and proclaiming the Christian duty to hate them. "I hate the Jews because they violate the law," he proclaimed, adding, "I hate the Synagogue because it has the Law and the Prophets."[29] Chrysostom depicted Jews as "children of the devil" and was appalled by the respect and goodwill they enjoyed among Christians, harping on the grave danger they represented. In his words they were "living for their belly, mouth forever gaping, the Jews behave no better than hogs and goats in their lewd grossness and the excesses of their gluttony."[30] These diatribes, which depicted the synagogue as a whorehouse, helped to provoke attacks

26. Franklin Hamlin Littell, "Uprooting Antisemitism: A Call to Christians," *JCS* 17 (winter 1975): 17–18.

27. Rousmaniere, *Bridge to Dialogue*, 52–53; Henri Fesquet, *The Drama of Vatican II: The Ecumenical Council, June 1962–December 1965*, trans. Bernard Murchland (New York: Random House, 1967), 229.

28. Waagenaar, *Pope's Jews*, 69; Fesquet, *Drama of Vatican II*, 229.

29. Wood, "Editorial," 204–5.

30. Quoted in Carmichael, *Satanizing of the Jews*, 46.

like the Christian slaughter of the Jews of Alexandria early in the fifth century.

While it is true that during the course of the conflict Christians and Jews neglected the theological truths and spiritual heritage they shared, their estrangement did not always result in persecution. Some Jewish as well as Christian writers have denounced the myth that the Church and the papacy preached and discriminated against Jews throughout the Middle Ages. This myth prevailed despite the meticulous research of Edward A. Synan, published in *The Popes and the Jews in the Middle Ages* (1965), and the publication over the years of papal documents relating to the Jews. Serious scholarship reveals that the Church could not and did not ignore the fact that Holy Scripture depicted the Jews as a "called and chosen people," nor did it deny the bond of spiritual kinship between the old faith and the new. Paul, in Romans 1:26, asserted that "all Israel will be saved." This belief also found expression in the teachings of St. Augustine of Hippo (354–430), who refused to dismiss the Scriptures, the covenant, and the Jews—all of which he saw as playing a key role in God's plan. In his *City of God* (427), viewing the Jews as "unwilling witnesses" to the message of Jesus, Augustine urged that the Jews be allowed to "survive but not thrive" as witnesses to the authenticity of the Bible of Israel. In his view, the Jews had survived so as to provide eternal witness to the truth of the prophecies of their own Scriptures and the triumph of the Church.[31]

Augustine announced that the scriptural prophesy that Israel would be divided in two meant that it would be split into Israel the enemy of Christ and Israel the worshipper of Christ.

> We see that by these words an utterly irrevocable sentence was divinely proclaimed concerning this division of the people of Israel, a sentence absolutely perpetual. For all those who have passed over from that people to Christ, or who are now passing over, or who will pass over, were not of that people according to God's foreknowledge. . . . Moreover, all those of the Israelites who attach to Christ and continue steadfastly in his fellowship will never be associated with those Israelites who persist in their hostility to him to the end of his life; in fact, they will continue for ever in that state of separation which is prophesied here. For the old covenant from Mount Sinai which has "children destined for slavery" is of no value except in so far as it bears witness to the

31. Norman Roth, "Bishops and Jews in the Middle Ages," *CHR* 80 (Jan. 1994): 1.

new covenant. Otherwise, as long as "Moses" is read, "a veil is laid on their hearts," on the other hand, whenever anyone passes over from that people to Christ, the veil will be taken away.[32]

Augustine's call for the toleration of the Jews was based on two convictions he shared with Paul. First, they had introduced the Scriptures to Christians, and second, their conversion would usher in the second coming. Furthermore, he argued that the Jews were to be brought to the baptismal font by the "sweetness of lips" and inducements rather than by persecution.[33] Although some questioned Augustine's theological arguments for invoking a qualified toleration, their impact in the Christian world was profound and helped to assure the survival of the Jews over the centuries.[34] Church practices and papal pronouncements often reflected Augustine's sentiments. A number of popes made universalist claims—for example, Gelasius I (492–96), who put forward the notion of the "two swords," so influential in the Church-state controversies of the Middle Ages; Gregory VII (1073–85), who issued the *Dictatus Papae* of 1075; and Boniface VIII (1294–1303), whose *Unam Sanctum* of 1302 insisted on the transcendent role of the papacy and its universal mission.

However, no pope claimed jurisdiction over the unbaptized or asserted religious authority over the Jews. Nonetheless, various popes had much to say about the social, economic, and political interactions between Christians and Jews in Christian states, and tended to adhere to the restrictions imposed by the Justinian code (529–35), on the one hand, and St. Augustine's teaching, on the other. Papal decrees on Jews were protective as well as restrictive.[35] In the Papal States the popes also defended the right and duty to impose taxes on their Jewish subjects.[36] These and other papal pro-

---

32. St. Augustine, *City of God,* ed. David Knowles, trans. Henry Bettenson (Baltimore: Penguin, 1972), 733.

33. Kenneth R. Stow, *Taxation, Community and State: The Jews and the Fiscal Foundations of the Early Modern Papal State* (Stuttgart: A. Hiersemann, 1982), 62.

34. Rousmaniere, *Bridge to Dialogue,* 50–52.

35. Guido Fubini, *La condizione giuridica dell'ebraismo Italiano. Dal periodo Napoleonico alla Repubblica* (Florence: Nuova Italia, 1974), 9.

36. The most important of these was the combined income and capital tax called the Vigesima (one-twentieth). In addition, the Jews of Rome had to make a contribution to the Roman *domus catechumenorum* and had to submit to additional sundry fees such as those for the Lenten carnival games and for the maintenance of the port at Fiumicino. Stow, *Taxation, Community and State,* 2–3.

visions reflected the divided attitude toward the Jews that would prevail throughout the centuries.

Pope Gregory I (590–604), known as Gregory the Great, embraced both a restrictive and a protective position toward Jews. Reflecting the teachings of Augustine and Paul, he affirmed that Jews were entitled to legal rights. How these should be assured was another matter. On the one hand, he prohibited Jews from keeping Christian slaves, servants, or employees—thus commencing the campaign to keep Jews and Christians apart.[37] On the other hand, he argued that Christians could better influence the Jews through Christian kindness and paternal love than through threats and violence. His advice was followed by Cautinus, bishop of Clermont-Ferrent, who remained on friendly terms with the Jews and did not press for their conversion.[38] Gregory's stance was elaborated in his proclamation of 598, which followed the Augustinian mandate that Jews were not to be destroyed. During the fourteen years of his pontificate, Gregory often protected Jews against unjust treatment, ordered the rebuilding of synagogues destroyed by Christian violence, and denounced their forced baptism. These protections were concretized in canon 60 of the Council of Toledo (633). After Gregory's death in 604, however, his letters and pronouncements were not generally cited until the tenth century, at which time canonical collections reiterated the right of Jews to reside peacefully in Christian communities. Documents of the tenth and eleventh centuries warned against forced baptism.[39] These provisions were incorporated in the bull *Sicut Iudeis* (1120) of Callistus II (1119–24), which guaranteed Jews legal protection and proclaimed:

> Just as the Jews ought not be allowed to do more in their synagogues than the law permits, so too they should suffer no reduction in the privileges that have been previously granted them. That is why, though they prefer to remain obstinate rather than acknowledge the words of the prophets and the secrets of their own scripture and come to a knowledge of Christianity and Salvation,

37. Sandra Tozzini, "Legal Discrimination against Italian Jews: From the Romans to the Unification of Italy," in *The Most Ancient of Minorities: The Jews of Italy*, ed. Stanislao G. Pugliese (Westport, Conn.: Greenwood Press, 2002), 18.

38. Roth, "Bishops and Jews in the Middle Ages," 2.

39. Kenneth R. Stow, "Conversion, Apostasy, and Apprehension: Emicho of Flonheim and the Fear of Jews in the Twelfth Century," *Speculum: A Journal of Medieval Studies* 76 (Oct. 2001): 919–20.

because they have sought our protection and aid, and in accordance with the mercy of Christian piety . . . we grant them their petition and offer them our shield of protection. We also decree . . . that no Christian shall use violence to force them to be baptized if they are reluctant or unwilling; but if any of them seeks refuge among Christians because of his faith, after his willingness has been made clear, he shall become a Christian without suffering any calumny. For it is impossible to believe that one who comes to baptism unwillingly truly possesses the Christian faith.[40]

The prohibition against coerced baptism of Jews and the other guarantees accorded the Hebrews in *Sicut Iudeis* were reissued by popes Eugenius III, Alexander II, and Clement III, among others. In fact, Pope Gregory IV (827–44) warned the bishops of Gaul and Germany that Jews were not to be forcibly converted.[41] This tolerant attitude was also evident in the writings of St. Bernard of Clairvaux (1090–1153), who warned the people and clergy of France, on the basis of Scripture, that Jews were not to be slaughtered, persecuted, or even driven out. In his homilies and letters he argued that the Church triumphed more if it converted rather than destroyed the Jews. For this reason the Church had established "the universal prayer which is offered up for the faithless Jews from the rising of the sun to its setting, that the Lord God may remove the veil from their hearts, that they may be rescued from their darkness into the light of truth."[42] St. Thomas Aquinas (1224–74) concurred with Pope Callistus II and St. Bernard that the children of Jews were not to be baptized against the will of their parents, deeming this a violation of natural justice. Citing the mandate of natural law, Aquinas defended the right of Jewish parents to determine the upbringing of their children. Once a person reached the age of reason, however, "he can consent to the faith and be baptized even against the will of his parents."[43] Aquinas's "tolerant" position toward the Jews did not overcome the stereotypes that he and other theologians had fostered by

---

40. Quoted in John Y. B. Hood, *Aquinas and the Jews* (Philadelphia: University of Pennsylvania Press, 1995), 29–30.

41. Gary Lease, "Denunciation as a Tool of Ecclesiastical Control: The Case of Roman Catholic Modernism," *JMH* 68 (Dec. 1996): 822–23; Roth, "Bishops and Jews in the Middle Ages," 2.

42. Quotation from http://listserv.american.edu/catholic/church/papal/benedict xiv/b14aquo.html, accessed 7 April 1999.

43. Hood, *Aquinas and the Jews*, 43–56; St. Thomas Aquinas, *St. Thomas Aquinas on Politics and Ethics*, trans. and ed. Paul E. Sigmund (New York: W. W. Norton, 1988), 63.

branding the Jews infidels and Christ killers. Consequently their protective measures often failed to provide the Jews security. Despite invocations, prayers, and protective proscriptions on behalf of Jews, so many synagogues were appropriated by Christian authorities that a special prayer was elaborated for their purification.[44]

Although Pope Innocent III (1198–1216) felt that the Jews were bound to wander until they repented and should not hold public office until they did, his constitution of 1199 prohibited forced baptisms and persecution. He also issued an explicit command prohibiting Christians from accusing Jews of using Christian blood in their religious rites.[45] They were not to be molested, for their presence established the truth and birth of Christianity. These admonitions were repeated in the "Declaration on the Protection of Jews" (1429) of Martin V (1417–31), which recognized that Jews were made in the image of God and that some of them would eventually be saved, while specifying that they were not to be molested in their religious services, baptized by force, or hindered in their business relations with Christians.[46] An objective examination of the papal documents of the Middle Ages on Jews reveals a conflicted stance, with some imposing restrictions upon them while others invoked clemency and provided protection.

While Church law, papal pronouncements, and patristic theology called for the protection of Jewish practice and religious life, making it an excommunicable offense to disrupt Jewish prayer services, undeniable hostility on the part of a series of other popes may have helped fan the flames of popular prejudice. Many resented the Jewish rejection of the Trinity, which Jews perceived as a denial of the oneness of God, and their condemnation of the Incarnation as virtual idolatry. Furthermore, it was charged that the Jews had not only been blind to the teachings of Jesus, their Messiah, but had put him to death! The charge emerged that Jewish "faithlessness" and "obstinacy" had provoked divine wrath, which led to the destruction of the Temple and subsequent Jewish suffering and disper-

---

44. Hood, *Aquinas and the Jews*, 111; Lapide, *Three Popes and the Jews*, 47.

45. Lapide, *Three Popes and the Jews*, 48, 81; Wistrich, *Antisemitism*, 25.

46. See the "Medieval Sourcebook," http://www.fordham.edu/source/ mart5-Jews, accessed 2 Feb. 2004. For a comprehensive documentary history of the relationship between the popes and the Jews during the Middle Ages, consult the work of Shlomo Simonsohn, *The Apostolic See and the Jews*, vol. 1, *Documents, 492–1402* (Toronto: Pontifical Institute of Medieval Studies, 1988).

sion. Within the Church and its leadership, some hoped to convert this "obstinate" people, viewing conversion as the solution to the "Jewish problem." When Christians failed to effect conversion, some moved toward separation, which soon turned to oppression.

In 1902 Pope Leo XIII (1878–1903) wrote that the Church always defended the feeble and the oppressed against the arrogant domination and excesses of the strong.[47] This may have been the papal intention, but the reality often varied, especially in the matter of ecclesiastical policy toward the Jews. The record reveals that after the conversion of Constantine I (306–37) in 312, the declaration of Christianity as the state religion in 315, and the spread of Christianity throughout the Roman Empire, legislation restricting Jewish activity increased dramatically.[48] The Edict of Caracalla of 212, which accorded Jews full citizenship in the empire while protecting them from legal abuses, was abandoned. In the Christian era, Jews lost the status of free citizens enjoyed by their Christian counterparts. Subsequently, it was prescribed that any Jew who demonstrated against a Jewish convert to Christianity was subject to death by burning, and in 339 Constantine II criminalized conversion to Judaism. Christianity was transformed from a persecuted faith into one that joined in the persecution of proscribed religions such as Judaism. The Synod of Gerona of 517 constrained Jews to pay taxes to support the Church. Then, in 531, the emperor Justinian forbade Jews from offering testimony against Christians. The Council of Orleans (533–41) supported the imperial anti-Judaic decrees by imposing its own proscriptions against conversions from Christianity to Judaism, while encouraging the conversion of Jews and forbidding intermarriage between Jews and Christians. In 545 a Church council restricted Jewish property rights while prohibiting Christians from selling real estate to Jews.[49] Some groups within the Church provoked religious animosity toward the Jews, who they condemned for rejecting and killing their Messiah and for continuing to proclaim their chosenness.[50]

The expansive Church supported the imposition of economic, political, social, and religious restrictions on the Jewish community, pursuing a

47. Pope Leo XIII, *Annum ingressi,* 19 March 1902, *ASS* 31, 513–32.
48. See the appendices in James William Parkes, *The Conflict of the Church and Synagogue: A Study in the Origins of Anti-Semitism* (New York: Meridian Books, 1961).
49. Tozzini, "Legal Discrimination against Italian Jews," 13, 15, 22, 27, 28.
50. Bernardini, "Origins and Development of Racial Anti-Semitism," 433.

policy of "supersessionism," which saw Christians as superseding the Jewish people in God's plan of human salvation.[51] The position of Jews was far from secure in the Holy Roman Empire under Charlemagne (768–814), who in 800 restricted citizenship to members of the Church. Charlemagne appointed a *magister Judaeorum*, or master of the Jews, to protect them from clerical abuse, and his son Louis the Pious (814–40) made no distinction between faithful and infidel. However, St. Agobard (769–840), the Archbishop of Lyons, conducted a bitter campaign against imperial toleration of the "cursed" Jews, producing a tract entitled *The Insolence of the Jews*. Pope Leo VII (936–39) urged Archbishop Frederick of Mainz to preach more diligently to effect the conversion of the Jews and to expel them should they refuse to convert, thus contravening canon law. Agobard was not alone in violating canonical strictures. In 1010 Bishop Alduin of Limoges offered the Jews of Limoges the option of conversion or expulsion. Two years later, all Jews were temporarily expelled from Mainz.[52]

The ecclesiastical opposition to imperial toleration of Jews did not deter the emperors, who allowed certain Jews to reside at court, while others were accorded special protection. In fact, Emperor Henry IV (1084–1105), in a decree of 1084, allowed Jews to exchange gold and silver, to govern themselves, to employ Christian servants, to engage in commerce by buying and selling, and to move about freely.[53] His generosity was seconded by some of the bishops of the empire. In 1084 Bishop Rudizer of Speyer sought to have Jews settle there. He granted the Israelites many favors, which the Jews recorded. His successor, John of Speyer (1090–1104), proved even more zealous in the defense of Jews, protecting them when they were attacked by criminals during the course of the First Crusade. The Hebrew chronicles report that he saved the majority of Jews in Speyer.[54] These actions aroused Pope Gregory VII (1073–85), who charged Henry IV with undue favoritism toward the Jews and in a Roman synod renewed the canonical proscriptions prohibiting Jews from exercising authority over Christians. Like many other churchmen, Gregory, consid-

51. Michael B. McGarry, "The Holocaust: Tragedy of Christian History," in Shermis and Zannoni, *Introduction to Jewish-Christian Relations*, 73.

52. Rousmaniere, *Bridge to Dialogue*, 54; Roth, "Bishops and Jews in the Middle Ages," 5–8.

53. Carmichael, *Satanizing of the Jews*, 51.

54. Roth, "Bishops and Jews in the Middle Ages," 8–9.

ered one of the greatest popes, believed that the Jews were responsible for their own plight.

No less a figure than Thomas Aquinas, one of the Church's most influential philosophers and theologians, believed that Jewish participation in the crucifixion placed a curse upon them and foretold the end of Judaism as a legitimate religion.[55] Nonetheless, as we have seen, he favored toleration by Christians. "Thus it is good that the Jews observe rites that once prefigured the true faith that we hold," he wrote, "because we have a testimony of our faith from our enemies and our belief is represented to us as prefigured."[56] In an ambitious study Jeremy Cohen of Tel Aviv University has chronicled how Christian writers from Augustine to Aquinas helped to shape the negative image of Jews, which influenced Western thought and practice.[57] Negative teachings about the Jews and the failure to combat the numerous accusations against them—in 1021 they were accused of having caused the Tiber to overflow and the earth to quake—contributed to continual violence against them in Christian Europe.[58]

To be sure, a number of popes sought to stem this tide of violence. "It is the duty of all good Christians to fight the Saracens who persecute the true believers," warned Pope Alexander II (1061–73), "and to save the Jews, who are peaceful and inoffensive."[59] Likewise Pope Urban II (1088–99), who called for the First Crusade, urged toleration toward the Jews. Some maintain that his words were not heeded during the frenzy of the crusade that commenced in 1096, which witnessed the slaughter of many Jews in Gaul, Germany, and the Low Countries, followed by pogroms in Palestine. Some estimate that one-quarter to one-third of the Jews of northern France and Germany were slaughtered or committed suicide in the first year of the crusade.[60] Others insist that the Jews of France were untouched by the First Crusade.[61]

---

55. Hood, *Aquinas and the Jews*, 62–63.

56. *Aquinas on Politics and Ethics*, 62–63.

57. Jeremy Cohen, *Living Letters of the Law: Ideas of the Jew in Medieval Christianity* (Berkeley and Los Angeles: University of California Press, 1999).

58. Eugene J. Fisher, "Jews and Catholicism," *HarperCollins Encyclopedia of Catholicism*, ed. Richard McBrein (San Francisco: HarperCollins, 1995), 706; Küng, "From Anti-Semitism to Theological Dialogue," 11.

59. Quoted in Waagenaar, *Pope's Jews*, 92.

60. Paul Blanshard, *Paul Blanshard on Vatican II* (Boston: Beacon Press, 1966), 125–26.

61. Roth, "Bishops and Jews in the Middle Ages," 5.

Disagreement persists about the impact of the papal call for toleration of the Jews and the overall influence of the Crusades upon them. Some writers deem the Crusades disastrous for the Jews. "They said in effect that it was unjust to permit enemies of Christ to remain alive in their own country," reported the chronicle of Richard of Poiters, "when they taken up arms to drive out the infidels abroad."[62] The massacre continued in Germany. "As the latter [crusaders] passed through the cities on the Rhine, the Main, and the Danube," contemporary German historians noted, "they tried to prove their zeal for Christianity but also endeavoring to destroy completely the accursed Jews . . . or to drive them into the arms of the church."[63] Other deny that the Crusades represented a turning point in Jewish-Christian relations.[64]

There is general agreement that the position of Jews worsened in medieval Europe after the middle of the twelfth century. In twelfth-century England a monk called Thomas claimed that a young boy whose corpse was found in Norwich had been murdered by the Jews of the city. This was the origin of the notorious "Jewish blood libel myth," which charged that the Jews would drain the blood of Christian children for use in their religious rituals. This horrific story motivated a rash of accusations, first in medieval England and then on the Continent, that resulted in mass hysteria and the massacre, over the years, of many Jews. As a consequence of this and other fabrications, Jews went from being a tolerated minority to enemies of the Christian faith and civil society. Following the coronation of Richard I in 1189, Christian mobs in London attacked the Jews of the city.[65]

A century later, in 1290, Jews were expelled from England by Edward I, and some three hundred Jewish communities were annihilated in the German empire in the mid-fourteenth century, during the course of the Black Death. Most of these atrocities were not sanctioned by the Church leader-

---

62. Quoted in Rousmaniere, *Bridge to Dialogue*, 59.

63. Seiferth, *Synagogue and Church in the Middle Ages*, 69.

64. Roth, "Bishops and Jews in the Middle Ages," 9.

65. Hugh Levinson, "What Are the Origins of the Jewish Blood Libel Myth?" published in BBC News, 23 Jan. 2004. For the evolution of perceptions of Jews, see Michael Goodich, ed., *Other Middle Ages: Witnesses at the Margins of Medieval Society* (Philadelphia: University of Pennsylvania Press, 1998). For attacks on Jews following Richard I's coronation, see Roger of Hoveden, *The Annals Comprising the History of England and of other Countries of Europe from AD 732 to AD 1201*, trans. Henry T. Riley (London: H. G. Bohn, 1853).

ship. However, the Fourth Lateran Council of 1215, presided over by Innocent III, issued canon 68, which insisted on distinctive dress for both Jews and Muslims, hoping thus to limit their interaction with Christians. Although the wearing of the yellow badge was prescribed for Jews and Muslims in all of Christendom, it was only sporadically imposed.

Even as the papacy proceeded against heretical movements within the Church in the twelfth and thirteenth centuries, it preached tolerance toward Jews.[66] A number of bishops did likewise. Archbishop Albrecht of Magdeburg intervened in 1206 when the Christians of Halle sought to expel the Jews, offering them one thousand silver marks to reconcile themselves with the Jews. As Archbishop of Narbonne, Guy Foulques or Guido Fulcodi, later Pope Clement IV (1265–68), preserved cordial relations with the Jews there, agreeing to almost all of their petitions and requests.[67] Although the Church consistently favored conversion, its ecclesiastical courts for trying and punishing heretics had no jurisdiction over Jews who had not converted to the faith. It did have jurisdiction over the Marranos, Jewish converts to Catholicism, to assure that they did not revert to their old practices. Nonetheless, from the sixth to the sixteenth century, the Church became increasingly tolerant of the practice of Judaism and softened its attitude toward Jews. This may have contributed to the shift in Jewish population from Asia and North Africa to Europe from the eighth to the twelfth century, so that by the fourteenth century most Jews lived within the bounds of Christendom.[68] At the end of the twelfth century, when the Vatican threatened excommunication against any Christian who lent money for interest, it provided an opportunity for Jews to step into the breach, and thus the basis for new accusations against them as usurious moneylenders.

The popes were prepared to confer a wide variety of privileges upon the Jews, convinced that by so doing they magnified apostolic charity and hastened conversion. "In 1530, Clement VII freed a Jewish banker from custom duties on goods he was about to transfer from one locale to another," one author has noted. "It was not, however, business interests that

66. Seiferth, *Synagogue and Church in the Middle Ages*, 68.

67. Roth, "Bishops and Jews in the Middle Ages," 5, 10.

68. Tozzini, "Legal Discrimination against Italian Jews," 16; Carmichael, *Satanizing of the Jews*, 50.

prompted the transfer, but the imminent conversion of the banker, who as the pope duly noted had been carrying on a fruitful dialogue with various Christian theologians." But many criticized this papal policy of toleration. In 1539 Cardinal Jacobo Sadoleto complained to Pope Paul III (1534–49) that Jews were accorded honors, awards, distinctions, and privileges denied their Christian counterparts. Although the cardinal may have exaggerated, researchers have discovered that Jews in the first half of the sixteenth century were granted a number of unique privileges.[69] Still, the Jews in the Papal States, as elsewhere in Christian Europe, endured burdensome restrictions as well.

Although some strictures of canon law restricted Jewish life and activity, popes consistently refused to sanction popular violence against them. Gregory IX (1227–41), an expert in canon law and theology, in his bull *Etsi Judarorum* (1233) insisted that Jews in Christian countries be treated with the same respect that Christians expected in non-Christian lands. During the plague Jews became the scapegoats for the frenzied masses and were massacred from the Mediterranean to the Black Sea—but not in Avignon, where they received papal protection. In fact, Pope Clement VI (1342–52) courageously defended them, denying that they had poisoned the wells and explaining that their isolation and hygiene, rather than witchcraft or Satanism, accounted for their lighter causalities during the plague. The Spanish Inquisition, which was often notoriously abusive toward Jews, operated autonomously and often in contradiction to papal directives. Later, in 1524–25, Pope Clement VII supported the efforts of the self-proclaimed Jewish leader and messianic pretender David ben Shelomoh, also known as David Reubeni, to launch a crusade to liberate the Holy Land from the Muslims. Although never realized, this scheme provided the interesting prospect of Jewish-Christian cooperation with papal blessing.[70] At the end of the fourteenth century, when Jews were barred from Russia because the Orthodox Church feared a "judaizing heresy," large numbers of Jews found refuge in Catholic Poland.[71]

Even earlier a series of popes had attempted to halt the Christian persecution of Jews, arguing that they were to be preserved in the position

69. Stow, *Taxation, Community and State*, 58, 1.
70. Waagenaar, *Pope's Jews*, 144–51.
71. Carmichael, *Satanizing of the Jews*, 76.

they enjoyed in the time of their predecessors. Thus in the thirteenth century Tebaldo Visconti, Pope Gregory X (1271–76), drawing upon the earlier admonitions of Innocent III and Innocent IV (1243–54), repudiated the charge of the "blood libel" that Jews seized, killed, and ate Christian children. To repudiate the rumor that at Passover they murdered Christian children and mixed their blood in their unleavened bread, Pope Innocent IV issued a bull in 1247 informing Christians that Jews were not allowed to touch a dead body at Passover. Pope Gregory ordered Jews seized under this "silly pretext" immediately released from prison, commanding the faithful not to stir up anything new against them.[72] Pope Clement VI also called for an end to the accusations of the blood libel and attacks against the Jews, but he likewise was not heeded. Although a series of popes denied the charge of Jewish ritual murder, the accusation was launched by part of the lower clergy and remained embedded in the psychology of the masses for centuries.

Many papal pronouncements and theological discourses on behalf of the Jews had little impact on the poorly educated lower clergy and the illiterate masses. The intricacies of their expositions confused the broad public, especially since these exhortations did not effectively confront the institutional anti-Judaism fed by Scripture, the Church Fathers, and popular beliefs. The Passion plays that originated in the ritual of the Church and were sanctioned by it reinforced the negative popular image of the Jews, who were portrayed as scheming, cruel, and perfidious. Small wonder that persecution continued, as Jews were increasingly viewed in Europe not as the "descendants of patriarchs and prophets" but as "murderers of Christ."[73]

Jews were expelled from France in 1394, from Prague in 1400, from Vienna in 1421, from Cologne in 1424, and from Augsburg in 1440. These expulsions were followed by others—from the Tyrol in 1493, from Nuremberg in 1499, from Spain in 1492, and from Portugal in 1497. Jews were exiled from the Kingdom of Naples in 1541, from Genoa and Venice in 1555, and from papal Bologna in 1593. In 1596 they were forced out of the Duchy of Milan. These expulsions of the fifteenth and sixteenth centuries reflected a mingling of popular religious fanaticism with emerging nationalist

72. Rousmaniere, *Bridge to Dialogue*, 61; Tierney, *The Middle Ages*, 1:230–31.
73. Seiferth, *Synagogue and Church in the Middle Ages*, 73.

identities.[74] In a sense they foreshadowed the merging of anti-Judaism and anti-Semitism in the nineteenth and twentieth centuries. In 1670 Jews were once again expelled from Vienna, but were soon allowed to return.

While Christian theology and papal policy repeatedly proclaimed that Jews were not to be molested, Rome from time to time adhered to the Justinian principle of preventing Jewish social intercourse with Christians. Although there is considerable continuity in the policies of the popes, there are also remarkable instances of discontinuity. Both were reflected in Rome's policies toward the Jews. The Fourth Lateran Council of 1215, called by Innocent III, reaffirmed Gregory VII's ban on Jews holding public office and positions of authority. At the same time, it reiterated the notion of Christian superiority over Jews, forbidding marriage and sexual relations between them. It also imposed special tax burdens, requiring that Jews wear distinctive clothing and a ring-shaped badge. John XXII (1316–34) sanctioned the investigation of heresy among converted Jews and renewed old papal proscriptions against the Talmud. After 1363 Jews in Rome had to wear a red cloak. Other provisions prohibited Jews from sporting their best garments on Sundays, while mandating that they remain locked in their homes on Easter and other Christian holidays. The latter stipulation had a twofold inspiration. In addition to protecting Christian sensibilities, it sought to prevent mob outbursts and violence against those deemed the "killers of Christ" and desecrators of the host.

Canon 68 of the Fourth Lateran Council decreed that "Jews and Saracens of both sexes in every Christian province and at all times shall be marked off in the eyes of the public from other peoples through the character of their dress." The Church Fathers did not deem this oppressive for Jews, "Particularly since it may be read in the writings of Moses [Num. 15:37–41] that this very law has been enjoined upon them."[75] At any rate, the initiative for these dress codes apparently came from the French bishops rather than the pope. In Spain the provision was totally ignored.[76] It has been alleged that many Jews did not resent being confined to Jewish quarters, which seemed to assure their social, religious, and security needs.[77] Jews allegedly recognized that Innocent III had protected them

---

74. Ruether, *Faith and Fratricide*, 212.
75. Canon 56 of the Fourth Lateran Council, in Tierney, *The Middle Ages*, 1:229–30.
76. Roth, "Bishops and Jews in the Middle Ages," 11.
77. Katz, *Exclusiveness and Tolerance*, 132–33.

against the violence of the French crusaders even though he protested Philip Augustus's royal protection to Jewish moneylenders in 1204. Jews did not appreciate this papal interference. They also had reason to regret ecclesiastical interference in Jewish religious questions, although this was partially provoked by divisions within Judaism and the appeal of rival Jewish factions to Catholic authorities. In the early thirteenth century Orthodox Jews in Montpellier attacked the writings of the celebrated Jewish rationalist Maimonides. They implored the Dominicans and the Franciscans to condemn his works and to treat Jewish "heretics" in the same manner that they treated Christian ones. As a consequence, in late 1233 all of Maimonides' books were seized and ceremonially burned.[78] Nor did most Jews appreciate being constrained to listen to the Christian sermons imposed by Pope Nicholas III (1277–80), who sought their conversion. The failure of these ventures provoked more stringent clerical and papal measures.

In states and regions where Jews remained they were restricted to certain quarters. Not surprisingly, such segregation was not always opposed by Jews who feared assimilation. "The church does not forbid believers to associate with unbelievers who have never accepted the Christian faith—that is pagans and Jews," St. Thomas wrote. "Believers are forbidden to associate with someone for two reasons—first to punish the one who is cut off from association with the faithful and secondly, for the protection of those who are forbidden to associate with him," he added. This may have influenced the papal determination to establish ghettoes, which in its perspective had a twofold aim—to protect Catholics from too close an association with those of the Jewish faith, and to protect Jews from mob violence. While St. Thomas questioned the validity of the first premise, he supported the second.[79]

In 1540 Pope Paul III, following St. Thomas, catalogued Jewish privileges, stating that "Jews would be permitted to live wherever they pleased in a city, even among Christians."[80] Some saw this papal protection as too little, too late, for the beleaguered Jews, especially since, at other times, Rome continued to champion Jewish isolation from Christian communi-

78. Carmichael, *Satanizing of the Jews,* 66.

79. Owen Chadwick, *A History of the Popes, 1830–1914* (Oxford: Clarendon Press, 1998), 128–29; *Aquinas on Politics and Ethics,* 61.

80. Stow, *Taxation, Community and State,* 59.

ties. Thus restrictions were imposed upon the Jews by Popes Nicholas IV (1288–92), Boniface VIII (1294–1301), Paul IV (1555–59), Pius V (1566–72), Gregory XIII (1572–85), and Clement VIII (1592–1605), among others. An edict of Pope Boniface VIII stipulated that Christians who converted to Judaism be treated as heretics. In 1344 papal legates were authorized by Pope Clement VI to take action against Jewish converts in Sicily who reverted to the old faith.[81] Subsequently, Pope Paul V (1605–21) persuaded the University of Pisa not to grant Jews degrees in medicine. These restrictive and.at times oppressive measures were not seen as contravening papal prohibitions against the molestation of the Jews but as legitimate mechanisms for protecting the faithful.

Although papal measures were taken to preserve the faith and were religiously motivated, anti-Judaism from time to time had recourse to proto-nationalist or racial arguments. For example, Spanish laws on "the purity of blood" were eventually applied to prevent individuals who had "Jewish blood" from occupying certain Church offices—a move apparently sanctioned by Pope Paul IV (1555–59). Furthermore, many of the religious orders discriminated against the descendants of Jews. Ignatius of Loyola (1491–1556), however, refused to exclude converted Jews from the Society of Jesus he founded, which was recognized by Paul III (1534–49) in 1540.[82] In 1593, however, after the death of Loyola, the Jesuits prevented men of Jewish ancestry as far back as five generations from entering their order. Neither the theological basis of clerical persecution nor protection of the Jews was understood by the masses.

The papacy had recourse to other coercive measures vis-à-vis the Jews. In 1240 Gregory IX was presented with a list of charges against the Talmud, the commentary on Jewish practices and requirements. Complaining that it permitted Jews to practice deception and violence against Christians, he commanded the kings of France, England, Aragon, and Castile to confiscate all Jewish books. Most monarchs ignored the invocation, but Louis IX of France allegedly had some twenty-four wagons of Jewish books destroyed. A number of subsequent popes reversed course, however, and or-

81. Tozzini, "Legal Discrimination against Italian Jews," 16.
82. James Bernauer, S.J., "The Holocaust and the Catholic Church's Search for Forgiveness," http://www.bc.edu/research/cjl/meta-elements/texts/articles/bernauer.htm, accessed 2 Feb. 2004.

dered the remaining books returned to their owners. This did not prevent Pope Eugenius IV (1431–47) from issuing instructions prohibiting Jews from studying the Talmud, or the Inquisition's condemnation of the Talmud in 1553. Although Pope Julius III (1550–55) had strong reservations about the condemnation, he had to capitulate, and in May 1554 he issued the bull *Cum sicut nuper,* giving papal sanction to the Inquisition's Talmud decree, though he specified that only books that insulted the Christian faith should be burned.[83] Since most of the rulers, bishops, and other magistrates instructed to confiscate the Talmud were not familiar with Hebrew, all Hebrew works were deemed dangerous, and the papal order degenerated into a wider confiscation and destruction of Jewish books, religious and otherwise.[84] During the tenure of Pius V (1566–72) thousands of additional copies of the Talmud were destroyed in the Papal States. This edict was later reversed by Sixtus V (1585–90), who permitted the possession as well as the printing of the Talmud. Clement VIII in turn rescinded the decree of Sixtus. The path pursued by his successors proved no more consistent, and though other campaigns against the Talmud were conducted by the papacy, no perpetually binding canon against it was ever issued.[85]

The papal position on contact with Jews also remained inconsistent, and stories circulated that a number of medieval popes were actually Jewish.[86] In fact, the antipope Anacletus II (1130–38) of the Pierleoni family was of Jewish descent (Baruch-Benedict family). Opposition to Anacletus flowed not so much from his Jewish background as from the rivalry of Rome's powerful families, the divisions in the College of Cardinals between its newer and older members, and his relations with the empire and the other powers. As temporal and spiritual leaders, the policies adopted by the popes toward the Jews were at once protective and restrictive.

Ironically, the popes were among the first to violate the prohibitions on Christian-Jewish interaction, having recourse to Jewish financiers as well as Jewish physicians, even as they publicly endorsed a form of apartheid. Thus a series of papal exemptions allowed Jews to practice medicine on Christians, while Jewish moneylenders often thrived with express papal

83. Stow, *Taxation, Community and State,* 66.
84. Waagenaar, *Pope's Jews,* 166.
85. Hood, *Aquinas and the Jews,* 35.
86. See Joachim Prinz, *Popes from the Ghetto: A View of Medieval Christendom* (New York: Horizon Press, 1966).

permission. Pope Boniface IX (1389–1404) in 1392 honored his Jewish doctor, Angel ben Manuel, by making him not only his personal physician but also a member of his household. Innocent VII (1404–6) in turn honored his Jewish doctor by making him a Roman citizen. The Borgia Pope Alexander VI (1492–1503) likewise had a Jewish physician, who was retained by his successor, Julius II (1503–13). A number of Renaissance popes granted the Jews expansive privileges and proved accommodating toward Jewish moneylenders. Eugenius IV was not unique in issuing an explicit authorization, in 1437, of Jewish moneylenders within the walls of Florence.[87] Popes, no less than bishops and monarchs, required the services of Jews.

Pope Martin V, called to power by the Council of Constance (1414–18) after the Great Schism (1378–1417), expressed broad tolerance of Jews. He reasserted the principles set forth by Gregory the Great in 598 and cautioned friars not to incite mob violence against Jews. In a letter of 1422 Martin ordered a halt to the incendiary practices of Franciscan preachers, indicating that such threats would deter those who would more readily come to the faith through Christian kindness and generosity.[88] He officially permitted the Jews of the Papal States to attend universities and granted a number of concessions to the Jews of the Duchy of Savoy. Martin agreed that Jews there should be allowed to practice their faith so long as they adhered to papal orders. He also stipulated that no Jew was to be baptized before the age of twelve without the consent of the parents. He deplored violence against Jews, charging that those who oppressed Jews were not true Christians. "Whereas the Jews are made to the image of God, and a remnant of them will one day be saved, and whereas they have sought our protection: following in the footsteps of our Predecessors," read his Declaration on the Protection of the Jews (1419), "We command that they be not molested in their synagogues; that their laws, rights and customs be not assailed; that they not be baptized by force, constrained to observe Christian festivals, nor to wear new badges, and that they not hindered in their business relations with Christians."[89]

---

87. Michele Luzzatti, "Florence against the Jews or the Jews against Florence?" in Pugliese, *Most Ancient of Minorities*, 65.

88. Stow, *Taxation, Community and State*, 63.

89. "Medieval Sourcebook," "Martin V: From the Declaration on the Protection of the Jews (1419)," http://www.fordham.edu/halsall.source/mart5-jews.html, accessed 2 Feb. 2004.

Rather than call for the segregation that many of his predecessors and successors did, Martin confided that contact with the Jews was useful. In his bulls of 1418, 1422, and 1429 he conferred or confirmed a series of privileges, while removing burdensome restrictions from Jews. A number of subsequent popes, including Nicholas V (1447–55), Sixtus IV (1471–84), and Alexander VI, continued his conciliatory course. Sixtus IV repeatedly sought to curtail the zeal of the Spanish Inquisition and prohibited the worship of the child Simon Unverdorben (Simon the Unblemished), also known as Simon of Trent, whom the Jews of that city were falsely accused of having murdered in a religious rite (1474). Sixtus suspected foul play, believing that the thirteen Jews executed were innocent and they had been charged with the crime so as to facilitate the expulsion of Jews from Trent and the expropriation of their property. Despite a papal investigation of the incident, Sixtus proved unable to reverse the decision of the local court. Indeed, Sixtus V proved even less able to withstand popular pressure and officially recognized the sanctity of San Simonino.[90]

In a sense, those popes who were favorably inclined toward Jews found themselves constrained by popular prejudice. In a sense they were the victims of their own negligence and inability to reverse centuries of Christian intolerance. Nonetheless, a number of popes sought conciliation, even though the overall papal policy toward Jews and Judaism remained inconsistent.

Pope Alexander VI confronted popular opposition for allowing Jewish refugees from Spain to settle in the Papal States and permitting the Jewish population of Rome to increase dramatically. In the next century Pope Leo X (1513–21), who was favorably inclined toward Jews and employed Jewish physicians and artists at his court, overcame the skepticism of some and accorded Hebrew literature recognition as an academic discipline. Leo granted the Hebrews a series of dispensations and privileges in the hope and expectation that this would lead them to convert to the Christian religion. "We—hoping that the use of such magnanimity, which the Apostolic See has always followed in your case, will at some point soften your bonds and excise the blindness from your eyes so that you should see and accept your creator in the saving bath of regeneration, and inclined to fulfill your request—accordingly quiet you (on your payment) and liberate and ab-

90. Waagenaar, *Pope's Jews*, 127–30.

solve you (from any claim of unpaid taxes), and so too we confirm your privileges."[91] In March 1524 Clement VII confirmed the privileges of the Jews of Rome.

Pope Paul III, who established the Congregation of the Inquisition in 1543, revealed his clemency in 1535 by confirming for the Jews of the Romagna all of the privileges they had hitherto enjoyed. He bestowed a number of favors upon the Jews residing elsewhere in his state, welcoming those who were expelled from the Kingdom of Naples (1541) into the Papal States. Among other things, he ended the Passion plays performed at the Coliseum, which were often followed by mob violence against the Jews.[92] In a letter of 1542 he cautioned the clergy of Milan against using incendiary language against Jews, who were to be tolerated and won over by Christian kindness rather than subjected to hostile attacks. Pope Paul, like most popes of the sixteenth century, made conversion of the Jews a central goal.[93] Even Julius III, who reluctantly ordered copies of the Talmud found within his state seized and burned, imposed a fine on any Christian who baptized a Jewish child against the wishes of its parents. Subsequently, Pius IV (1559–65) resisted applying many of the repressive measures flowing from the Counter-Reformation against the Jews.

Papal toleration was countered by papal persecution, as other popes showed themselves less sympathetic and at times hostile to Jews. Pope Eugenius IV revoked many of the concessions granted Jews by Martin V, including their right to attend universities, while severely restricting the number of professions they could enter. At the same time, he forbade Jewish physicians to attend Christian patients, while again constraining them to listen to Christian sermons. During the course of the Council of Basle (1431–49), Eugenius decreed (in 1434) that Jews should live in separate quarters—a call he repeated in his bull of 1445. Many of these proscriptions were adopted by his successor, Nicholas V, who in 1451 barred Jews from all "honorable walks of life."[94]

The Church continued to follow the teaching of St. Thomas Aquinas on conversion. "There are some unbelievers such as the Gentiles and the Hebrews who have never accepted the Christian faith," St. Thomas wrote.

91. Stow, *Taxation, Community and State,* 53.
92. Waagenaar, *Pope's Jews,* 104.
93. Stow, *Taxation, Community and State,* 45, 54, 63.
94. Tozzini, "Legal Discrimination against Italian Jews," 19.

"These should in no way be forced to believe, for faith is a matter of the will."[95] In the 1530s the influential cardinal and professor of canon law Pier Paolo Pariseo judged that the forced baptism of Portuguese Jews in 1497 had not been valid and that they should not be deemed property baptized. For those who freely chose to convert, Pope Paul III granted the Jesuits permission to open two houses or "Case dei Catecumeni" in Rome in 1543 for the instruction of Jewish men and women who sought conversion to Catholicism. Initially the synagogues of the city were burdened with the responsibility of funding these conversion centers, and finally responsibility for their funding was thrust upon the Jewish community of the Eternal City.[96] Although Pope Paul restricted the unjust inquisitorial prosecution of Spanish and Portuguese Jews, he appointed the anti-Judaic Gian Pietro Carafa to preside over the revived Roman Inquisition.

As the Counter-Reformation continued, Gian Pietro Carafa, who became Paul IV, had recourse to more stringent measures. Convinced that the papal policy of kindness and dispensations had been abused by the Jews and had resulted in few conversions, he had recourse to a policy of discrimination that he hoped would weaken Jewish communities and stubborn adherence to Judaism. He frankly acknowledged that the papacy tolerated Jews to the precise end that they converted, and to encourage such conversion he felt that Jews should be made to feel the full brunt of their servitude. He thus resurrected all the restrictions and dismantled all the dispensations on Jews in the Papal States. His papal bull of 1555 (*Cum Nobis Absurdem*), issued soon after his accession, restored the most repressive prohibitions on the Jews in his state. It restricted both their financial and commercial activities, rendering the lending of money far less profitable by imposing stringent controls on interest rates. At the same time it allowed Jews to deal only in old clothes and secondhand goods, while again forbidding Jewish physicians from treating Christian patients. It once more prohibited Jews from employing either male or female Christian servants, while barring most associations between members of the two faiths.

Cum Nobis Absurdem also prescribed that Jews in the Papal States were to be allowed no more than one synagogue per community, and required

95. *Aquinas on Politics and Ethics,* 61.
96. Stow, "Conversion, Apostasy, and Apprehension," 923; Waagenaar, *Pope's Jews,* 164.

that their accounting books be in Italian rather than Hebrew.[97] The bull forbade the future ownership of real property by Jews in the Papal States, while constraining them to sell their current property. It also called for the Jews of Rome to be shut in the ghetto, which was chained shut every night, and it mandated that they wear distinctive garb.[98] In many ways this bull was a watershed, and many of Paul IV's restrictions and prohibitions remained in effect until the middle of the nineteenth century. It represented the opposite of the lenient papal legislation of the first half of the sixteenth century. To be sure, the papacy still sought the conversion of the Jews, but it moved from employing the carrot to using the stick in its campaign. Segregation and conversion were the two sides of papal policy toward Jews. In 1556 a ghetto was also established in papal Bologna. Ghettoes spread throughout Italy in the sixteenth century and became fixtures in England and Germany in the seventeenth. Paradoxically, many of Paul IV's repressive measures, rather than disrupt the Jewish communities of the Papal States, stabilized those that survived. Furthermore, Jews were not alone in resenting Pope Paul IV. At his death, the joyful people of Rome set a fire in the Castel Sant' Angelo upon hearing the "good news."[99]

The celebrations in the Jewish communities proved short lived, however. The inflexible Michele Ghislieri, who had been named commissioner general of the Roman Inquisition in 1561, became Pope Pius V in early 1566. In a bull of 19 April 1566 (*Romanus Pontifex*), he renewed the anti-Jewish edicts of Paul IV, thereby canceling most of the mitigations allowed by his predecessor, Pius IV. He re-imposed the "badge of shame"—the obligation of Jews to wear yellow hats—while excluding Jews from banking and shutting them in ghettoes. Pius V, who was canonized in 1712, imposed restrictions on the Jews of Rome during his moral campaign. Accusing the Jews of divination and witchcraft as well as of usury, he sought to separate them from Christians by returning them to the ghetto.[100] His anti-Judaic provisions were more easily catalogued than enforced, however, because the Jewish population was widely scattered throughout the state. This led Pius to resort to other measures, including the imposition

97. Tozzini, "Legal Discrimination against Italian Jews," 16, 18.
98. Kertzer, *Popes against the Jews*, 27, 101, 139; Chadwick, *History of the Popes*, 128.
99. Stow, *Taxation, Community and State*, 67, 26, 38.
100. Sergio Pagano, "Pius V (1566–72)," in *Great Popes through History: An Encyclopedia*, ed. Frank J. Coppa (Westport, Conn.: Greenwood Press, 2002), 2:341.

of new and heavy taxes and fines upon the Jewish communities of his state. In 1569 he issued the bull *Hebraeorum gens,* which mandated the expulsion of all Jews from the cities of the Papal States, except for Rome and Ancona, within three months.[101] It proved ineffective and short lived, as Jews were permitted to return by his successors, Gregory XIII and Sixtus V.

Upon their return, however, Sixtus V imposed an entrance fee of two *scudi* on all males between the ages of fifteen and sixty, as well as an additional 1.2 *scudi* for each year of residence thereafter. In return, these males were exempt from all other forms of taxation, and the pope also granted them permission to open a lending bank as well as to engage in commerce.[102] Pope Clement VIII later issued another order of expulsion, which was itself overturned. The Reformation that began in 1517 did not improve the position of Jews or change their status in Catholic countries, including the Papal States, or in Lutheran ones. During these turbulent times the popes lost their traditional and primary source of income—the many spirituality taxes paid by the clergy. To compensate for their decreased income at a time of increased expenses, the popes relied more on the taxation imposed upon the population of the Papal States. The Jews, like other papal subjects, were adversely affected, although their overall tax burden was not unduly oppressive.[103] The Jews fared no better in Germany.

Early in his career Martin Luther had had a favorable opinion of Jews, writing that they "were blood relations of our Lord; if it were proper to boast of flesh and blood, the Jews belong more to Christ than we." Finding them opposed to conversion, however, he later complained that one could sooner convert the devil than the Jews, and he turned violently against them, judging their rejection of the truth as nothing less than "satanic demonism." He called them morally depraved, "devilish," and "vermin." He warned Christians to guard themselves against the "poisonous activities" of this "miserable and accursed people."[104] Luther's hatred of Jews endured

101. Abraham David, "The Expulsion from the Papal States in Light of Hebrew Sources," in Pugliese, *Most Ancient of Minorities,* 91–99.

102. Stow, *Taxation, Community and State,* 33.

103. In 1552, for example, the Jews provided less than 2 percent of the total papal income. Ibid., 19.

104. "Medieval Sourcebook," "Martin Luther (1483–1546): The Jews and Their Lies (1543)," http://www.fordham.edu/halsall/source/luther-jews.html, accessed 2 Feb. 2004; Carmichael, *Satanizing of the Jews,* 81–84.

to the end. He condemned them in his last sermon, and even on his deathbed, on 18 February 1546, he blamed the Jews for his plight.[105] Still, Luther's explosive, often coarse language against the Jews should be not be taken out of context. He was equally venomous in his condemnation of Catholicism, the papacy, the Anabaptists, the German peasantry, and all others he perceived as enemies.[106] Calvinism proved far less hostile to Judaism than Lutheranism was.

A number of Luther's followers adopted the anti-Judaic stance revealed in his 1543 pamphlet denouncing "The Jews and Their Lies." Luther's seven-point solution to the "Jewish problem" did not display the contradictions inherent in the papal program. He advised the princes and people to (1) set fire to their synagogues and schools and cover their remains with dirt so that there would be no sign of them; (2) destroy their houses so they would have to live like gypsies; (3) destroy their prayer books and Talmudic writings, which preached blasphemy and idolatry; (4) forbid rabbis to teach, on pain of death; (5) abolish all safe conduct for Jews on the highways; (6) prohibit Jews from practicing their usury and confiscate all their gold and silver; and finally (7) put all Jews to honest labor so that they could earn their bread by the sweat of their brow. "If this does not help," he wrote in conclusion, "we must drive them out like mad dogs, so that we do not become partakers of their abominable blasphemy and other of their vices and thus merit God's wrath and be damned with them."[107] His position and policies denied Jews the theological mitigation and protection they had long received from the Church.

Despite Luther's prosecutorial program and outburst of vituperation, there were those on the Catholic side who charged that the Jews were responsible for the Protestant Reformation! During the Counter-Reformation, by contrast, Paul's successor, Pius IV, who completed the work of the Council of Trent, commenced a theological rapprochement with Judaism by commissioning a new catechism that specified that the death of Jesus was caused not so much by external violence—whether by Romans or Jews—but by internal consent. It stipulated that Christ's sacri-

---

105. Carroll, *Constantine's Sword*, 428.

106. On Luther and the Jews, see Hans Hillderbrand, "Martin Luther and the Jews," in *Jews and Christians: Exploring the Past, Present, and Future*, ed. James Charlesworth (New York: Crossroad, 1990), 133–43.

107. Ibid., 6.

fice was meant to expiate the sins of all mankind, who were in a sense all responsible for the crucifixion. Furthermore, his bull of 1562 permitted Jews in the Papal States to acquire land valued up to 1,500 ducats and to trade in things other than old rags.[108] Paul VI (1605–21) supported the teaching of Hebrew by members of the religious orders in the universities of early modern Europe. The papal position toward the Jews remained contradictory, as did that of the *philosophes* of the Enlightenment.

The Enlightenment, which worshipped reason rather than revelation, led to Deism, which rejected the established religions and challenged the authority of the institutional Church as well as the practices of Judaism. In the mid-eighteenth century there were some 3 million Jews in a European population of about 150 million. About one-half lived in eastern Europe and especially in Poland, while in central Europe they were concentrated in commercial centers and cities such as Vienna, Berlin, Frankfurt, and Leipzig, with smaller numbers found in France, the Low Countries, England, and Italy. Almost everywhere they were subject to legal disabilities and popular mistrust. While religious toleration was championed in the salons of the intellectual elite, it was not popular with the masses or with most political and religious figures. Indeed, prior to the French Revolution, discrimination against the Jews remained pervasive in the major states of Europe.

As late as the middle of the eighteenth century, Pope Benedict XIV (1740–58), who condemned Freemasonry in 1751, sought to keep Christians and Jews apart, going so far as to decree that Jews were not to have their linens washed by Christians—unless they were transported by specially licensed porters.[109] His anti-Judaism also emerged in his encyclical to the Poles, decrying the call for the principle of freedom of conscience throughout much of Europe and the indiscriminate mingling of Christians and Jews in Poland. In his letter, Benedict praised the efforts of the bishops in aiding the Poles in resisting Jewish "domination." Some of his accusations descended to the level of popular stereotype.

> The Jews are cruel taskmasters, not only working the farmers harshly and forcing them to carry excessive loads, but also whipping them for punish-

108. Lapide, *Three Popes and the Jews*, 76.
109. Tozzini, "Legal Discrimination against Italian Jews," 19.

ment. So it has come about that those poor families are the subjects of the Jews, submissive to their will and power. Furthermore, although the power to punish lies with the Christian official, he must comply with the commands of the Jews and inflict the punishments they desire. If he doesn't, he would lose his post. Therefore, the tyrannical orders of the Jews have to be carried out.[110]

Benedict denounced the employment of Christians as domestics by Jews and the promotion of Jews to public office, and reaffirmed the decrees of the Apostolic See forbidding Jews to live in the same cities as Christians. During his pontificate, in 1753–54, the police in Rome searched ghetto homes for forbidden books, including those designed for liturgical use in the synagogues.[111] Still, it is unlikely that the police confiscated thirty-eight wagon loads of books, as one writer reports,[112] unless they were very small wagons. This does not excuse Benedict, who warned the clergy not to do any business or indeed have any dealings with these "faithless" people, and especially to avoid borrowing from them. Subsequent popes were among the first to violate this papal proscription. Determined to quarantine and restrict the Jewish presence, Benedict disdained the zeal of the famous monk Radulph, who in the twelfth century incited Christians to destroy Jews, whom he branded treacherous enemies of the faith. Instead, this pope concurred with Saint Bernard (1090–1153), who, even as he preached the crusade, opposed the persecution of the Jews in Mainz. Mixed sentiments toward the Jews prevailed in Rome in the eighteenth century and continued throughout much of the following one as well.

The papacy continued to disapprove of the elimination of Jews as a violation of Church doctrine. Nor did the Church ever espouse or second the call for a racially pure society that emerged in the nineteenth century, which was likewise contrary to its theology. Even critics acknowledge that from the thirteenth century on the papacy periodically acted to protect Jews from Christians. When Clement XIV (1769–74) assumed the triple tiara in 1769, he ended the Inquisition's control over Rome's ghetto, assigning the task to the cardinal vicar of the Eternal City, while ending some of the occupational restrictions Jews faced, allowing them to prac-

---

110. *A Quo Primum* (encyclical of Pope Benedict XIV on Jews and Christians living in the same place), 14 June 1751, *PE* 1:42.
111. Tozzini, "Legal Discrimination against Italian Jews," 17.
112. Waagenaar, *Pope's Jews*, 168.

tice medicine and work as artisans among other things. In 1773 Clement XIV issued a brief suppressing the Jesuit Order.

The papal pendulum soon swung again in the opposite direction, as the curia continued to proclaim "no salvation outside the church" and preserved the right to suppress all ideas of which it did not approve.[113] Much of Clement XIV's liberalization was undone by his successor, Gianangelo Braschi, Pius VI (1775–99), who was elected pope after a 134-day conclave. Although critics found the new pope more handsome than holy and were appalled by his initial frivolity and nepotism, Pius VI from the first challenged the Enlightenment culture of the age and sought to restore the most repressive measures against the Jews of his state. That these anti-Judaic measures had to be reintroduced time and again suggests two things. First, the popes were inconsistent in their resolve regarding their policies toward the Jews, and second, the most oppressive measures were almost never rigidly enforced for any length of time.

Pius VI's edict of 20 April 1775 sought to return Jews to the ghettoes in Rome, Ancona, Ferrara, Lugo, Cento, Urbino, Senigaglia, and Pesaro and to force them to wear yellow badges, while constraining the Jewish community, once again, to pay for and listen to Christian sermons. It stipulated that no one buy, sell, translate, or possess any codex or volume on the Talmud or any book critical of the Christian faith. The edict also banned Christian silversmiths from producing any seven-branched candelabras, while prohibiting Jews from having any public cortege for their funerals.[114] Finally, it restricted their right to own property, kept them from enlarging their synagogues, and even denied them tombstones on their graves. Subsequently, in 1779, this pope restored some of the carnival rites that disparaged and humiliated Jews.[115] Pius VI proved no more successful than his like-minded predecessors in securing the implementation of his anti-Jewish measures at home and abroad, once again revealing the limits of papal authority and influence. To make matters worse, from the anti-Judaic papal perspective, Rome's anti-Jewish actions no longer found a receptive audience in the eighteenth-century culture of the Enlightenment, whose overall agenda was secular and often antireligious.

113. Robert R. Palmer, *Catholics and Unbelievers in Eighteenth-Century France* (Princeton: Princeton University Press, 1967), 5.

114. Tozzini, "Legal Discrimination against Italian Jews," 17.

115. Kertzer, *Popes against the Jews,* 5, 26–29, 75.

The Papal States and the papacy had to confront an age of toleration and liberalism that increasingly denounced the restrictions on the Jews as an anachronism fostered by blind ignorance and blatant superstition. In the second half of the seventeenth century Baruch Spinoza (1632–77) championed freedom of thought and religion in a major work published in Amsterdam in which he concluded that the true aim of government was liberty.[116] The Church concurred with the Orthodox Jewish community of Amsterdam, which excommunicated Spinoza in 1656 for looking to natural philosophy rather than religious revelation or the Scriptures as the basis for truth and ethics. The condemnation did not curtail philosophical speculation, of course. At the end of the seventeenth century and opening of the eighteenth, John Locke (1632–1704) drafted a series of tracts on religious toleration. "A Letter Concerning Toleration," which Locke first published in Latin (1685) but which was soon translated into English and other languages, deeply influenced other enlightened thinkers. Locke posited that neither pagan nor Jew should have his civil rights abridged on the basis of religion. "Nobody, therefore, in fine, neither single persons nor churches, nay nor even commonwealths," he admonished, "have any just title to invade the civil rights and worldly goods of each other upon pretense of religion."[117] Locke emphasized not only the justice of religious toleration but the many benefits that flowed from it.

Locke's work on religious toleration had a tremendous impact in England and on the Continent. In England the Jews were accorded limited toleration following the Glorious Revolution of 1688. In France Locke's ideas were elaborated by Charles de Secondat, the Baron de Montesquieu. "To kill Jews for not believing what Christians believe is not merely cruel, but un-Christian as well," Montesquieu wrote, posing as a Jewish author. "You want us to be Christians, and you don't want to be Christians yourselves. But if you don't want to be Christians, at least be human beings."[118] Both Locke and Montesquieu found ready support for their notion of reli-

---

116. Spinoza, *A Treatise on Religion and Politics Containing Several Discussions Which Show That to Philosophize Not Only Can be Granted Without Detriment To Piety and Public Peace, But Cannot Be Destroyed Without Destroying Them as Well*, trans. R. M. N. Elwes (Amsterdam, 1670). See David Sidorsky, ed., *The Liberal Tradition in European Thought* (New York: Capricorn Books, 1971), 31–33.

117. Sidorksy, *Liberal Tradition*, 51.

118. Quoted in Peter Gay, *The Party of Humanity: Essays in the French Enlightenment* (New York: W. W. Norton, 1971), 99.

gious toleration of the Jews among thinkers of the German Enlightenment, or *Aufklarung*. Gotthold Ephraim Lessing (1729–81) issued an impassioned appeal for religious toleration of the Jews in his drama "Nathan the Wise" of 1779. He, like other German *philosophes*, sought Jewish liberation and assimilation, if not a Jewish makeover. Moses Mendelssohn (1729–86), on the other hand, perceived no conflict between civic equality and the practice of a particular religious observance.[119] King Frederick William I of Prussia (1713–40) assumed the lead in assuring Jews some protection. He was followed by Joseph II of Austria (1780–90), who assumed full power following the death of his mother, Maria Theresa.

Joseph's edict of toleration of May 1781 legalized Jews as residents of Vienna, lower Austria, Hungary, and Moravia, while expanding their civil rights. Joseph gave Jews as well as other non-Catholics full rights as citizens and allowed the private exercise of religion. The edict also granted them permission to attend the public schools and admission to all of the university faculties—save that of theology. At the same time it opened all occupations to them, expanding their areas of residence, while eliminating past discriminatory signs and clothing requirements. This edict, following one that curtailed the privileges and prerogatives of the Catholic clergy and the papacy's control of the Austrian Church, aroused Pius VI.[120] It contributed to his decision to venture to Vienna in 1782, the first pope in centuries to travel beyond the borders of Italy, to urge Joseph to reconsider and rescind these measures, but Pius proved unable to alter Austria's reformist course. Nor did the emperor back away from his toleration of non-Catholics during his 1783 visit to Pius VI in Rome. Joseph's toleration of non-Catholics and his imposition of restrictions on the Church were emulated by his younger brother, the grand duke of Tuscany, who encouraged the Synod of Pistoia (1786), which challenged Rome's centralization. The same year, 1876, even the prince-bishop of Cologne and Treves issued the Punctuation of Ems, flouting Rome's authority. The ensuing papal protests fell upon deaf ears.

The Enlightenment that nourished Joseph's reformism and challenged the Church did not prove entirely beneficial to the Jews and Judaism.

---

119. Carroll, *Constantine's Sword*, 417.

120. Fubini, *Condizione giuridica dell'ebraismo Italiano*, 1; Carmichael, *Satanizing of the Jews*, 112.

There was a Jewish variant of the new liberal culture called Haskalah, which emerged in German-speaking Europe under the leadership of Moses Mendelssohn. Although Mendelssohn remained a devout member of the Jewish congregation, like other *philosophes* he favored the assimilation of Jews into the broader national culture. Thus, though the enlightened elite favored Jewish civil emancipation, its rationalism proved no less critical of Jewish ritual than Christian authorities did, and because most of these figures were less familiar with Judaism, they found it more baffling, superstitious, and bizarre. The *philosophes* also criticized Jewish parochialism, which they found even more wanting than the universalism of the Church. Indeed, there were those who suspected that the pro-Jewish stance of many of the *philosophes* was simply another means of attacking the Church, in this case by using Jews as witnesses to the errors of Christianity.[121]

François-Marie Arouet (1694–1778), better known as Voltaire, was repelled by all organized religion and sought to liberate himself and others from its irrational grasp.[122] He was particularly critical of Jews, whom he derided as a "wretched" and "little people," who could not be used as role models, for "(putting aside religion) [they] were never anything but a race of ignorant and fanatic brigands."[123] But Voltaire's antagonism toward the Jews did not flow from the anti-Judaism of Christianity over the centuries. Indeed, he flatly rejected the portrayal of Judaism as a harbinger of Christianity as well as the contention that the source of Jewish suffering was their rejection of the new covenant. "It has been pretended that the dispersion of this people had been foretold, as a punishment for their refusal to acknowledge Jesus Christ as the Messiah," Voltaire wrote. But this neglected the fact "that they had been dispersed throughout the known world long before Jesus Christ."[124] He thus refused to accept the presence of Jews as testimony to the perils of heresy and found no real rationale for their preservation. As an ex-Christian, Voltaire ignored the religious attacks on Jews as deicides, faulting them instead for their "innate character."[125] Some

---

121. Carmichael, *Satanizing of the Jews,* 108.
122. See Carroll, *Constantine's Sword,* 421–22.
123. *The Portable Voltaire,* ed. Ben Ray Redman (New York: Viking Press, 1963), 167.
124. From Voltaire's *Philosophical Dictionary* (1764), reprinted in Richard S. Levy, ed., *Antisemitism in the Modern World: An Anthology of Texts* (Lexington, Mass.: D. C. Heath, 1991), 42.
125. Carroll, *Constantine's Sword,* 427.

have perceived his critique of the Jews and Judaism as a precursor to the racism and anti-Semitism of the following century.

A number of these prejudices were shared by his fellow *philosophes*. Denis Diderot (1713–84) claimed that one found among Jews "all the faults that mark an ignorant and superstitious people."[126] They are all born with the fury of fanaticism in their hearts, Voltaire warned, "just as the Bretons and the Germans are born with blond hair."[127] On the basis of these and similar condemnations, some have charged Voltaire with being anti-Semitic. At the same time, however, he deplored Jewish persecution by the Spanish and Portuguese Inquisitions, but perhaps more out of hatred of Christian fanaticism than sympathy for the Jewish plight. He continued to deplore Jewish greed, urging Jews to be less "calculating animals" and more "thinking ones."[128] Hannah Arendt has noted that the Christian suspicion of Jews for essentially religious reasons was transformed during the Enlightenment into a secular, racial hatred of the Jews.[129]

It is not surprising that Voltaire, who sought to discredit the Church as the implacable enemy of progress and rationality, should also strike at its Jewish roots. Peter Gay has concluded that many of Voltaire's diatribes against the Jews were inspired by anti-Christian rather than anti-Jewish convictions. "Despicable as the history of the Jews appears to Voltaire," Gay writes, "the history of the Christians, their disciples, is even more despicable." In Gay's view of Voltaire, "the vileness and absurdity of the Biblical Jews," reflects "the vileness and absurdity of Christianity."[130] Nonetheless, Voltaire and his fellow *philosophes* provided an escape for the Jews as the Christians had earlier, although they sought their conversion to the god of reason rather than to Christianity. They therefore encouraged the Jews to renounce their "superstitious" beliefs and historical "pretensions" and adopt the principles of rational thought. Frederick II of Prussia (1740–86), who lured Voltaire to Berlin and Potsdam for three years (1750–53), shared his mentor's outlook on the religious issue. In his *Political Testament* of 1768 he called Christianity "an old metaphysical fairy tale,

---

126. Quoted in Rousmaniere, *Bridge to Dialogue*, 76.
127. Quoted in Carroll, *Constantine's Sword*, 422.
128. Gay, *Party of Humanity*, 101–2.
129. Hannah Arendt, *The Origins of Totalitarianism* (New York: Harcourt, Brace and World, 1968), 8, quoted in Carroll, *Constantine's Sword*, 423–24.
130. Gay, *Party of Humanity*, 106.

full of miraculous legends, paradoxes, and nonsense."[131] Like Voltaire, Frederick disliked Jews, and in his *Political Testament* he urged his successors not to permit their increase in the state or allow them to dominate trade.

Thus, while Jews were offered the prospect of civil emancipation, they were to lose the protection the Church had provided on the basis of theological arguments and historical precedents that the rationalists judged ludicrous. Unquestionably, liberation and secularization proved to be a double-edged sword for the Jews. While Enlightenment thinkers espoused equality and toleration, they found Jewish fanaticism irrational and Jewish customs and practices bizarre. The rationalism of the eighteenth century sought to undermine both Judaism and Christianity. By challenging the latter, it also struck at its attitude toward its religious rival, which it had long restricted by theory and practice but always acknowledged as its seedbed. Rationalism rejected this religious view of the matter and the Christian conception of the Jewish role in history, viewing the Jews in purely secular terms. This led to positive results in parts of eighteenth-century Germany but had less fortunate consequences in the twentieth century. Rome, for its part, resisted the Enlightenment's secular evaluation of the Jews and religion in general, clinging tenaciously to its traditional interpretation and separatist solution.[132] Critics complained that the clock of Europe had stopped in Rome and predicted disastrous consequences for the papacy.

That prophesy seemed to materialize following the outbreak of the French Revolution in 1789, in which the Church eventually struggled for its survival in France and the countries of the Continent overrun by their forces. The "Jewish question" formed one part of this broader struggle that challenged the Church's role and primacy in state and society. French Jews were accorded full citizenship in 1792, as were Jews throughout most of Europe, occupied by the armies of revolutionary and Napoleonic France. In Rome as elsewhere the French dismantled the Jewish ghettoes they encountered. This was often accomplished in the face of papal and Church opposition, which continued to champion segregation as the only sure

---

131. Quoted in Hajo Holborn, *A History of Modern Germany, 1648–1840* (New York: Knopf, 1967), 239.

132. Katz, *From Prejudice to Destruction,* 24–25.

way to protect the Christian faith from Jewish beliefs. For the papacy and other champions of traditionalism, the emancipated Jews represented the very incarnation of the despised modernity that undermined their privileged position.

The long and erratic papal treatment of the Jews, and the history of Christian anti-Judaism over the centuries, unquestionably had some impact on the anti-Semitism that erupted in the nineteenth century. Following the French Revolution, however, the papacy found itself locked in a struggle with the competing ideologies of liberalism and nationalism, confronting the threat of secret societies and Freemasonry. Its attitude toward the Jews was increasingly reflected through the prism of this broader conflict.

2

ANTI-JUDAISM IN THE CHURCH

From the French Revolution to the Mid-Nineteenth Century

Now We consider another abundant source of the evils

with which the Church is afflicted at present: indifferen-

tism. This perverse opinion is spread on all sides by the

fraud of the wicked who claim that it is possible to obtain

the eternal salvation of the soul by the profession of any

kind of religion, as long as morality is maintained.*

THE PAPAL RESPONSE to the ideological transformation initiated by the French and Industrial Revolutions reflected a clash of cultures. The popes from Pius VI (1775–99) to Gregory XVI (1831–46) were pressed to reconcile the traditionalism of the Church and papal transcendent claims with the liberal and nationalist innovations of the age. It proved a difficult and at times an impossible task. It is within this context that the Church's attitude toward Jews and the separate, though related, issue of its response to Jewish emancipation during the nineteenth and twentieth centuries must be examined. After the Nazi genocide, however, the relationship between the Church and the Jews has been increasingly influenced by the attempt to explore the roots of the Holocaust in the anti-Judaism of Christianity. This chapter traces the historical evolution of papal anti-Judaism in the

* Gregory XVI, *Mirari vos*, 15 August 1832, *PE* 1:237.

first half of the nineteenth century within the context of the papal struggle against modern civilization and the Jews, who increasingly appeared to be the virtual incarnation of modernity.

At the opening of the nineteenth century, the Church's major preoccupation was not its relationship with the Jews but revolutionary social and political upheaval, which provoked a conflict between its traditionalism and the liberalism of the modern age.[1] The age of revolution struck at the papacy's religious rationale as well as its political base. Papal authority was questioned, its mission reviled, and its power curtailed by tumultuous events that often profaned the spiritual while extolling the material. In response, the popes warned that the absolute individualism and religious indifferentism that flowed from political and economic liberalism would inevitably lead to chaos and moral confusion. Early on, Rome rejected self-interest as an appropriate motivation for human conduct. From the papal perspective, the Jewish issue represented one part of its broader confrontation with the unfortunate consequences of modernity.[2] While the papacy concurred with Marx that capitalism "drowned the most heavenly ecstasies of religious fervor,"[3] it rejected the collectivism and communism that emerged as a reaction. Not surprisingly, the five popes, from Pius VI through Gregory XVI, refused to sanction either, while waging a conflict against modern doctrines, including religious freedom for all faiths, which they denounced as indifferentism.

The outbreak of the French Revolution in 1789, which challenged the traditional order, posed new and frightening problems for Rome and cast a shadow on the pontificate of Pius VI. The papacy, confronted with the revolutionary call for liberty, equality, and fraternity, harbored serious reservations about all three. Although the revolutionary upheaval in France was not initially inspired by antireligious sentiments, distressing developments soon took shape in Paris, despite the fact that a majority of the French were Catholic. As early as 1789 an unruly mob attacked the religious house

1. In this regard consult the ASV, SS, files on emigranti della rivoluzione, those of the epoca Napoleonica, Francia, and epoca Napoleonica, Italia, among others.

2. Renato Moro, *La Chiesa e lo stermino degli ebei* (Bologna: Mulino, 2002), 48–49; Marina Caffiero, *La nuova era. Miti e profezie dell'Italia in Rivoluzione* (Genoa: Marietti, 1991), 26–27.

3. Karl Marx, *The Communist Manifesto*, ed. Frederic L. Bender (New York: W. W. Norton, 1988), 57.

of the Lazzarists and another menaced the Archbishop of Paris, Monsignor Juigone.[4] The situation deteriorated further following the National Assembly's passage, in 1790, of the civil constitution of the clergy, which provided that bishops were to be elected not only by the Catholic faithful but by Protestants, Jews, agnostics, and even atheists. The revolutionaries made various attempts to secularize society, including the eventual introduction of civil matrimony and divorce and the abolition of clerical control of education.[5] The assembly's unilateral attempts to reorganize and restrict the Church alarmed Rome and led to an eventual clash.

The system of thought guiding Rome's conduct differed radically from that emanating from Paris, where the new political elite equated Catholic orthodoxy with rigidity bolstered by stupidity. The confiscation of Church property in October 1789, which undermined the Church's fiscal security, was followed by measures that threatened its religious primacy. While Pius VI did not wish to meddle in internal French affairs, he could not tolerate the proposition that Catholicism should be placed on an equal footing with Protestantism, Judaism, and atheism, and he did not hesitate to reveal his sentiments. The papal position may have contributed to the reaction in the Catholic countryside, where a "white terror" was later launched against the Revolution, Protestants, and Jews.[6] For the moment, the assembly's refusal to approve a declaration that Catholicism was the religion of state "with the exclusive right of public worship" portended future difficulties.[7]

Pius VI was further displeased by the assembly's actions and laws of 27 September and 13 November 1791, which eliminated the legal discrimination that had weighed upon the Jews for centuries and assured them full civil and political rights.[8] In this fashion liberty, equality, and fraternity were extended to the "pariah people" of Europe. Thus, initially, it seemed that while the Roman Catholic Church was one of the greatest casualties

4. Henri Daniel-Rops, *The Church in an Age of Revolution, 1789–1870*, vol. 1, trans. John Warrington (Garden City, N.Y.: Image Books, 1967), 16.

5. Owen Connelly, *French Revolution/Napoleonic Era* (New York: Holt, Rinehart and Winston, 1979), 6.

6. Ibid., 172.

7. John McManners, *The French Revolution and the Church* (New York: Harper, 1970), 25.

8. Giacomo Martina, *Pio IX e Leopold II* (Rome: Pontificia Università Gregoriana, 1967), 195–96.

of the revolutionary regime, the Jews were among its greatest beneficiaries. This discrepancy angered and aroused conservatives. In fact, it was a misconception that the Revolution treated Judaism better than Catholicism. As heirs of the Enlightenment, the revolutionaries called upon the Jews to renounce their particularism and merge into the nation. In the words of one deputy, "To the Jew as an individual—everything," but "to the Jews as a nation—nothing."[9] This position would eventually prove a mixed blessing for Jews. The revolution brought problems as well as benefits to France's Jews, as old hatreds reemerged and Jewish property was attacked. In 1791, when the assembly accorded citizenship to the Askenazi Jews of Alsace and Lorraine, it did so only once Jews had left their communities and forgiven loans to non-Jews.[10]

Friends of the Jews in revolutionary France believed that Jews had to change. Their theory of emancipation was integral to their broader program to eliminate internal divisions and orders in the new nation, in which all would enjoy an equal status.[11] Increasingly, opposition to Jews was based less on their religious convictions and more on their stubborn refusal to renounce their particular practices and separateness. This had unfortunate consequences in the secular age that followed, although for the moment Rome's position appeared more precarious. From the papal perspective the revolution's "libertarian" measures represented one aspect of the attack on the faith's privileged position. It contributed to the antirevolutionary riots in Rome, including an attack on the Jewish ghetto. To quell the disturbances and restore order, papal authorities resisted the French libertarian measures and sought to reimpose all of the anti-Jewish regulations cataloged in the Edict of 1775.[12] Tensions were momentarily eased in Rome, but the stage was set for a future confrontation with the French.

The religious conflict continued as the new cult of reason displaced Catholicism, and it intensified after France declared war on Catholic Austria in April 1792. In the massacres of the following September, three bish-

9. Carroll, *Constantine's Sword*, 415.

10. Connelly, *French Revolution*, 84, 93.

11. Carmichael, *Satanizing of the Jews*, 111–12.

12. Cecil Roth, *The History of the Jews of Italy* (Philadelphia: Jewish Publication Society of America, 1946), 426.

ops and more than two hundred priests perished. The proclamation of the republic the same month, the execution of Louis XVI in January 1793,[13] and the replacement of the Christian calendar by the Republican one at the end of 1793 led to a further deterioration of relations between Paris and Rome. Pius VI's moral support for the first coalition against France (1793) did little to ingratiate Rome with the Paris government. Pius assumed a more determined course in 1794 when he condemned the more than eighty articles of the Synod of Pistoia of 1786. Robespierre's fostering of the cult of the Supreme Being in 1794 and the French Directory's support of theophilanthropy in 1795 strained relations further. In fact, Napoleon Bonaparte, who assumed command of the army of Italy in 1796, was encouraged by the Directory to undermine the temporal and spiritual authority of the papacy by pushing into Rome, "the center of fanaticism." Cautious as first, after defeating the Austrians at Lodi and signing the Armistice of Cherasco with Piedmont (1796), Napoleon overran and plundered the papal provinces of Ravenna, Ferrara, and Bologna. Rome's future appeared precarious.

When Napoleon informed the people of Italy that the French army had come to break their chains and ensure their liberation, he included the Jews in that promise and demolished the ghetto walls in the French-occupied peninsula. By the end of 1796 his forces threatened Rome itself, forcing the pontiff to negotiate.[14] Pius pragmatically accepted the harsh conditions imposed in the Armistice of Bologna because they preserved part of his temporal power and left Rome in his hands. He resisted the demand to revoke all papal bulls issued since 1789, including his denunciation of the civil constitution of the clergy. His refusal led to a suspension of the armistice and the prospect of a further French incursion into the remaining papal realm.

Napoleon responded in January 1797 by declaring war on what remained of the Papal States, occupying Faenza and Ancona, systematically plundering as he pushed south toward Rome. The frightened pontiff, fear-

---

13. In a consistory of 17 June 1793, Pius VI condemned the barbarism in Paris and the beheading of Louis XVI on 21 January 1793. See the *Magnum Bullarium Romanum Continuatio,* 10:318–27.

14. Ludwig Freiherr von Pastor, *The History of the Popes,* trans. E. F. Peeler (St. Louis: B. Herder, 1953), 40:295–96.

ing the consequences for both Church and state, had to negotiate to prevent a French occupation of the capital, agreeing to the Peace of Tolentino in February 1797. Its terms proved more onerous than those earlier outlined at Bologna, constraining the pope to renounce a large part of his temporal patrimony in order to safeguard his spiritual authority. Possessing no other option at this juncture, Pius submitted.[15] The Directory wanted still more, however, proclaiming its goal to be nothing less than the total collapse of the pope's temporal power. Napoleon, conscious of the religious sensibilities of the Italian people, avoided making himself the instrument of the papacy's demise, hoping it would self-destruct.[16] It did not.

Difficulties between Paris and Rome accelerated once Napoleon left Italy. In February 1798 French forces pushed into Rome, proclaiming the end of papal rule and establishing a Roman republic.[17] Article 343 of its constitution of March 1798 eliminated any preferential treatment for one religion over another, while prohibiting any impositions contrary to man's natural rights. This was one of the few of the epoch which declared not only the equality of citizens but also that of religions.[18] This was likewise established in the Cisalpine constitution of 1798, which guaranteed equality to citizens of all religious persuasions.[19] In Rome as elsewhere, the revolutionary French forces abolished the ghettoes. During this time the Jews of Rome laid their obligatory yellow badges, or *sciamanni,* aside, illuminated their quarter, and erected a tree of liberty in the ghetto. The French and their allies plundered palaces, looted shrines and churches, waged war on the Church, liberated the Jews, and opened the gates of the ghetto in the capital and other cities of the former papal territory. The French declared all special regulations abolished and counted the Jews as citizens with equal rights. In fact, a Jew, Ezechiele Morpurgo, was elected senator of the city, alongside Prince Borghese and Count Cesarini. The sudden prominence of some Jews, and the fact that others offered confiscated church

---

15. J. Derek Holmes, *The Triumph of the Holy See: A Short History of the Papacy in the Nineteenth Century* (London: Burns and Oates, 1978), 24, 31; Owen Chadwick, *The Popes and European Revolution* (Oxford: Clarendon Press, 1981), 448, 462.

16. Gugliemo Oncken, *L'Epoca della Rivoluzione, dell'Impero e delle Guerre D'Indipendenza, 1789–1815* (Milan: Società Editrice Libraria, 1887), 1134.

17. See index no. 1189 in the ASV for Repubblica Romana I (1798–99).

18. Fubini, *Condizione giuridica dell'ebraismo Italiano,* 2.

19. Ibid.

vessels for sale, inflamed many Italian Catholics and reinforced their anti-Judaic sentiments.[20] Conservatives in the curia fanned the flames of this resentment, complaining that the world had been turned upside down.

Rome's intransigence was resented in Paris, where the director Lare-villere Lepaux called for the destruction of the spiritual and temporal power of the papacy and its replacement by a "theophilanthropist" church based on rational principles that would preach the worship of the father-land. The pope, who of course resisted this scheme, was arrested and dragged into exile. He died a prisoner of the French at the close of August 1799, ending the longest pontificate to date. Some believed his demise por-tended the death of the papacy. The obituary proved premature, however, as the Camaldolese monk and future pope, Gregory XVI, predicted in his tract *The Triumph of the Holy See and the Church against the Attacks of In-novators* (1799). In fact the French triumph in Italy was transitory, under-mined by the formation of the second coalition (June 1799) and a peasant insurrection in Calabria and the Abruzzi orchestrated by the Army of the Holy Faith, led by Cardinal Fabrizio Ruffo. As the French retreated, an undisciplined peasant army vented frustration on the Jews and Italian Ja-cobins who were accused of summoning and collaborating with the ene-my.[21] The conservative triumph in Italy and Europe proved transitory.

Napoleon's coup d'etat of 9 November 1799 established the French Consulate, with power in his hands as first consul. The pragmatic Bona-parte, always suspicious of ideologues, revealed a more accommodating attitude toward the Church and the papacy than his predecessors had. Meanwhile, at the end of November, the cardinals of the Church ventured to Habsburg-controlled Venice to elect a successor to Pius VI. The 1799–1800 conclave led to the election of the moderate Bishop of Imola, Grego-rio Luigi Barnaba, Count Chriamonti, on 14 March 1800. Because the French had seized the Vatican jewels, the new pope reportedly was crowned with a papier-mâché tiara. The Roman community of Jews, through the rabbi in Venice, offered its congratulations to the new pope, presenting him with a gift of homage.[22] Although he chose the name Pius

---

20. Hermann Vogelstein, *The Jews of Rome*, trans. Moses Hadas (Philadelphia: Jewish Publication Society of America, 1940), 329–30.

21. Roth, *History of the Jews of Italy*, 434–35.

22. Vogelstein, *Jews of Rome*, 331.

VII, this pope was not a retrograde, or *zelante*, who opposed every aspect of the revolutionary upheaval of the age. He had earlier preached that liberty, fraternity, equality, and democracy could be reconciled with Christianity.[23] The selection of the reform-minded Ercole Consalvi as his secretary of state and his decision to return to Rome directly displayed his determination to pursue a moderate course, preserving his freedom of action vis-à-vis both friends and enemies, as he confirmed with his reform decree of October 1800.[24]

The moderation of Pius VII was appreciated by the Jews of Rome, for whom a new age seemed to have dawned. It was prescribed that members of the Jewish community's board of trustees were to be elected and that all were to be bound by its strictures. Consalvi, meanwhile, authorized the expenditure of three hundred *scudi* for aid to the Jewish poor. Furthermore, on hearing Consalvi's report of the financial distress of the community, the pope canceled Jewish carnival dues, amounting to some sixteen thousand *scudi*, while granting a grace period for the tax payment of 1802.[25] Some believed that Consalvi's moderate course was the harbinger of a new relationship and reconciliation between the papacy and the Jews. This proved an overly optimistic appraisal.

Pius VII's charity to the Jews formed part of the papacy's traditional Christian mission rather than any radical modification of its stance toward Judaism. Rome clung tenaciously to past practice and perceived neither the need nor the desirability of altering Christian-Jewish relations at home or abroad. Confronted with radical changes in the political, social, economic, and religious spheres, the Church sought solace in the stability of tradition. In fact, in his first allocution to the cardinals, in March 1800, Pius predicted that the Church would overcome its current problems, as it

23. Holmes, *Triumph of the Holy See*, 41; Chadwick, *Popes and European Revolution*, 455; E. E. Y. Hales, *The Catholic Church in the Modern World* (Garden City, N.Y.: Hanover House, 1958), 54; Margaret M. O'Dwyer, *The Papacy in the Age of Napoleon and the Restoration: Pius VII, 1800–1823* (Lanham, Md.: University Press of America, 1985), 24–25; Vittorio E. Giuntella, "Cristianesimo e democrazia in Italia al tramonto del Settecento," *Rassegna Storica del Risorgimento* 42 (1955): 291.

24. Raffaele Colapietra, *La formazione diplomatica di Leone XII* (Rome: Instituto per la storia del Risorgimento Italiano, 1966), 92–105; also see Ercole Consalvi, *Memorie del Cardinale Ercole Consalvi*, ed. Mario Nasalli Rocca (Rome: Signorelli, 1950). For Pius VII's reform decree of 31 Oct. 1800, see *Magnum Bullarium Romanum Continuatio*, 10:49–79.

25. Vogelstein, *Jews of Rome*, 331.

had past adversities, if it remained steadfast in its principles. Likewise, in his first encyclical, *Diu satis* of May 1800, the pope praised the virtues of his predecessor but at the same time invoked peace.[26] Napoleon, for his part, appreciated the advantage of regular relations with Rome. "My firm intention is that the Christian religion, Catholic and Roman, shall be maintained untouched," he reported to an assembly of priests he had convoked in Milan. He further promised to "put everything in operation to secure and guarantee the faith," and proposed negotiations.[27] Long anxious to restore Catholicism in France, Pius immediately seconded the idea and dispatched representatives to Paris to negotiate.[28] Serious negotiations commenced in November 1800, aimed at ending the schism in France while reconciling Roman religion and the Revolution. Both sides found it prudent to ignore the thorny question of the truncated temporal power of the papacy. There was no such harmony over Rome's determination to have Catholicism proclaimed the religion of state and Paris's reluctance to do so.

Despite differences, by mid-July 1801 two declarations and seventeen articles had been approved.[29] In the first declaration the French Republic recognized the Catholic apostolic and Roman religion as that of the great majority of the French people, although it was not accorded any legal priority. Nonetheless, the second declaration promised that the Catholic religion could expect the greatest good from the restoration of public worship. The articles arranged for the reorganization of the Church, with sixty dioceses instead of the 135 under the *ancien regime*. Provision was made for the resignation of all the existing bishops of the constitutional Church and those who had remained loyal to Rome; their replacements were to be

26. "Dius Satis," *PE* 1:189–93; Erasmo Pistolesi, *Vita del Somo Pontefice Pio VII* (Rome: F. Bourlie, 1824), 1:76–80; Giuseppe Hergenrother, *Storia universale della Chiesa*, ed. G. P. Kirsch, trans. P. Enrico Rosa (Florence: Libreria Editrice Fiorentina, 1911), 362.

27. Napoleon Bonaparte, *The Corsican, A Diary of Napoleon's Life in his Own Words*, ed. R. M. Johnson (Boston: Houghton Mifflin, 1910), 135.

28. *Documents sur la négociation du concordat et sur les autres rapports de la France avec le Saint-Siège en 1800 et a 1801*, 6 vols., ed. A Boulay de la Meurthe (Paris: E. Leroux, 1891–1905), 1:21–26.

29. The developments leading to the conclusion of the concordat of July 1801 and the final text can be found ibid., and in the two volumes edited by J. Crétineau-Joly, *Mémoires du Cardinal Consalvi, secrétaire d'état du Pape Pie VII, avec un introduction et des notes*, 2 vols. (Paris: Plon, 1864).

named by the first consul but instituted by the pope.[30] In August 1801, in accordance with article 5 of the concordat, Pius called for the resignation of the entire French hierarchy to make way for the new appointments.[31]

Neither Paris nor Rome was totally satisfied with the agreement, although both benefited by it. Pius appreciated the reestablishment of the Catholic hierarchy in France, the restoration of Catholic worship, and the end to the schism, but resented the exclusion of the Church from education and the concessions granted to other religious groups, including Protestant and Jews. Napoleon in turn was disturbed by what he perceived as clerical pretensions, but by ending the religious conflict he deprived the royalist opposition of Catholic mass support.[32] In February 1802 Napoleon allowed the remains of Pius VI to be transported from Valence to St. Peter's Cathedral in Rome. This concession was balanced in April 1802, when the French legislature, in approving the concordat, appended a number of "organic articles" for its implementation. These measures, which sought to establish control of the state over the Church while restricting the rights of the Holy See in France, were criticized by Rome.[33]

In 1803 the pope, who preferred to settle ecclesiastical matters in Italy unilaterally, was constrained to conclude a concordat with the Italian Republic, but this agreement proclaimed Catholicism the religion of state, as provided in the January 1802 constitution of the Italian republic. Article 117 of that constitution also assured all its citizens the free private exercise of their religion of choice, to the dismay of the clerical party.[34] To assure the continuation of this and other provisions, Count Francesco Melzi D'Eril, the vice president of the Italian republic, stipulated in two decrees

---

30. A copy of the concordat of 1801 can be found in E. E. Y. Hales, *Revolution and Papacy, 1769–1846* (Notre Dame: University of Notre Dame Press, 1966), 298–300; and more recently in Frank J. Coppa, ed., *Controversial Concordats: The Vatican's Relations with Napoleon, Mussolini, and Hitler* (Washington, D.C.: Catholic University of America Press, 1999), 191–93.

31. *Tam multa*, 15 Aug. 1801, *PP* 1:19.

32. For a positive evaluation of the concordat from the papacy's perspective, see P. Ferraris, "Il Concordato Francese e il Card. Fesch," *CC* 87 (1936): 497, while a less positive evaluation is provided in Luigi Sturzo, *Church and State* (Notre Dame: University of Notre Dame Press, 1962), 2:378–81.

33. Hergenrother, *Storia universale della Chiesa*, 375; Cardinal Jean Caprara, *Concordat, et recueil des bulles et bres de N.S.P., le Pape Pie VII, sur les affaires actuelles de l'Église de France* (Liege: Lemarié, 1802), 23–31.

34. Fubini, *Condizione giuridica dell'ebraismo Italiano*, 3.

published in January 1804 that the laws of the republic would prevail in all matters not specifically enumerated in the concordat. Rome denounced this as another attempt to curtail Church influence.

At the end of April 1804 the empire was proposed in France, approved by plebiscite, and proclaimed in mid-May. Preparing for his coronation as emperor, Bonaparte recognized that papal participation in the ceremony would confer legitimacy and assure broad support in Catholic France. In Rome Cardinal Joseph Fesch, the French ambassador, pressed Consalvi and Pius to accede to his nephew's request. The pope, eager to have the emperor's support against the Melzi decrees in Italy, favored attending the coronation, as did a majority of the cardinals. Pius prayed that the visit would prove advantageous for the Church as he departed Rome in early November 1804.[35] Although the pope received the details of the ceremony only belatedly, he knew beforehand that he would only anoint the emperor, who would crown himself in the 2 December ceremony in Notre Dame.[36] Pius nonetheless, seeking to illustrate the centrality of the Church in the empire and win the new emperor's goodwill for the papacy and the Church, participated in the coronation ceremonies.

Pius remained in Paris until spring, petitioning for a modification of the organic articles in France and the Melzi decrees in Italy—but to no avail. Although he had participated in Napoleon's coronation, the new emperor refused to remove the limitations placed upon Church and papacy in his realm. In mid-March Napoleon transformed the Italian republic into the Italian Kingdom and became its king. To Rome's dismay, he proved no more willing to make concessions to the Church than had the republic he replaced. The pope was further distressed to learn that the French civil code, with its provision for divorce and religious toleration, would be imposed in Italy, complaining that such religious liberty was incompatible with the proclamation of Catholicism as the religion of state. Nor was the curia pleased by Napoleon's convoking an assembly of Jewish notables in Paris—a sort of culmination of Jewish emancipation. In 1807 Napoleon convoked a European-wide Sanhedrin of rabbis to advise him

35. O'Dwyer, *Papacy in the Age of Napoleon*, 83–86; Caprara, *Concordat*, 2–15.

36. Richard Metternich-Winneburg, *Memoirs of Prince Metternich, 1773–1815*, trans. Mrs. Alexander Napier (New York: Howard Fertig, 1970) 1:289–90; see the correspondence of Cardinals Pacca and Gabrieli on the Pope's visit to France for the coronation of Napoleon, ASV, Archivio Particolare Pio IX, Ogetti vari, no. 909, fascicolo 3.

on relations with the Continent's Jews, winning him the broad support of European Jewry.[37] Clerical circles accused him of "indifferentism."

However, as war clouds gathered, papal concerns shifted from opposition to religious indifferentism to fear for the survival of the temporal power. To assure the latter, as a third coalition against France materialized by the treaty of St. Petersburg (April 1805) and the resumption of hostilities in Europe threatened, Pius strove to preserve his neutrality.[38] His efforts proved vain, for Napoleon treated the pope like a satellite, demanding the expulsion from Rome of the English and his other enemies. Pius rejected Napoleon's demands, refusing to recognize any higher authority in his state. Further conflict appeared inevitable, as other developments disturbed Rome.[39] Following the creation of the Confederation of the Rhine (1806), the churches in the Grand Duchy of Frankfort were placed under state control, while its monastic orders were dissolved.[40]

In January 1808 Napoleon dispatched troops to Rome, provoking Pius's protests. Napoleon responded by a decree of 2 April 1808 providing for the irrevocable incorporation of the pontifical provinces of Urbino, Ancona, Macerata, and the Camerino into the Kingdom of Italy, and, as the successor to Charlemagne, he withdrew the donations of Pepin and the confirmation of Charlemagne.[41] The following July Pius denounced the French outrages against the temporal and spiritual power of the papacy.[42] Unrepentant, in mid-May of the following year Napoleon incorporated the remainder of the Papal States into France and declared Rome an imperial city. The French, who regained control of Rome, reopened the gates of the ghetto, demolished its walls, and once again accorded the Jews equal civil rights.[43] In clerical circles the liberation of the Jews was linked to the hu-

---

37. Roth, *History of the Jews of Italy,* 442; Connelly, *French Revolution,* 227.

38. Project for a political treaty between the Holy See and the Emperor Napoleon, ASV, Archivio Partiolare Pio IX, Oggetti vari, no. 909, facscioli 4–5.

39. Alexis Artaud de Montor, *Histoire du pape Pie VII* (Paris: Le Clere, 1836), 1:126; Ilario Rinieri, *Napoleone e Pio VII, 1803–1813* (Turin: Unione Tipografico Editrice, 1906), 1:331–32, 377–85; Daniel-Rops, *Church in an Age of Revolution,* 130–31; Chadwick, *Popes and European Revolution,* 511; Hergenrother, *Storia universale della Chiesa,* 380–82; Bartolomeo Pacca, *Historical Memoirs,* trans. George Head (London: Longman, 1850), 1:124–26; Joseph Schmidlin, *Histoire des papes de l'époque contemporaine,* trans. L. Marchal (Paris: E. Vitte, 1938), 1:108.

40. Connelly, *French Revolution,* 305.

41. For Napoleon's decree of 2 April 1808, see ASV, Archivio Particolare Pio IX, Oggetti Vari, no. 909, fascicolo 1.

42. Pistolesi, *Vita del Somo Pontefice Pio VII,* 4:106–18; Schmidlin, *Histoire des papes* 115.

43. Kertzer, *Popes against the Jews,* 31; Connelly, *French Revolution,* 293.

miliation of the papacy, and some even suggested that this humiliation had been at the instigation of the Jews. Responding to the annexation and its consequences, Pius issued a bull of excommunication. In July 1809 French forces broke into the Quirinal Palace, seized the pope, and brought him to southern France. Later he was transferred to Savona, where he was placed under house arrest. While the pope was imprisoned, the reform movement in Prussia liberated the Jews, and freedom of religion was enforced in the Confederation of the Rhine.[44]

In early June 1812, as his army stood poised to attack Russia, Napoleon transferred Pius from Savona to the chateau of Fontainebleu. In September the emperor entered Moscow unopposed, but Alexander would not submit, and on 17 October the French made preparations for withdrawal. In Paris Cardinal Fesch, learning that the French-led coalition forces had all but vanished in the ensuing flight, commented that while his nephew was lost, the Church was saved.[45] The Jews of Rome did not fare as well. The emperor hastened back to Paris in December to mend his relations with the opposition, including the pope. In 1813 Napoleon and Marie Louise ventured to Fontainebleu, where in less than a week the emperor and pontiff hammered out the basis for an eleven-article accord between Church and state. Pius apparently considered these points the basis for a future arrangement, or later claimed he did, while Napoleon regarded it as a definitive agreement and labeled it the Concordat of Fontainebleu. The pope's reservations were reinforced by the cardinals, who were now allowed to meet with the pontiff and opposed the declarations. Cardinals Consalvi, Pacca, and Di Pietro advised the pope to rescind the articles because they contained unacceptable provisions and because Napoleon in mid-February had presumptuously presented them to the senate as a final concordat. Pius followed their suggestion.[46] Only Napoleon's defeat by the forces of the quadruple alliance in October 1813 led him to release the pope and restore his temporal sovereignty.

Although Napoleon had been defeated, the revolutionary and Napoleonic wars strengthened the concept of national identity, so that Jews were again perceived as outsiders, not only on a religious basis but increasingly from a national perspective. At the end of May 1814 Pius returned to

---

44. Connelly, *French Revolution*, 314, 317.
45. Daniel-Rops, *Church in an Age of Revolution*, 154.
46. Pacca, *Historical Memoirs*, 2:233–83.

Rome, preceded by Monsignor Antonio Rivaroli, who set the stage for the rigid restoration championed by the conservatives in the curia.[47] It is estimated that the population of Rome declined from 153,000 in 1800 to 117,000 at the time of the restoration.[48] Rivaroli suppressed the French civil code in Rome, and in August Pius restored the Society of Jesus amid cries for a complete restoration of traditionalism in Church and state. Metternich, among others, questioned whether the Holy See had acted wisely in resurrecting the Jesuits.[49] From the first, the Austrian minister counseled the reformation of the administrative and juridical life of the Papal States as the best means of self-preservation.[50] He also urged moderation toward its Jewish minority, but conservatives in Rome were little inclined to follow his suggestions.

Rome was not unique in assuming an antirevolutionary and anti-Judaic stance. A number of conservatives and members of the ultramontane faction, such as Joseph De Maistre, claimed to have unearthed a new truth—that behind all the anti-Christian sects lurked the Jews.[51] Small wonder that, following Napoleon's defeat, the Jews who had prospered during the revolutionary period in much of Europe suffered a series of setbacks. Obvious beneficiaries of the revolutionary legislation, they were now made scapegoats and identified with the negative consequences and turmoil of the French imperium. In the restoration world, the liberation of the Jews was perceived as part of a broader program of social and cultural innovation and upheaval that conservatives deemed dangerous and destructive. Both the leadership and the masses of the restored regimes sought redress. As a consequence, throughout much of Europe, Jews were deprived of the right to own real property, to attend public schools, to at-

---

47. Alberto Aquarone, "La restaurazione nello Stato Pontifico ed i suoi indirizzi legislativi," *Archivio della Società Romana di Storia Patria* 78 (1955): 123–25.

48. Nicholas Patrick Wiseman, *Recollections of the Last Four Popes and of Rome in Their Times* (New York: Wagner, 1858), 64.

49. "Sollicitudo omnium ecclesiarum," *PP* 1:20; Metternich-Winneburg, *Memoirs of Prince Metternich,* 4:243.

50. Angelo Filipuzzi, *Pio IX e la politica Austriaca in Italia dal 1815 al 1848* (Florence: Felice Le Monnier, 1958), 10. A good synopsis of the philosophy and practice of the restoration in the Church and Papal States is provided in Cosimo Semeraro, *Resaurazione chiesa e società. La "seconda riclupera" e la rinascita degli ordini religiosi nello Stati pontificii* (Rome: Libreria Atenes Salesiano, 1982).

51. Moro, *Chiesa e lo stermino degli ebei,* 49.

tain academic positions, or to enter public service, and were prohibited from entering a number of professions, including law and medicine. In Piedmont-Sardinia the ultra-Catholic Victor Emmanuel I reimposed the anti-Judaic restrictions that had prevailed prior to the French incursion.[52] Its Jews were again shut in the ghetto, where they would remain until 1848. Many conservatives claimed that this righted the wrongs and excesses of the revolutionary age. Rome was delighted that the charter granted by the restored Louis XVIII reestablished Catholicism as the religion of state in France, and looked forward to playing a major role there and in the rest of Catholic Europe.

Cardinal Ercole Consalvi, who was dispatched to represent the papal position at the Congress of Vienna, also had to plan for the reorganization of the Papal States after years of dismemberment. He did not believe that the pope could or should fully reestablish the old ecclesiastical regime.[53] He would have liked to see the pope follow the lead of Ferdinand III of Tuscany, who upon his restoration in 1814 renewed the patent of 1593, preserving the privileges of his Jewish subjects—or of Parma, which likewise retained the provisions that guaranteed Jewish rights.[54] He was disheartened by the news from Rome, where the pope left much of the political restoration to the *zelanti*, or retrograde party, in the curia, which aimed to revive the worst features of the *ancien regime*, including its treatment of the Jews. They assumed an uncompromising stand against "dangerous elements" in the secular world and unbendingly opposed compromise or concessions.[55] Reports reached Consalvi that Jewish students had been dismissed from the university and Jewish pupils from the ordinary schools, that prohibitions had been reimposed on the Jewish ownership of real estate, and that Jews had again been denied access to public services and entry into the liberal professions.[56] Cardinal Bartolomeo Pacca, acting secretary of state in Consalvi's absence, proceeded systematically to undermine

---

52. Martina, *Pio IX e Leopold II*, 198.

53. See Gellio Cassi, *Il Cardinale Consalvi ed i primi anni della restaurazione pontificia (1815–1819)* (Milan: Società Editrice Dante Alighieri, 1931).

54. Andrew M. Canepa, "L'Atteggiamento degli ebrei italiani davanti alla loro secondo emancipazione. Premesse e analisi," *Rassegna Mensile di Israel* (Sept. 1977): 425.

55. John Tracy Ellis, *Cardinal Consalvi and Anglo-Papal Relations, 1814–1824* (Washington, D.C.: Catholic University of America Press, 1942), 147.

56. Martina, *Pio IX e Leopold II*, 199.

the French reforms of the previous decade, beginning by suppressing the French civil code, which had provided a measure of civil and religious equality. For the *zelanti*, "true Jewish emancipation" could be attained only through baptism. Metternich appreciated Pacca's strong character but found him "somewhat too severe."[57] The restored Jesuits were showered with privileges and the Roman inquisition was reestablished, while the Jews were again shut in the ghetto.[58] Some believed that Rome's unwillingness to grant parity to non-Catholics encouraged repression elsewhere in the Italian peninsula and in Catholic Europe.

The successful recovery of Roman art, which capped the restoration of the Papal States at Vienna, as well as the disillusionment with war and revolution that led many to seek solace in the traditional faith, was perceived by some as the complete triumph of the Holy See. Consalvi, more than anyone else responsible for Rome's diplomatic achievements and good fortune, remained cautious. Critical of the reaction of the *zelanti*, he warned that though the task of recovering the Papal States had been difficult, retaining and preserving them would prove even more so.[59] Aware that the world had changed, he called for the Church to respond to the new circumstances, urging the pope to humanize and illuminate the temporal government, including its treatment of the Jews, and opposing the restitution of Pius VI's 1775 restrictions on them. To restore the repressive measures of the prerevolutionary period would court increasing diplomatic isolation, he warned, and would have unfortunate political and economic consequences.[60] Although Consalvi's message was prophetic, in restoration Rome his was a voice crying in the wilderness. Even moderates like Cardinal Tommaso Bernetti deemed the old restrictive system "best in every way" and sought its restoration in "its entirety."[61] Conservatives deplored the fact that following emancipation the pressure on Jews to convert had dissipated. They hoped this unfortunate trend could be reversed with the restoration of restrictions on Jewish life and activities.

---

57. Metternich-Winneburg, *Memoirs of Prince Metternich*, 3:92.

58. Pistolesi, *Vita del Somo Pontefice Pio VII*, 4:7–9; Aquarone, "Restaurazione nello Stato Pontifico," 123–25, 163; Alan J. Reinerman, *Austria and the Papacy in the Age of Metternich* (Washington, D.C.: Catholic University of America Press, 1979–89), 1:37–40.

59. Reinerman, *Austria and the Papacy*, 1:35.

60. Alesandro Roveri, *La Sante Sede tra rivoluzione francese e restaurazione. Il cardinale Consalvi, 1813–1815* (Florence: Nuova Italia, 1974), 143–44.

61. Brunetti to Consalvi, 4 Nov. 1815, ASV, Segretaria di Stato, rubrica 25.

Not everyone shared their vision. Consalvi, like Metternich, deplored obscurantism. He was especially concerned that repressive measures against Jews would provoke dissension in the legations, and he issued instructions that the existing Jewish rights and situation be respected there—so long as it did not cause public scandal.[62] This was not supported by the *zelanti* clerics, who condemned the alleged Jewish materialist pursuit of profit and power and attempts to subvert Christian principles and society. They proclaimed the moral duty to return to the status quo *ante bellum*, including the visible subordination of Jews. Furthermore, they judged absolutely ludicrous and manifestly inadmissible the notion that the state should be neutral in religious matters and operate impartially for the benefit of all its subjects, regardless of their religious convictions. Their program called for a curtailment of Jewish economic activities, social status, and even their "superstitious" and "scandalous" rites in the capital as well as the provinces.[63] The monk, later Cardinal Giuseppe Sala, who was closely associated with Cardinal Pacca urged Pius to curtail the Jewish liberties he said degenerated into license. He was appalled and outraged that Jews in parts of the Papal States lived "in perfect communion with Christians," and scandalized that they "obtained full freedom and protection for the exercise of their superstitions."[64] Consalvi disagreed, deeming the monk's proposal impractical and counterproductive for both Christians and Jews.

Pius VII sought to steer a middle course between reformers and reactionaries. He allowed Consalvi to prevail over conservatives such as Sala, and in July 1816 adopted part of Consalvi's reformist program, which provided a new civil and penal code, incorporated many of the French innovations, and introduced the principle of equality before the law. Consalvi's code eliminated torture and arbitrary arrest, while separating civil and criminal tribunals from the ecclesiastical courts. From Vienna, Metternich praised Consalvi for inaugurating an enlightened form of government and adhering to moderate principles that averted a violent reaction, which might have provoked a new revolutionary outburst.[65] In fact, Consalvi re-

---

62. Martina, *Pio IX e Leopold II,* 199.
63. Roveri, *Sante Sede,* 143.
64. Kertzer, *Popes against the Jews,* 32.
65. Reform of the Public Administration of the Pontifical State, 6 July 1816, *Magnum Bullarium Romanum Continuatio,* 14:47–79; Massimo Petrocchi, *La restaurazione, il Cardi-*

stricted but proved unable to permanently overturn the governance by priests in the Papal States. Nonetheless, his ability to overcome entrenched and intransigent opposition earned him the title "the Siren of Rome." In the words of Cardinal Wiseman, "the government of Pius VII, through his minister Consalvi, was just, liberal, and enlightened."[66] Unfortunately, not all were seduced by his common sense, and his accomplishments did not delight conservatives in Rome, who criticized Consalvi's moderation from the first—including the attempt to provide leniency toward the Jewish population.

Very probably the *zelanti*'s anti-Judaic campaign played a part in deterring Pius from proceeding further along the path of modernization and issuing a decree providing parity for his Jewish subjects, as Consalvi urged. The most that the pope would concede to Consalvi on the Jewish issue was to permit them, de facto, to enjoy many of the privileges they had during the past two decades. Considering the vocal and vehement *zelanti* opposition to toleration, this was the best Consalvi could do for Jews and for the image of the papacy abroad. "As much as the circumstances of the time may suggest that it is not appropriate to return the Jews to that precarious state in which they were found in 1796," Consalvi wrote Metternich at the end of 1815, "His Holiness does not believe it opportune to issue a solemn, public decree, as the Jewish supplicants would like, that they be put on an equal footing with the other Pontifical subjects."[67]

Ghettoes were reestablished in much of restoration Europe, and in Rome the *zelanti* pressed for the reconstruction of the walls demolished by the French—in order to contain Jewish "contagion." Some in the Church identified Jews with liberalism, skepticism, humanism—in a word, with modernism, which challenged Catholic truths and tradition. Their diatribes complicated Consalvi's determination that the restored Papal States not impose all the former restrictions on its Jewish population. The pope likewise faced a dilemma, caught between the strident anti-Judaic accusations of the *zelanti* and the counsel of moderation by Metternich and Consalvi. Pius hesitated to incur the wrath of the *zelanti*

---

nale Consali, e la riforma del 1816 (Florence: Felice Le Monnier, 1941), 265–67; Metternich-Winneburg, *Memoirs of Prince Metternich*, 3:92.

66. Wiseman, *Recollections of the Last Four Popes*, 97.

67. Quoted in Kertzer, *Popes against the Jews*, 35.

by displaying an "excessive generosity" toward the Jews. Nonetheless, following Consalvi's directives, and to a chorus of conservative criticism, Pius used moderation in restoring anti-Jewish measures. As part of the compromise, Jews were not totally confined to the ghetto in Rome and were allowed to have shops outside. The wearing of the Jewish badge, though nominally prescribed, was not enforced. Furthermore, Jews continued to live and work in other cities within the Papal States, including Bologna, from which they were technically banned. Despite the rhetoric of the *zelanti* and their allies, in the Papal States as well as the rest of Italy, anti-Jewish laws were not as rigidly enforced as elsewhere, and the impositions on the Jews proved less burdensome.[68] Although papal policy shied away from according the Jews full legal equality, Metternich and the Austrians applauded Pius VII for his willingness to combat "the exorbitant pretensions of the Roman Curia."[69]

Consalvi in turn looked to Austria for inspiration and leadership regarding moderation toward Jews. In all the German states of Austria, the reform edict of Joseph II—which Pius VI had vainly sought to scuttle—remained in effect. Schools existed for Jews of both sexes, and in those areas where the community was small, Jews were at liberty to receive their education in Christian schools. Their parents could become landed proprietors, were subject to military conscription alongside Christians, and were eligible for all sorts of distinctions and honors. Finally, they were free to enter any profession, including the civil service. In Metternich's view, the laws of Joseph II had served his state well and proved immensely beneficial for its Jewish population.[70] Metternich's optimism was not shared by the *zelanti* in Rome or by Joseph de Maistre (1754–1821) of Piedmont-Sardinia, who published his *Du Pape* in 1819.

The lax enforcement of the anti-Judaic proscriptions disturbed the conservatives in the curia, who complained about events in their state and other Catholic countries. They were dismayed in 1817 when the secretary of state thwarted their aggressive campaign in the capital for the mass arrest of Jews and members of sects who flagrantly violated the prescribed restrictions. They sought more active involvement of the Inquisition and

---

68. Lapide, *Three Popes and the Jews,* 78; Martina, *Pius IX e Leopold II,* 198.
69. Metternich-Winneburg, *Memoirs of Prince Metternich,* 3:271.
70. Ibid., 209–10.

later persuaded Pius to write Ferdinand VII of Spain, protesting the abolition of the Inquisition there.[71] Although increasingly isolated by the *zelanti* in the curia, Consalvi refused to align his state with the conservative course during the revolutionary upheaval of 1820. Following the outbreak of a *carbonari* revolution in Naples early in July, Consalvi pursued a pragmatic policy. Unwilling to provide Naples with any pretext for launching an attack on the Papal States or to hinder the mission of the Church in that realm, he pronounced that the pope was obliged to protect the interests of religion, and accorded the constitutional regime de facto recognition. However, he proved unable to deter a papal condemnation of the Carbonari and the excommunication of its members in 1821.[72] The position of Jews of papal Rome likewise proved precarious. Consalvi's pragmatism and moderation toward them disappeared following the death of Pius VII in August 1823. Consalvi sold almost all of his precious art objects to have Antonio Canova erect a monument for the patron and sovereign he had served long and loyally. He also sought to continue his legacy by promoting the election of the like-minded Francesco Saverio Castiglioni. But Castiglioni was not elected once he made it known that he would retain Consalvi as his secretary of state.[73] Forewarned, the conservatives in the curia vetoed both, as they championed a rightward change of course.

The Austrians, by contrast, sought a pope who would manifest "an enlightened piety" and "a conciliatory spirit and moderate principles."[74] This did not materialize, however, because the conclave of September 1823 was dominated by *zelanti* cardinals who disapproved of the political reformism of Consalvi, which they deemed detrimental to the spiritual life of the Church. They likewise believed that Pius's conciliatory approach to the powers and the Jews had been attained at the expense of their ecclesiastical mission. The Austrians used their exclusive, which gave them the right to exclude one cardinal from the election[75] (such vetoes were elimi-

---

71. Pius VII to Ferdinand VII, 30 April 1820, ASV, Epistolae ad Principes, vol. 223, *fascicoli* 11 and 12.

72. W. Maziere Brady, ed., *Anglo-Roman Papers*, vol. 3, *Memoirs of Cardinal Erskine, Papal Envoy to the Court of George III* (London: Alexander Gardner, 1890), 13; "Ecclesiam a Jesu Christo" (on the carbonari), 13 Sept. 1821, *PP* 1:20.

73. Metternich-Winneburg, *Memoirs of Prince Metternich*, 4:617.

74. Ibid., 64.

75. Reinerman, *Austria and the Papacy*, 1:117.

nated by Pius X in 1904), to prevent the election of the *zelanti* leader, Cardinal Gabriele Severoli. At this juncture the *zelanti* majority turned to one of his disciples and secured the election of the reactionary cardinal Annibale della Genga, the former nuncio to Cologne, who assumed the name Leo XII.[76] Although Leo XII was a graduate of the Pontifical Ecclesiastical Academy, the Vatican School of Diplomacy founded by Clement XI in 1701, his rigid convictions and refusal to yield to the "madness of the age" undermined all diplomatic initiatives. The conclave of 1823 and the election of Genga as Leo XII earmarked a watershed in papal history, as the moderation and reformism of Consalvi were replaced by the intransigence of the *zelanti*.

Although Leo appeared fatigued and feeble, he proved energetic in his attempts to affect a more complete return to the *ancien regime,* restoring most of the prerevolutionary impositions on the Jews and attempting to force them back into the ghetto in Rome. In 1823 he reimposed the obligation of Jews to attend and pay for Christian sermons, although the number was reduced to five per year. Leo also commissioned the Holy Office of the Inquisition to investigate Jewish violations of the lawful restrictions imposed upon them in the Papal States. Responding to a litany of complaints against alleged Jewish abuses, Leo's government sought corrective measures. Among other things, the Holy Office reimposed a series of restrictions on Jewish attendance at universities.[77] These measures were applauded by Leo's intransigent allies, who urged more stringent prohibitions on the Israelites.

To assist him in his traditionalist—some said reactionary—program, Leo immediately replaced the moderate Consalvi with the conservative and unyielding Cardinal Giulio della Somaglia. Leo was now prepared to wage war against the liberal and revolutionary currents of the age that he believed the former secretary of state had coddled. He and the other *zelanti* denounced Consalvi's "useless innovations," such as vaccination, street lighting, and the new firefighting company.[78] Although Consalvi's departure delighted the *zelanti*, his moderation was sorely missed not only by

76. Raffaele Colapietra, "Il Diario Brunelli del Conclave del 1823," *Archivio Storico Italiano* 120 (1962): 76–146.

77. Martina, *Pio IX e Leopoldo II,* 199.

78. Reinerman, *Austria and the Papacy,* 1:120.

the Jews of Rome but by the ministry in Vienna. "He had an uncommon understanding and a fine temper, such as we seldom meet with," noted Metternich on Consalvi's death in January 1824, "like an Italian, hot-blooded and vehement, he was yet full of deliberation, like a German."[79]

Insisting on the public primacy of Catholicism at home and abroad, Leo XII, in his first encyclical (*Ubi Primum*, 5 May 1824) condemned de-Christianization, indifferentism, toleration, and Freemasonry, tracing many of the contemporary problems to the contempt for Church authority. He warned the bishops of the sects, which under the guise of philosophy and liberalism spread innumerable errors, and railed against the indifferent, who under the pretext of toleration undermined the faith. At home, education was reformed to reinforce, indeed impose, its moral and religious message, while a decree of October 1824, issued on the first anniversary of his coronation, reformed Rome's administrative and judicial systems, purging them of many of Consalvi's innovations and restoring the prerevolutionary regressive provisions.[80]

Leo's 1824 decree benefited the nobility at the expense of the masses, especially Jews. The jurisdiction of ecclesiastical tribunals, restricted to spiritual matters by Consalvi, was again extended to secular affairs, provoking confusion over civil and canon law to the detriment of Jews, other non-Catholics, and the Catholic laity as well.[81] During the summer of 1824 Leo restored the Gregorian University to the Jesuits. He also required the use of Latin in the universities and law courts. Leo's actions stood in stark contrast to those of Leopold II, who ascended the throne of Tuscany in 1824 and immediately recognized the privileges the Jews in his state had long enjoyed.[82] During Leo XII's tenure the Papal States were burdened by a series of intrusive, reactionary, antimodern measures, championing a social and political order that was slowly but surely disappearing throughout much of Europe. The state, in his view, had not only to educate its subjects in Christian truth but to provide mechanisms and legislation that would assure that they adhered to its precepts and teaching. At the same time, it

79. Metternich-Winneburg, *Memoirs of Prince Metternich*, IV, 99.
80. Ubi Primum *PP* 1:21; Filipuzzi, *Pio IX e la politica Austriaca*, 95.
81. Lucio Toth, "Gli ordimenti territoriale e l'organizzazione periferica dello Stato Pontificio," in *Studi in occasione del Centenario. Scritti sull' amministrazione del territorio romano primo dell'unita* (Milan: Giuffrè, 1970), 101–3; Reinerman, *Austria and the Papacy*, 1:127.
82. Quod divina sapieta, *PP* 1:21; Martina, *Pio IX e Leopoldo II*, 203.

had the responsibility of marginalizing the critics of Catholicism. He renewed the condemnations against the *carbonari* and Freemasons, charging them with conspiring against both Church and state. This pope also
did his best to revive the anti-Jewish edicts that had existed prior to the
revolution and, in the words of one author, "made troubling the Jews his
chief interest in life."[83]

In 1825, with Leo's apparent blessing, a scurrilous treatise on the Jews
by the Domincan father Ferdinando Jabalot appeared in the *Ecclesiastical
Journal* and soon afterward was published as a booklet.[84] This work per-
petuated many of the negative stereotypes and myths about Jews and created new ones, accusing them, among other things, of planning the
destruction of Christianity. Many believed that Leo appreciated and seconded Jabalot's accusations, for after the publication of his pamphlet he
appointed Jabalot head of the Dominican Order.[85] Continuing his conservative campaign, in 1826 Leo created a permanent congregation of vigilance to supervise the activities of all governmental and judicial employees
of the Papal States.[86] At the same time he resurrected the 1775 Jewish ordi-
nance of Pius VI and introduced measures to prohibit Jews from employing Christian domestics in the Papal States. And while papal policy had
long opposed forced conversions of Jews, this principle was not always followed in practice.

During Leo's pontificate, Jews, like Christians, were subject to arrest
for conducting business on Sunday or selling meat on Friday in the Papal
States. Jews were not alone in complaining about the policies of Leo; most
Romans were offended by Leo's crude attempts to control public morality
by placing restrictions on the public sale of wine, closing taverns, cafés,
restaurants, and theaters during Lent, and even implementing intrusive
measures regarding women's wardrobe and the proximity in public between unmarried men and women. In his zeal, Leo even banned the waltz
as obscene.[87] There was a tendency to report even trivial matters to the In-

83. *Pro gravia mala, PP* 1:22; Vogelstein, *Jews of Rome,* 334.

84. Ferdinando Jabalot, *Degli ebrei nel loro rapporto colle nazioni cristiane* (Rome: Poggioli, 1825).

85. Kertzer, *Popes against the Jews,* 64–65.

86. Leo XII's motu proprio of 27 Feb. 1826, *Magnum Bullarium Romanum Continuatio,*
16:409–11.

87. Reinerman, *Austria and the Papacy,* 1:127; Maurice Andrieux, *Rome,* trans. Charles
Lam Markmann (New York: Funk and Wagnalls, 1968), 417–18.

quisition, which scrupulously investigated all Jewish violations of the restrictions imposed upon them. In 1826 Jews were again confined to ghettoes in Rome and witnessed yet another attempt to confiscate their property. This led many Jews and others to flee, to the detriment of Rome's
political reputation and economic well-being. The following year Jews
were constrained to sell their accumulated real estate within a period of
five years, but this provision was implemented only in Rome. Elsewhere in
the Papal States, the authorities had to cede before strong public opposition to the measure.[88] In fact, Cardinal Tommaso Bernetti, the new secretary of state, pleaded for a mitigation of the government's anti-Jewish restrictions but encountered opposition in clerical circles, and the laws
remained, though they were not always enforced. Thus Leo's coercive attempts to impose religious uniformity proved more sporadic than consistent and, though often ruthless in conception, were generally moderate in
implementation.

The plight of the Jews was catalogued in the musical drama La Juivre,
composed by the Franco-Jewish musician Jacques Halevy, who studied for
three years at the Academie de France in Rome. This work, which revealed
the prevailing anti-Judaism that burdened the Jews of the ghetto by the
Tiber, premiered at the Paris Opera in 1835.[89] Jews were joined by other
Romans who resented the restrictions and prohibitions of the pontificate,
and few mourned Leo following his death on 10 February 1829. Giovanni
Maria Mastai Ferretti, the Archbishop of Spoleto and future Pope Pius IX,
was one of the few who praised not only his religious life and devotion to
the Holy See but his government as well. This may be confirmation of
Mastai's later assertion that he knew little about political matters, or
maybe simply the subordination of sound judgment to institutional loyalty. As the archbishop delivered his oration for Leo, he reportedly could not
hold back his tears, so great was his attachment to the deceased pontiff.[90]
Others greeted Leo's death with tears of joy. He was certainly not missed
by his Jewish subjects, for his animosity toward Jews had unfortunate economic, social, and political consequences, during his pontificate and after-

88. Martina, Pio IX e Leopoldo II, 200.

89. Waagenaar, Pope's Jews, 255.

90. Giovanni Maria Mastai's funeral oration for Leo XII, 21 Feb. 1829, ASV, Fondo Particolare Pio IX, cassetta 9, no. 46; Pierre Fernessole, Pie IX Pape (Paris: Lethielleux, 1960–63),
1:61.

ward.[91] Some Christian Romans were upset that he had died at the height of the carnival, in death as in life frustrating their quest for pleasure. They expressed this frustration by breaking into the Jewish ghetto and plundering several shops.

Most of the cardinals in the conclave of 1829 still vehemently opposed "modern civilization" and the toleration it entailed, differing mainly on how best to combat it. They therefore resented the lecture of the French ambassador, Chateaubriand, who called upon the cardinals to elect a pope better attuned to the spirit of the age and prepared to second its support of liberty. Cardinal Castiglioni, authorized to respond to the French ambassador and present the conclave's position, noted that the Church had no need to adapt to the modern world in essentials for it was solidly established on divine authority. Rather than follow current trends or popular positions, its policy was based on Holy Scripture and venerable tradition—the only school of good government. It was the world that should follow and adapt to the Church! The ascendancy of such sentiments in the conclave undermined the position of the moderate contenders and virtually eliminated the prospects of "progressive" cardinals.

On 31 March 1829, sixty-eight-year-old Francesco Saverio Castiglioni, Bishop of Frascati and prefect of the Congregation of the Index, was elected pope. Although he had moved in a more conservative direction, he was not a reactionary, and he recognized the need for some reforms in the Papal States, though not in the Church. Since a majority of the cardinals were more conservative than he, Pius VIII's initial actions were confined to suspending or revoking the most unpopular measures of his predecessor. Perhaps to further reassure the skeptical *zelanti,* in his first encyclical, *Traditi humilitati* of 24 May 1829, Pius launched an attack on the enemies of Church and state.[92] Commencing with a condemnation of those who attacked the Church's spiritual mission, he denounced indifferentism, calling this heresy, which claimed that salvation might be reached by means of any religion, a contrivance of sophists. To prevent "religious pollution," he forbade Jews from entering any relations with Christians, except during the course of business.[93] At the same time, he revived the earlier papal con-

---

91. For the unfortunate economic consequences, see Leone Carpi, *Alcune parole sugli Israeliti in occasione di un decreto* (Florence, 1847).

92. *Litteris Altero, PP* 1:23.

93. Roth, *History of the Jews of Italy,* 451.

demnations of Freemasonry, denouncing its impact on education and its contribution to the lax morals of the new generation.

The papal secretary of state, the octogenarian Cardinal Giuseppe Albani, assured the public that there would be no meaningful departure from the conservative course outlined by Leo XII.[94] Like his predecessor, Pius VIII called upon the authorities to ensure that all Jews in the Papal States remain enclosed in the ghettoes, but he was no more able to enforce this injunction. Nonetheless, the attempted repression of Jews provoked censure in liberal circles. Opposition to this papal policy toward the Jews formed only a small part of the broader disenchantment with the policies of this pontificate at home and abroad. In France critics of the restored regime deplored the unholy alliance between throne and altar. Not surprisingly, the revolutionary outbreak of 1830 against the monarchy also took aim at its clerical allies. Although distressed that the July Revolution in Paris was directed against the Church as well as the legitimist regime, the pope shied away from sanctioning Lamennais's call for the separation of Church and state and continued to champion their union. He finally seemed to recognize the need to moderate his state's conservative course, however, in order to avert a similar revolutionary cataclysm at home. Pius VIII's death after a reign of only a year and eight months spared him the grief of seeing the revolution and its principles spread to his state. His promise of future reform and his sudden death led some to suspect he had been poisoned, but an autopsy deemed his death natural. The Romans did not mourn his passing, "The eighth Pius was Pope," they sang out, "he lived and died and no one took note."

The conclave to elect a successor opened on 14 December 1830 following an abortive coup in Rome. The prospect of upheaval did not inspire the cardinals to end their personal bickering and ideological disputes, and the conclave deadlocked, which only encouraged the revolutionaries. Early in February 1831, under the orchestration of Bernetti, the parochial Camaldolese monk Bartolomeo Alberto Cappellari was elected pope, assuming the name Gregory XVI, and selected Bernetti as his secretary of state. Gregory was the last monk as well as the last nonbishop to be so elected. While some *zelanti* found him too moderate, reformers branded him a re-

94. Toth, "Gli ordimenti territoriale," 104.

actionary.[95] All agreed that the new pope was otherworldly, shunned innovation, and relied on his pragmatic secretary of state, who was a cardinal though not a priest, for political decisions. He trusted Bernetti, who he claimed had "an arm of Iron and a heart of gold."[96] In light of the troubled current situation, Gregory needed all the help he could get.

Gregory's election was followed by uprisings in Parma, Modena, and papal Bologna, overturning the legitimate regimes and pressing for the creation of an Italian republic in north central Italy. Thus the pontificate of Gregory XVI opened in the midst of crisis. Gregory immediately denounced the rebels.[97] Bernetti hoped to rely on a counterrevolutionary militia to regain the provinces, but this strategy proved futile and Gregory was constrained to appeal to Metternich, who responded promptly to suppress the revolutionary tempest. Liberals and nationalists in France complained that Louis Philippe had virtually surrendered Italy to the Austrians. Their outcry was echoed by the other powers when Bernetti issued an edict that imposed burdensome penalties on the revolutionaries. Indeed, the secretary of state was constrained to issue a revised and substantially more liberal amnesty.[98] To appease French national sentiment, Metternich supported changes in the Papal States to eliminate the conditions that had led to the outburst, but he could not prevent a conference of the major powers (France, England, Austria, Russia, and Prussia) to suggest reforms to the papal government.

In May 1831 the conference of ambassadors submitted a memorandum, cataloguing the changes the powers deemed essential for a modernization of the Papal States, including the creation of a national consultative assembly. The secretary of state, Bernetti, rejected the call for such a body, asserting that the principles inspiring it were contrary to the special nature of the papal regime.[99] This moderate minister found himself

95. Reinerman, *Austria and the Papacy*, 2:7–9.

96. Daniel Rops, *Church in an Age of Revolution*, 250; See Index no. 1175 in the ASV for Archhivio Particolare Gregorio XVI.

97. Gregory XVI decried the rebellion in his 9 February 1831 statement; *Magnum Bullarium Romanum Continuatio*, 17:1–2.

98. See Reinerman, *Austria and the Papacy*, 2:49–53.

99. Frank J. Coppa, *The Origins of the Italian Wars of Independence* (London: Longman, 1992), 17; Filipuzzi, *Pio IX e la politica Austriaca*, 100–105; Luigi Rodelli, *La Repubblica Romana del 1849* (Pisa: Domus Mazzininiana, 1955), 35–36; Alexandre de Saint-Albin, *Pie IX*

caught between the calls for progressive reforms coming from abroad and the insistence on the preservation of tradition issued by clerical groups at home, which had the ear of the pope. Repeating many of the arguments they had launched to counter Bernetti's earlier call for a relaxation of anti-Jewish measures, they denounced the Hebrew alliance with the forces of modernity. Indeed, they charged that this alliance craved modernization, secularization, individualism, and that it ultimately sought to unravel the fabric of Christian society. Small wonder that Bernetti, who was constrained to promise reforms to satisfy liberal opinion abroad, proved unable to implement many changes in the face of a determined clerical and conservative domestic opposition.[100]

When rebellion again erupted at the end of 1831 in the legations, the papacy called for Austrian intervention, which prompted a French occupation of Ancona to preserve a balance of power in the peninsula. Vienna was disappointed by Rome's inability or unwillingness to introduce meaningful reform and modernization that would quiet the unrest. "You can prop up a corpse," the Austrians complained, "but you can't make it walk." Metternich did not despair, and continued to seek reforms that could save Rome "in spite of itself."[101] Rome proved less than cooperative. Despite increasing criticism, Gregory remained committed to past practice and critical of revolutionary movements at home and abroad, including that of the Catholic Poles against their Russian Orthodox masters, urging submission to legitimate authority.[102] His sentiments were reflected in the "catechism on revolution," which maintained that any revolution against constituted authority represented a rebellion against God and religion as well.[103] Critics complained that this pope was an intransigent obstacle to progress. Even moderate conservatives feared the worst. "Here they are so convinced of the indestructibility and infallibility of this government," the exasperated Austrian ambassador to Rome complained, "that its rulers of-

(Paris: E. Dentu, 1860), 35; Carlo Ghisalberti, "Il Consiglio di Stato di Pio IX. Nota storia giuridica," *Studi Romani* 2 (1954): 56; Reinerman, *Austria and the Papacy*, 2:70.

100. Filipuzzi, *Pio IX e la politica Austriaca* 109; Edgar Quinet, *La questione romaine davant l'histoire, 1840–1867* (Paris: Armand Le Chevalier, 1868), 16.

101. Reinerman, *Austria and the Papacy*, 2:135.

102. *Cum Primum*, 9 June 1832, *PP* 1:25.

103. *Catechismo sulle rivoluzioni* (1832), ASV, Fondo Particolare Pio IX, cassetta 5, busta 4.

ten abandon themselves calmly to inaction, counting upon the aid of God and the miracles He will work to support the state against its enemies."[104]

The European situation proved increasingly hostile to the restoration of past practice or even the preservation of the status quo. The introduction of a separation of Church and state in Belgium as well as in France, in 1830, alarmed Rome but inspired Félicité de Lamennais, who perceived the advantages of constitutionalism and republicanism, which allowed Catholics the liberty to defend their rights in the political arena. With a circle of friends he founded the daily *L'Avenir*, which championed the separation of Church and state. Gregory was not converted, needless to say, and abhorred the movement's slogan, "tout les libertés pour tous." To papal ears this smacked of indifferentism, which would inevitably lead to incredulity and license. The crusading Breton priest, certain of the justice of his cause, failed to accurately assess Gregory's adverse reaction. At the end of 1831 Lamennais decided to present his case personally to Rome and to plead on behalf of freedom of conscience. After waiting for two months, Lamennais was finally received by Gregory, who diplomatically chose not to discuss his work and mission but appointed a congregation to examine his movement.[105] Its report was reflected in Gregory's encyclical of 15 August 1832, the *Mirari vos*, which implicitly condemned both the ideas of *L'Avenir* and the international organization Lamennais had founded.[106]

Rejecting the call for religious freedom, Pope Gregory remained convinced that outside the Church there was neither truth nor salvation. He condemned liberty of conscience as "false," "absurd," "mad," and "one of the most contagious of errors."[107] He had expressed a similar view in his first encyclical letter, which excoriated false enlightenment and blind innovation as well as the "pestilence of indifferentism" and the "pretensions of unrestrained religious liberty." Denouncing the pretended right of *L'Avenir* to publish everything and anything, Gregory defended the Holy See's right not only to condemn but to remove harmful books from circu-

---

104. Quoted in Reinerman, *Austria and the Papacy*, 2:47.

105. Francesco Andreu, "Un aspetto inedito nel raporto Ventura-Lamennais," ed. Eugenio Guccione (Florence: Leo Oschki, 1991), 2:635–36.

106. Ellen Evans, "Joseph Gorres and Félicité de Lammenmais: Early Catholic Politics," *Consortium on Revolutionary Europe, 1750–1850: Proceedings, 1991*, ed. Karl A. Roider Jr. and John C. Horgan (Tallahassee: Florida State University, 1992), 197.

107. Quoted in Carroll, *Constantine's Sword*, 441.

lation. Denying that the Church needed regeneration, he proclaimed its need to oppose the fashionable "insanities" of the age. One of the "intolerable innovations" was the separation of Church and state, which Gregory considered dangerous for religion and the well-being of a Christian people. The pope catalogued the difficulties the Church confronted and the problems posed by the enemies of God, who camouflaged their evil intent under the guise of liberty of conscience and freedom of the press. Complaining of the campaign to oppose the authority of the Church and the papacy and the attempts to curtail their rights, he invoked a crusade against the common enemies of the Church and religion.[108] Some in the curia placed Jews in the enemy camp, applauding the papal prohibition on Catholics uniting with non-Catholics to achieve political aims.

Gregory's *Mirari vos* was the forerunner of Pius IX's *Quanta cura* and his "Syllabus of Errors" of 1864, and it further alienated progressive opinion, which continued to challenge the legitimacy of papal political power. Brushing criticism aside, Gregory again denounced the concept of freedom of conscience. Although his call for Catholic primacy achieved at the expense of other religious groups found favor in the clerical conservative camp, it alienated liberal opinion at home and abroad. Conservatives also applauded the letter Gregory issued later in the year condemning contemporary revolutionary principles and their sources. Among other things, it charged that the halls of the universities rang with "new and monstrous opinions." Denouncing the idols worshipped by "modern civilization," Gregory was particularly outraged by the emerging indifferentism, which claimed that members of society had a right to select their own beliefs and follow whatever practices they desired. Lamennais, who refused to submit to the papal position, was singled out for particular condemnation in 1834. The following year the pope struck out against the rationalist ideas and tendencies of Georg Hermes, who also championed freedom of conscience.[109]

The traditionalist pontiff insisted that restrictions be maintained on non-Catholics such as Protestants and Jews in Catholic countries, and of course in the Papal States. Under his guidance the Holy See continued to

108. *PE* 1:235–38.
109. *E principio certo PP* 1:26; *Singulari nos,* 24 June 1834, *PP* 1:26; *Dum acerbissimas,* 26 Sept. 1835, *PP* 1:27.

discourage, if not forbid, mixed marriages between Catholics and non-Catholics, tolerating such unions only to avoid greater scandal. However, Gregory insisted that it was incumbent upon the Catholic partner in such a union to make every effort to withdraw the non-Catholic from error and educate all children in the Catholic faith.[110] Conversion and segregation still remained the cornerstones of his policy toward Jews. Thus, in his negotiations with the Austrians in the 1830s to eliminate the remnants of Josephism, Gregory insisted that the bishops there should be allowed to baptize Jews without government consent. He also sought government support of the Church position that any Catholic minor adopted by a non-Catholic must be raised in the Catholic faith. In turn, Catholic priests were no longer to assist at the funerals of non-Catholics, who were to be exempt from the tax paid to priests for this purpose. This concession proved insufficient to satisfy the emperor and the Austrians, who rejected the agreement, so that the Church in Austria remained under close governmental control and scrutiny.[111]

Catholic Austria was not unique in its refusal to adhere to Rome's unyielding position. The papal outlook, which earlier had found a large and receptive audience, was increasingly considered obscurantist and hopelessly outdated in nineteenth-century Europe. Consequently, Gregory's determination to preserve the restrictions on Jews was perceived as not only morally unjust but as economically unsound. In 1835 Carlo Cattaneo published a work attributing the social degradation of the Jews to the massive discrimination against them, and urged changes in this "medieval" mentality and the alteration of the public perception. Many of Cattaneo's themes were repeated in the widely read *Primato morale e civile degli Italiani* (1843) of Vincenzo Gioberti, in which this priest invoked liberty of conscience. His call was supported by a series of other writers and the Piedmontese press, which called for an end to the discrimination against the Jews. A number of Jewish writers also entered the fray.[112]

Gregory, who believed that as pope he had been delegated the supreme power of nourishing and directing the Church, remained divided in his

---

110. Summo Iugiter Studio, 27 May 1832, *PE* 1:229–31.

111. Reinerman, *Austria and the Papacy*, 2:280.

112. Carlo Cattaneo, *Ricerche econimiche sulle interdizioni impose dalla legge civile agli Israeliti* (Milan, 1835); Martina, *Pio IX e Leopoldo II*, 208–10; Sabatino Sacredoti, *Al dottor Samuele Liuzzi di Reggio. Lettere riguardante gli Israeliti Italiani* (Parma, 1843).

position toward Jews, reflecting past papal principles and practices. For Gregory the treatment of Jews was only one of the many problems he confronted. He was especially troubled by his inability to curb the growing disorder in the provinces and his helplessness in the relentless forward march of modernization. He opposed the lighting of streets and the building of railways, dubbing the latter *chemins d'enfer* (roads of hell) rather than *chemins de fer* (roads of iron). The backwardness of the state facilitated and encouraged disturbances that the government found difficult if not impossible to contain. The solution proposed by Bernetti—a counterrevolutionary peasant force—was questioned even by staunch supporters of the regime. The violence provoked by Bernetti's "Centurians" led to further unrest and resentment in the provinces, and aroused concern in Vienna. Cardinal Spinola, commissioner of the legations, complained of the anarchy and disorder the militia brought on, concluding that it represented "a cure worse than the disease."[113]

The attempted "reform" of the papal administration in the mid-1830s proved long, detailed, and entirely ineffective.[114] The suggestions emanating from Vienna were essentially ignored, except for Metternich's insistence on the dismissal of Bernetti. This was sanctioned only because the *zelanti* shared Vienna's perception that his regime had proved ineffective—but whereas Vienna proposed a more moderate course, the *zelanti* hoped for a more repressive regime. Under the circumstances, Cardinal Luigi Lambruschini's selection as the new secretary of state represented a compromise. Disbanding Bernetti's militia, the Centurians, Lambruschini relied on older institutions to curb the growing dissatisfaction in the state, but he was no more effective than Bernetti in restoring law and order. By this time even loyal sons of the Church such as Cardinal Mastai-Ferretti privately criticized the ineffective Roman administration and recognized the need for real reform.[115] Outside Rome, criticism of papal policies was more severe.

During Gregory's pontificate the papacy's diplomatic reach was neither wide nor influential. In 1840 Rome sent its nuncios to only eleven

113. Cardinal Spinola to Cardinal Bernetti, 12 Feb. and 5 April 1835, ASV, SS, rubrica 190.

114. Proposals for reform of the administration and judicial system of the Papal States, 10 Nov. 1834, *Bullarii romani continuatio*, 6:490–563.

115. Giovanni Maioli, ed., *Pio IX da Vescovo a Pontefice. Lettere al Card. Luigi Amat. Agosto 1839–Luglio 1848* (Modena: Società Tipografico Modenese, 1943), 42.

countries, nine of them in Western Europe and the remaining two in South America. Neither London nor St. Petersburg housed nuncios, who were likewise absent from all of Africa, Asia, the Middle East, and North America.[116] At any rate, Gregory was no more inclined to listen to the call for change emanating from outside his state than to that coming from within. Instead, he continued to look to the past for guidance. His 1838 edict on the Jews sought to reimpose the proscriptions of Pius VI's 1775 edict, but under the existing circumstances this proved even more difficult than it had been before. In fact, the pope found it necessary to make all sorts of concessions, but he always insisted that these were by way of exception and did not compromise official Church policy. This dichotomy was also reflected in his reaction to the alleged Jewish ritual murder of Father Tommaso in Damascus in 1840—the so-called Damascus Affair. Some have seen Vatican duplicity in spreading the publication that implicated a group of Jews in the murder, but making sure it was not published in Rome. Others, however, have praised Gregory for his refusal to have these outrageous charges launched in Rome, and for agreeing to have the incendiary inscription on Tommaso's grave, which specified that the Capuchin priest had been assassinated by the Jews, removed. Still, Gregory could not be persuaded to issue a formal declaration against the myth of Jewish ritual murder.[117]

Wedded to past practice, Gregory proved reluctant to criticize his predecessors' policies—a characteristic shared by most popes in the modern age. He also hesitated to abandon previous ecclesiastical regulations that imposed restrictions on the Jews, and he prohibited their mingling with Christians. Nonetheless, neither he nor the curial institutions were entirely insensitive to Jews' personal plight, dispensing charity and ministering to them during the cholera epidemics. Then, in 1845, the Roman rota ruled in their favor, judging that Jews no more than Christians could be arrested during their religious services. "The Jews are not to be treated as heathens," it ruled. "They pray to the same God as Christians."[118] On the other hand, neither Gregory nor his successors could acknowledge the equality of Catholicism and Judaism. Financial exigencies bolstered, if

116. David Alvarez, *Spies in the Vatican: Espionage and Intrigue from Napoleon to the Holocaust* (Lawrence: University Press of Kansas, 2002), 17.

117. Kertzer, *Popes against the Jews*, 86–105; Vogelstein, *Jews of Rome*, 337.

118. Quoted in Chadwick, *History of the Popes*, 129.

they did not inspire, papal sensitivity toward the suffering of Rome's Jews. Early on, Gregory had recourse to Jewish banking houses, above all the house of Rothschild, whose leaders pled on behalf of their coreligionists in Rome. In 1831, through the intervention of Metternich, a loan was made, and shortly thereafter Carl Rothschild, head of the bank in Naples, was received by Gregory in a private interview and granted the newly established Order of Saint George. Perhaps this later encouraged the Rothschilds to appeal to Gregory on behalf of the Jews of Ancona, upon whom the papal regime and Inquisition had sought to reimpose a series of burdensome restrictions.

In an extraordinary move, Metternich presented the Jewish case to the Holy See in 1843. Among other things, the Austrian minister indicated that the ancient ecclesiastical restrictions that burdened the Jews of Ancona and other cities of the Papal States were no longer in harmony with present conditions and the needs of the moment. He earnestly pressed Rome for change. To encourage it to abandon its restrictive course, he reported that modern Jews had evolved from their fanaticism and no longer posed a threat to the faith. "It seems to me," Metternich advised, "that the Holy Pontiff has nothing to lose and everything to gain in treating his Jewish subjects with a mercy that is far from being seen as a sign of weakness." Gregory did not agree, noting that the prohibitions on Jews were inspired by the sacred canons and aimed to guarantee Christian religion and morality. Gregory, who perceived a link between the Jews and modernity, also contested Metternich's claim that Jews no longer represented a danger. "Nor does the loss of the Jews' primitive fanaticism [regarding Jewish law and practices] render the observance of the Canonical sanctions on them any less necessary," Gregory warned, because "they certainly do not lose their national hatred for the Religion of Jesus Christ, and for the Christian name itself."[119] In his view, the Jews were implicated in the war waged against the Church and the papacy, and to accord them liberty and equality would undermine the faith.[120] In this manner Gregory pinpointed the "religious" considerations underlying his political actions.

Although Gregory confronted problems at home and abroad, he re-

---

119. Metternich's letter of 3 Aug. 1843, ACDF, Santum Officium, Stanza Storica, TT.3, f.5, quoted in Kertzer, *Popes against the Jews*, 81, 83.

120. Martina, *Pio IX e Leopoldo II*, 205.

mained unreceptive to the pleas of the powers for political reforms, ignoring most of the recommendations of their memorandum, which he shelved in the Vatican Archives. It was said of Cardinal Luigi Lambruschini, his secretary of state during the last decade of the pontificate (1836–46), that he was "liberal chiefly in his employment of spies and prisons."[121] To make matters worse, another outbreak of cholera struck Rome and its environs in 1837, sparking disturbances and disorders. During this difficult time the pope responded to the Jewish plight in Rome with Christian kindness, forgiving their debts and providing medical aid during the crisis.[122] Unfortunately, many of the problems of the ghetto and of his Jewish subjects—which had been highlighted by the report of the papal commission following the 1835 epidemic—remained unresolved. His paternalism did not extend to granting the Jews civil equality or anything approaching it. Religious equality he found detrimental to the "one true faith."

In the last years of his pontificate, from 1840 to 1846, Gregory continued to battle the "forces of evil" that sought to diminish the influence of the Roman Church. As before, he saw religion under attack by errors of all kinds, spearheaded by "the unbridled rashness of renegades," and he resisted most change, preferring piety to progress, obedience to liberty.[123] The position of the Jews in Rome did not much improve during his pontificate, as we learn from a memorandum transmitted by the Baron Salomone Rothschild to the nuncio at Vienna for transmission to Rome. This report highlighted the difficulties of the Roman Jewish community of some 3,800, of which some 2,000 were indigent. Among the difficulties they faced was the closing of the eight gates of the ghetto every evening and the need for a special passport to leave Rome. Jewish life in the Eternal City was further restricted by the prohibition against owning real property outside the ghetto walls, the prohibition on entering the liberal professions, the regulations that prevented them from printing, the burdensome array of taxes that made it difficult for them to fund their schools, and, when they fell ill, their exclusion from the hospitals.[124]

These problems Pope Gregory was not prepared to tackle, insofar as

121. Lease, "Denunciation as a Tool of Ecclesiastical Control," 820.

122. Giacomo Antonelli to Filippo Antonelli, 28 June and 13 Aug. 1837, ASR, Fondo Famiglia Antonelli, busta 1, no. 1, no. 116; Chadwick, *History of the Popes*, 129.

123. *Probe nostis*, 18 Sept. 1840, *PP* 1:28.

124. Martina, *Pio IX e Leopoldo II*, 200–201.

they required some revision of papal policy toward Jews. His unwillingness to reconsider the papal treatment of Jews was not unique but formed
part of his broader stubborn adherence to tradition. Like the tsar of Russia, Nicholas I, who visited Rome at the end of 1845, Gregory failed to understand the direction in which the world was moving, and what he recognized, he did not like. Considering himself a priest first and a sovereign
second, this hierarchy was reflected in his priorities as well as his political
and spiritual decisions. Not surprisingly, Christians as well as Jews hoped
his successor would be more amenable to an accommodation with modernity. An air of expectation led many to believe that Gregory's death in
1846 represented a turning point in the history of the papacy, and that the
selection of his successor was of crucial importance.

3

PIO NONO AND THE JEWS

From Reform to Reaction, 1846–1878

*The Roman Pontiff can and ought to reconcile and har-
monise himself with progress, with liberalism, and with
modern civilization.*[*]

GIOVANNI MARIA MASTAI-FERRETTI was elected pope on 16 June 1846, assuming
the name Pius IX (Pio Nono), in honor of Pius VII, who had issued the
dispensation that allowed the epileptic Giovanni to enter the priesthood.[1]
Ordained in 1819, he received holy orders not to make a career but to serve
as a pastor of souls. His first assignment as a priest was at a Roman or-
phanage, where he remained until 1823. From 1823 to 1825 he accompanied
the apostolic delegate to Chile and Peru, in a venture he initially thought
would be more missionary than diplomatic.[2] Following his return from
Latin America, Giovanni was appointed director of the Hospice of San
Michele in Rome. Named Archbishop of Spoleto in 1827, he served there
until 1832, when he was appointed Bishop of Imola, where he remained
until 1846, even though Gregory XVI had brought him into the College of
Cardinals six years earlier.

[*] The 80th Proposition condemned in the "Syllabus of Errors" of Pope Pius IX, found in
Frank J. Coppa, *The Papacy Confronts the Modern World* (Malabar, Fla.: Krieger Publishing,
2003), 139. An earlier version of this chapter was published in *CHR* 89, no. 4 (2003): 671–93.
1. See ASV, SS, Morte di pontefici e Conclavi, Pio IX.
2. "Breve relazione del viaggio fatto al Chili dal Canoninco Giovanni Maria Mastai-
Ferretti di Sinigaglia," Memorie. Viaggio al Chile, Biblioteca Apostolica Vaticana Latina, no.
10190, sala studio manoscritti, 19–25.

In his various pastoral posts and ecclesiastical positions, he had little interaction with Jews, as is attested by the biographers of his prepapal career, and for most of these years he was little known in Rome.[3] That he had friends and acquaintances in the liberal and nationalist camp led some to judge him as more progressive than conservative. Rumors circulated that, unlike his predecessor, he was not opposed to "progress," and word spread that in 1845 he had outlined a reformist program for the Papal States.[4] Although his fifty-eight-point program, set forth in his "Thoughts on the Public Administration of the Papal State," did not include the civil emancipation of the Jews, Giovanni's liberal reputation flowed largely from his social interactions with reformers and his call for administrative change and a cautious modernization of the Papal States. Those who favored political, Jewish, and national liberation saw a glimmer of hope.

The pontificate of Pio Nono (1846–78), the longest in history, opened with an air of expectation that was reinforced by the amnesty of July 1846, earning Pius a liberal image at home and abroad.[5] Liberals, nationalists, and Jews hoped that the new pope would reconcile liberty and religion, unite Italy, and ameliorate the position of the Jews in the Papal States. Initially Pio Nono seemed to fulfill this mission, emerging in the eyes of many as the pope-liberator prophesied by the Piedmontese priest Vincenzo Gioberti in his work *On the Civil and Moral Primacy of the Italians* (1843). Following the revolutionary upheaval of 1848–49, however, the pope who had been hailed as a liberal was denounced as the high priest of reaction and chief protagonist of the Counter-Risorgimento. Thus, while Mazzini, Garibaldi, and Cavour were respectively dubbed the "heart," "sword," and "brains" of unification, Pio Nono emerged as the "cross" of liberals, nationalists, and Jews.

In the year 2000, when John Paul II beatified Pius IX, the pope who

3. See Alberto Serafini, *Pio IX, Giovanni Maria Mastai Ferretti dalla giovinezza alla morte nei suoi scritti e discorsi editi e inediti*, vol. 1, *Le vie della Divinia Provvidenza (1792–1846)* (Vatican City: Tipografia Poliglotta Vaticana, 1958); and Carlo Falconi, *Il giovane Mastai* (Milan: Rusconi, 1981).

4. "Pensieri relativi alla Amministrazione pubblica dello Stato Pontificio," in Serafini, *Pio IX*, 1:1397–1406.

5. "Amnistia accordata dalla Santità di nostro Signore Pio IX nella Sua exaltazione al Ponificato," 16 July 1846, in *Atti del Sommo Pontefice Pio IX, Felicemente Regnante. Parte seconda che comprende I Motu-proprii, chirografi editti, notificazioni, ec. per lo stato pontificio* (Rome: Tipografia delle Belle Arti, 1857), 1:4–6.

convoked Vatican I (1869–70) and waged war against the modern world, alongside John XXIII, who convoked Vatican II (1962–65) and sought an accommodation with it, there was a trinity of opposition from liberals, Italian nationalists, and Jews. Many knew of Pio Nono's fierce opposition to Italian unification and his role in the Counter-Risorgimento, which aroused nationalists, as well as his war against modern civilization, concretized in the "Syllabus of Errors," which angered liberals. Although some mentioned his role in the Mortara affair,[6] others wondered why Jews opposed his canonization. Not all aspects of Pius IX's reversal of course have been fully explored, including his relationship to the Jews—the focus of this chapter. Pio Nono's Jewish policies are examined in light of the traditional anti-Judaism within the Church, his early reformist program, and, finally, his conflicts with Italian nationalism and European liberalism and unsuccessful attempts to preserve the temporal power. Some contend that had Pius continued on his reformist course, Catholic-Jewish relations might have been improved a century earlier and would not have had to wait for John XXIII (1958–63) and the Second Vatican Council. Why did this reconciliation fail during the pontificate of Pius IX?

It failed for a number of reasons, and above all because, from the first, Pius IX saw neither the need for nor the desirability of Christian-Jewish reconciliation. Nor did he suppose that Jews could or should enjoy the same rights as Catholics in Rome or any Catholic country. In the nineteenth century neither the papacy nor the Church was prepared to sanction such equality. Pius IX's initial reforms were designed to correct abuses and offer assistance rather than to change prevailing structures in either the Roman Church or the Papal States. Pio Nono assumed the Christian nature of Italy and Europe, believed that the clerical nature of his government should and would continue, and saw no reason why the clergy should not retain their privileged position in the social and political spheres as well as in the religious realm.[7] Determined to provide for the well-being of all his subjects, including Jews, from the first Pius sought to do so only by methods compatible with the ecclesiastical nature of his state. His differences with Gregory XVI were political rather than reli-

6. David I. Kertzer, *The Kidnapping of Edgardo Mortara* (New York: Knopf, 1997).

7. Leopold G. Glueckert, *Between Two Amnesties: Former Political Prisoners and Exiles in the Roman Revolution of 1848* (New York: Garland, 1991), 26–27.

gious, for unlike his predecessor he believed in the prospect of a conciliation of sorts between religion and progress, between the Catholic faith and
some liberal programs, if not liberal principles.[8] "Theology is not opposed
to the development of science and industry," he confided to friends, but
added cautiously, "I know nothing about politics and maybe I am wrong."[9]

During his pastoral and episcopal career Pius never questioned, much
less challenged, the Church's religious practices or even recognized its prevailing anti-Judaism, which for him was more institutional than individual.[10] During his tenure at Imola, when the Holy Office in Rome instructed him to remove a child from its relatives in the ghetto of Lugo, Giovanni
complied without expressing doubt or scruple. While at Spoleto his personal library, like his sermons, avoided controversial subjects. It contained
no volume of speculative philosophy, political or historical theory, or even
critical theology. Instead his books focused on devotional matters such as
Christian love and charity.[11] As Bishop of Imola, his talks almost always
dealt with devotional and disciplinary matters, which reflected the traditional Church position.[12] This perspective inspired his early reformism in
the Papal States. Since he initially sought some conciliation between the
Church and the modern world, there were those who hoped he would
moderate the papacy's anti-Judaism and possibly introduce Jewish emancipation.

The Jewish community in Rome was encouraged to petition the pope,
pleading for the removal of some of the burdensome restrictions imposed
by his immediate predecessors.[13] The pope, following his natural inclina-
tions and humanitarianism, took steps to remedy the most grave and urgent needs of his Jewish population. He also appointed a committee to examine their plight, and in the interim ordered an end to the degrading
carnival ceremonies and the compulsory sermons, while permitting Jews
to erect tombstones over their graves. He perceived no danger to the faith

8. Maioli, ed., *Pio IX da Vescovo a Pontefice*, 44–45.

9. Giuseppe Pasolini, *Memorie. 1815–1876*, ed. Pietro Desiderio Pasolini (Turin: Bocca, 1887), 57.

10. See ASV, Fondo Particolare Pio IX, cassetta 10, busta 1, fascicoli 1–75.

11. List of books belonging to Giovanni Maria Mastai-Ferretti, Archbishop of Spoleto, ASV, Fondo Particolare Pio IX, cassetta 5, busta 1.

12. Ibid., cassetta 9, buste 1–2.

13. See breve racconti degli avventimenti successi in Roma, ASV, Archivio Particolare Pio IX, ogetti vari, no. 515.

in these modifications. He introduced other practical measures to ameliorate the plight of Rome's Jews. At the end of 1846, dismayed by the flood-
ing of the Tiber into their overcrowded and disease-ridden quarter, he allowed a number of Jewish families to reside outside the ghetto.[14] He
provided the stricken community the sum of three hundred *scudi* for
flood damage, and later provided that Jews, too, were eligible for public
charity. His government also extended public subsidies to Jewish families
that had twelve or more children.[15] These moderate measures did not differ much from past acts of papal generosity toward the Jews, but they were
given an entirely new and exaggerated meaning in light of the euphoria
and unrealistic expectations surrounding the initial phase of his pontificate. In the words of the Jewish writer Salvatore Anau, Pius IX was "the
new beneficent genius called by Providence."[16] Thus a sense of expectation, and the prospect of reform, infused the ghetto as well as the rest of
Rome, which hoped for a new era after the sterile restoration years and the
stagnation of Gregory XVI's pontificate.

The hope for change was fueled as well by the abolition of internal
passports and of mandatory attendance of Jews at conversionary sermons,
and by the closure of the House of Catecumens, which fostered conversions.[17] This "liberal" interlude witnessed the dismantling of extraordinary tribunals and the first steps toward a reform of the criminal justice
system, which benefited Jews as well as Christians. Meanwhile a new press
law did away with much censorship, which had hitherto prohibited the
publication of liberal and national sentiments, and plans were drafted for
the creation of a council of ministers.[18] For these initiatives and modest
measures, Pius was praised in Rome, in Italy, and abroad. Across the Atlantic, at the end of 1847, U.S. President James Polk urged Congress to establish diplomatic relations with Rome.[19] The admirers of Pius not only

14. Martina, *Pio IX e Leopoldo II*, 211–13.
15. Domenico Demarco, *Pio IX e la rivoluzione romana del 1848. Saggio di storia
economica-sociale* (Modena: Società Tipografica Modenese, 1947), 70.
16. Quoted in Canepa, "Atteggiamento degli ebrei italiani," 426.
17. Martina, *Pio IX e Leopoldo II*, 212; Lapide, *Three Popes and the Jews*, 78.
18. Rapporto a Sua Santità per l'udienza del 30 settembre 1846, ASR, Fondo Famiglia
Antonelli, busta 3.
19. Leo F. Stock, ed., *Consular Relations between the United States and the Papal States:
Instructions and Despatches* (Washington, D.C.: Catholic University of America Press, 1945),
92, 114.

exaggerated his concessions but tended to confuse his roles as priest and prince, accentuating the latter, while Pius, from the first, stressed the former. In thanking the cardinal electors, he revealed his priorities by promising to focus on the glory of God and the honor of the Church and the Holy See, and to work for the well-being of his people.[20] Committed to defending the faith, and a traditionalist in most Church matters, Pius harbored reservations concerning Jewish emancipation.[21] That Pius was neither a revolutionary nor a liberal can be gleaned from his first encyclical of 9 November 1846, *Qui pluribus,* on faith and religion, in which Pius attacked the incredulous and the enemies of Christian truth, condemning rationalism, indifferentism, latitudinarianism, and other modern errors, and repeating Gregory's proscriptions against liberalism.[22] In many ways this first encyclical was a precursor to his later "Syllabus of Errors" (1864). It reflected his underlying traditional convictions and the philosophical preconceptions he accepted without question.

Although Pius was far from a revolutionary, preferring limited and timely political reform to outright reaction, Metternich feared that the new pope did not appreciate the political consequences of his actions or the deliberate distortion of his aims. "Warm hearted, with little imagination, he has since his election to the Papacy, allowed himself to be entangled in a net from which he is no longer able to escape, and if events pursue their natural course, he will get himself turned out of Rome," Metternich warned.[23] In fact, Pius was dismayed by many of the demands made upon him. He was prepared to increase lay participation in his ministry but balked at the notion of secularizing his administration or recognizing religious equality, which, like his predecessors, he denounced as indifferentism. This pope accepted the idea of limited lay and popular input into state affairs but not affairs of the Church. Displaying a benevolent paternalism, he favored improving the material position of the Jews but did not envision their civil emancipation or equality with Christians. He sanc-

20. Fernessole, *Pie IX Pape,* 1:131.

21. For Pius IX's traditionalism, see Frank J. Coppa, "Pessimism and Traditionalism in the Personality and Policies of Pio Nono," *Journal of Italian History* 2 (autumn 1979): 209–17; for his reservations about Jewish emancipation, Martina, *Pio IX e Leopoldo II,* 211.

22. *PE* 1:277–84; *Acta Pio IX. Pontificis Maximi. Pars prima acta exhibens quae ad Ecclesiam universam spectant (1846–1854)* (Rome: Artium, 1855), 1:4–24.

23. Metternich, *Mémoires,* 7:572.

tioned broader liberty of the press but denounced license, insisting on the preservation of all of his and his government's prerogatives. Finally, he opposed arming the people by creating a civic guard.[24] The public in Rome was not satisfied with the pope's administrative reforms and benevolent paternalism, and called upon his government to make more substantial changes.

To placate the middle classes, who desired some input into the political process, the pope promised to form an advisory council, the need for which had long been recognized by the Memorandum of 1831 of the powers. The papal secretary of state, Cardinal Pasquale Gizzi, accepted the proposal for an advisory council only after being assured that it would not evolve into a representative chamber, and in April 1847 he published the edict on the consulta di stato.[25] While the pope and his secretary of state considered this consultative chamber the capstone of their reforms, his subjects demanded much more. Word spread that the kind-hearted and "liberal" pope was inclined to make further concessions but was restrained by the *zelanti* in the curia and administration surrounding him. When the pope permitted a civic guard and Cardinal Gizzi resigned, this conviction seemed confirmed. The guard created in Ferrara was open to Jews, and this distressed the pope as much as those around him; Pius had his new secretary of state write the legate there, calling for their exclusion. This "arbitrary and unjust exclusion," in the words of the reformist, some said radical, Leone Carpi, created new tensions. In Rome Jews were admitted into the guard but segregated into a separate unit to insulate its Christian members from Jewish skepticism and unbelief. Meanwhile, additional demands, including the call for Jewish emancipation, were made on the pope and his government.[26]

Early in July 1847 a man named Favella, from the Trastevere district, entered the ghetto with a group of his friends and invited the Jews to join them for a drink in a nearby tavern. To show his support for their emancipation, he and his friends paid for the wine of their Jewish guests. On 6 July one Luigi Caraccioli, with another group of Christian men, entered the ghetto to demonstrate Roman solidarity with the Jews of the district.

24. Maioli, *Pio IX da Vescovo a Pontefice*, 111.
25. *Atti del Sommo Pontefice Pio IX*, 1:147–48.
26. Canepa, "Atteggiamento degli ebrei italiani," 431.

Later, they joined the Mazzinian Angelo Brunetti, who orchestrated yet another demonstration of Roman solidarity with the Jews. These moves formed part of a broader campaign for Jewish emancipation, which the pope continued to question.[27] Pius sought to discourage the widespread expectation of new and more radical change. "Everybody must understand the difficulty encountered by him who united two supreme dignities," Pius informed the members of the Roman municipality who wanted representative constitutional government. "What can be effected in one night in a secular state cannot be accomplished with mature examination in Rome in consequence of the necessity to fix a line of separation between the two powers."[28]

The pope's belief that the issue of restrictions on Jews was religious as well as political led him to ignore the suggestions of Massimo D'Azeglio's "On the Civil Emancipation of the Jews," which the statesman-philosopher directed to Pius in 1847.[29] The pope did not share D'Azeglio's vision or the ideas put forward by father Luigi Crescioli's 1847 article, which not only expressed sympathy for the Jews but called for an end to all of the restrictions imposed upon them. Scandalized by this program, the pope had the article seized and all further circulation prohibited. He found the 1847 pamphlet of father Amerigo Borsi, which championed liberty of conscience, equally objectionable. In Rome, even talk of liberty of conscience generated fear and opposition, and Borsi's work was denounced as being in conflict with Gregory XVI's *Mirari vos* of 1832, which denounced indifferentism. The Holy Office found the goal of Jewish emancipation in conflict with a long and consistent series of decrees from synods and apostolic constitutions, as well as with Holy Scripture.[30] This undoubtedly reinforced the pope's opposition to Jewish emancipation. The discreet papal hesitation was largely ignored, observers preferring to focus on Pio Nono's incremental and modest measures on behalf of the Jews, which, like so much else he did, were blown out of proportion.

Following the outbreak of revolution in Palermo and Paris in early

---

27. Demarco, *Pio IX e la rivoluzione romana del 1848*, 70; Martina, *Pio IX e Leopoldo II*, 213.

28. Quoted in John Gilmary Shea, *The Life of Pope Pius IX and the Great Events in the History of the Church during his Pontificate* (New York: Thomas Kelly, 1878), 107.

29. See Roth, *History of the Jews of Italy*, 464.

30. Martina, *Pio IX e Leopoldo II*, 215–16.

February 1848, Pius, who was neither a political figure nor a diplomat, promised to develop the political institutions of his state but cautioned that he could not violate his obligations as head of the Church. Only when an ecclesiastical committee ruled that there was no theological hindrance to the introduction of constitutionalism in the temporal realm did Pius support it.[31] Cardinal Giacomo Antonelli and the priest Giovanni Corboli Bussi were assigned the task of drafting the constitution for the Papal States. Neither laymen nor non-Catholics played any role in its drafting, as Pius deemed such participation inappropriate.[32] The clergymen who drafted the constitution confronted the difficult task of preserving the spiritual power of the pope in its entirety while limiting his political role. The document they published in March provided for two deliberative councils for the formation of law: a high council and a council of deputies. Both were expressly prohibited from even discussing the diplomatic-religious relations of the Holy See, with the statute specifying that the new governmental form must in no way infringe upon the rights of the Church.[33] It included a prohibition that prevented the chambers from dealing with "mixed matters"—including political and administrative matters that touched upon the moral and religious mission of the Church—judging such an intervention in conflict with the papacy's religious responsibilities.

The reforming pope's new institutions were balanced and challenged by the older ones preserved in the ecclesiastical tribunals, by a host of clerical privileges, and by the extraordinary influence exercised by the apostolic chambers and the Roman curia. Among other things, this clerical establishment opposed the concessions made to Jews and the increased interaction between them and Catholics, which they deemed detrimental to the faith. They maliciously pointed out that the revolutionary Mazzini had an affinity for Jews, and they one for him.[34] Conservatives denounced

31. Arturo de Grandeffe, *Pio IX e l'Italia* (Turin: Reviglio, 1859), 44; Pasolini, *Memorie*, 77; Giacomo Martina, *Pio IX (1846–1850)* (Rome: Università Gregoriana Editrice, 1974), 209–12.

32. Rodelli, *Repubblica Romana del 1849*, 44.

33. "Statuto fondamentale del governo temporale degli Stati di S. Chiesa," in *Atti del Sommo Pontefice Pio IX*, 1:223–24, 229–32.

34. Demarco, *Pio IX e la rivoluzione romana del 1848*, 22; Martina, *Pio IX e Leopoldo II*, 409–11; Waagenaar, *Pope's Jews*, 258.

Jewish liberation as part of the nefarious, anti-Christian revolutionary scheme. Their vociferous opposition, among other things, led Pius to move cautiously on the Jewish issue and to shun innovation, which had religious implications.

The papal constitution of 1848 did not follow the lead of the Piedmontese statuto, which granted Jews full civil rights at the end of March 1848 and paved the way for their emancipation.[35] Although article 4 of the Roman constitution of 14 March 1848 spoke of equality before the law, article 25 stipulated that the profession of Catholicism was essential for the enjoyment of full political rights in the Papal States.[36] This created considerable confusion and encouraged a group of Jews to petition the Roman Parliament for a clarification and resolution of their status. Eventually, in July, the government presented a declaration stipulating that as of 5 June 1848, the day the constitution went into effect, all the Jews of the Papal States enjoyed full civil rights. In mid-August 1848, in its report on the ministerial declaration, the chamber in Rome noted that Jewish emancipation was a general European phenomenon that marked the end of the blind spirit of superstition and race hatred, and overwhelmingly approved the ministerial declaration.[37] Privately, Pius harbored reservations about this resolution, and he did not applaud the provisions of the Tuscan constitution, which accorded Jews equal political rights.

Despite papal concerns, the Roman constitution and its logical consequences contained the germ of social revolution. On 17 April 1848, the first night of Passover, celebrating Jews were startled to hear the pounding of axes, and watched in amazement while a crowd under the direction of Angelo Brunetti, called Ciceruacchio, or "big ugly Caesar," tore down the gates to the ghetto. They quickly joined in the effort, displaying solidarity with their Christian brethren. Although the action was spontaneous, it had been sanctioned by the pope with the approval of his minister of police, who reluctantly seconded what they found difficult to prevent. Nonetheless, members of the curia questioned the wisdom of this action, and

35. Martina, *Pio IX e Leopoldo II*, 220, Fubini, *Condizione giuridica dell'ebraismo Italiano*, 18.

36. "Statuto fondamentale del governo temporale degli Stati di S. Chiesa," in *Atti del Sommo Pontefice Pio IX*, 1:224, 229.

37. Demarco, *Pio IX e la rivoluzione romana del 1848*, 104.

some expressed concern for the Jews, others for the Christians.[38] Opponents of papal reformism warned of the economic and religious consequences of dismantling the ghetto and provoked a number of hostile demonstrations on the edge of that quarter. These attempts at violence were suppressed by the actions of Ciceruacchio and the papal police, who, working together, managed to calm the people of the neighboring district. Subsequently those ghetto gates that remained in the other cities of the Papal States were also torn down. By this time Jews were able to move about Rome at will, without papal opposition. Pius neither applauded nor condemned this development.

Most Jews were delighted by their newfound freedom. To commemorate the occasion, David Levi composed an ode hailing the pope as liberator, calling upon him to assume the lead in the regeneration of Italy's Jews.[39] Nationalists called upon the pope to act as liberator of the Italian peninsula, but Pius did not intend to assume either role, considering both in conflict with his religious responsibilities. If emancipation and equality of the Jews were deemed necessary for the unification and modernization of Italy, the pope wanted neither the one nor the other.[40] The approval, in July 1848, of legislation that recognized the full civil rights of Jews was one of the measures that brought the pope into conflict with the ministry of Terrenzio Mamiani and contributed to that ministry's collapse shortly thereafter.[41] Throughout, the Holy See remained resolutely opposed to having any non-Catholic vote on matters that might affect the Catholic faith.

A conflict between this pope and his subjects was virtually inevitable, for Pius would brook no interference with his spiritual authority and found it difficult to submit to any limitation of his temporal authority. "He knew only one way of ruling," observed a critic, and "that was the free enactment of his own will."[42] Not surprisingly, Pius opposed joining the

---

38. A. R. Gilardi to A. Rosmini, in Gianfranco Radice, *Pio IX e Antonio Rosmini* (Vatican City: Libreria Editrice Vaticana, 1974), 17.

39. Roth, *History of the Jews of Italy*, 459.

40. See Giacmomo Dina, "Desidereii e speranze," 26 Nov. 1847, quoted in Canepa, "Atteggiamento degli ebrei italiani," 434.

41. Martina, *Pio IX e Leopoldo II*, 219; Frank J. Coppa, *Pope Pius IX: Crusader in a Secular Age* (Boston: Twayne, 1979), 85–86.

42. Guglielmo Gajani, *The Roman Exile* (Boston: John P. Jewett, 1856), 398.

war of national liberation against Austria, fearing it would provoke a German schism. He made his position known in an April allocution, which asserted that the common father of all Catholics could not wage war against Catholic Austria. This provoked a revolution in Rome.[43] Pius fled his capital on the evening of 24 November 1848. "Among the causes which has moved us to take this painful step," he later explained, "was the need to enjoy full liberty in the exercise of the supreme power of the Holy See, which in the existing situation was impossible."[44] He undoubtedly lamented the fact that Jews from throughout the peninsula identified with the Roman republic, while several Jews from Bologna and Ferrara were elected to the assembly that deposed him. He was not wrong in suspecting that Jews had joined the carbonari, Masons, Mazzini's Young Italy, and other revolutionary groups.[45] Furthermore, conservatives were quick to complain that a number of the revolutionaries, including Daniele Manin, were Jewish.

Deploring the revolutionary events in Italy, the pope in exile publicly repudiated the February 1849 constitution of the Roman republic, which provided for religious equality. Pius now tended to see the Jews fomenting anarchy and Masonry, while assuming their general aversion to the Church.[46] Soon thereafter, he made it clear that he would not follow the lead of Piedmont, whose constitutional structure preserved the emancipation of the Jews. The events of 1848–49 led this pope to abandon his early reformism and to conclude that constitutionalism was incompatible with the government of the states of the Church. Following the restoration of papal power in Rome by the Catholic powers (Austria, France, Spain, and Naples), Pius deemed freedom of the press and liberty of association subversive and branded liberalism a dangerous delusion.[47] He therefore resis-

43. Frank J. Coppa, "Cardinal Antonelli, the Papal States and the Counter-Risorgimento," *JCS* 16 (autumn 1974): 461–63; Great Britain, *British and Foreign State Papers*, (1848–49), 37:1065.

44. "Allontamento temporaneo del S. Padre dai suoi Stati, protesta per le violenze usate e creazione di una commisione governativa," *Atti del Sommo Pontefice Pio IX*, 1:252.

45. Vogelstein, *Jews of Rome*, 341; Ester Capuzzo, "Gli ebrei e la Repubblica Romana," *Rassegna Storica del Risorgimento* 86, no. 4 (1999): 285, 270.

46. See Index no. 1190 in the ASV for Repubblica Romana II, 1849; Moro, *Chiesa e lo sterminio degli ebrei*, 50.

47. Antonio Rosmini, *Della missione a Roma* (Turin: Paravia, 1854), 143–44; Pius IX to Archbishop Dupont, 10 June 1849, ASV, Archivio Particolare Pio IX, Francia, Particolari, no. 18; SSE, corrspondenza da Gaeta e Portici, 1848–50, rubrica 248, fascicolo 2, sottofascicolo 4.

ted the exhortations of the French and Piedmontese to preserve his earlier liberal institutions. The French foreign minister called for an amnesty, a law code patterned on that of France, abolition of the tribunal of the Holy Office, substantial modification of the rights of ecclesiastical tribunals in civilian jurisdictions, and granting the consulta a veto on financial issues, among other things. These suggestions were rejected by the acting secretary of state, Cardinal Giacomo Antonelli, who specified that the Holy Father would make no concession that compromised his temporal power.[48]

Pius now deemed such political concessions incompatible with the exercise of the papacy's spiritual power. He deplored the politics of the Piedmontese government, which he felt attacked the position of the Church and which led him to wonder if all constitutional governments sought to undermine the ecclesiastical order.[49] Pius believed that the lay state posed a danger to the eternal salvation of its subjects. When Count Cavour's newspaper, *Il Risorgimento,* called for the separation of Church and state in Catholic Piedmont, Pius denounced this as a frontal assault upon the faith. The newspaper in turn called developments in Rome "the restoration of obscurantism and in its worst form—the clerical."[50] In liberal circles Pius IX, who had formerly been hailed as the apostle of reform, was now denounced as the symbol of European reaction.

Fearful of further revolutionary upheaval, the pope tightened the reins of power in his state as well as upon ecclesiastical life, developing a siege mentality. Despite Piedmontese and French pressure, he refused to base his laws on the Napoleonic Code, which supported religious equality, and he resisted the rapid secularization of his administration. In July Roman Jews were again restricted in their movement, the pontifical government stipulating that they would not be permitted to leave their usual residence without a permit from the Holy Office.[51] Attempts at conversion also followed. Some believed it was the intervention of the Rothschilds, whose financial assistance the restored regime required, that mitigated the repres-

48. ASV, SSE, corrispondenza da Gaeta e Portici, 1849, rubrica 242, sottofascicolo 76; Emile Bourgeois and E. Clermont, *Rome et Napoleon III (1849–1870)* (Paris: Librarie Armand Colen, 1907), 91–93.

49. Nicomede Bianchi, *La politica di Massimo d'Azeglio dal 1848 al 1859* (Turin: Roux e Favale, 1884), 75; Martina, *Pio IX e Leopoldo II,* 431–33.

50. "Affari di Roma," *Il Risorgimento,* 10 Aug. 1849.

51. Dispatch of the Holy Office on the movement of Jews in the Papal States, 29 July 1849, ASV, Archivio Nunziatura Parigi, 1849, no. 77.

sion of the Jews in the Papal States.[52] This banking house saved the papacy from financial ruin after the Revolution of 1848 and the restoration of 1849. In fact, Pius was able to return to Rome aided by a loan of 15 million francs from the house of Rothschild.[53] Among other concessions, the chained gates of the ghetto were not rebuilt, nor were the insulting rites inflicted upon Jews at carnival times restored. In practice, Jews were permitted to live where they wished in the Rome of the second restoration. Their ghetto was self-governing and contained four small synagogues— the only non-Catholic houses of worship in the city.[54] Still, Pius, like his predecessors, would not confer legal equality upon his Jewish subjects. In April 1850, when he returned to Rome, there was no rejoicing among the Jews.

The restored pope proved no more tolerant of non-Catholic Christians—perhaps even less so, for they were not allowed to have a house of worship within the walls of Rome. He permitted a Protestant church only outside the city. Pius condemned religious toleration and liberty for Protestants just as he did for Jews, insisting that the principles of the Church were eternal and unchangeable. "There is no salvation out of the Roman Church, yet I, the pope, do think that some Protestants may by the special grace of God be saved," he told the Protestant English representative Odo Russell. But he quickly added, "I mean those Protestants who by peculiar circumstances have never been in a position to know Truth. For those who, like yourself, have lived at the very fountain of Truth, and have not recognized and accepted it, there can be no salvation."[55]

Rome perceived the restored restrictions on Jews as part of a broader need—to preserve the traditional order and Christian society—and opposed the constitutional system that seemed to threaten both. Not surprisingly, the pope and curia were little inclined to follow the stance of the Roman constituent assembly, which had earlier proclaimed that political and civil rights were not linked to religious beliefs. The pope revealed the con-

52. Jews of Rome to the Baron de Rothschild, 10 Sept. 1849, ibid., 1849, no. 77.
53. Chadwick, *History of the Popes*, 378; Lapide, *Three Popes and the Jews*, 78; Kertzer, *Popes against the Jews*, 115.
54. Chadwick, *History of the Popes*, 129–30.
55. Noel Blakiston, ed., *The Roman Question: Extracts from the Despatches of Odo Russell from Rome, 1815–1870* (London: Chapman and Hall, 1962), 307.

servative institutions he would grant his people in a decree of 1849.[56] The papal retreat from reformism and the curia's intransigence on Church-state issues antagonized the Piedmontese as well as the French. In liberal and radical circles in Turin, clericalism was denounced as the vanguard of absolutism and the pope as the personification of Italian reaction.[57]

Pius, for his part, distrusted liberal and constitutional Piedmont, which restricted ecclesiastical control over education and placed supervision of the curriculum in state hands. The papal nuncio to Sardinia frankly confided to its king, Victor Emmanuel II, that the Holy See got along better with absolute monarchs rather than with constitutional rulers because it could appeal to their religious piety—as it had with Carlo Alberto prior to 1848. It could not do so with constitutional monarchs, who placed all responsibility in the hands of their ministers, who might be Protestants, Jews, or even Muslims![58] Papal-Piedmontese relations did not improve following the Turin government's unilateral emancipation of Jews and other non-Catholics and the passage of the Siccardi Laws in March 1850, which, despite Rome's protests, abrogated the various forms of ecclesiastical jurisdiction enjoyed by the clergy, eliminated the Church's ancient right of asylum, provided for the suppression of mortmain, and restricted the official observance of Catholic holidays in Piedmont. Liberals elsewhere were invariably anticlerical champions of secularism, and were by and large supported by Jews who appreciated the protection they provided. In turn, the *Civiltà Cattolica* praised the anti-Judaic work of Father Antonio Bresciani.[59]

To preserve the privileged position of the Church over other religious sects, the pope favored the conclusion of concordats, and one was approved by Leopold II in the summer of 1851. That year, in addition, the Madrid government approved an accord that pronounced Catholicism the religion of state to the exclusion of all others and invested the clergy

56. Martina, *Pio IX e Leopoldo II*, 219, 228; "Motu proprio di Sua Santità sulla insitutzione del Consignlio di Stato e della Consulta di Stato per le Finanze" (12 Sept. 1849), in *Atti del Sommo Pontefice Pio IX*, 1:287–89.

57. Frank J. Coppa, "Realpolitik and Conviction in the Conflict between Piedmont and the Papacy during the *Risorgimento*," *CHR* 54 (Jan. 1969): 592–93.

58. Report of Monsignor Antonucci, 25 Nov. 1849, ASV, Archivio Particolare Pio IX, Particolari, Sardegna.

59. Moro, *Chiesa e lo stermino degli ebei*, 50.

with broad powers and rights. Subsequently, talks were opened with the Vienna government, which resulted in the 1855 concordat that strengthened the position of the Church in the Habsburg state.[60] The Turin government refused similar concessions and responded to Rome's intransigence by unilaterally revising Church-state relations. The *connubio* or marriage of the center-right, led by Cavour, and the center-left, led by Urbano Rattazzi, provided the parliamentary basis for antiecclesiastical legislation and the downfall of the D'Azeglio government at the end of 1852. Cavour, who emerged as prime minister of Piedmont and worked closely with his Jewish secretary and collaborator, Isaaco Artom, insisted on freedom of action on religious legislation.[61]

Papal relations with the Grand Duchy of Tuscany were much better, especially after the grand duke abrogated the constitution in March 1852. Before doing so, he consulted Pius IX, informing him that article 2 of that constitution had assured equality under the law for all citizens, regardless of their religious affiliation. With its pending abrogation that provision would also be eliminated, and Leopold had serious reservations about curtailing the rights of Jews and Protestants in his state. Not surprisingly, Pius proved far less scrupulous on this matter and did not hesitate to state his position. Tuscan Jews and Protestants also voiced their opinions. The former revealed that when the grand duke's cousin in Vienna, Franz Joseph, had abandoned his constitution, he had subsequently issued a patent preserving the rights of Jews and providing for their equality under the law. They petitioned Leopold II to do likewise.

The grand duke was personally inclined to grant some measure of equality to non-Catholics but feared the reaction of Rome. This led him to transmit conflicting messages. He indicated to the Jewish community that Jewish rights would be preserved, while promising Pio Nono that he would not admit any non-Catholics to public office in Tuscany. As a compromise, Leopold suggested that the decree abolishing the constitution contain a provision recognizing the equality of all citizens under the law,

60. Martina, *Pio IX e Leopoldo II*, 439; Franz Josef to Pius IX, ASV, Archivio Particolare Pio IX, Sovrani, Austria.

61. Michelangelo Castelli, *Ricordi di Michelangelo Castelli*, ed. Luigi Chiala (Turin: Roux e Favale, 1888), 66; Pietro Pirri, *La laicizzazione dello stato sardo, 1848–1856* (Rome: Università Gregoriana, 1944), 79–80; Waagenaar, *Pope's Jews*, 271.

regardless of their religion, and rendering all eligible for entry into the professions—except those specifically closed to them. Pius IX found Leopold's compromise unacceptable. He pointed out that the Grand Duchy was a Catholic country in the middle of Catholic Italy, where the pope was primate. The reference to "Tuscans of whatever faith" he found personally offensive and smacking of indifferentism. He could not and would not sanction granting Jews and other non-Catholics the same rights accorded to believers, allowing them to enter practically all of the professions. He found such equality subversive of the faith and detrimental to the faithful, and therefore steadfastly refused to sanction it.

Pius offered his own solution, based on his understanding of Church law and his own experience in Rome. He was prepared to accept various exemptions for the Jews, but he hesitated to grant them full legal rights and equal status. He opposed religious equality not only because he feared that non-Catholics would abuse these rights and influence the faithful, but also in the desire to adhere to what he perceived as past papal practice and the anti-Judaism that prevailed in the Church. He suggested that the grand duke, acting on the basis of Christian charity rather than law, grant certain exemptions from the restrictions imposed on non-Catholics. In this way he might allow non-Catholics to practice certain professions under close control and scrutiny. Eventually Leopold accepted the papal "compromise"; Tuscan Jews could study and practice law and medicine, so long as it was understood that they would minister only to other Jews. Rome continued to deem dangerous and unacceptable any association between Catholics and non-Catholics in which the latter were able to exercise a moral influence over the former.[62]

Pio Nono's increasingly conservative stance, and his fear that the faithful could be "contaminated" by nonbelievers, colored his stance in the Modiai case in Florence (1851–52), as well as papal protests regarding the Tuscan educational system. In the first matter, a Protestant couple, Francesco and Rosa Modiai, were arrested and imprisoned for holding "religious services" in their home and were accused of proselytizing to the detriment of the "religion of state." Liberal and Protestant Europe was scandalized by the Tuscan government's actions, which provoked public

---

62. Martina, *Pio IX e Leopoldo II*, 231–44, 252–55, 449–59.

protests in England, Prussia, Holland, and even the United States—but Rome supported Leopold in the matter, approving the jail sentences imposed upon the convicted couple, whom he deemed "miserable apostates and propagandists of error."[63]

Pius was less pleased with the Tuscan educational reforms of the early 1850s, which ensured that the Church would supervise religious instruction but left the selection of teachers and books entirely in lay hands. The pope foresaw abuses in this system, which he deemed unacceptable in a Catholic country, and complained to the grand duke, who again sought some compromise. To appease the pope, the ministry of public education in Tuscany promised to consult with the bishops concerning the moral conduct of prospective teachers prior to their appointment. It also created a commission, which included two bishops, to provide input on both curriculum and texts for courses.[64] Although this issue had been satisfactorily resolved, Pius feared that other attempts would be made to undermine the faith and erode papal leadership, and he instructed papal representatives to exercise constant vigilance. Behind the political agitation in the Italian peninsula and the rest of Europe, the pope saw hostility to religion, the Church, and the papacy. Indeed, this was his major concern.

Pius decried the "evil currents" that "schemed" to place other religious beliefs on the same plane with those of "the one true Faith," and he deplored the unleashing of unbridled desires.[65] He was disturbed by Italian nationalists, who posed a threat to his temporal and spiritual power, and believed Piedmont championed the cause of Italian Jewry to the detriment of Catholicism. Consequently he perceived the Risorgimento as a spiritual as well as a political threat, deeming the Sardinian ecclesiastical legislation contrary to the rights of the Church and accusing the Turin government of interfering in the administration of the sacraments.[66] The pope was suspicious of Piedmont's participation in the Crimean War

63. Ibid., 268–72.

64. Ibid., 267.

65. *Excultavit cor Nostrum*, 21 Nov. 1851, *PP* 1:32.

66. Report of 20 Jan. 1852, ASR, Miscellanea di Carte Politiche o Riservate, busta 121, fascicolo 4214; memorandum of 23 June 1852, ibid., fascicolo 4213; *L'Osservatore Ligure-Subalpino*, 25 June 1852; Consistorial Allocution of 1 Nov. 1850, in *Papal Teachings on Education compiled by the Monks of Solesmes*, trans. Rev. Aldo Rebeschini (Boston: St. Paul Editions, 1960), 43–44.

alongside England and France, suspecting that the Piedmontese sought to undermine the papal regime. Pius continued to insist that his mission was more religious than political, that he sought the glory of God, the salvation of souls, and the propagation of the faith. This religious mission earned him the love of the faithful of his state. The cardinal secretary of state sought to capitalize on this popularity by having Pius tour the northern provinces of his state in 1857, thus negating the image that only French and Austrian bayonets upheld his regime. Upon his return to the capital, the pope did not exclude the Jews from his largesse, distributing two hundred *scudi* to the poor Jews of Rome.[67] Pio Nono's position remained Christian charity to the Jews, yes; Jewish equality, no!

The goodwill generated by the papal visit and Pio Nono's generosity was squandered by his stance during the Mortara affair of 1858. That June, a six-year-old Jewish boy, Edgardo Levi Mortara, of Bologna, supposedly baptized secretly by a Christian servant of the household during a childhood illness years earlier, was spirited from his parents by the papal police, allegedly to assure the salvation of his soul. Although this was not the first time papal authorities had disregarded the wishes of Jewish parents and "kidnapped" children who allegedly had been "secretly baptized," the political climate in Italy and Europe had changed drastically, and such abuses were no longer quietly sanctioned or tolerated. The seizure of Mortara provoked Europe-wide protests, and the controversy reached Pius in Rome, who took a special interest in the child and his case. The Jewish family denied that a baptism had occurred and said they would certainly have opposed such a thing, and begged the police to return their child. English, French, and more than forty Prussian and German rabbis petitioned the pope on behalf of the Mortara family. Their pleas were reinforced by a wide range of private and political groups, who condemned the "medieval mentality" that permitted such an "outrage." Thus the "Mortara affair" widened the chasm between the liberal and Catholic worlds.[68]

Pius perceived the global protests denouncing the boy's seizure as part

---

67. R. De Cesare, *The Last Days of Papal Rome, 1850–1870*, trans. Helen Zimmern (London: Constable, 1909), 173.

68. Salomone Mortara to Pius IX, 19 Sept. 1858, ASV, Archivio Particolare Pio IX, Oggetti Vari, no. 1433; Prussian and German rabbis' petitions to Pius IX, ASR, Archivio Particolare Pio IX, Oggetti Vari, 1858, no. 1433, 109–16; Moro, *Chiesa e lo stermino degli ebei*, 51.

of a concerted campaign to discredit the Church and undermine the papacy, which only made him more defensive and intransigent. When requests poured in for the release of the child, and when many questioned the truth of this "coerced baptism," Pius responded that Edgardo's wishes had to be considered. Obviously pope and curia were aware of the many papal proscriptions against the forced baptism of Jews, and that Julius III had even imposed a fine on any Christian who baptized a child against its parents' wishes.[69] Perhaps this is why Rome now argued that the boy's intentions had to be respected. Not surprisingly, there were conflicting reports about what the child wanted. According to his parents, who were allowed to visit him in the House of Catechumens in Rome, the frightened six-year-old wanted to return home to his family. The papal authorities told another story, reporting that the boy begged to remain a Christian and urged that his parents be kept away. Miraculously transformed, the child allegedly cried out, "I have been baptized, my father is the pope."[70] Outside the papal curia, few were convinced of this "spontaneous conversion." Nonetheless, the alleged desire of the child to remain a Christian provided a pretext of sorts for Rome to instruct him in the faith without completely or clearly violating the many papal prohibitions against forced baptism.

Critics, however, complained that if the original baptism were valid and justified the boy's seizure, then why was he baptized a second time by papal authorities? Rome would not, perhaps could not, provide an adequate response. Protests from the family, the Jews of Italy and Europe, and the various courts continued, to no avail.[71] Pius was shocked by the outcry, attributing it to liberal hostility toward the Church and the papacy. He especially lamented the ingratitude of the Jews, after "all he had done for them." He refused to bow to the mounting criticism, claiming that it was "impossible for the head of this Church, for the Representative of Jesus Christ on earth, to refuse this child, for he begged me with an almost supernatural faith to let him share in the benefit of the Blood that Our Lord

69. Waagenaar, *Pope's Jews*, 165.

70. Kertzer, *Popes against the Jews*, 122; "Breve cenni e riflessione . . . relative al Battesimo conferito in Bologna al fanciullo Edgardo, figlio degli Ebrei Salomone e Marianna Mortara," ASV, Archivio Particolare Pio IX, Oggetti Vari, no. 1433.

71. Prussian and German rabbis to Pius IX.

shed for his Redemption."[72] Pius proclaimed that his irrevocable decision was in conformity with God's will, pontifical legislation, and Catholic doctrine, and that therefore he would not and could not relent. Despite the condemnation by world opinion and the unfortunate publicity it generated, Pius would not budge. Rather than conciliate public opinion, he preferred to preserve his principles. He knew his responsibility, he confided to the Neapolitan ambassador, and would rather have his hands cut off than shirk his duty. When the French ambassador explained to him the depth of public opposition to his action, the pope pointed to the crucifix and announced confidently, "He will defend me."[73] The fact that Mortara eventually became a priest and a missionary pleased the curia but scandalized liberal Europe.

The nearly universal outrage provoked by Pio Nono's determination to raise Mortara as a Catholic and keep him away from his Jewish parents undermined the moral and diplomatic position of the papacy. Nonetheless, neither the pope nor the Roman curia was inclined to change course. The "abuses" of the Mortara affair were presented in Rome after 1870 in the drama *A Hebrew Family,* the performance of which had to be halted because it provoked riots against the Church and the clergy.[74] This compelling incident continues to generate interest and recently was adopted for the stage in the play *Edgardo Mine,* and in the Emerging Artists Theatre production of *A Ritual of Faith.* The "forced baptism" depicted in these productions was far from a unique event in the Papal States. Thus, some five years after the seizure of Mortara, a young Jewish girl named Graziosa Cavagli was found weeping near the ghetto and taken to the House of Catechumens, where she was instructed in Catholic principles and baptized—despite the opposition of her parents and the Jewish community. A year later, in 1864, Giuseppe Cohen, found wandering outside the ghetto district, was likewise brought to the House of Catechumens and baptized following a period of instruction, despite the protests of his parents and the intervention of the French ambassador. Giuseppe was liberat-

72. Kertzer, *Popes against the Jews,* 127, 122.

73. Mariano Gabriele, ed., *Il Carteggio Antonelli-Sacconi (1850–1860)* (Rome: Istituto per la Storia del Risorgimento Italiano, 1962), 1:xiii, Giuseppe Massari, *Diario delle cento voci* (Bologna: Cappelli, 1959), 67.

74. De Cesare, *Last Days of Papal Rome,* 179.

ed only after the fall of Rome in 1870. In 1870 the Italians also offered Mortara the opportunity to revert to Judaism, but he chose to remain a Catholic.[75] Pius was more scandalized than surprised by the fact that the Mortara family sought and found refuge in anticlerical Turin. After studying at Brixen in the Tyrol and Poiters in France, Edgardo was ordained a priest in 1873.[76]

Among other things, these actions pointed to the primacy of "religious" over "political" considerations in Pio Nono's policies, while revealing that there was some wisdom in the long-standing though laxly enforced prohibition on Christian domestics in Jewish households. Finally, and perhaps most important, they further undermined the legitimacy of the papal regime in the eyes of liberal Europe, facilitating the collapse of the pope's temporal power. Unquestionably, Cavour used the Mortara affair to discredit Rome, and secretly schemed with Napoleon III at Plombières in late July 1858 to wage war on Austria, reorganize Italy, and diminish the territory of the Papal States. The nuncio in Paris warned his government that the emperor resented Rome's refusal to return the Mortara boy to his family and that this might have unfortunate consequences. Subsequently, he reported that the French government proposed that the pope have a smaller state so that he would be less embarrassed by the burdens of power.[77] The pope disagreed. When war erupted at the end of April 1859, Napoleon III declared that he would uphold the cause of the Holy See and the sovereignty of the Holy Father. His pledge, like that of King Victor Emmanuel II of Piedmont, was not kept.[78]

Pius saw the second war of Italian liberation (1859–60), and Sardinia's occupation of papal territory, as a war against the Church and the papacy

75. Waagenaar, *Pope's Jews,* 272; Lease, "Denunciation as a Tool of Ecclesiastical Control," 823.

76. He earned a reputation as a preacher in the many countries in which he served, including Italy, Austria, Belgium, France, Spain, England, and even America. He died unnoticed in 1940, at the age of eighty-eight. Lease, "Denunciation as a Tool of Ecclesiastical Control," 823.

77. Gabriele, *Il Carteggio Antonelli-Sacconi,* 1:5, 26; Massari, *Diario delle cento voci,* 84, 93; Castelli, *Ricordi di Michelangelo Castelli,* 75–77; Marco Minghetti, *Miei Ricordi,* 3d ed. (Turin: Roux, 1888), 3:219.

78. Napoleon III to Pius IX, 1 May 1859, ASV, Archivio Particolare Pio IX, Sovrani, Francia, #42; "Proclamation L'Empereur au Peuple Francais," *Le Moniteur Universel. Journal Officiel de L'Empire Francais,* 3 May 1859; Victor Emmanuel to Pius IX, 25 May 1859, ASV, Archivio Particolare Pio IX, Sovrani, Sardegna, #52.

and he issued more than a dozen condemnations of Cavour and his colleagues, whom he saw as responsible for unification. The Piedmontese annexation of the greater part of the peninsula into the emerging Italian
Kingdom extended Turin's legislation and broadened the emancipation of
the Jews to most of the peninsula—including the former papal territory. It
also witnessed the entry into public life of significant numbers of Jews.
Throughout 1859–60, the pope catalogued the ills afflicting the peninsula,
including an irreligious and subversive press, the excessive liberty granted
to men of ill will and other enemies of the faith, and above all the restrictions and impositions placed upon the Church of God. In an allocution of
March 1861 he noted that the adherents of "modern civilization" demanded that he reconcile himself with "progress" and "liberalism," while those
who defended the rights of justice and religion understood his need to
preserve the "immovable and indestructible principles of eternal justice"
intact. He rejected the call to come to terms with this modern civilization,
repeating he could not consent to the "vandalous" aggression without violating his beliefs and principles.[79]

The pope resented French pressure to reach an accommodation with
modern civilization in general and the Turin regime in particular. Jewish
equality was only one of the many features of modernity that Pius IX deplored. Rumors were rife of secret Franco-Italian negotiations to end the
French occupation of Rome, entrusting the Italians with the pope's security. This actually happened on 15 September 1864, when the Minghetti government signed the September convention with the French. It provided
that Napoleon would withdraw his forces from Rome within two years,
while the Italian government promised not to attack the patrimony of St.
Peter, and to prevent others from doing so, from its territory. Pius complained that this was like sending the wolves to guard the sheep.

In response Pius issued the encyclical *Quanta cura* (8 December 1864),
to which was appended a "Syllabus of Errors" listing eighty errors drawn

79. Martina, *Pio IX e Leopoldo II*, 344–45; Pius IX to Archduke Ferdinand Maximilian, 7
Aug. 1860, ASV, Archivio Particolare Pio IX, Sovrani, Austria, #35; C. Cadorna, *Illustrazione
giuridica della formula del Conte di Cavour, Libera Chiesa in Libero Stato* (Rome: Badoniana,
1882), 101–2; "Allocuzione di N.S. Papa Pio IX, 18 March 1861, *CC*, series 4, 10 (1861): 17; P.
Pietro Pirri, ed., *La Questione Romana. Parte seconda, I documenti* (Rome: Pontirfica Università Gregoriana, 1951), 164; Pius IX to Leopold II, 10 Aug. 1862, ASV, Archivio Particolare Pio
Nono, Sovrani, Toscana.

from previous papal documents and condemning various movements and beliefs. It recapitulated the papacy's catalogue of complaints against the modern, liberal agenda over the past century. Under ten headings the syllabus condemned pantheism, naturalism, materialism, absolute as well as moderate rationalism, indifferentism, and false tolerance in religious matters, all of which were pronounced incompatible with the Catholic faith. Thus Pius made it clear that the age-old restrictions against the Jews in his state and in other Christian countries should be maintained. In addition, socialism, communism, secret and Bible societies were denounced. Likewise condemned were errors regarding marriage, as well as those on the temporal power of the pope. The broad critique of the errors of the liberalism of the day caused the greatest controversy, and especially the condemnation of the eightieth and final error, which called for the Roman pontiff to reconcile himself with progress, liberalism, and recent civilization.[80] Pio Nono's syllabus proved to be another public relations nightmare for his secretary of state, Antonelli, whose task was the preservation of the Papal States.

Distressed by contemporary developments wrought by a virtually "bewitched and bewildered generation," the pope also proposed convoking a council to reaffirm the doctrines of the Church challenged by modern thought and practice.[81] On 6 December 1864, two days before issuing the "Syllabus of Errors," he consulted the cardinals in curia on the prospect. Encouraged by their response, in June of 1867, when the upper clergy ventured to Rome to commemorate the martyrdom of Saints Peter and Paul, Pius publicly revealed his decision to convoke a condemnatory council, indicating that much of the groundwork had been established. While awaiting its opening, Pius took other measures to combat the naturalism and secularism of the age, while reinforcing the traditional papal position toward Jews. Among other things, he named more saints than any pope had ever done (or would do until the pontificate of John Paul II).[82] Thus in 1867 the pope had Pedro d'Arbues, the first inquisitor of Aragon, who was

80. *Quanta cura* and "Syllabus of Errors," *ASS* 3:160–76; "The Syllabus of Errors," *Documents in the Political History of the European Continent, 1815–1939*, ed. G. A. Kertesz (Oxford: Clarendon Press, 1968), 233–41.

81. See Henri Rondet, *Vatican I, le Concile de Pie IX. La preparation, les methodes de travail, les schemas reste en suspens* (Paris: P. Lethielleux, 1962).

82. Chadwick, *History of the Popes*, 557.

instrumental in the coerced conversion of Jews after Ferdinand and Isabella had ordered their expulsion, proclaimed a saint. Contemporary Jews held him responsible for the execution of countless people as heretics, which reportedly led a small group of Jews to murder him in the choir of the Cathedral. Pio Nono's decision to canonize this hated figure represented to some a repudiation of Jewry and a validation of the Inquisition.[83]

For others the canonization of Spain's grand inquisitor seemed to reflect a certain insensitivity, revealing the mindset of this pope and of the nineteenth-century curia.[84] Indeed, the curia suspected that liberal Jewry was behind the opposition to this canonization, and they said as much in the proclamation of canonization, which read, "The divine wisdom has arranged that in these sad days, when Jews help the enemies of the Church with their books and money, this decree of sanctity has been brought to fulfillment."[85] It also reflected the pervasive anti-Judaism in the nineteenth-century Church, which some branded pathological and determined not so much by conscious choice as by forces hidden in the institution. Thus neither pope nor curia questioned the story that on Good Friday 1866 the fifteen-year-old Lorenzino of Marostica was allegedly seized by a crazed mob of Jews, crucified, and drained of his blood. In fact, when miracles reportedly occurred at his gravesite in 1867, there was a call for recognition and celebration of the new martyr. Whereas Sixtus IV (1471–84) had prohibited the worship of the child Simon of Trent, whom the Jews of that city were falsely accused of having murdered in a ritual, in the second half of the nineteenth century Pius acted otherwise and recognized the cult of the new martyr. In this way he provided a validation of sorts for the ritual murder charge against the Jews. In 1869 he praised the anti-Judaic work of the French writer Gougenot des Mousseau, *Le Juif, le Judaisme et la Judaisation des peuples chretiens,* which stimulated anti-Semitism in France.[86]

Pius resented those who questioned his policies as head of state and even more those who challenged his actions as head of the Church. Political circumstances rather than criticism of his plans delayed the convoca-

83. Carroll, *Constantine's Sword,* 484.

84. Giacomo Martina, *Pio IX (1851–1866)* (Rome: Editrice Pontificia Università Gregoriana, 1986), 701–4.

85. Quoted in Chadwick, *History of the Popes,* 555.

86. Kertzer, *Popes against the Jews,* 127–28; .

tion of the Church council he planned. Its projected opening was frustrated first by the war waged by Prussia and Italy against Austria in 1866, and than by Garibaldi's incursion into the Papal States in 1867. In June 1868, however, the papal bull of convocation was issued, explaining the general purpose of the council as the combating of error, the defining and developing of doctrine to negate "these absurdities," and finally the upholding of ecclesiastical discipline and the fighting of corruption.[87] Its opening was set for 8 December 1869, as Pius resolved to unmask the enemies of Christian society and free it from the grasp of "Satanic forces." He played a key role in the proceedings, nominating the cardinals who presided over the five congregations of the council.[88] These committees outlined fifty-one categories or schemata for consideration, but only two were discussed— Dei Filius, divided into four chapters, on God, revelation, faith, and reason; and De ecclesia, on the Church. Dei Filius, adopted by a unanimous vote on 24 April 1870, aimed not simply to condemn rationalism, modern naturalism, pantheism, materialism, and atheism, but elaborated the positive doctrines that these "errors" violated. Rejecting naturalism, which discounted and denied what is not evident to the senses, it reaffirmed the reasonableness of the supernatural character of Christian revelation. De ecclesia, which contained three chapters on the pope's primacy and one on his infallibility, generated even greater controversy.

From mid-May to early July there were more than 160 speeches for and against the proposed dogma. On the final vote, taken 18 July 1870, 535 members assented to infallibility while only two opposed—the Bishop of Little Rock, Edward Fitzgerald, and the Bishop of Caizzo, Luigi Riccio.[89] The dogma, defined and pronounced divinely revealed, read, "that the Roman Pontiff, when he speaks ex cathedra, that is, when in discharge of the office and doctor of all Christians, by virtue of his supreme Apostolic authority, he defines a doctrine regarding faith or morals to be held by the universal Church . . . is possessed of that infallibility with which the divine Redeemer willed that his Church should be endowed for defining doctrine regarding faith and morals."[90] Then and later Pius denied that the procla-

---

87. See Index no. 1172 (I and II) in the ASV for Vatican Council I.
88. *Multiplices Inter,* 27 Nov. 1869, *PP* 1:40; Coppa, *Pius IX: Crusader in a Secular Age,* 159–61.
89. Hergenrother, *Storia universale della Chiesa,* 613–17.
90. Kertesz, *Documents in the Political History of the European Continent,* 243.

mation undermined or replaced the power of the bishops, asserting that papal jurisdiction did not absorb the episcopal one.[91] The council, cut short by the outbreak of the Franco-Prussian War on 19 July, proved vulnerable to the vagaries of war, as did the pope's remaining temporal power. The departure of French troops from Rome and the fall of the empire were followed by an Italian proclamation revealing the decision to make Rome the capital.[92]

On 20 September, when the Italians bombarded the three gates of the city, Pius protested this "sacrilegious" action to the ministers of the powers, who remained in Rome, and withdrew into the Vatican, considering himself a prisoner of Victor Emmanuel, while Jews were free to live wherever they pleased. From within the Vatican walls he excommunicated all those who had perpetrated the invasion and occupation of the papal domain, as well as those who had aided or counseled the "pernicious" action.[93] His condemnations were not deterred by the consideration that this might provoke a crisis for Italians, who were at once nationalist and Catholic. Unlike Pius XII, who later had such qualms about placing German Catholics in a difficult position, Pius saw no prospect of cooperation or even neutrality between the forces of "good" and "evil," and he used all the spiritual weapons in his arsenal against his opponents. No one, past or present, accused Pius IX of being silent!

In a series of subsequent messages, he warned of other hardships that threatened the Church.[94] His prediction proved prophetic, for following the loss of Rome the Church confronted the *Kulturkampf,* which undertook a series of measures against the Church in Prussia and the new German empire as early as 1871. Pius responded in an allocution at the end of 1872, protesting against the secret and public persecution of the Church there, fuming that those who neither profess "our religion" nor even know it should attempt to determine its dogmas and rights.[95] Pius praised the clergy of Prussia and German Catholics for their constancy, exhorting

---

91. Blanshard, *Blanshard on Vatican II,* 60.

92. *DDI,* vol. 13, no. 580.

93. *Respicientes,* 1 Nov. 1870, *PE* 1:393–397.

94. *Beneficia Dei,* 4 June 1871, *PP* 1:41; Pasquale De Franciscis, ed., *Discorsi del Sommo Pontefice Pio IX Pronunziati in Vaticano ai fedeli di Roma e dell'orbe dal principio della sua prigionia fino al presente* (Rome: G. Aurelj, 1872), 1: 89, 137–40.

95. Allocution to cardinals, 23 Dec. 1872, De Franciscis, *Discorsi del Sommo Pontefice Pio IX Pronunziati,* 2:130.

them to stand firm in the face of persecution, as he had before the abuses of the Italian revolution. He unequivocally declared the bulk of the legislation against the Church in Prussia and the German empire null and void, excommunicating those who accepted the misdeeds and obnoxious laws.[96]

The pope was not the only opponent of the liberals' agenda. A series of anti-Judaic and anti-Semitic articles emerged in the press, protesting the laicization of the schools of Rome and warning of dire consequences.[97] Pius remained convinced that revolutionaries and the "synagogue of Satan" aimed to destroy the Church and professed his confidence they would not succeed, and that the papacy had to provide guidance to a world gone astray. He continued to champion the Christian state and even opposed the Spanish constitution of 1876, which established limited toleration of Jews.

When a group of Catholic women visited him in the Vatican, he related a story that betrayed his anti-Judaism as well as his growing conviction that Jews were embroiled in the current campaign against the Church's primacy. A Canaanite woman, he told them (paraphrasing Matthew 15:22–28), had asked Jesus to free her daughter from a demon and Jesus supposedly responded to this Gentile that it was not proper to take the bread of one's children (the Jews) and feed it to the dogs (the Gentiles). She answered that Jesus had come to them also, because dogs gather the crumbs that fall from the table of the master. Jesus relented, cured her child, and in the process the women was transformed from a dog into a daughter. He interjected the widespread conviction in the Church that the Jews, who had been children in the house of God, had became dogs and outcasts because of their obstinacy and refusal to believe in Jesus.[98] Ironically, Pius was now locked in the Vatican, while the Jews of Rome were fully emancipated by the Italian government and free to move about.

Both Pio Nono's reformist program vis-à-vis the Jews in the first two years of his pontificate, as well as the policies of his restored regime after 1849, have been misinterpreted and distorted. His efforts from 1846 to 1848

96. *Quod nunquam,* encyclical of Pope Pius IX on the Church in Prussia, 5 Feb. 1875, *PE* 1:447–49; De Franciscis, *Discorsi del Sommo Pontefice Pio IX Pronunziati,* 3:562–65.

97. See Moro, *Chiesa e lo stermino degli ebei,* 52.

98. Pius IX to the Union of Catholic Women of Rome, 24 Aug. 1871, in De Franciscis, *Discorsi del Sommo Pontefice Pio IX Pronunziati,* 1:222.

to improve the life of his Jewish citizens did not question or challenge the Church's teaching that the Jews had seized and slain Jesus, or its supersessionist notion that Christianity had replaced Judaism, claiming the Old Testament as the precursor of the New. Nonetheless, he did not favor their persecution. Like others in the Church, he envisioned that eventually Jews would be converted, and he perceived their present suffering as flowing from their hard-heartedness and obstinacy rather than from Christian hostility.

At the same time, Pius IX, like countless of his predecessors, in principle adhered to the papal decrees that prescribed that the Jews were not to be forcibly converted. In theory these decrees were followed, but Church practice and papal leadership sometimes violated the principle, as the Mortara case clearly demonstrates. Jewish separation from the Christian community was not deemed a punishment but was judged necessary for two reasons: to guard the faithful from their persistent disbelief and to protect Jews from Christian violence. Pius never challenged or questioned the anti-Judaic principle on which such decrees rested, which he accepted as a given. It was not until the horrors of the Holocaust that the Church and the papacy recognized the danger of these anti-Judaic sentiments and finally took steps to reverse them, twenty years after that, during the Second Vatican Council, 1962–65.

During the liberal era of his pontificate, when the influence of the Jews expanded dramatically throughout most of Italy and Europe, Pio Nono found no reason to question, much less change, his or the Church's traditional attitude toward them. If anything, his perception of Jewish collaboration in the liberal onslaught against the Church and Christianity very probably reinforced his anti-Judaism. His intransigence earned him a reputation as the "unmoved and immovable" colossus of the nineteenth century.[99]

On the other hand, it would be a mistake to overemphasize Pio Nono's hatred of the Jews by taking his reference to them as "dogs" out of context.[100] Likewise, one should not exaggerate the impositions he put on Jews in his state following the restoration of 1849. To be sure, a number of the

99. Foreign correspondent, "The Death of Pius IX: The Conclave and the Election," *Catholic World* 27 (April 1878): 129.

100. See David van Biema, "Not So Saintly?" *Time* magazine, 4 Sept. 2000, 58.

old restrictions in Rome were theoretically restored, but, as in the past, they were not rigidly enforced. Nor can his conduct during the Mortara affair be seen solely in terms of the degradation of the Jews, but must be viewed in light of his understanding of the canon law of the period as well as his dual responsibility as ruler of the state and head of the faith. Furthermore, his intransigence on this and other issues flowed from his conviction that the papacy and the Church were under assault and that to compromise was to concede. Pio Nono's intransigence in the religious realm had unfortunate political and diplomatic consequences, and increasingly isolated Rome. Indeed, in 1878, at the end of his pontificate, the Vatican preserved diplomatic relations with only fifteen states: seven were Western European and the remaining eight were Latin American.[101]

Finally, Pio Nono's most formidable opponents were liberalism, nationalism, socialism-communism, and those who called for modernization of the Church that would limit its role in state and society. Insofar as Jews were seen to be in alliance with these forces, they were deemed guilty by association and earned the pope's ire. Unlike Richard Wagner, whose critical *Jewry in Music* (1850) condemned Jews on racial grounds,[102] the pope's opposition remained religious. Thus, while for many he symbolized the anti-Judaism of the Church, he did not reflect the anti-Semitism of a secular age that he abhorred and upon which he waged war for some three decades following the revolutionary upheaval of 1848.

101. Alvarez, *Spies in the Vatican*, 58.
102. Levy, *Antisemitism in the Modern World*, 49–50.

4

ANTI-JUDAISM IN AN AGE OF ANTI-SEMITISM, 1878–1922

If you come to Palestine and settle your people there,

we shall have churches and priests ready to baptize all

of you. *

THE TASK OF THE 1878 CONCLAVE, the first following the papal loss of Rome, and the papacy's self-imposed "imprisonment" in the Vatican, did not prove easy.[1] The pontificate of Pius IX, Pio Nono (1846–78), had witnessed problems with Italy, Germany, Austria, France, and Switzerland, among other powers. Serious ideological dissension complicated the picture, with some resentment of papal policy within the church, and more outside. These were those who questioned the policies of the "unmoved and immovable" Pio Nono, who had arrayed the powers of the Church against the social, scientific, and political trends of contemporary civilization, and called for his successor to lift his "reactionary veil." It was hoped that his successor, the sixty-eight-year-old Gioacchino Vincenzo Rafaelle Pecci, elected on 20 February 1878, would prove better attuned to the modern world, even though he assumed the name Leo in memory of the ultraconservative, some said reactionary, Leo XII.

There was reason for hope. While Archbishop of Perugia, Pecci had explained that the condemnations of Pio Nono's "Syllabus of Errors" did not anathematize the modern state or contemporary civilization. Once pope,

* Pius X to Thedor Herzl in January 1904, quoted in Andrej Kreutz, *Vatican Policy on the Palestinian-Israeli Conflict: The Struggle for the Holy Land* (Westport, Conn.: Greenwood Press, 1990), 33.

1. In the ASV, SS, see the documents in Morte di Pontefici e Conclavi, Leone XIII (Index 1186, I–IV).

his appointment of the moderate Cardinal Alessandro Franchi was perceived as a positive step.[2] Another followed when Leo supported the Belgian constitution, concluding that the system of liberty enshrined therein would be beneficial to the Church. Both actions contributed to the initial positive reaction to his pontificate.[3] Although Leo sought to show that the Church was not an implacable enemy of progress, he remained a staunch traditionalist in interpreting the nature of progress. Thus, though Leo has been called the "first modern pope," this is only partly true. In fact, his accommodation with the modern world and other religions was partial at best.[4]

Those who hoped that the new pope would quickly bring about a reconciliation between Rome and the modern world, or the papacy and the Risorgimento, were to be disappointed. In his first encyclical, of April 1878, Leo bewailed the evils of the day and the rejection of the authority of the Church. At the same time, he stressed the need for the temporal power of the papacy, renewing the catalogue of complaints and condemnations of his predecessor.[5] In Leo's view, any civilization that conflicted with the doctrine and laws of the Church was virtually worthless. "Of this, those people on whom the Gospel light has never shone afford ample proof," he wrote, adding, "since in their mode of life a shadowy semblance only of civilization is discoverable, while its true and solid blessings have never been possessed."[6] He also assumed a contentious stance in his second encyclical, at the end of the year, in which he condemned socialism, communism, anarchy, and nihilism, and offered Christian principles as the cure.[7] To combat contemporary evils, Pope Leo appealed to rulers, even those who were not bound to the Church by religious ties.[8]

2. "What's Going on at the Vatican? A Voice from Rome," *Littell's Living Age* 139 (14 Dec. 1878): 650; foreign correspondent, "The Coronation of Pope Leo XIII," *Catholic World* 28 (May 1878): 284–85.

3. William C. Langdon, "The Old Pope and the New," *Atlantic Monthly* 41 (May 1878): 658; editorial, *New York Times,* 21 Feb. 1878, 4; "The Position of Leo XIII," *Nation* 27 (24 Oct. 1878): 251.

4. Consult the selection of papers in the Spoglio Leone XIII, housed in the SS of the ASV.

5. "Inscrutabili Dei Consilio," *PE* 2:5–10; Harry C. Koenig, ed., *Principles for Peace: Selections from Papal Documents from Leo XIII to Pius XII* (Washington, D.C.: National Catholic Welfare Conference, 1943), 3–6.

6. Quoted in Koenig, *Principles for Peace,* 5.

7. "Quod Apostolici Muneris," 28 Dec. 1878, *PE* 2:15.

8. Letter "Da Grave Sventura," 27 Aug. 1878, in Koenig, *Principles for Peace,* 7.

In his campaign against the evils of modernity, he invoked Thomistic thought and philosophy—with its anti-Judaic bias—to inculcate sanity in a world gone astray.[9] Leo never doubted that the Church was "the sacred guardian of religion, the parent and teacher of the purity of customs and of all the virtues which spring from religion as their source."[10] Like Pio Nono, he believed that without Christian morality, liberty degenerated into license, and he branded those who rejected the teachings of Christianity as enemies not only of the Church but of the commonwealth as well.[11] Such sentiments did little to reassure Jews and other non-Christians. Like his predecessors, Leo perceived the Church of Christ as the only true teacher of virtue and guardian of morality.[12] Following Pius IX, Gregory XVI, and the other nineteenth-century popes, he was not prepared to embrace religious equality.

Leo's attitude toward the Jews in Italy and elsewhere continued to form part of the Church's broader conflict with secularism, radical social change, Freemasonry, socialism, and international finance. The emancipation of the Jews of Europe, in the words of one scholar, represented the first tentative step of radical social engineering on a large scale,[13] which unfortunately coincided with the papacy's loss of temporal power and what many in the Vatican perceived as a war on the Church. There were those who tended to associate the two, tracing the secular movement for social change to the Jews while calling for an end to their emancipation and their return to the ghettoes.[14] These themes were repeated in the Italian Catholic press and even in the journals closely associated with the Holy See, *L'Osservatore Romano* and *La Civiltà Cattolica*, which waged a series of campaigns against Jews during Leo's pontificate. In large measure their denunciations represented an indirect counterattack against the Italian liberalism and secularization that had destroyed the pope's temporal power, as much as an attack on the Jews.[15] Whatever the motivation, Jews found the clerical accusations offensive.

9. "Aeterne Patris," 4 Aug. 1879, *PP* 1:43–44.

10. Encyclical "Quod multum," 22 Aug. 1886, in Koenig, *Principles for Peace*, 36.

11. Encyclical "Etsi nos," 15 Feb. 1882, ibid., 16.

12. Encyclical "Immortale Dei," 1 Nov. 1885, ibid., 28.

13. Canepa, "Atteggiamento degli ebrei italiani," 421.

14. Bernardini, "Origins and Development of Racial Anti-Semitism," 434.

15. Andrew M. Canepa, "Pius X and the Jews: A Reappraisal," *Church History* 61, no. 3 (1992): 370.

During Leo's pontificate the papal campaign against secularism and Judaism in Italy was paralleled by a racist anti-Semitic campaign that emerged in much of Europe north of the Alps, in an age of fervent nationalism. The anti-Semitic ideology first arose at the end of the 1870s in the recently united Germany, and the new terminology of anti-Semitism, rather than the traditional anti-Judaism, suggests that it was not so much the Jewish religion that aroused opposition as the perception that Jews were members of another race. This was precisely the argument presented by Eugen Dühring in his pamphlet "The Jewish Question as a Question of Race, Morals, and Culture with a World Historical Answer" (1875). Dühring depicted the Jews as a unique human race with negative moral and physical characteristics quite distinct from their creed and religious practices. In his opinion the act of baptism made no difference whatsoever; race, not religion, was the basis of his anti-Semitism. This belief was shared by Wilhelm Marr, the second-rate Viennese journalist, who likewise insisted on the exclusion of religion from the definition of the Jewishness.[16]

Marr's pamphlet "The Victory of Judaism over Germanism" appeared in February 1879, claiming that between Jews and animals stood only primitive beings such as blacks and red Indians, and brimming with political, cultural, and racial hostility toward the Jews.[17] Marr's screed became the first anti-Semitic best-seller, going through twelve editions. His compatriot Paul de Lagarde (1827–91) combined deep-seated criticism of both Protestantism and Catholicism with a racist animosity toward Jews. Anticipating the Nazi racial program and Hitler's critique of Judeo-Christianity, Lagarde claimed that the German "religion of the future" had to be created in line with Germans' own intrinsic nature to the exclusion of foreign elements introduced by Christianity. Houston Stuart Chamberlain, in his *Foundations of the Nineteenth Century,* provided another racist interpretation of Christianity.[18] This anti-Semitism was not seconded, for political as well as moral reasons, by the Catholic-led German Center Party. "We, as a minority in the Reich, have not forgotten what happened to us," one of

16. See Katz, *From Prejudice to Destruction,* 20, 265–69; Uriel Tal, *Christians and Jews in Germany: Religion, Politics, and Ideology in the Second Reich, 1870–1914* (Ithaca: Cornell University Press, 1975), 223–82.

17. Moro, *Chiesa e lo sterminio degli ebrei,* 39.

18. Katz, *From Prejudice to Destruction,* 305–6.

the leaders of the party noted, recalling the *Kulturkampf,* "and for that reason, even if more elevated considerations and more fundamental motives did not restrain us, we cannot offer to forge the weapon to be used against the Jews today, the Poles tomorrow and the Catholics the day after that."[19]

Rome also received disconcerting reports on Karl Lueger's Christian Socialist Party, which emerged in 1891, with the nuncio to Vienna complaining that the movement spouted racial theories rather than religious principles and made no attempt to convert the Jews. Nonetheless, a series of articles in the *Civiltà Cattolica* eventually supported much of its program.[20] Similar thoughts were expressed in France, which saw the publication of Ernest Renan's *Histoire du peuple d'Israel* in 1887, a book that borrowed heavily from the work of Arthur Gobineau (1816–82), who developed a theory of race to explain the superiority of Europeans over the yellow and black races. In 1886 Eduard Drumont published *La France Juive. Essai d'histoire contemporanie,* which claimed that the Jews, who were members of an inferior race, had made themselves masters of France though duplicity and intrigue. Similar charges were later launched in Russia following the publication of "The Protocols of the Elders of Zion," which appeared at the end of the 1890s.

In these works and programs, race rather than religion was the primary factor. Thus in Austria the anti-Catholic and anti-Judaic Georg von Schoener (1842–1921) did not believe that baptism changed anything, asserting "you cannot resign from your race."[21] Drumont, too, believed that a Jew was a Jew was a Jew, and that conversion to Christianity changed nothing. This position was in direct conflict with the theological position of the Church, which maintained that a person baptized as a Christian could no longer be considered a Jew. Nonetheless, this did not prevent the Assumptionist religious order in France from spewing an anti-Judaism that paralleled the secular anti-Semitism in their review *La Croix,* which emerged in 1880, becoming a daily newspaper in 1883. Although it claimed to be Catholic, apostolic, and Roman, its views on racial matters were clearly in conflict with the tenets of the faith and mirrored the anti-Semitism of the emerging secular racism. Indeed, in September 1890 *La*

---

19. Quoted in Carroll, *Constantine's Sword,* 493.

20. Kertzer, *Popes against the Jews,* 187–96.

21. Quoted in Joachim Remak, ed., *The Nazi Years: A Documented History* (Prospect Heights, Ill.: Waveland Press, 1990), 7.

Croix proudly proclaimed itself the most anti-Jewish journal in France.[22] Its blatant anti-Semitism was aped by others.

The notion of the radical difference between anti-Judaism and anti-Semitism has been challenged both within and outside the Church. Catholicism's antimodernism and opposition to liberalism nourished an anti-Judaism in the Church that had social, political, and economic aspects in addition to the traditional religious opposition that was often mistaken for anti-Semitism.[23] Clearly, the thought of the Jesuit father Raffaele Ballerini (1830–1907), writer for the *Civiltà Cattolica*, was dangerously similar to that of the anti-Semites. This did not hinder his close relationship to Pope Leo, who also remained tied to Umberto Benigni, the anti-Judaic editor of the Catholic newspaper *La Voce della Verità* of Rome. Nor did religious scruples and the differences between anti-Judaism and anti-Semitism stop the writers of the *Civiltà Cattolica* from supporting many of the propositions advanced at the First International Anti-Semitic Congress of Dresden in 1882.[24] In November 1885 the *Osservatore Cattolico* claimed that Jews dominated the Masonic lodges, and that in their relentless drive for domination they provoked the revolutionary upheaval that rocked the continent.[25]

On the other hand, even critics of the Church acknowledged that in principle its anti-Judaism differed from the contemporary anti-Semitism, for it was not unqualified and provided relief for Jews who converted to Christianity.[26] In fact, the blatantly anti-Semitic *La Croix* refused to sanction or support the Russian pogroms of the 1880s, insisting that good Catholics could not condone the murder of Jews.[27] The Vatican journal *L'Osservatore Romano* repeatedly took pains to spell out the crucial differences it perceived between traditional anti-Judaism and the emerging secular anti-Semitism. Others countered that anti-Semitism flowed from a long evolution to which the Church's anti-Judaism contributed.[28] For var-

---

22. Moro, *Chiesa e lo stermino degli ebei*, 55.

23. Martin Rhonheimer, "The Holocaust: What Was Not Said," *First Things* 137 (Nov. 2003): 18–28.

24. Kertzer, *Popes against the Jews*, 142.

25. "Gli ebrei nel mondo," *L'Osservatore Cattolico*, 11–12 Nov. 1885, in Moro, *Chiesa e lo stermino degli ebei*, 54.

26. Katz, *From Prejudice to Destruction*, 323.

27. Kertzer, *Popes against the Jews*, 175.

28. Moro, *Chiesa e lo stermino degli ebei*, 39.

ious theological reasons, Leo stood aloof from anti-Semitism, even avoiding the occasional anti-Judaic outbursts of his predecessor.[29]

Leo had political and diplomatic as well as religious reasons for his reluctance to be identified with secular anti-Semitism.[30] This pope sought some accommodation with the contemporary world, striving to shed the retrograde image many had of the Vatican. Part of this program, as well as his effort to enlist France's support for the Holy See's claim to Rome, required a reconciliation with the French Republic, and this meant shedding the Church's medieval and blatantly illiberal image. Leo commenced his campaign for a rapprochement with the French by explaining that the Church was not opposed to any particular form of government that did not infringe upon her freedom of action.[31] In this fashion the Vatican revealed that it was not opposed to all aspects of modernity and did not totally reject its political manifestations. In 1880 Leo XIII wrote to the Archbishop of Paris, decrying Catholic support for the various demonstrations in favor of "Henry V" and the restoration of the monarchy, explaining that in all its dealings with governments, the Church's main objective remained to preserve Christianity.[32] He also reassured Alexander of Russia that the Catholic religion sought to promote peace and harmony between subjects and rulers in all countries.[33] An agreement of 1882 between the Vatican and St. Petersburg promised greater freedom to Catholic seminaries in Russia, and the Russian *chargé d'affaires* promised that the prosecutorial degree of 1865 would be suppressed. Relations were also improved with Bismarck's Germany, which terminated the most oppressive anti-Catholic measures of the *Kulturkampf.*

While papal relations with France, Russia, and Germany improved, there was a deterioration in relations with Italy, which fueled clerical opposition against liberalism, secularism, and Judaism in the last two decades of the nineteenth century. The identification of Italy's Jews with liberalism and modernism added another dimension to the Vatican's anti-Judaism, as some Catholic journals abandoned all restraint and freely

---

29. "Antisemitismo in Francia," *OR*, 1–2 July 1892.

30. Kertzer, *Popes against the Jews*, 168.

31. Eduardo Soderini, *Leo III, Italy and France* (London: Burns, Oates and Washbourne, 1935), 143.

32. Leo XIII to Archbishop of Paris, 22 Oct. 1880, in Koenig, *Principles for Peace*, 12.

33. Ibid., 11–12.

merged religious and racial critiques. In the words of one observer, "those Jews who left the orthodox fold chose secularization, irreligion and apostasy rather than adapting their liturgy and doctrine and so preserve their religious affiliation."[34] This development was deplored in the columns of the Jesuit *Civiltà Cattolica,* whose former director, Father Giuseppe Oreglia, published a series of thirty-six articles denouncing the Jews who had poured out of the ghettoes and taken part in the liberal campaign against the Church and Christianity. In his view, Jews who abandoned their religion, or pretended to, still represented a danger to Church, state, and society. In language that was essentially anti-Semitic he charged that Jewishness was based not only religion but also, and especially, on race, culture, and attitude. Although a number of Jesuits also denounced the Jewish "race," they did not go as far as the secular anti-Semites, but continued to uphold the millennial papal belief that Jews could be saved through conversion.[35]

In Italy the hostility toward Jews of some forty major Catholic newspapers and periodicals "was intimately tied to both traditional religious anti-Judaism and Catholic opposition to modernity."[36] This clerical campaign against the Jews was reinforced by the fact that there were five Jewish firms among the country's major publishing houses and that Jews had a prominent profile in the newspaper industry of liberal Italy; one Jew alone had a controlling interest in six of the country's leading newspapers, while five of the sixteen Italian dailies in Rome had Jewish managing editors.[37] By 1900, Italian Jews, who made up less than 2 percent of the population, accounted for more than 6 percent of the liberal professions. This distressed clerical and conservative circles, whose publications opposed most of the measures introduced by the liberal state, including its emancipation of the Jews. They used the Jews as scapegoats as a means of garnering mass support for their less than popular illiberal and antinationalist campaigns.

Relations between the Vatican and the liberal state reached a low point in July 1881, when a violent demonstration was orchestrated against the

34. Quoted in Andrew M. Canepa, "Reflections on Antisemitism in Liberal Italy," *Wiener Library Bulletin* 31, nos. 47–48 (1978): 104.
35. Kertzer, *Popes against the Jews,* 136–38.
36. Canepa, "Reflections on Antisemitism," 109.
37. Ibid., 106–7, 109.

papacy as the body of Pio Nono was transported from St. Peter's to its final resting place in San Lorenzo, outside the city walls. The crowd's attempt to dump the casket into the Tiber led Leo to call for foreign intervention. He deplored the wounds inflicted on the Church on the
peninsula and condemned secular interference in ecclesiastical activities,
the expulsion of religious from their convents, the confiscation of Church
property, the sanctioning of civil matrimony, and the elimination of
Catholic supervision over education. Leo insisted that Christianity had to
remain integral to public life, serving as the source of unity and the guar-
antor of justice. He called upon Italian Catholics to assume their responsibility by founding a wide range of benevolent and educational organizations, later dubbed Catholic Action, in opposition to the secularizing
efforts of the sects and the state. He also urged the faithful to sustain a
Catholic press that would combat the lies and perfidy of the anticlerical
journals.[38] It is in this context that Leo XIII tolerated, if he did not encourage, the scurrilous attacks of part of the Catholic press against the Jews.

While Leo carefully avoided personal outbursts against Jews,[39] he did
not hesitate, in April 1884, to denounce the Freemasons—who some de-
monized as Jewish fellow travelers—as a danger to Church, state, and society, and he drew on the condemnations of some nine predecessors over
the course of more than a century. Commencing with the critique of
Clement XII in 1738, Leo XIII contributed his own negative assessment of
the "pernicious" sect he deemed destructive of religious values and moral
laws. He denounced both Masonic society and the organized groups—
many conservative Catholics and clerics included Jews within this catego-
ry—that shared its subversive philosophy and purpose. Preaching that
their aim was to overturn the Christian order while replacing the authority of the Church with that of human reason, Leo was scandalized by the
naturalism of a sect that refused to acknowledge the certainty of God and
immorality. In their "insane and wicked endeavors" Leo perceived the "implacable hatred" and "spirit of revenge" of Satan himself. State and Church
together must overcome the evil designs of the sects, and protect and preserve public order and tranquillity.[40]

Leo's paranoia and virtual obsession regarding the Freemasons, with

---

38. "Etsi Nos," PE 2:63–68.   39. Kertzer, Popes against the Jews, 168.
40. "Humanus genus," PP 1:46.

whom he and others in the Vatican saw the Jews allied, was fueled by the disclosures of the controversial French journalist, pamphleteer, and author Gabriel Jogand-Pages, better known by his pen name, Leo Taxil. Apparently abandoning his atheism and earlier campaign against the Church and the papacy, in the mid-1880s Taxil met Pope Leo and commenced a crusade to expose the conspiracies of the "secret brotherhood." In a series of pamphlets, articles, and books he portrayed the Masons as Satanists whose demonic agenda plotted to undermine Christianity and its leadership. His lurid account of Masonic rituals and clandestine activities captured the public imagination in France and abroad, as his works were translated into Italian, German, Spanish, and English. A comparison of texts and styles reveals that the author or authors of the original version of the *Protocols of the Elders of Zion,* which first appeared in Russia around 1898, apparently borrowed freely from Taxil, applying his diatribes against the Masons to the Jews. Even after Taxil confessed that he had fabricated his stories in order to expose the gullibility of the Church and its leaders, the lies he fostered about the Freemasons and Jews persisted. Recently they have been revived in parts of the Middle East and Africa.[41]

Leo remained preoccupied by the issue of Church-state relations and returned to it in his encyclical on the Christian constitution of states. Proclaiming the chief task of the Church as the saving of souls, he acknowledged that this had an impact on the temporal world. He repeated the Church dictum that the right to rule was not bound to any specific form of government, one being as legitimate as another. Developing themes he had earlier expressed, Leo observed that the condemnations of his two immediate predecessors, Gregory XVI and Pius IX, had not discriminated between various forms of government but had laid blame equally on all secularizing tendencies. What the Church could not and would not accept were "opinions verging on naturalism or rationalism, the essence of which is to do away with Christian institutions and to install in society the supremacy of man to the exclusion of God."[42] And he continued to contest the concept of religious liberty, and the indifferentism and license it allegedly promoted.

41. Dan Gilgoff, "The Lie about the Freemasons Lives On," *U.S. News and World Report,* 26 Aug.–2 Sept. 2002, 46.
42. "Immortale Dei," *PE* 2:117.

Nonetheless, Leo recognized the need to bring the papacy and Church into some accommodation with the modern world. He proved willing to cooperate with secular governments of all types, but he insisted on the preservation of Catholic principles in states as diverse as France and Bismarck's Germany. He alerted the bishops of Hungary that the Catholic religion represented the best foundation for peace, exhorting them to combat rationalism, naturalism, and socialism, and he urged a crusade against civil matrimony. He also called on the bishops of Portugal to preserve the Christian bases of their society. In the process, Leo sought to keep Catholics from all developments not sanctioned by Christian rules or morals.[43] He had reservations about liberty of speech and the press and stipulated that these should exist only in moderation, claiming that it was "absurd to suppose that nature has accorded indifferently to truth and falsehood, justice and injustice."[44] In the same encyclical of 1885, he branded freedom of worship "a liberty totally contrary to the virtue of religion." "The state cannot treat all religions on an equal basis or indiscriminately accord them the same rights."[45] Unquestionably, this belief colored his attitude toward the role and position of Jews in Christian countries.

Similar sentiments were echoed in the columns of *Civiltà Cattolica*, which argued that the separation of Jews and Christians was in the best interest of both.[46] The anti-Jewish articles of Raffaele Ballerini (1830–1907), published in the *Civiltà Cattolica* in 1890, were bound together the following year in the pamphlet "Della questione ebraica in Europa." Publicly Leo neither approved nor condemned this work.[47] He did, however, continue to denounce religious liberty as indifferentism.[48] The case of Captain Alfred Dreyfus (1859–1935), which erupted in 1894, presented the Vatican with a dilemma. On the one hand conservative Catholics and clerics commenced a bitter campaign against the French Republic and the Jews; on the other hand, the case inspired Theodor Herzl (1860–1904) to move away

43. See "Quod multum" and *"Pergrata,"* PP 1:48; Koenig, *Principles for Peace,* 35–36; "Saepe nos," 24 June 1888, PE 2:183–85.
44. Encyclical "Libertas Praestantissimum," 20 June 1888, in Koenig, *Principles for Peace,* 44.
45. Quoted in Festquet, *Drama of Vatican II,* 241.
46. Kertzer, *Popes against the Jews,* 134.
47. Ibid., 143–44; Lapide, *Three Popes and the Jews,* 80.
48. "Pastoralis," 25 June 1891, PP 1:52.

from Jewish conversion and integration and to seek a home for the Jewish people in Palestine—founding the Zionist movement in the process.

During the Dreyfus Affair the greater part of the Catholic press, from Italy to England, including journals tied to the Holy See, expressed hostility to Jewish capitalism and finance. This complicated the efforts of Theodor Herzl to garner Catholic support for a Jewish homeland in Palestine. As early as May 1896 Herzl met with the papal nuncio to Vienna in the hope of securing Vatican support for his program, reassuring him and Pope Leo that the Jewish homeland he envisioned would not include Jerusalem, Bethlehem, or Nazareth, and that the Christian shrines would be accorded extraterritorial status. Neither the nuncio nor the pope showed any interest in the project.[49] In fact, as news of the Zionist goal spread, *Civiltà Cattolica* opposed the creation of a Jewish state in Palestine as contrary to Christ's predictions.[50] Leo concurred with the Jesuits in opposing Jewish control of the Holy Land.

The Jesuit journal as well as the official *Osservatore Romano* appeared to be more sympathetic to the anti-Judaic campaign that the Dreyfus Affair provoked in the conservative Catholic press in France than it was to the Zionist program. One article in the *Osservatore,* borrowing shamelessly from anti-Semitic propaganda, identified Jews and the Jewish race with treason. Another biased article in the Vatican journal indiscriminately accepted the racist stereotypes, and tied the Panama scandal to the Dreyfus Affair, portraying Jews as the connecting link.[51] Combining anti-Semitism and anti-Judaism, the Vatican journal branded the Jews an "accused race" condemned to wander the earth. The *Osservatore*'s one-sided reporting on the affair continued well into the new year, its reporters tying this and other scandals to the Jewish-Masonic alliance that they claimed sought to undermine Christianity. The Jesuits who wrote for the *Osservatore* warned that Jews and other malcontents sought to sow discord in Christian France and Europe.[52]

The Jesuits were even more irresponsible and racist in their own jour-

49. Kreutz, *Vatican Policy on the Palestinian-Israeli Conflict*, 32.
50. "La dispersione degli Israelli pel mondo moderno," *CC,* 20 April 1897; see also Kreutz, *Vatican Policy on the Palestinian-Israeli Conflict*, 32, 51.
51. "Tradimenti e traditori," *OR,* 1–2 Dec. 1897, and "Un altro Panama. Cose del Giorno," *OR,* 23–24 Nov. 1897, both in James F. Brennan, *The Reflection of the Dreyfus Affair in the European Press, 1897–1899* (New York: Peter Lang, 1998), 403.
52. "La razza giudaica. Cose del Giorno," *OR,* 9–10 Dec. 1897, ibid., 405, 418; "La Coeren-

nal, *La Civiltà Cattolica*, as they described the "dastardly Jewish plot" to free Dreyfus and cripple the real—the Catholic—France.[53] Returning incessantly to their charge of a Masonic-Jewish alliance to undermine Christian France, they had no doubt of Dreyfus's guilt or of his supporters' determination to sow discord. The writers of this journal charged that while the Jews were made the equal of Christians in Germany, Austria-Hungary, and Italy, in France they were allowed to dominate. Accepting Taxil's bogus accounts, they perceived French Masonry as totally subordinate to Jewish goals and charged that the Jews controlled the political life and economy of France. In fact, the *Civiltà Cattolica* concluded that the Republic in Paris was more Jewish than French! As the campaign against the Jews and Dreyfus merged with attacks on the Republic, Leo's Vatican, which sought a rapprochement with France for political more than religious reasons, urged caution. Indeed, following the suicide of Lieutenant Henry, some restraint was placed on the writers of the *Osservatore Romano*, who were informed that the Dreyfus Affair should be depicted as an internal French matter.[54] This was precisely the stance that Leo took during the course of another interview with the journalists of *Le Figaro*, as he sought to extricate the Church from the political wrangling and deep divisions in the Republic.[55]

Leo was not prepared to support the racist and monarchist right in France to the detriment of the Vatican's broader diplomatic goals.[56] In fact, he was visibly disappointed that his attempt to get Catholics in France to rally to the republic (*Ralliement*) had not succeeded. Monsignor Domenico Ferrata, the nuncio in Paris, and Cardinal Mariano Rampolla del Tindaro, the papal secretary of state, were convinced that if the parliamentary right accepted Leo's call to rally to the republic, breaking the mischievous alliance of the French Church with the royalist and racist cause, the anticlerical policies of the radicals and radical socialists would lose support. Neither thing occurred. The "Declaration of the Monarchist Right" pronounced that as Catholics they bowed to the Holy Father's infallible au-

---

za giudaica-masonica," *OR*, 25–26 Feb. 1898, "La giustizia in Francia," *OR*, 5–6 April 1898, and "Il Processo Zola," *OR*, 12–13 Feb. 1898, ibid., 412.

53. "Cronoca Contemporanea. Cose Straniere, Francia," *CC*, 18 Dec. 1897, ibid., 405, 418.

54. "Cose straniere. Francia," *CC*, 6 Aug. 1898, ibid., 429, 439; "Il Caso di Alfredo Dreyfus," *CC*, 24 Jan. 1898, ibid., 411; "Cronoca del Giorno," *OR*, 5–6 Sept. 1898, ibid., 431, 439.

55. Moro, *Chiesa e lo stermino degli ebei*, 58.

56. In the ASV, SS, see the files on Francia, indices 134, 1024.

thority on matters of faith, but that as citizens they exercised their individual political option. Despite papal concern, *La Croix* spewed out a slew of anti-Judaic, anti-Semitic, antirepublican articles, and defined itself as "the most anti-Jewish newspaper in France."[57] This Catholic journal, with a circulation of more than half a million, was a thorn in the side of the republic. The vast majority of conservative Catholics refused to bow to the strictures of Leo and rally behind the republic. Leo's futile initiative revealed the limits of papal authority on "political" issues and probably influenced the cautious policies of his more diplomatic successors, such as Pius XII.

During the Panama Canal scandal and the Dreyfus Affair, the clerical alliance with the royalist right, deplored by the pope, proved unfortunate for the position of the Church in France. Some in the Vatican concurred with the conclusion of Charles Maurras's Action Française, formed in 1898, that France had fallen into the hands of Jews, Protestants, Freemasons, and recently naturalized foreigners, and the more intransigent writers of the *Osservatore Romano* continued to link Jews, Protestants, Masons, and socialists in an unholy alliance. The Jesuits who composed the third editorial of the *Osservatore* harped on the link between Judaism and Masonry, charging that only the unbaptized descendants of the crucifiers of Christ could nourish such hatred of the Catholic Church.[58] For its part, the *Civiltà Cattolica* claimed that all of Emile Zola's advocates were Protestants, Jews, and Judaized anarchists, radicals, and socialists.[59] Its writers were quick to see anticlerical and Jewish plots behind all actions against the Church and its ministers, and in an article of January 1898 traced the problem to the emancipation of the Jews during the revolutionary period.[60] They charged that the accusations that a teaching brother in Lille had raped and murdered a young boy were part of broader campaign to discredit the Catholic schools and religious orders of France.[61] Furthermore, the Holy Office refused to issue a solemn declaration of the falsity of the belief that Jews took part in ritual murder. For some this provided proof positive that anti-Ju-

57. Kertzer, *Popes against the Jews*, 175.

58. "Giudaismo e socialismo," *OR*, 26–27 Jan. 1898; also see this journal for 28–29 Jan. 1898, in Brennan, *Dreyfus Affair in the European Press*, 410; "Giudaismo e Masoneria. Cose del Giorno," *OR*, 3–4 Jan. 1899, ibid., 449.

59. "Cose straniere. Francia," *CC*, 5 March 1898, ibid., 415, 422.

60. Chadwick, *History of the Popes*, 385.

61. "L'Innocenza di un frate ed I suoi calunniatori," *OR*, 12–13 July 1899, in Brennan, *Dreyfus Affair in the European Press*, 454.

daism and anti-Semitism were alive and well in Rome as in Paris.[62] The 1890s thus witnessed an intensification rather than a diminution of the anti-Judaic campaign of clericals and conservative Catholics.

Pope Leo did not sanction this racist campaign, and in 1898 he wrote a letter condemning the anti-Semitic movement in Algeria.[63] Leo was moved not only by religious scruples but also by political considerations. He feared the retaliation that this bitter antirepublican, anti-Jewish, and promonarchist campaign would provoke, and supposedly called in the superior general of the Jesuit Order to ask him to mitigate the Jesuits' campaign against Dreyfus and the Jews. Pope Leo had reportedly even prepared an encyclical against anti-Semitism.[64] This was only partly true, for the overt focus of the encyclical *Depuis le Jour,* dated 8 September 1899 but released a week later, was on ecclesiastical education in France.[65] In fact, it represented Leo's belated and indirect attempt to discipline the clergy for their anti-Semitic polemic during the Dreyfus Affair. In the encyclical Leo cited Saint Bernard of Clairvaux (1090–1153), who advocated peaceful conversion rather than blatant violence against the Jews. The encyclical also admonished the French clergy for their language, which was out of harmony with "the sacredness of the word of God," and criticized them for exciting "the passion of the wicked."[66] Unfortunately, few could decipher the "hidden message" of this encyclical, and most of those who did tended to ignore it. The papal message found greater resonance in Vienna than in Paris, and in the Austrian capital one cardinal after another sought to block race hatred and anti-Semitism among the faithful.[67]

Meanwhile, the Vatican journal emphatically denied that the Church was anti-Semitic, noting that the Holy See had long been the defender of the Jews.[68] In fact, not all French Catholics, or indeed even those who tended to harbor anti-Judaic sentiments, supported the anti-Semitic cam-

62. Moro, *Chiesa e lo stermino degli ebei,* 58–59.

63. Carroll, *Constantine's Sword,* 456.

64. For reports on Leo XIII's concerns, see Boyen d'Agen, "Une Visite a Leon XIII," *Le Figaro,* 15 March 1899; and "The Pope Alarmed," *Daily Mail,* 29 Aug. 1899, both in Brennan, *Dreyfus Affair in the European Press,* 472.

65. Koenig, *Principles for Peace,* 100.

66. Brennan, *Dreyfus Affair in the European Press,* 113.

67. Chadwick, *History of the Popes,* 379.

68. "Gli oppressori degli Ebrei," *OR,* 14–15 Sept. 1899, in Brennan, *Dreyfus Affair in the European Press,* 472.

paign unleashed by the scandals at the turn of the century. Although he believed that Jews were cursed by God, Leon Bloy, author of *Salut par les Juifs* (1892), ridiculed the notion that Jesus was not a Jew and deplored the violence launched against Jews. Furthermore, Edgar Demange, the lawyer who assumed the defense of Dreyfus at great personal cost, remained a fervent Roman Catholic. The bishops, in turn, while they did not join in the anti-Semitic excesses, failed to condemn them, thus providing tacit approval. The Vatican did not follow suit, but its message was diluted by its diplomatic language and its refusal to abandon its long-standing anti-Judaism. Paradoxically, Doellinger, who denounced the Christian roots of anti-Judaism, was excommunicated, but those who pronounced his sentence remained anti-Judaic.[69]

Nonetheless, Pope Leo eventually urged the Assumptionists to cease publication of their anti-Judaic, anti-Semitic, antirepublican paper *La Croix*.[70] The papal call for moderation was not well received by the writers of *La Croix* or by other Catholic journalists who did not see the linkage between their own anti-Judaic, antirepublican crusade and the reaction it provoked in France and Italy. Surprisingly, the Jesuits were stunned by the bitter outburst in France against them following the second trial and condemnation of Dreyfus in 1899. They felt that the Jews and Masons, who precipitated this second trial, rather than their order, should have borne the brunt of the anger. They were also shocked when French public opinion suspected that they were behind the attempted assassination of Fernado Labori, the lawyer for both Dreyfus and Zola.[71] Their failure to heed the papal counsel of moderation eventually led to the expulsion of many of the religious orders from France, which contributed to the bitter Church-state conflict during the next pontificate.

The pope had greater success in reaching an accommodation with the working classes. In 1891 Leo showed his sensitivity to the problems faced by labor by issuing his *Rerum novarum* on the rights and duties of capital and labor. The best known of Leo's encyclicals, it condemned socialism and the civilization that had produced it. While he professed to under-

69. Carroll, *Constantine's Sword*, 456–58.

70. Chadwick, *History of the Popes*, 383–86.

71. "Cronoca Contemporanea," *CC*, 7 Oct. 1999, and "Cronoca Contemporanea. Cose Straniere. Francia," *CC*, 2 Sept. 1899, both in Brennan, *Dreyfus Affair in the European Press*, 473.

stand that the vast expansion of industrial society had changed relations between workers and employers for the worse, the socialist solution of eliminating private property was a cure worse than the disease. But *Rerum novarum* did proclaim the worker's right to protection against economic exploitation and social injustice, and submitted that when workers could not defend their own rights it was up to the state to intervene on their behalf. The pope specifically recommended associations that could help the distressed, including societies for mutual help, benevolent foundations to provide for the workingman, and institutions for the welfare of the young and the aged. This encyclical, dubbed the "social *Magna Carta* of Catholicism," inspired Catholic social action in Europe and abroad.[72]

In his desire for a Christian solution to the social question, Leo did not entirely abandon the conservative outlook of his predecessors, and he warned the laity in Italy to shun nonreligious societies. He expected laws in Catholic counties to reflect Church teaching and discourage mixed marriages. Throughout his pontificate, he continued to denounce the contemporary evils of the age—the subversion of truth, the opposition to authority, dissension within and between nations, contempt for law, and materialism—all evil fruits of the rejection of Church authority.[73] Leo called attention to the dangers of religious indifference in *Pastoralis* (June 1891) and the attacks on dogma in *Octobri mense* (September 1891). Although not clearly spelled out, these letters were critical of religious equality and, by extension, of the emancipation of the Jews. Subsequently, in *Officiorum ac numerum* (1897) Leo amended, but did not eliminate, the Index of forbidden books.[74] Meanwhile, the anti-Judaic campaign in the Catholic press continued. Although Leo did not take the lead in combating racist bigotry, he steadfastly refused to sanction it. "The brotherhood of Christ indeed is greater than that of blood," he wrote, "for brotherhood of blood shows a likeness of body only, but the brotherhood of Christ shows a oneness of heart and soul."[75]

Less hostile to contemporary civilization and more open to some cur-

---

72. "Rerum Novarum," 15 May 1891, *PE* 2:241–61; see also Francis L. Broderick, "The Encyclicals and Social Action: Is John A. Ryan Typical?" *CHR* 55 (April 1969): 1–6.

73. "Custodi di quella fede," 8 Dec. 1892 *PP* 1:53; "Constanti Hungarorum," 2 Sept. 1893, *PP* 1:54; "Inscrutabili dei consilio," *PP* 1:43.

74. *PP* 1:43–44, 51–53, 57–58; John J. Wynne, ed., *The Great Encyclical Letters of Pope Leo XIII* (New York: Benziger Brothers, 1903), 407–20.

75. Letter *Reputantibus*, 20 Aug. 1901, in Koenig, *Principles for Peace*, 106.

rent developments than his immediate predecessors, this pope's condemnation of racist and religious bigotry lacked the clarity and intensity of his
denunciations of Freemasonry and indifferentism. Leo's conservative sentiments and earlier criticism of modern philosophical movements were
repeated in his Easter message of 1902, which was a review of the twenty-
five years of his pontificate and a last testament of sorts. In it he reiterated
his earlier denunciations of current affairs and their unfortunate consequences. Scandalized by the "vast conspiracy of hostile forces" aimed at
"destroying" the work of Christ, he described the disorders in social relations and again listed the dangers posed by Freemasonry. Echoing Pius IX,
he warned the faithful that liberty and peace were illusory when separated
from religion, adding that liberty should not be granted indiscriminately
to truth and error, good and evil. The pope called on public officials to
demonstrate firmness in defense of principles, and on parents to provide
their children with a Christian education.[76]

No less determined than Pius IX to preserve papal power and the Vatican's centralization, Leo was concerned about the emergence of a liberal
party in the American Church, subsequently known as Americanism. The
pope recognized that Catholicism had flourished in the United States but
opposed the separation of Church and state there. Indeed, he suggested
that the Church might have borne more abundant fruit in America if liberty had been bolstered by the patronage of public authority.[77] In 1895 he
cautioned his apostolic delegate there, Archbishop Francesco Satolli,
against any American Catholic participation in interfaith congresses such
as had occurred in Chicago in 1893.[78] His concern increased after the talk
delivered by father Denis O'Connell in August 1897 at the International
Catholic Scientific Congress in Fribourg, Switzerland. O'Connell seemed
to indicate that the separation of Church and state in America was more
beneficial to Catholicism than the theoretical integralism championed by
traditionalists, hinting that the Church should be reorganized along democratic lines.[79] Such views thoroughly alarmed the Vatican, and Leo appointed a committee to investigate them.

76. "Annum ingressi," 19 March 1902, *PP* 1:62–63.
77. Gerald P. Fogarty, *The Vatican and the Americanist Crisis: Denis J. O'Connell, American Agent in Rome, 1885–1903*, Pontificia Universitas Gregoriana (Rome: Università Gregoriana Editrice, 1974), 165; "The Pope's American Encyclical," *Independent* 47 (7 Feb. 1895): 10.
78. "Pope Leo XIII on Religious Congresses," *Literary Digest* 12 (9 Nov. 1895): 50.
79. Fogarty, *Vatican and the Americanist Crisis*, 257–59, 279–81.

Following the committee's critical report of developments on the other side of the Atlantic, Leo responded in a letter of 22 January 1899 to Cardinal Gibbons, condemning the alleged Americanist attempt to reconcile the Church with the age. Without criticizing the American system of government or the American separation of Church and state, the pope pointed to the difference between the Church, founded on divine right, and other associations, which subsist by the free will of man. Leo let it be known that the Vatican could not sanction the notion of a Church in America different from that which prevailed elsewhere, and called for the unity of doctrine and governance. He strongly resisted the suggestion that external spiritual direction or the centrality of the infallible pontiff could be abandoned. He likewise rejected the introduction of a new apologetic to explain the faith, as well as the new approach to non-Catholics.[80] Among other things, these last strictures provided for the preservation of the status quo in Catholic-Jewish relations in American and worldwide. As Leo's pontificate came to an end in the first years of the twentieth century, some hoped that the new pope would be better attuned to developments across the Atlantic.[81]

In the conclave of 31 July 1903, Cardinal Mariano Rampolla, Leo's secretary of state, emerged as the leading candidate. His candidacy was torpedoed when the Cardinal of Krakow invoked the veto of the Austrian emperor, who considered Rampolla too much of a Francophile and not sufficiently friendly to the dual alliance between Austria-Hungary and Germany. Some have suggested that Rampolla was vetoed because he had seemed to befriend the anti-Semitic party of Karl Lueger of Vienna.[82] Whatever the motivation, the veto proved an important factor in the search for an alternative, a less political and more pastoral candidate, who was found in the patriarch of Venice, Cardinal Giuseppe Melchiore Sarto, on 4 August 1903.[83] Sarto, who chose the name Pius Decimus (Pius X) in memory of Pius IX, asked the conservative Cardinal Rafaelle Merry del Val to serve as his secretary of state, and on Sunday, 9 August 1903, was

80. "Testem benevolentiae nostrae," 22 Jan. 1899, in Wynne, *Great Encyclical Letters of Pope Leo XIII*, 445.

81. Documents in the Archivio della Delegazione Apostolica negli Stati Uniti through January 1922 are available in the ASV.

82. Chadwick, *History of the Popes*, 381.

83. In ASV, SS, see the documents in Morte di Pontefici e Conclavi, Pio X, index 1186.

crowned with the triple tiara.[84] From peasant stock, Pius, like his name-sake, had long shown himself staunchly opposed to secular liberalism and to the notion that there could be a compromise between rationalism and religion, defining himself as "intransigent to the core."[85] At the same time, this warm-hearted pope deplored ceremony and ostentation, refused to eat meals alone, and would not permit visitors to remain on their knees during audiences.[86]

Although ultraconservative and suspicious of innovation, Pius was not hostile to Jews or Judaism. Unlike his more aloof, aristocratic, and diplo-matic predecessor, Sarto had formed close relations with a number of in-dividual Jews—the oldest and closet of these was with Leone Romanin Jacur and his family—and had close and cordial relations with a number of Italian Jewish communities.[87] Indeed, while at Mantua he had relied on the generosity of a number of Jewish families, as he later did in Venice. Thus, when Sarto was asked by Pope Leo who were the best Christians in the city, the bishop supposedly responded, "To tell the truth, as far as char-ity is concerned, the best Christians are the Jews." Sarto was familiar with, and respectful of, Jewish law and practice. When a Jewish peddler called at the bishop's residence in Mantua on the Sabbath, he reportedly rebuked him, saying, "You are a bad Jew because you don't respect your religion," and warned him, "if I catch you working on Saturday again, I'll bar you from the bishopric." He continued to have a high opinion of Jews after be-coming pope and was not burdened by the traditional anti-Judaic stereo-types prevailing in the Vatican. In fact, he told the editor of *L'Osservatore Romano* that he "often found them [the Jews] to be upright and trustwor-thy people." He was particularly close to conservative Jews who shared his religious outlook; there is no evidence that he ever said anything to dis-parage the Jewish faith. And there is evidence that he was instrumental in ending the twenty-year anti-Judaic campaign waged in Italy by the clerical

84. Hartwell de La Garde Grissell, *Sede Vacante, Being a Diary Written during the Con-clave of 1903* (London: James Parker, 1903), 48; Amleto Giovanni Cicognani, *A Symposium on the Life and Work of Pope Pius X* (Washington, D.C.: Confraternity of Christian Doctrine, 1946), 13–14; Cardinal Merry del Val, *Memories of Pope Pius X* (Westminster, Md.: Newman Press, 1951), 1–8.

85. Merry del Val, *Memories of Pope Pius X*, 35, 58; Ernesto Vercesi, *Il movimento catolico in Italia (1870–1922)* (Florence: La Voce, 1923), 99.

86. Chadwick, *History of the Popes*, 345.

87. Moro, *Chiesa e lo stermino degli ebei*, 59.

party.[88] Pius X's attitude toward the Jews was reflected in the *Civiltà Cattolica,* which in 1903 adopted a less polemical and more positive approach toward Jews.[89]

Liberals discounted Pius X's humane attitude toward Jews, harping instead on his overall conservative attitude. He proved to be surprisingly moderate, however, not only on the Church's relations with the Jews but also on the Vatican's stance toward the Kingdom of Italy. To be sure, he was not prepared to challenge head on the traditional Catholic attitude toward Jews, but he discouraged disparagement of their faith or their person. On the political conflict with the Kingdom of Italy, he concluded that the old antagonistic course had been detrimental to both Church and state and proposed a new approach. Critics of the Church were not satisfied, complaining that anti-Judaism and anti-Semitism must be denounced in clearer and stronger language and that Pius X's antimodernism on other issues was deplorable.

In his first encyclical, of October 1903, the new pope expressed his concern with "the disastrous state of human society today." He insisted that there could be no peace without God and that mankind could be brought back to God only through Christ. The way to Christ was through his Church, and Pius called for a return to Catholic teaching not only in doctrine but in economics and social life, in family, in school, in the use of private property, and in government.[90] More of a pastoral than a diplomatic pope, his style contrasted sharply with that of the more urbane Leo and seemed to portend a return to the intransigence of Pio Nono. The negative assessment by the "progressive forces" transcended his position on doctrinal questions and was extended to his relationship with the Jews. Likewise, his meeting with Theodore Herzl was cast in a negative light, coloring the perception of his attitude towards the Jews. Although Pius X opposed those who sought to modernize the Church by adapting Catholicism to the intellectual, moral, and social needs of the time, as well as those who sought to emancipate the faithful from ecclesiastical authority, science from dogma, and the state from the Church, he remained sensitive to human needs.

88. This account of Leo X's relations with the Jews is taken from Canepa, "Pius X and the Jews," 366–72.
89. Moro, *Chiesa e lo sterminio degli ebei,* 59.
90. "E Supremi," 4 Oct. 1903, *PE* 3:8.

Pius repeated his conservative convictions in an encyclical of March 1904, marking the thirteenth centenary of Pope Gregory the Great. There he reiterated his belief that peace in the state depended on the Church, and he catalogued the causes of the rift between the world and the Church, citing heresies, schisms, denial of the supernatural, the abandonment of true philosophy, and the development of a false historical criticism. Those who made concessions to "modern or false" science under the illusion that they could thus win converts did more harm than good. Pius considered the denial of the supernatural order the chief error of his time, from which so many others flowed. He was also critical of Christian democrats who championed the cause of the lower classes but who, in their mania to promote their material well-being, ignored their spiritual welfare. "The times are indeed greatly changed," he wrote, but "nothing is changed in the life of the Church."[91] And in spite of his personal friendliness toward Jews, and his appreciation of Judaism as the basis of Christianity, he followed a string of popes, from Gregory XVI to Leo XIII, in his opposition to the religious liberty the papacy termed indifferentism.[92]

Like his predecessors, Pius was concerned about the Church's position in the Holy Land, the cradle of Christianity, whose indigenous Christian population remained among the oldest in the world.[93] At the opening of his pontificate, the Vatican supported some thirty orders and associations there, some twenty convents and monasteries, and eighteen hospices and five hospitals.[94] Although the founder of Zionism, Theodore Herzl, again promised extraterritorial status for the Christian shrines in the Holy Land, Pius had serious reservations about his movement. Nonetheless, at the beginning of 1904, the pope decided to meet with Herzl, though Pius's Jewish friend Leone Romanin, who opposed Zionism, would not.

Some were unhappy with the position the pope took during the course of the interview, but even critics acknowledged that it was significant that Pius X received Herzl, who was campaigning for a Jewish state in Palestine. Herzl described Pius as an "honest, rough-hewn village priest." Pius was honest in his response to Herzl's plea for papal assistance in establish-

91. *PE* 3:27.

92. "Acerbo Nimis," 15 April 1905, *PP* 1:69.

93. Kreutz, *Vatican Policy on the Palestinian-Israeli Conflict*, 19.

94. Sergio I. Minerbi, *The Vatican and Zionism: Conflict in the Holy Land, 1895–1925*, trans. A. Schwarz (New York: Oxford University Press, 1992), 6.

ing a Jewish homeland in Palestine, making it clear that as head of the Church he could never favor such a development, though neither was it in his power to stop it. At the end of the interview he told Herzl, "If you come to Palestine and settle your people there, we shall have churches and priests ready to baptize you all." This banter reflected Pius X's close relationship to the Jews rather than any hostility to them. "I have always been on good terms with Jews," he confided to Herzl during their meeting. "After all, there are other bonds than those of religion: courtesy and philanthropy. These we do not deny to the Jews. Indeed, we also pray for them." Likewise Pius's secretary of state, Merry del Val, had good relations with Jews, confessing that "the history of Israel is our heritage, it is our foundation." Some weeks after the pope met with Herzl and Merry del Val, the latter met with Herzl's associate, Heinrich York Steiner, promising that if the Jews wished to establish agricultural colonies in Palestine, he would deem it a humanitarian effort and would not attempt to impede it.[95] He kept this promise.

Papal opposition to Zionist assumption of political control over the Holy Land did not reflect a negative attitude toward Jews, nor did it indicate Pius X's position on the "Jewish problem."[96] In fact, the following year Pius dispatched a letter to the bishops of Poland asking them to restrain the faithful from attacking Jews.[97] Likewise, Pius X's opposition to the election of Ernesto Nathan in June of 1907 stemmed not from any concern about his Jewish family background but from his status as an atheist and a Freemason. Indeed, Pius openly intervened against Nathan only when the mayor of Rome delivered a violently anticlerical speech on 20 September 1910, in which he attacked papal infallibility and the Vatican's suppression of modernist movements. Although Pius condemned the discourse as "blasphemous," he never attacked the person or ethnic background of Nathan.[98]

Pius X, who perceived a grave and pernicious conspiracy against the Church of Christ, reacted strongly against those he considered suspect.[99]

95. The account of Pius's meeting with Hertzl, including quotations, are from Kertzer, *Popes against the Jews*, 223, and Kreutz, *Vatican Policy on the Palestinian-Israeli Conflict*, 33.
96. Canepa, "Pius X and the Jews," 364.
97. *ASS* 38 (1905–6): 321–27.
98. Canepa, "Pius X and the Jews," 364–65.
99. Consult the papers in the Spoglio Pio X, SS, ASV, as well as those of the Archivio Particolare Pio X of the ASV.

Many of his condemnations were catalogued in the decree *Lamentabili* of July 1907, in which he denounced the erroneous propositions heralded as progress. But this was a condemnation of errors within the Church rather than an attack on those outside its domain, such as the Jews. Pius encouraged, if he did not publicly support, the work of the anti-Semitic Umberto Benigni, not because he shared his dislike of the Jews and Judaism but because he favored Benigni's clandestine campaign against the modernist movement within the Church by means of his *Soldalitum pianum*.[100] Benigni, who railed against "Jewish-Masonic" sects, ended his life as a Fascist.

Lamentabili condemned sixty-five propositions, exposing misconceptions about the authority of the Church, Holy Scripture, revelation, the faith, dogma, the person of Christ, the sacraments, and the principles of evolution.[101] This was followed in September 1907 by Pius X's encyclical *Pascendi dominici gregis*, on the modernists, whom he accused of a foolish infatuation with ideas and practices that contradicted Church principles. Here the pope grouped a number of heresies under the term modernism, which he defined as the "synthesis of all heresies." He warned that the partisans of error were found not only among the Church's enemies but in her very clergy. He could not concur with those who demanded a rationalistic theology, a democratization of the government of the Church, and a decentralization of its administration.[102] Reaffirming the decree *Lamentabili* and the encyclical *Pascendi*, Pius prescribed excommunication for those who contradicted them, denouncing both the persecution of the Church from without and the civil war waged from within.[103] In 1910 he constrained the clergy to take the modernist oath against innovative philosophy and practice, which survived until 1967, when Paul VI abolished it.[104]

The papal war against modernism widened the rift between the Vatican and the world that Leo had sought to close, and it virtually undermined the *Ralliement*. It contributed to the republic's separation of Church and state in France in 1905, which Pius denounced as disastrous to

100. The records of the Fondo Umberto Benigni of the ASV are partially open up to January 1922.

101. Hergenrother, *Storia universale della Chiesa,* 767; Igino Giordani, *Pius X: A Country Priest,* trans. Thomas J. Tobin (Milwaukee: Bruce Publishing, 1954), 154.

102. "Pascendi dominici gregis," 8 Sept. 1907, *PE* 3:71–98; Giordani, *Pius X: A Country Priest,* 154–56.

103. "Haerent animo," 4 Aug. 1908, *PP* 2:73.

104. Chadwick, *History of the Popes,* 355.

society as well as religion.[105] The pope viewed that separation as another attempt to destroy the Church, de-Christianize France, and undermine the position of Catholics there.[106] To add to his consternation, in 1911 the Portuguese republic promulgated a similar law separating Church and state, provoking another papal condemnation.[107] The sense that Catholicism was under siege in much of Europe led Pius in 1904 to partially lift the *non-expedit*, prohibiting Catholics from taking part in national elections in Italy. This move was made concrete in an encyclical of June 1905, which allowed the bishops to decide whether Catholics in their care should participate in national elections.[108] It represented a first tentative step in the resolution of "the Roman question." Pius also dispatched a letter to the Polish bishops, publicly condemning the new pogroms against the Jews in Russia.[109]

Pius X's reconciliation with the Italian state led him to curb the Catholic press campaign in the peninsula against liberalism, secularism, and Judaism.[110] He also questioned the basis of Action Française's anti-Semitism, which he saw as more racial than religious. Thus, while many of Charles Maurras's anti-Semitic political views found resonance in Rome, his theological positions, including that on the Jews, were perceived to be in glaring violation of Church doctrine. Under the pope's direction, the Congregation of the Index had decided to condemn Maurras's works, and Pius in his last year of life signed the condemnation of the Action Française but withheld its publication.[111] In the words of one Jewish historian, his relations with the Jews were "exemplary."[112] This pope was also critical of anti-Semitism in eastern Europe. He deplored the calumnies

105. "Vehementer nos," 11 Feb. 1906, *PE* 3:45–51; Giordani, *Pius X: A Country Priest*, 105; Katherine Burton, *The Great Mantle: The Life of Giuseppe Melchiore Sarto, Pope Pius X* (Dublin: Clonmore and Reynolds, 1950), 176–82.

106. "Gravissimo officii munere," 10 Aug. 1906, *PE* 3:63–65; "Une fois encore," 6 Jan. 1907, *PE* 3:67–70; Giordani, *Pius X: A Country Priest*, 108.

107. "Iamdudum," 24 May 1911, *PE* 3:127–30; Cicognani, *Symposium on the Life and Work of Pope Pius X*, 30–31.

108. G. Suardi, "Quando e come I Cattolici poterono partecipare alle elezioni politiche," *Nuova Antologia* 306 (Nov.–Dec. 1927): 118–23; "Il fermo proposito," 11 June 1905, *PE* 3:37–44.

109. Moro, *Chiesa e lo stermino degli ebei*, 59.

110. Canepa, "Pius X and the Jews," 370.

111. R. E. Balfour, "The Action Française Movement," *Cambridge Historical Journal* 3, no. 2 (1930): 197–98, 202.

112. Lapide, *Three Popes and the Jews*, 83.

hurled at the Jews of Kiev who were accused of ritual murder in 1913, and promised that the Holy See would use all its means to prevent harm to the poor and falsely accused population. Pius was likewise distressed by the Beilis affair (1911–13), which exposed the depth of anti-Semitism in Russia. At his death, Italy's leading Jewish periodical, *Il Versillo israelitico,* noted that Pius X had been the only European sovereign to protest the pograms in Russia.[113]

Pius's moderation toward the Jews won him little support in Italy or abroad, while his war on modernism and continuing conflict with a number of states undermined both his reputation and his health, contributing to his death in 1914. During his last years, he foresaw the outbreak of a disastrous war of horrific consequences, predicting that it would erupt before the close of 1914. When the conflagration began at the end of July 1914, Pius's nightmare materialized.[114] His prayer for peace unanswered, he prayed for his successor, who would have to confront the disastrous consequences.

The conclave that opened in Rome at the end of August met while the war raged in Europe, and the cardinals sought a pope who could address the threats confronting the peoples of Europe and the Church. Both inside and outside the conclave there was talk of the need for an interventionist pope such as Leo XIII, who had addressed international concerns, rather than a pastoral one like Pius X, who had focused more on internal Church issues. On 3 September the sixty-year-old Giacomo Giambattista Della Chiesa, Archbishop of Bologna, was elected pope.[115] Giacomo had studied as a day student in the diocesan seminary, and then at the University of Genoa law school, receiving a degree in civil law in 1875. Determined to enter the priesthood, he enrolled in the Roman Seminary of the Capranica, while studying theology, history, and canon law at the Jesuit University of the Gregoriana. He was ordained a priest in December 1878 and received a doctorate in theology in 1879, and another, in canon law, in 1880. While at the Academy of Noble Ecclesiastics in Rome training for a diplomatic career, Della Chiesa impressed Monsignor Mariano Rampolla del Tindaro, who in 1882 named him an apprentice in the Congregation of Ex-

113. Canepa, "Pius X and the Jews," 369.
114. Merry del Val, *Memories of Pope Pius X,* 19–20; Giordani, *Pius X: A Country Priest,* 197–98; "Guerra (1914–1918)," ASV, SS.
115. ASV, SS, "Morte di Pontefici e Conclavi, Benedetto XV," index 1186 (I–IV).

traordinary Affairs. At the end of that year, when Rampolla was appointed nuncio to Spain, he brought Della Chiesa along as his secretary. When the archbishop was recalled to Rome as secretary of state and cardinal in 1887, Della Chiesa returned with him and in 1901 was named undersecretary of state. In 1907 he was appointed to the cardinalate See of Bologna, but he was not made a cardinal until May 1914, just in time to participate in the conclave of 1914, and to secure election as Benedict XV.

Benedict confronted two major problems: internationally the horror of the world war, and internally the tension within the Church provoked by integralism, which championed a close union between Church and state.[116] To assist him in dealing with these issues, Benedict chose the Francophile Domenico Cardinal Ferrata for his secretary of state, but Ferrata died almost immediately from appendicitis. Within days Benedict selected another Francophile, and a disciple of Rampolla, Pietro Gasparri (1852–1934). Both nominations were based on the papal desire to improve relations with the French republic and enhance the Vatican's diplomatic position. Diplomatic considerations as well as religious convictions may have led the new pope to sever all connections with the anti-Semitic Benigni. Clearly, Benedict XV sought to chart a new course for papal-Jewish relations, and during his pontificate the anti-Jewish campaign in the *Civiltà Cattolica* and the *Osservatore Romano* was curtailed.[117]

Two days after his coronation, Benedict released an exhortation, *Ubi primum*, to the Catholics of the world, expressing his determination to hasten the end of the war he branded "the scourge of the wrath of God." Determined to preserve papal impartiality, he did not believe the Church should or could take sides. Benedict urged the charitable treatment of all captives, regardless of religion or nationality.[118] On numerous occasions Cardinal Gasparri explained that the Holy Father sought to mitigate the consequences of the war for all, without distinction of party, nationality, or religion.[119] His search for common ground among the belligerents earned him the scorn and abuse of both sides.

116. In the ASV, see Archivio Particolare Benedetto XV, and in the SS of the ASV, the Spoglio Benedetto XV.

117. Kertzer, *Popes against the Jews,* 240–41.

118. "The Pope and the War," *Times* (London), 6 Sept. 1914; Koenig, *Principles for Peace,* 128–30.

119. Cardinal Gasparri to Cardinal Amette, Archbishop of Paris, 23 April 1915, in Koenig, *Principles for Peace,* 164.

Concerned with the war against modernism within the Church, Benedict's main focus remained bringing the world war to an end. He explained that the Holy See was not and did not wish to be neutral in the European war, but had the duty to remain impartial. The distinction was understood by neither camp, and paradoxically both accused the Holy See of favoring the other side.[120] Moved by the suffering of the Belgians, the pope prayed for the end of their misfortunes, but he did not condemn the German aggression.[121] This "silence" on the part of the pope, coupled with the fact that he openly supported German efforts to keep Italy neutral, aroused angry public sentiment in the allied countries. Word spread that Benedict had advised Franz-Josef, by means of his nuncio in Vienna, to cede the Trentino to Italy to avert Italian intervention. Nor were the Allies pleased by the pope's directive to Monsignor Eugenio Pacelli, secretary of the Congregation of Extraordinary Ecclesiastical Affairs, to instruct bishops and the clergy to care for the spiritual and material welfare of prisoners of war in their countries.[122]

In the spring, the pope prayed that Italy would not become embroiled in the conflict, issuing new prayers for peace to be recited during May devotions. On 26 April 1915 the Italian government signed the Treaty of London, which called for Italian intervention and prohibited the Vatican, under article XV, from having a seat at the peace conference.[123] On 24 May Italy declared war against Austria, creating new difficulties for the Vatican. Although Sidney Sonnino, the Italian foreign minister, assured full liberty to the representatives of the enemy powers to the Vatican,[124] the representatives of the Central Powers, appreciating the difficulty of their position, left the Vatican for Lugano, Switzerland. Benedict was haunted by the war's devastation. In September he asked President Woodrow Wilson to appeal to the warring nations to stop the bloodshed. The *New York Times* reported that the pope had asked Wilson to present the belligerents with a

120. In this regard, see G. Anaud d'Agnel, *Benoit XV et le conflit Europeen* (Paris: Lethielleux, 1916), and Anthony Brennan, *Pope Benedict XV and the War* (London: King, 1917); "Pope Eager to Convince the World at Large of His 'Absolute Impartiality' in the War," *New York Times*, 24 July 1916.

121. "The Pope's Sympathy with Belgium," *Times* (London), 17 Dec. 1914.

122. Koenig, *Principles for Peace*, 140–44.

123. Thomas E. Hachey, ed., *Anglo-Vatican Relations, 1914–1939: Confidential Reports of the British Minister to the Holy See* (Boston: G. K. Hall, 1972), 19.

124. Sidney Sonnino, *Diario, 1914–1916*, ed. Pietro Pastorelli (Bari: Laterza, 1972), 101.

proposal for a cessation of hostilities in the hope that in time a resolution of their differences might be ironed out.[125]

Pope Benedict regretted the persecution of the Jews in the Polish territories by the retreating Russian forces, and he reportedly denounced this violence in a series of secret meetings with Jewish representatives from France, Great Britain, and the United States. During his discussion with the French Jew Lucien Perquel in May 1915, Benedict supposedly revealed his willingness to defend the Jews and denounce the Russian persecution in an encyclical marking the first anniversary of the war's outbreak. In return, the pope allegedly asked the Jewish communities of France, Britain, and America to use their influence to persuade their governments to offer the Holy See a seat at the postwar conference, and to support an independent Poland. The plan allegedly collapsed because the French and British Jewish groups eventually rejected the papal bargain, which they felt might "involve the whole Jewish community in extremely serious dangers." Although this episode is based on documentation found in the Archives Alliance Isralie Universelle (AAIU) and the exposition of Pawel Korzec, it does not ring true.[126] It would be uncharacteristic of the cautious Benedict to assume a partisan stance that compromised his cherished impartiality. Moreover, by May he was probably privy to the Treaty of London signed by Britain, France, and Russia in April, which assured Italy that the Vatican would not be invited to the peace conference. In addition, it would have been extremely difficult to draft and edit a major encyclical in a mere two months. And finally, the projected encyclical would have antagonized the Allies and undermined papal attempts to mediate a peace—Benedict's major preoccupation.

At the end of 1915 the pope called for an exchange of ideas, as well as the willingness of the belligerents to make concessions, thoughts he repeated in his Christmas allocution.[127] The new year brought little relief to the stricken pontiff, who continued his campaign to alleviate the suffering

125. "Pope Asks Wilson to Send Peace Appeal to the Warring Powers, but President Awaits Their Call," *New York Times*, 3 Sept. 1915.

126. Kertzer, *Popes against the Jews*, 242. Kertzer cites Korzec's article "Les relations entre le Vatican et les organisations juives pendant la premiere guerre mondiale," in *Revue d'historire moderne et contemporaine* 20 (1973): 301–33, and the Korzec volume *Juifs en Pologne. La question juive pendant d'entre-deux guerres* (Paris: Presses de la Fondation Nationale des Sciences Politiques, 1980).

127. "E pur troppo vero," 24 Dec. 1915, in Koenig, *Principles for Peace*, 193–97.

and slaughter. Early in February 1916 his secretary of state, Cardinal Gasparri, responded to the pleas and petitions of the American Jewish Committee of New York, which had called on the pope to use his moral authority to halt mistreatment of the Jews. At Benedict's behest, Gasparri wrote back that the Holy Father, like the 3 million Jewish U.S. citizens whom the committee represented, deplored the suffering of Jews and others during the terrible conflagration.

> The Supreme Pontiff . . . on principle, as Head of the Catholic Church, which faithful to its divine doctrine and to its most glorious traditions, considers all men as brothers and teaches them to love one another, he never ceases to inculcate among individuals, as well as among people, the observance of the principles of natural law and to condemn everything which violates them. This law must be observed and respected in the case of the children of Israel, as well as of all others, because it would not be conformable to justice or to religion itself to derogate from it solely on account of divergence of religious confessions.[128]

Gasparri concluded by saying that Pope Benedict rejoiced in the religious harmony that prevailed in the United States, convinced that it contributed to the peaceful prosperity there. Unwilling to contradict earlier Church criticism of religious liberty, Gasparri and Benedict diplomatically skirted the issue in their statement, though most regarded it as the bedrock of American religious harmony.

Gasparri's letter was given wide publicity and published in the *Civiltà Cattolica* and in the *Tablet* of London. The *New York Times* exaggerated its nature and impact in an article published under the headline "Papal Bull Urges Equality for Jews." For one thing, this was a private letter, not a papal bull. For another, while the letter called for observance of the principles of natural law toward all people, it said nothing about equality of civil rights, much less about religious equality. It also studiously avoided condemning either belligerent camp. The Holy See, seeking a voice in future peace negotiations, cautiously sought to preserve the strictest impartiality, an approach that influenced Pius XII's actions during World War II as well. Benedict's Christmas appeal for peace of 24 December 1916, like his earlier ones, avoided any form of partisanship.[129]

128. Cardinal Gasparri to the American Jewish Committee of New York, 9 Feb. 1916, in Koenig, *Principles for Peace*, 199.
129. Rhonheimer, "Holocaust: What Was Not Said," 4; "Ancora una volta," 24 Dec. 1916,

In April 1917 Benedict appointed Eugenio Pacelli nuncio to Bavaria, and in May his envoy presented his credentials to King Ludwig III and met with the German chancellor, Theobald von Bethmann-Hollweg. On 1 August Benedict transmitted his peace note to the belligerents. Commencing with the overriding proposition that the moral force of right should be substituted for the material force of arms, the pope proposed a number of points to achieve this goal, including (1) a simultaneous and reciprocal decrease in armaments, (2) the institution of international arbitration as a substitute for armies, (3) free intercourse of peoples and true liberty of the seas, (4) the reciprocal renunciation of war indemnities, (5) the evacuation and restoration of all occupied territories, and finally, (6) the resolution of political and territorial claims, undertaken in a spirit of equity and justice. The pope prayed that his invitation to make peace would be accepted.[130] Public opinion on both sides of the war recognized the importance of the pope's initiative. The *New York Evening Post* called it "a diplomatic and international event of the first rank."[131]

Although the note said nothing about the future of Palestine, an issue that very much interested the Vatican, and ignored the "Roman question," it was not as well received by the belligerents as by the press and public. One of Benedict's few happy moments during the war came with the British liberation of the Holy Land from the Turks at the end of 1917, although the pope, curia, and clericals throughout Europe remained suspicious of Jewish ambitions in the Holy Land.[132] Abandoning the Vatican's impartial stance, Cardinal Gasparri dispatched his congratulations to the British envoy on 16 December 1917, while the *Osservatore Romano* proclaimed the liberation a "victory for Christian civilization."[133] This riled the Central Powers, who complained that it was a violation of the Vatican's self-professed impartiality. Cardinal Gasparri admitted as much when he replied that in dealing with the liberation of the Holy Land from the infidel, the Holy See perforce had to take sides.

Although he was delighted by the liberation of Palestine, Pope Benedict expressed concern about the impact of the "British Declaration of

---

in Koenig, *Principles for Peace,* 221–22; Walter H. Peters, *The Life of Benedict XV* (St. Paul, Minn.: Bruce Publishing, 1959), 140–45.

130. "Des le Debut," 1 Aug. 1917, in Koenig, *Principles for Peace,* 232.

131. "The Pope Acts," *New York Evening Post,* 14 Aug. 1917.

132. Moro, *Chiesa e lo stermino degli ebei,* 61.

133. *OR,* 15 Dec. 1917.

Sympathy with Zionist Aspirations" issued by the British foreign secretary, Lord Arthur James Balfour, on 2 November 1917, which seemed to promise the Jews territorial rights in the Holy Land. Benedict expressed his benevolence toward the Jews to the British representative, but he opposed conceding them direct control over the area to the detriment of Christian interests.[134] Thus the pope, who had earlier viewed the Jewish return to Palestine as providential and miraculous, followed his predecessors in opposing the creation of a Jewish state there. Cardinal Gasparri was even more outspoken. "It is hard to take back that part of our heart which has been given over to the Turks in order to give it to the Zionists," he complained.[135] The talk of a British mandate over the area led the pope and his secretary of state to fear that their rights in the Holy Land would be ignored and their position undermined. Furthermore, since the Treaty of London excluded their participation at the peace conference, they could not represent their own interests directly, as Consalvi had done at the Congress of Vienna in 1815.

Meanwhile, the Vatican was pleased by President Wilson's address to the American Congress early in January, in which proposed his "fourteen points" as a basis for negotiation.[136] Both the pope and Cardinal Gasparri were optimistic about the impact of Wilson's speech. The cardinal secretary of state hoped it would lead to talks, providing the starting point for negotiations for a just and lasting peace. Benedict lamented that his attempts to bring about peace had been scandalously misinterpreted by the enemies of the Church, although he predicted that these efforts would be understood by all those who were fair-minded, once the war was over.[137]

134. Kreutz, Vatican Policy on the Palestinian-Israeli Conflict, 36, 39–40.

135. Quoted in Minerbi, Vatican and Zionism, xiii.

136. Wilson's fourteen points called for (1) agreements to be openly arrived at and the renunciation of secret diplomacy, (2) freedom of the seas in war and peace, (3) efforts to remove economic barriers between nations, (4) the reduction of armaments, (5) the impartial adjustment of colonial claims, (6) evacuation and restoration of Russian territory, (7) restoration of Belgian sovereignty, (8) the evacuation of France and the return of Alsace-Lorraine, (9) redrawing the Italian frontier along national lines, (10) autonomy for the peoples of Austria-Hungary, (11) the evacuation of Montenegro, Romania, and Serbia, and access to the sea for Serbia, (12) self-determination for the peoples of the Ottoman Empire and freedom of navigation through the Dardenelles, (13) establishment of an independent Poland with access to the sea, and (14) the creation of a general association of nations to guarantee the independence of all.

137. "Address Pleases Vatican," New York Evening Post, 15 Feb. 1918; Koenig, Principles for Peace, 246–54.

To assist in that endeavor, Benedict authorized the publication of a papal white book to gather all the diplomatic efforts and correspondence of the Vatican since the opening of the war.[138]

In his Easter message to the United States, Pope Benedict expressed the hope for a lasting settlement and the creation of a new organization of peoples and nations aspiring to a "nobler, purer, and kinder civilization." Likewise, in his talk to the delegates from Finland, Benedict proclaimed that the Holy See recognized the same rights for small nations as for large, and hoped to see this more universally accepted in the postwar period.[139] At the beginning of December, Benedict wrote an encyclical on the general armistice of 11 November 1918, which brought about what the faithful had advocated for years. Looking ahead, he called upon Catholics to pray for divine assistance for all those who would take part in the peace conference, that they might produce a true peace founded on Christian principles of justice. He covered the same ground in his Christmas Eve allocution, which stressed that social unity and international harmony had to be based on benevolence rather than hatred.[140]

On 4 January 1919 the pope met with President Wilson, the first chief of the United States ever received by the supreme pontiff. Despite rumors, the "Roman question" was not broached, nor did Benedict attempt to gain a seat at the impending peace negotiations. This was confirmed by the British representative at the Vatican, Viscount John Francis De Salis, who noted that Cardinal Gasparri had not tried to interject himself and that the Holy See would serve as mediator only when both sides requested its participation.[141] It is very likely that allegations that the Vatican had tried to force itself into the peace process were fed in part by the paranoia of the Italians, which was aggravated when Benedict dispatched Monsignor Bonaventura Cerretti to Versailles. In fact, the task of this papal envoy was to safeguard the position of the missions in the former German colonies and make known the papal stance on the Holy Land and the position of

138. "Papal White Book Soon," *New York Times*, 2 Feb. 1918; "Pope Works on White Book," ibid., 10 Feb. 1918.

139. "Papal Peace Message Is Sent to America," ibid., 23 March 1918; "Discourse to the Delegates from Finland," 2 March 1918, in Koenig, *Principles for Peace*, 247.

140. "Quod Iam Diu," *PE* 3:161–62; "E la Quinta Volta," 24 Dec. 1918, in Koenig, *Principles for Peace*, 261–65.

141. Peters, *Life of Benedict XV*, 167; "Report on Mission to Holy See, Count de Salis to Marquis Curzon," 25 Oct. 1922, in Hachey, *Anglo-Vatican Relations, 1914–1939*, 12.

Catholics and Jews there. The concern for the missions inspired Benedict's apostolic epistle on the propagation of the faith throughout the world at the end of 1919, the charter of the missionary movement of modern times.[142] Benedict was ecumenical in his outreach, even appealing to Lenin and the Soviet Union through his secretary of state, who telegraphed the Soviet leader, imploring religious toleration for all faiths. "The Holy Father abjures you to give strict orders that the servants of every religion be respected," Gasparri wrote, adding, "humanity and religion will be grateful to you."[143] Benedict and Gasparri increasingly moved away from the Vatican's nineteenth-century insistence on the primacy of Catholicism and the subordination of other faiths—including the Jewish one. Unwilling to expose contradictions or sow discord within a Church where the condemnation of indifferentism still prevailed, they did so without releasing a specific encyclical or statement on the subject.

Both the pope and his secretary of state were much more explicit in supporting the creation of a new international order, as Benedict made clear in his Easter message of 1918. But Benedict was less than pleased with the results of the peacemaking process and its discussion of the future administration of the holy places in Jerusalem and the rest of the Holy Land. In his encyclical at the end of the war, he continued to urge nations to resume cordial relations as soon as possible by clearing their hearts of bitterness and opening them to mutual love, concord, and Christian charity.[144]

The treaties emanating from Paris did little to reassure the pontiff, who feared that the embers of war still smoldered. He was upset by the emergence of communism in Russia and radical movements in Germany. Neither he nor the Church could sanction the program of the new Nazi Party, born 25 February 1920, which specified that only those of German blood, regardless of religion, could be considered members of the nation. Benedict also continued to be concerned about the situation in Palestine, long considered holy by Christians and one of the great pilgrimage places of the world. He was determined to assure the "inalienable rights" of the Church there. With this end in mind, in May 1917 he founded the Congregation for Eastern Churches, which he personally directed, and in June

142. "Maximum illud," 30 Nov. 1919, *PP* 1:83.
143. Gasparri to Lenin, 12 March 1919, in Koenig, *Principles for Peace,* 269.
144. Minerbi, *Vatican and Zionism,* 17, 28; "Pacem Dei Munus Pulcherrimum," 23 May 1920, *PP* 1:171–75.

1919 he had a branch of the Biblical Institute at Rome erected in Jerusalem.[145] Regarding the British mandate in Palestine, in an allocution of 13 June 1921 Benedict expressly stated, "We do not wish to deprive the Jews of their rights; we want, nevertheless, that they be not in any way preferred to the just rights of the Christians."[146] Indeed, Cardinal Gasparri complained about the draft British proposal Lord Balfour presented on 7 December 1920, which he believed would establish the economic and political predominance of the Jews in the Holy Land. At the same time, the Vatican considered the prospect of an Arab administration there unreliable and therefore unacceptable.[147]

There was some hope in the Vatican that the conflicting positions of the Church and the Zionists over the Holy Land would be resolved at the international conference held at San Remo in April 1920. Among other issues to be considered was that of preserving the special status of the French regarding the holy places, and the possible creation of a special international commission to administer these sites. Although the conference granted Britain the mandate for Palestine, neither of the other two objectives was attained. A number of Vatican aims were thwarted, including the internationalization that would have accorded Catholic countries, especially France and Belgium, special protective rights. Instead, the British were accorded exclusive control. Furthermore, there was some concern at the Vatican when the British appointed Sir Herbert Samuel as first high commissioner in Palestine, not so much because he was a Jew as because he was known to be sympathetic to the Zionist program. To allay these fears, Samuel visited Rome on the way to his new post and was received by both Benedict XV and Cardinal Gasparri on 25 June 1920.[148] Rome was not reassured by the promises provided for its position in the Holy Land, and this encouraged it to facilitate the reopening of relations with the Paris government, whose support on this issue it hoped to garner. Disappointed by the position accorded the Church in the Holy Land and the other consequences of the peace, at the end of December 1921 Benedict caught a cold, which he neglected and which developed into a bronchial infection. He died on 22 January 1922.

145. "Pontificium," 29 June 1919, *PP* 1:82.

146. Quoted in James H. Ryan, "The Vatican's World Policy," *New York Times Magazine,* Dec. 1922, 437; *Brooklyn Tablet,* 25 June 1921.

147. Kreutz, *Vatican Policy on the Palestinian-Israeli Conflict,* 44.

148. Minerbi, *Vatican and Zionism,* 32.

5

PIUS XI AND THE JEWS IN AN AGE OF DICTATORS,
1922-1939

The banner is at last unfurled:
Chief Rabbi of the Christian World. *

AFTER THE DEATH OF BENEDICT XV IN JANUARY 1922, Achille Ratti, the Cardinal Archbishop of Milan, was elected pope and assumed the name Pius in honor of Pius IX, whom he admired. Ordained a priest at the end of 1879, following study at the Gregorian University and the Sapienza in Rome, he received degrees in philosophy, theology, and law. He was summoned to Rome in 1910 to serve as vice-prefect of the Vatican Library, becoming its prefect in 1914. Ratti had to abandon this refuge in 1918, when he was appointed apostolic visitor to Poland. During his visit to Sandomierz, Ratti met with its rabbi and the leaders of the synagogue, reminding Polish Jews, about one-tenth of the population, of "the justice and charity that the pontiff had always shown [the Jews], including in Rome itself."[1]

Following the creation of the Polish state in 1919, Ratti was dispatched there as nuncio.[2] Queried about the pogroms against Polish Jews, Ratti described the situation as unclear, noting, "the Jews blame the Christians,

---

* Concluding lines of the poem in *Das Schwarze Korps,* critical of Pius XI's efforts on behalf of the Jews, in *The Persecution of the Catholic Church in the Third Reich: Facts and Documents* (London: Burns and Oates, 1940), 427.

1. Quoted in Kertzer, *Popes against the Jews,* 250.

2. Documents up to January 1922 are available in the Archivio della Nunziatura Apostolica in Varsavia of the ASV.

and the Christians blame the Jews."[3] Perhaps influenced by the Judeophobic members of the hierarchy, he hesitated to condemn the brutal persecution. Ratti focused on "matters strictly ecclesiastical," seeking to determine the changes required in the church structure in the new state.[4] Violence against the Jews was not his primary preoccupation. In fact, during his days in the Polish republic he became increasingly obsessed with the communist menace. By 1921, when he became archbishop of Milan and a cardinal, he was a confirmed anticommunist, and like many in the Polish hierarchy perceived a link between the Jews and the Communists. Claiming that most of the commissars of the Bolshevik regiments were Jews, he was convinced that de-Christianization in Russia was fueled by the Jewish aversion to Christianity.[5]

More academically inclined than politically astute, Ratti imbibed the anti-Semitic stereotypes that prevailed in certain Polish circles and the anti-Judaism that lingered in the Vatican, sometimes merging the two in his rhetoric. Suspicious of the political arena, after he became pope he preferred to secure ecclesiastical interests through concordats rather than political jockeying.[6] He has been criticized for concluding concordats with the Fascist state in 1929 and the Third Reich in 1933, and for legitimizing these regimes while abandoning the Popular Party in Italy and the Center Party in Germany.[7] Critics charge that Pius XI contributed to the success of the fascist dictatorships that championed territorial revision and racism. One scholar has written that this pope "offered few objections to the Italian racial laws," a view supported by others, who concur that he "failed to assume a determined opposition against the racism of Fascist Italy."[8] Presumably Pius XI's anti-Judaism and conciliatory approach toward Nazi Germany served as a precursor to that of Pius XII.

3. Kertzer, *Popes against the Jews*, 256.

4. Koenig, *Principles for Peace*, 249.

5. Renato Moro, "Le premesse dell'atteggiamento cattolico di fronte alla legislazione razziale fascista. Cattolici ed ebrei nell' Italia degli anni venti (1919–1932)," *Storia Contemporanea* 19 (Dec. 1988): 1118; Moro, *Chiesa e lo sterminio degli ebrei*, 67.

6. Concordats had earlier been concluded with a number of German states. ASV, SS, Rapporti con gli stati, AS; AAES, Germania, 1922–39, posizione 507, fascicoli 16–17.

7. For the Vatican's relations with the Center Party of Germany, see ASV, SS, Rapporti con gli stati, AS, AAES, Germania, 1922–39, posizione 523, fascicoli 33–35.

8. Susan Zuccotti, *The Italians and the Holocaust: Persecution, Rescue, and Survival* (New York: Basic Books, 1987), 61; Antonio Pellicani, *Il Papa di tutti. La Chiesa Cattolica, il fascismo, e il razzismo, 1929–1945* (Milan: Sugar Editore, 1964), 103.

It has been difficult for scholars to explore Pius XI's attitude toward the Jews dispassionately. Some equate the anti-Judaism of the Church with the racial anti-Semitism of Nazism and Fascism, and assume that because Pius XI's Vatican was tinged with the former, it was necessarily infected by the latter. Unquestionably, the Catholic press often expressed anti-Semitic sentiment. Thus, the *Civiltà Cattolica* in 1922, the year Ratti became pope, published an article alleging that 447 state functionaries in the Soviet Union were Jewish, as were seventeen of the twenty-one commissars.[9] Members of the World Jewish Congress, among others, perceived the dogmas and doctrines of Christianity as the breeding ground for anti-Semitism. Many concluded that the prevailing anti-Judaism in the Church facilitated, if it did not provoke, the anti-Semitism of Nazi Germany and Fascist Italy. Contemporaries such as Roberto Farinacci claimed that Mussolini's racist legislation represented the logical culmination of the anti-Judaism of the Church.[10] Such accusations led the pope to defend the Church and differentiate its religious anti-Judaism from racist anti-Semitism.

Clearly, Pius remained suspicious of both Judaism and Protestantism. Throughout the negotiations for the Lateran Accords, which were concluded with Mussolini's Italy in 1929, the pope was hostile to granting religious equality to Protestants and Jews.[11] Nonetheless, he understood that the dehumanization of Jews was anti-Christian, destructive, and dangerous long before he recognized that it might culminate in genocide. Those who stressed the chasm between the Church and Fascism insist that a majority of Catholics, including those who collaborated closely with Mussolini's regime, had serious reservations about its non-Christian methods, its neopagan convictions, and, eventually, its racism and anti-Semitism, asserting that few genuine Catholics held positions of power in the Fascist

9. "La rivoluzione mondiale e gli ebrei," *CC*, 22 Oct. 1922, in Moro, *Chiesa e lo sterminio degli ebrei*, 60.

10. Aryeh Leon Kubovy, "The Silence of Pope Pius XII and the Beginnings of the 'Jewish Document,'" in *Yad Vashem Studies of the European Jewish Catastrophe and Resistance*, ed. Nathan Eck and Aryeh Leon Kubovy (Jerusalem: Yad Vashem, 1967), 6:18; Meir Michaelis, *Mussolini and the Jews: German-Italian Relations and the Jewish Question in Italy, 1922–1945* (Oxford: Clarendon Press, 1978), 240; *Il Popolo d'Italia*, 8 Nov. 1938. For an examination of Fascist anti-Semitism, see Renzo de Felice, *Storia degli ebrei sotto il fascismo* (Turin: Einaudi, 1962); and Luigi Preti, *Impero fascista, africani ed ebrei* (Milan: Mursia, 1968).

11. Moro, *Chiesa e lo sterminio degli ebrei*, 60.

Party. They note that the Church began to disengage itself from the Fascist movement once its racism became clear. The debate continues today.[12]

At the end of his first year in office, Pius outlined the program of his pontificate. Reiterating Leo XIII's pronouncement that the Church could reconcile itself with any reasonable system of government, he warned that popular democratic governments were most subject to conflict and chaos.[13] Some interpreted these remarks as expressing approval of Mussolini's government, a perception reinforced by the fact that the Vatican did not oppose the entry of the Popular Party into it. Pius was clearly more concerned in the 1920s with the impact of communism than with fascism, as Moscow uncovered and suppressed Pius XI's efforts to consecrate new bishops and establish an underground ecclesiastical structure in the Soviet Union. Pius charged that liberalism had given birth to socialism and that bolshevism was its logical heir.[14] But Pius XI's authoritarianism and anticommunism did not include support for racism, which he believed was contrary to the faith.

Pius perceived biological hatred of the Jews not only as a violation of the moral law but as a rebellion against the reality of salvation history and the Jewish role as bearers of revelation.[15] This racism represented not only a danger to Jews but a challenge to Christianity. Papal opposition to anti-Semitism was clearly and publicly expressed to the Church curia, the Fascist Party, and the masses in Italy and abroad. As early as September 1922 the pope proclaimed that "Christian charity extends to all men whatsoever without distinction of race."[16] Still, the Church supported regimes that

12. Edward R. Tannenbaum, *The Fascist Experience: Italian Society and Culture, 1922–1945* (New York: Basic Books, 1972), 195; Giuseppe Dalla Torre, *Azione Cattolica e fascismo* (Rome, 1945), 7; Maria Cristina Giuntella, "Circoli Cattolici e organizzazioni Giovanili fasciste in Umbria," in *Cattolici e Fascisti in Umbria (1922–1945),* ed. Albertino Monticone (Bologna: Il Mulino, 1978), 31; J. Derek Holmes, *The Papacy in the Modern World, 1914–1978* (New York: Crossroad, 1981), 60; D. A. Binchey, *Church and State in Fascist Italy* (New York: Oxford University Press, 1941), 164; Michaelis, *Mussolini and the Jews,* 248–49; Georges Passelecq and Bernard Suchecky, *L'encyclique cachée de Pie XI . Une occasion manquée de l'Eglise face a l'antisémitisme,* preface, "Pie XI, les Juifs et l'antisemitisme," by Emile Poulat (Paris: Éditions La Découverte, 1995).

13. "Ubi Arcano Dei," 23 Dec. 1922, in Koenig, *Principles for Peace,* 334–35.

14. Alvarez, *Spies in the Vatican,* 228; "Quadragesimo anno" (May 1931), in Koenig, *Principles for Peace,* 435.

15. The attempt to purge Christianity of Judaism echoed the thought of Marcion (c. 85–160 C.E.), who was excommunicated in 144.

16. *Cum Tertio,* 17 Sept. 1922, in Koenig, *Principles for Peace,* 329.

championed Catholic canons while restricting other religious groups and practices, apparently approving the Spanish coup orchestrated by General Miguel Primo de Rivera in 1923. The general, who called for loyalty to religion, country, and monarchy, arranged for King Alfonso XIII (1902–31) to visit Pius XI. That the pope encouraged this visit, even though the papacy had long discouraged Catholics from visiting and thus sanctioning the Italian seizure of Rome, reflected his cordial relations with Italy.[17]

Relations with France also improved once it became apparent that Pius XI shared the republic's suspicions of the monarchical Action Française. In 1926 he condemned Charles Maurras's racist and reactionary movement, denouncing its pagan outlook and political agenda.[18] Although some eleven of the seventeen cardinals and archbishops of France were sympathetic to the Action Française, Rome persuaded Cardinal Paulin Andrieu, the Archbishop of Bordeaux, to condemn the movement in August 1926, a move Pius personally endorsed.[19] Two years later the Holy Office, with papal approval, struck out against anti-Semitism, when it suppressed the Friends of Israel, a group formed in 1926 that sought to bring about the conversion of Jews and combat anti-Semitism among Catholics. Some complained that the suppression condemned the organization's goal of overcoming the long-standing anti-Judaism in Church theology and liturgy.[20] Although the suppression seemed prompted by Vatican opposition to "unwarranted" reconciliation with the Jews, it also contained an explicit

---

17. Stanley G. Payne, "Spain: The Church, the Second Republic, and the Franco Regime," in *Catholics, the State, and the European Radical Right, 1919–1945,* ed. Richard J. Wolff and Jorg K. Hoensch (Boulder: Social Science Monographs, 1987), 183; "Il Benvenuto a Voi to the King of Spain, 19 Nov. 1923," in Koenig, *Principles for Peace,* 367–68; Hachey, *Anglo-Vatican Relations 1914–1939,* 40; Francesco Margiotto Broglio, *Italia e Santa Sede dalla grande guerra alla concilazione* (Bari: Laterza, 1966).

18. Consistorial allocution of 20 Dec. 1926, in *Discorsi di Pio XI,* ed. Domenico Bertetto (Turin: Società Editrice Internazionale, 1959), 1:647; Maurras's movement was condemned for both its excessive nationalism and the challenge it posed for papal authority. Peter Godman, *Hitler and the Vatican: Inside the Secret Archives That Reveal the New Story of the Nazis and the Church* (New York: Free Press, 2004), 46.

19. "Nous avons lu," 5 Sept. 1926, *PP* 2:95; Hachey, *Anglo-Vatican Relations, 1914–1939,* 104, 109, 119; Anthony Rhodes, *The Vatican in the Age of Dictators, 1922–1945* (New York: Holt, Rinehart and Winston, 1973), 106–8.

20. In 1928 the Friends of Israel was composed of eighteen cardinals, two hundred archbishops and bishops, and some two thousand priests. Godman, *Hitler and the Vatican,* 24. See *Decretum De Conosciatione Vulgo, "Amici Israel" Abolenda,* 25 March 1928, *AAS* 20:103–4; Moro, *Chiesa e lo sterminio degli ebrei,* 60; Rhonheimer, "Holocaust: What Was Not Said."

condemnation of anti-Semitism. "The Holy See has always protected the Jews against unjust vexations," it read, and "particularly reproves hatred against a people once chosen by God, known as Anti-Semitism."[21]

The condemnation of anti-Semitism did not silence the opponents of Judaism in the Vatican. In the *Civiltà Cattolica*, Father Enrico Rosa commented that while condemning racial anti-Semitism, the Church had not abandoned its religious anti-Judaism, nor was it ignoring the threat posed by Judaism to Christianity. Borrowing anti-Semitic slurs, he warned of the danger resulting from the Jews' "pernicious infiltration, their hidden influence, and their resulting disproportionate power." Despite this and other inflammatory articles, the *Civiltà Cattolica* slowly moderated its anti-Judaic polemic.[22] During the contentious debate on anti-Semitism and anti-Judaism, negotiations continued with the Mussolini government. On 11 February 1929, on the seventh anniversary of the pope's coronation, an accord was signed by Mussolini, on behalf of the king of Italy, and Cardinal Gasparri, on behalf of the Holy See. The tripartite agreement included a conciliation treaty that terminated the troublesome "Roman question" and declared Vatican City the papacy's neutral and inviolable territory; a concordat that regulated Church-state relations in Italy; and a financial convention to provide some compensation for papal territory and possessions confiscated during and after unification.[23] The treaty also established the Holy See as a sovereign state, according it some forty-four hectares (108 acres) of territory. Under its provisions, the Vatican secured its own currency and stamps, post office, wireless and telegraph stations, railway, guards and police, and, most important, the right to send its diplomats to foreign countries and receive foreign diplomats. In turn, the Holy See promised not to intervene in conflicts of a temporal nature or in international congresses.

The concordat regulated the Church's position in the Fascist state,

---

21. Passelecq and Suchecky, *Encyclique cachée de Pie XI*, 144; *AAS* 20 (1928): 103–4.

22. See Rhonheimer, "Holocaust: What Was Not Said," 5; Kertzer, *Popes against the Jews*, 270–73; Giovanni Miccoli, "Santa Sede e Chiesa Italiana di Fronte alle Leggi Antiebriache del 1938," *Studi Storici* 29 (Oct.–Dec. 1988): 829–33.

23. The text of the Lateran Accords can be found in Nino Tripodi, *Patti lateranese e il fascismo* (Bologna: Capelli, 1960), 267–79, and in Wilfrid Parsons, *The Pope and Italy* (New York: America Press, 1929), 81–114. For an analysis of the three documents, see Ernesto Rossi, *Il Managnello e l'aspersorio* (Florence: Parenti, 1958), 227–36.

making concessions that led some to complain it had converted Italy from a lay to a confessional state. Among other things it recognized Catholicism as the religion of state, made religious instruction compulsory in the secondary as well as the primary schools, accepted marriage as a sacrament, and sought the harmony of public policy, legislation, and moral behavior with Church principles. The Fascist state assumed the obligation of enforcing canon law among the Catholic population, revising its civil legislation so it would be in harmony with Church teaching on matters of faith and morals, and recognizing the Church holidays. Article 43 provided for the immunity of Catholic Action organizations from Fascist supervision.[24] Some Italian Jews expressed concern when the concordat restored Catholicism as the religion of state, but their fears were allayed when this was followed by a comprehensive law (no. 1731), which assured their rights.[25]

Despite the agreement, problems arose between Mussolini's Italy and the Vatican. Pius was displeased by Il Duce's speech in the Chamber of Deputies, which claimed that although Christianity had been born in Palestine, it had become Catholic in Rome. In an address printed on the first page of *L'Osservatore Romano* (16 May 1929), the pope denounced the speech as "worse than heretical." Mussolini responded by increasing surveillance over telephone calls to and from Vatican City. The Vatican increasingly found itself in conflict with a regime that challenged the faith and attempted to mold the future generation in its own image.[26] To counter the bellicose Fascist stance, the pope issued the encyclical *Divini Illius Magistri* (December 1929), "On the Christian Education of Youth." In it, he defended the Church's inalienable right to supervise the education of children in all institutions, both public and private, claiming that its mandate extended "to every other branch of learning."[27]

Papal relations with the Soviet Union also worsened. Pius XI deplored the Communist program and its flagrant violations of Christian morality.

---

24. "Il Nostro Più," 11 Feb. 1929, and "Vogliamo anzitutto," 13 Feb. 1929, *PP* 2:99; Tannenbaum, *Fascist Experience*, 190.

25. Michaelis, *Mussolini and the Jews*, 53.

26. Godman, *Hitler and the Vatican*, 15; Alvarez, *Spies in the Vatican*, 159; Ecco una, 14 May 1929, in Koenig, *Principles for Peace*, 388.

27. *AAS* 21 (1929): 730–53; "Rappresentanti in Terra," 31 Dec. 1929, in Koenig, *Principles for Peace*, 388.

In 1929 he established the Russicum in Rome, a pontifical college devoted to preparing priests for a missionary role in the Soviet Union. In February 1930 Pius spoke out publicly against religious persecution in the Soviet Union. His statement, written by the French Jesuit Michel d'Herbigny, condemned the Bolshevik attacks on religion. At the same time it reproached European governments for their virtual silence in the face of this persecution, and called for a "crusade of prayer" for the godless Soviet regime.[28] This preoccupation with communism did not deter Pius from objecting to the racism of the Fascist regimes. He believed it was his duty to caution the faithful against racism and made a clear distinction between secular anti-Semitism and the Church's anti-Judaism, which was motivated by religious concerns. "If there is in Christianity the idea of a mystery of blood," he observed in his Christmas message of 1930, "it is that not of a race opposed to other races, but of the unity of all men in the heritage of sin." This pope emphasized that Catholicism could not denounce the Jews, or any other people, on the basis of biology, for this would undermine the unity of humanity and the Church's mission of conversion.[29] The Fascists saw things differently, seeking to consolidate their "ethical state" by restricting the activities of Catholic organizations. In June 1931 Pius issued the encyclical *Non abbiamo bisogno*, which repudiated the regime's claim to control over the young and declared that this totalitarian notion could not be reconciled with Catholic doctrine.[30]

Although Pius denounced totalitarianism and racism, he preserved many of his anti-Judaic prejudices, in February 1932 confiding his concerns about the attacks on the Church by Protestants, Communists, and Jews. He was suspicious of international Jewry but claimed that Italian Jews were different, recalling his Jewish friends in Milan and his studies with the chief rabbi there.[31] While racism and anti-Semitism raged north of the Alps, the pope welcomed his old friend and collaborator Da Fano and a Jewish delegation to the Vatican on 12 May 1933, expressing concern

28. Alvarez, *Spies in the Vatican*, 45, 144; "Ci Commuovono Profondamente," 2 Feb. 1930, in Koenig, *Principles for Peace*, 393.

29. Lapide, *Three Popes and the Jews*, 98; Bernardini, "Origins and Development of Racial Anti-Semitism," 434.

30. *The Papal Encyclicals in Their Historical Context*, ed. Anne Fremantle (New York: G. P. Putnam's Sons, 1956), 249.

31. Moro, "Premesse dell' atteggiamento cattolico," 1118.

for the burdens imposed on German Jews. Da Fano, aware of the pope's opposition to racial anti-Semitism, thanked Pius for his appeals against religious persecution.[32] While Pius still believed that anti-Christian sentiment in Russia was provoked by Jewish aversion to Christianity, he did not hesitate to denounce those who fostered race hatred.[33] This was one of many factors that kept Mussolini from pursuing a racist course.

Since Pius and Mussolini both derived advantages from the concordat, both found it expedient to seek conciliation rather than conflict. Thus a compromise on Catholic Action was fashioned early in September 1931.[34] Nonetheless, Pius grew increasingly suspicious of Fascist intentions and even more so of the Nazi movement in Germany, sharing the sentiments of those German bishops who found Catholicism and Nazism incompatible. At the end of March 1931, the bishops of the Prussian provinces and Bavaria issued joint pastorals condemning the National Socialist party and forbidding Catholics to join a movement that espoused principles contrary to the faith. The bishops especially found fault with article 24 of the party program, which insisted that all religious creeds were subordinate to racial considerations. Equally odious, in their eyes, was the exaltation of nationalism over religion, the recognition of violence as a legitimate political weapon, the agitation for nondenominational education, the advocacy of artificial birth control, and the blatant anticlericalism of Nazi leaders.[35] Subsequently, the Fulda Episcopal Conference of 17–19 August banned membership in the party and forbade the clergy to offer communion to anyone wearing the swastika.[36] Pius, for his part, found blasphemous the suggestion that Jesus was an Aryan, and he would not accept the German-

32. Rhonheimer, "Holocaust: What Was Not Said," 14. Pius XI's opposition to Germany's racist policies has been confirmed by the partial opening of the papers of Pius XI in the Vatican Archives. See ASV, SS, Rapporti con gli stati, AS, AAES, Germania, 1922–39, posizione 643, fascicolo 158.

33. Moro, *Chiesa e lo sterminio degli ebrei*, 60; Lapide, *Three Popes and the Jews*, 98, 100.

34. The terms of the 2 September 1931 agreement between the Holy See and the Mussolini regime, or a copy of the same, is misfiled in the Vatican Archives among the papers that focus on the Reich concordat of 1933 in ASV, SS, Rapporti con gli stati, AS, AAES, Germania, 1922–39, posizione 645, fascicolo 163. Perhaps the settlement on Catholic Action in Italy was consulted during the negotiations with the Reich to avoid similar problems with Catholic Action in Germany. A printed copy may be found in Pellicani, *Il Papa di tutti*, 61–62.

35. Hachey, *Anglo-Vatican Relations, 1914–1939*, 190, 209.

36. Cesare Orsenigo to Eugenio Pacelli, ASV, SS, Rapporti con gli stati, AS, AAES, 1922–39, posizioni 641–43, fascicolo 157; Carroll, *Constantine's Sword*, 498.

Christian call to impose an "Aryan paragraph" excluding all clergy or Church officials of Jewish ancestry. Vatican officials in the secretariat of state, headed by Eugenio Pacelli after 1930, were more cautious, claiming that Catholic critics of the party in Germany were acting on their own initiative. For this and other reasons, ecclesiastical circles in Rome responded diplomatically to the accession of Hitler, avoiding any public expression of opinion. Nonetheless, in February, Cesare Orsenigo, the nuncio, observed that the Center Party should not support the new Nazi government, condemned by the bishops on the basis of religious principle.[37] Orsenigo changed his stance when he learned that some in the Vatican were urging a rapprochement with the National Socialists. The new course was probably influenced by the fact that out of 13 million or so Catholic voters in the Reich, 6 or 7 million voted for the Nazis in the election of 6 March, despite the opposition of the episcopacy to the regime. In light of this reality, Orsenigo and the secretariat of state questioned the wisdom of Catholic opposition. Indeed, the nuncio asked and received permission to attend the inauguration of the new government.[38] The rapprochement was incomplete, as the Vatican remained suspicious of the new regime, and the Nazi authorities in turn considered the Catholic Church an enemy and monitored its organizations. In 1933 there was sporadic violence against the Jews of Germany that the Nazi regime disowned, but this was followed by official discriminatory measures. Once the Nazi regime proposed its first racial laws, the *Civiltà Cattolica* condemned them as a violation of Church and natural law. It encouraged some ecclesiastical figures to reconsider the anti-Judaism that still prevailed among the clergy and laity.[39]

At this juncture the nuncio in Berlin favored an accommodation with the Nazis, writing Pacelli that despite the bishop's denunciation the Catholic population of Germany enthusiastically supported the new regime, which had shown toleration toward religious groups. Hitler in

37. Orsenigo telegraphs Pacelli, 30 Jan. 1933, ASV, SS, Rapporti con gli Stati, AS, Germany, 1922–39, posizioni 642–43, fascicolo 157, no. 60; Orsenigo to Pacelli, 16 Feb. 1933, ibid., 641–43, fascicolo 157, no. 6424.

38. Orsenigo to Pacelli, 16 March 1933, ibid., posizione 643, fascicolo 159, nos. 733–34; Orsenigo to Pacelli, 7 March 1933, ASV, SS, Rapporti con gli Stati, AS, AAES, Germania, 1922–39, 641–43, fascicolo 157, no. 6578; Orsenigo to Pacelli, 9 March 1933, ibid., no. 6610.

39. Alvarez, *Spies in the Vatican*, 196; Moro, *Chiesa e lo sterminio degli ebrei*, 77–78.

turn sought to reassure the Vatican, declaring that his government sought friendly relations with the Holy See and claiming that his failure to attend Catholic religious functions flowed from the episcopacy's condemnation of his movement, which he wanted revoked.[40] During the debate on the enabling act (23 March 1933), he reached out to the Church, promising that his government would protect the two Christian confessions and would "respect the agreements made between them and the states; their rights will not be interfered with." He also claimed that his government regarded "Christianity as the unshakable foundation of the moral and ethical life of our nation" and that he placed "the greatest value on the maintenance and development of friendly relations with the Holy See."[41] This promise was applauded by the Catholic party, which contributed to the two-thirds majority needed to pass the enabling act, establishing the Nazi dictatorship. The nuncio informed Pacelli that he was convinced that Hitler and the Nazis had achieved this victory only with the complicity of the Center Party.[42]

Not all approved of the Center's accommodation with the Hitler regime. In April 1933, weeks after the granting of extraordinary power to Hitler, Edith Stein, a convert from Judaism to Catholicism, wrote the pope, pleading with him to condemn Nazism's racist ideology and seeking help for the persecuted Jews of Germany. It was one of many pleas for assistance dispatched to Pius XI in 1933.[43] "In the name of all Sacred in Christianity," Rabbi Margolis of New York City wrote Pius, "I implore you to lift your voice in unreserved condemnation of the Hitlerite persecution." While he did not respond to the individual petitioners, the pope instructed the nuncio in Berlin to intervene on behalf of the persecuted Jews.[44] Orsenigo questioned the wisdom of the papal directive, noting that

40. Orsenigo to Pacelli, 22 March and 18 June 1933, ASV, SS, Rapporti con gli Stati, AS, AAES, Germania, 1922–29, posizione 641–43, fascicolo 157, nos. 6736, 7461; Orsenigo to Pacelli, 22 and 24 March 1933, ibid., telegram nos. 70–71.

41. *German Parliamentary Debates, 1848–1933,* ed. Michael Hughes and Mitchell Allen (New York: Peter Lang, 2003), 259, 263.

42. Orsenigo to Pacelli, 24 March 1933, ASV, SS, Rapporti con gli stati, AS, AAES, Germania, 1922–39, posizione 644–45, fascicolo 162, no. 844/33.

43. Edith Stein to Pius XI, 12 April 1933, ibid., posizione 643, fascicolo 158, no. 1092/33. Stein's letter is one of the many documents of the interwar period opened to scholars on 15 Feb. 2003. In this regard see the *Brooklyn Tablet,* 1 March 2003, 6.

44. Rabbi Margolis of Congregation Ohab Zedek to Pius XI, 22 April 1933, and Pacelli to

the anti-Semitic campaign had assumed a governmental character that would make intervention tantamount to protesting Nazi law. The nuncio discussed the matter with the Bishop of Berlin, who promised a general appeal on the basis of universal charity. Both believed that more direct protest would be dangerous. The Bishops of Cologne, Paderborn, and Osnabruck also appealed indirectly on behalf of the persecuted, asserting that God gave his only Son for the salvation of all of mankind.[45]

Hitler, of course, was unwilling to budge on the Jews, whom he denounced as "pernicious." At the same time he deplored the fact that liberalism failed to recognize the danger posed by this "race" to Church and state, and claimed that his measures served the interests of both. Confronted with this determined stance, the nuncio failed to challenge the Führer but assured Jewish suppliants that everything possible had been done on their behalf.[46] Pacelli's recently opened prewar correspondence reveals that he did not press the nuncio to do more. Although displeased by the anti-Semitic and neopagan course pursued by the Hitler regime, Pius, for practical reasons, pondered the prospect of a rapprochement between the Vatican and the Hitler regime. In the spring of 1933 the Reich vice chancellor, Franz von Papen, ventured to Rome and proposed the conclusion of a concordat. The project, conceived by von Papen, was seconded by Monsignor Ludwig Kaas, leader of the Center Party. Pius XI was not initially enthusiastic, although some ecclesiastics responded much more favorably, among them the Archbishop of Freiburg, Konrad Gruber, who proclaimed his adherence to the new Nazi order.[47]

Pius reconsidered the call for a concordat following Nazi harassment of the Church. He could not ignore the fact that some prominent Catholic

Orsenigo, 4 April 1933, both in ASV, SS, Rapporti con gli stati, AS, AAES, Germania, 1922–39, posizione 643, fascicolo 158, no. 1227/33.

45. Orsenigo to Pacelli, 9 April 1933, ASV, SS, Rapporti con gli stati, AS, AAES, Germania, 1922–39, posizione 643, fascicolo 158, no. 73.0; Orsenigo to Pacelli, 11 April 1933, ibid., posizione 641–43, fascicolo 158, no. 6953.

46. Orsenigo to Pacelli, 8 May 1933, ibid., posizione 641–43, fascicolo 157, no. 7173; Orsenigo to Pacelli, 28 April 1933, ibid., posizione 643, fascicolo 158, no. 1366/33; alo see posizione 585, fascicolo 93.

47. Orsenigo to Pacelli, 16 March 1933, ibid., posizione 643, fascicolo 159, no. 733/34; Orsenigo to Pacelli, 2 April 1933, ibid., posizione 644–45, fascicolo 162, no. 968/33; ibid., posizione 643, fascicolo 158, no. 1366/33; also see posizione 644–45, fascicolo 162, no. 1400/33; ibid., posizione 650, fascicolo 194; "Cronoca Contemporanea," CC, 7–20 April 1933.

figures in the Reich sought reconciliation with the Nazi regime.[48] The impending dissolution of the Center and the Bavarian People's Party also contributed to his reassessment. Determined to preserve Catholic youth organizations in Germany and provide a legal basis for the religious and educational freedom of the Church in the Reich, the pope sanctioned negotiations for a concordat, despite the fact that the Nazi "Law for the Restoration of the Civil Service," passed 7 April 1933, excluded Jews. In fact, the nuncio in Berlin warned the papal secretary of state that the Nazi campaign against the Jews continued unabated.[49]

Pius understood that Hitler hoped to remove the Catholic clergy from party politics, and it was later charged that the Vatican, lured by the prospect of guarantees for its schools and other institutions, negotiated the concordat by sacrificing the Center Party, which had fought the Kulturkampf. Rome was thus held responsible both for the accord and for the dissolution of the Center Party that followed. Furthermore, some have implied that approval of the Reich concordat, favored and facilitated by Pacelli, revealed the Vatican's sympathy for Nazism. Father Rosa, in the Civiltà Cattolica, emphatically denied that it expressed approval of Hitler's government or ideology.[50] It has also been charged that the Nazis' destruction of Jewish works in May 1933 was reminiscent of earlier Christian burning of Jewish texts, but Pius denounced the comparison as insidious and inappropriate. Meanwhile, the papal secretary of state, Pacelli, privately revealed his aversion to the anti-Semitism of the Nazi reign of terror. The Holy See had agreed to the accord, he confessed to the English representative, to preserve the Catholic Church in Germany.[51] In mid-

48. AAS 25 (10 Sept. 1933), no. 14; "Concordat of the Holy See and Germany," Catholic World, Aug. 1933; Hachey, Anglo-Vatican Relations, 1914–1939, 250; "Cronoca Contemporanea," CC, 23 June–6 July 1933. See also Donald J. Dietrich, "Catholic Theologians in Hitler's Reich: Adaptation and Critique," JCS 29 (winter 1987): 21–24.

49. Orsenigo to Pacelli, 28 April 1933, ASV, SS, Rapporti con gli stati, AS, AAES, Germania, 1933–34.

50. See articles 1, 2, 4, and 21 of the Reich concordat (1933), Italian translation, ibid., 1922–39, posizione 645, fascicolo 163; François Charles-Roux, Huit ans au Vatican (Paris: Flammarion, 1947), 94–95; Cardinal Gasparri to Cardinal Pacelli, 24 July 1933, ASV, SS, Rapporti con gli stati, AS, AAES, Germania, 1922–39, posizione 645, fascicolo 165; Carroll, Constantine's Sword, 505.

51. E. Rosa, "Il Concordato della Santa Sede con la Germania," CC 84 (1933): 345; Mr. Kirkpatrick (the Vatican) to Sir R. Vansittart, 19 Aug. 1933, Documents on British Foreign Policy, 1919–1939, 2d series, vol. 5 (London: H. M. Stationery Office, 1956), 524–25.

August 1933, James McDonald, the American who served as high commissioner for refugees of the League of Nations, met with Pacelli, who expressed sympathy for the persecuted Jews of Germany. But McDonald found the secretary of state preoccupied "with the church's problems with the German government," and concluded "that no vigorous cooperation could be expected from that direction."[52]

To assure Church interests, the Holy See transmitted a memorandum of understanding to Berlin, especially regarding the activity of Catholic Action groups in the Reich. Rome was also assured that if the Reich government reinstated compulsory military service, seminarians would be exempt. Such promises made were not always kept. No sooner had the concordat been signed than the Reich approved a sterilization law, in direct opposition to the doctrines established by Pius XI in his encyclical on Christian marriage.[53] In response, Pius and the Holy Office were prepared to condemn a book by Joseph Mayer, which approved of the legal sterilization of the mentally ill. Pacelli, seeking to avoid even this indirect confrontation with the Reich, proposed allowing Mayer the option of rewriting his volume in light of the papal position.[54] The call for moderation was undermined by Nazi actions, which disturbed Pius, who deplored the Nazi interpretation of the concordat. Although some Catholics sought to reconcile differences between the pope and the Nazi regime on the sterilization issue, Pius XI would not be silenced. He repeated that the sterilization legislation violated the moral order and publicly expressed his disapproval.[55]

Early in 1934 the Holy Office, under papal direction, condemned Ernst Bergmann's book *Die deutsche Nationalkirche* and Alfred Rosenberg's *The Myth of the Twentieth Century*, which was denounced as anti-Christian and antihuman.[56] At the end of October 1934, when the prospect of con-

52. Neuk A. Lewis, "Nazis and Jews: Insights from Old Diary," *New York Times*, 22 April 2004, A3.

53. ASV, SS, Rapporti con gli stati, AS, AAES, Germania, 1922–39, posizione 645, fascicoli 162–71; Dietrich, "Catholic Theologians in Hitler's Reich," 30.

54. Godman, *Hitler and the Vatican*, 60.

55. ASV, SS, Rapporti con gli stati, AS, AAES, Germania, 1922–39, posizione 647, fascicolo 191; Orsenigo to Pacelli, 30 Dec. 1933, ibid., posizione 650, fascicolo 197, no. 9198; Pacelli to Orsenigo, 10 Dec. 1933, ibid., posizione 650, fascicolo 195. See also the *Jewish Chronicle of London*, 1 Sept. 1933, ibid., posizione 643, fascicolo 158, no. 2574/33.

56. The condemnation of the former appeared in the *OR* of 14 Feb. 1934, and that of the latter a week earlier.

demning the errors of National Socialism was introduced at a meeting of the Holy Office, Pius approved the initiative and called upon the general of the Jesuits to commence the condemnation. Ledochowski assigned the task to the Jesuit father Franz Hurth, who had earlier condemned key elements of Nazi ideology and practice. He and Johannes Baptista Rabeneck, a colleague at the Seminary of Valkenbrug, drafted a pronouncement describing the Nazi doctrines of race and blood as heretical. Their report, which saw no prospect of reconciliation between racism and Catholicism, was presented to the Holy Office in March 1935.[57]

Not all in the congregation, curia, or German hierarchy concurred in this confrontational course. Acknowledging that what the Nazis were doing to the Jews was "so un-Christian that not only every priest but every Christian must protest," Cardinal von Faulhaber, the Archbishop of Munich, nevertheless, and paradoxically, concluded that this should not be denounced by Church leaders, who had more important matters to address, including "the preservation of our schools and Catholic organizations and the question of compulsory sterilization." Besides, the cardinal believed that the Jews could help themselves. Thus, in April 1933, von Faulhaber wrote Pacelli that the Church should not intervene on their behalf, for this would turn the battle against the Jews into a battle against Catholics.[58] The cardinal's strategy was to defend the Old Testament but not to contest the negative image of the Jews or the discriminatory measures introduced by the Nazi regime.

For similar tactical reasons, the German bishops did not speak out against the violence of the "Night of the Long Knives." In fact, the nuncio in Bavaria cautioned that following the purge of Roehm, Catholics might be the next victims.[59] Following the murder of the leader of Catholic Action in Berlin, Pius and Pacelli feared that an organized campaign was being launched against the Catholic Church, which they felt should seek some accommodation with the Nazis. Pacelli's conciliatory course was

57. Godman, *Hitler and the Vatican*, 48–49, 52–53, 57–59, 69; "The Holy Office's First Proposed Condemnation of National Socialism," ibid., appendix 1, 172–93.

58. Rhonheimer, "Holocaust: What Was Not Said," 7; ASV, SS, Rapporti con gli stati, AS, AAES, Germania, 1933–34, posizione 641–43, fascicolo 158.

59. Moro, *Chiesa e lo sterminio degli ebrei*, 78–82, 104–6; Nuncio in Bavaria to Pacelli, 17 Aug. 1934, ASV, SS, Rapporti con gli stati, AS, AAES, Germania, 1922–39, posizione 650, fascicolo 148, no. 2740/34.

questioned by part of the German clergy. Father Franziskus Stratmann, a leader of the German Peace League, charged as early as 1933 that the failure to bear witness to the truth revealed that "true Christianity is dying of opportunism."[60] The Bishop of Munster, von Galen, and the Bishop of Berlin, Preysing, shared his concern. Von Galen informed the pope that they confronted an adversary who appreciated neither loyalty nor truth, who in fact did not even worship God but some diabolical entity. His position was bolstered by Preysing, who called for a policy of public denunciation of Nazi excesses. Although Pius XI was receptive to their pleas, others in the German hierarchy shared the prevailing sentiment of the secretariat of state that the position of Catholics in the Reich was precarious, and that therefore caution was the best policy. Unquestionably, the pope's increasing public hostility toward Nazism undermined the diplomatic approach of the German bishops, making collaboration more difficult.[61]

The Nazis made a concerted effort to silence the pope and Church. Among other things, there were numerous arrests, the closing of Catholic organizations, and an increasing suppression of the Catholic press, which prompted a series of energetic papal protests. These protests were published in the *Osservatore Romano*, in which an article of 8 June 1934 defended the Old Testament attacked by the Nazi regime, noting that its revelations came from God. Pius, in a pastoral letter of April 1934 to the Catholic youth of Germany, decried developments in Germany.[62] As the attack on Catholic principles continued, Rome faced a real dilemma: should the pope remain silent so as to avoid the wrath of the regime, or should he speak out against Nazi abuses, exposing the institutional

60. Quoted in Rhonheimer, "Holocaust: What Was Not Said," 8.
61. Orsenico to Giusepe Pizzardo, secretary of the Sacred Congregation of Extraordinary Ecclesiastical Affairs, 12 Oct. 1934, ASV, SS, Rapporti con gli stati, AS, AAES, Germania, 1922–39, posizione 670–73, fascicolo 233, no. 3884/34; Moro, *Chiesa e lo sterminio degli ebrei*, 105–6.
62. "Nazi Government Persecutes Catholics and the Church, 1933–37," ASV, SS, Rapporti con gli stati, AS, AAES, Germania, 1922–39, posizione 650, fascicoli 194–200; ibid., posizione 666, fascicoli 220–24; posizione 693, fascicoli 264ff.; posizione 713, fascicolo 308; posizione 672, fascicolo 233; posizione 649, fascicolo 193, no. 2412/33; posizione 650, fascicolo 148, no. 2168/34, and posizione 650, fascicolo 195, no. 3475/33; "Dalla Germania. Voci dell'Episcopato," 8 June 1934, ibid., posizione 650, fascicoli 190ff; "Una lettera del Papa alla gioventù catttolica," *La Tribuna*, April 1934, ibid., posizione 650, fascicolo 199; "Pericolo pe la pace religiosa in Germania," *OR*, 14 Jan. 1934.

Church to grave peril? Papa Ratti, as he was known, and his secretary of state, Pacelli, the future Pius XII, disagreed on this and other matters. Angelo Roncalli, later Pope John XXIII, and others noted that the two differed in style as well as substance.[63] Pius XI agreed with von Galen and Preysing that Christianity had public as well as private responsibilities, and stressed that the Christian life required action.[64] Furthermore, he believed that the Nazi attack on the Jews was an attack on the Church's heritage. In this light silence could not be an appropriate option.

When the condemnation of Nazism was brought before the Congregation of the Holy Office, Pius called for a synthesis of the mistaken principles on which Nazi racism and totalitarianism were based. Pacelli, a member of the younger generation who favored a more diplomatic course, made no comment. His silence here formed part of his overall approach, for Pacelli, wanting to avoid confrontation, had even hesitated to make an issue of sterilization.[65] Pius disagreed and refused to remain silent on issues such as sterilization and the persecution of the Jews. In fact, between 1933 and 1936, Pius made more than thirty protests against Nazi actions.[66] While he did not renounce the Reich concordat, he reconsidered his attitude toward *Anschluss,* and now favored an independent Austria. Upset by the abortive Nazi coup there in 1934, Pius praised Mussolini for dispatching troops to the frontier and preserving Austrian independence. He approved the formation of the Popular Union of German Christian Culture, which included a large group of Catholics and some seventy ecclesiastics and which rejected both racism and class hatred, and he supported Bishop von Galen's protests against the Nazi regime's suppression of Catholic youth organizations.[67]

In September 1935, during the Nuremberg party rally, two measures

63. Michael Phayer, *The Catholic Church and the Holocaust, 1930–1965* (Bloomington: Indiana University Press, 2000), 222.

64. "Ai Superiori della Comagnia di Gesù," in Bertetto, *Discorsi di Pio XI,* 3:383.

65. Godman, *Hitler and the Vatican,* 24, 70, 76.

66. Cindy Wooden, "Archives Show Vatican Opposed Hitler's Anti-Jewish Laws," *Brooklyn Tablet,* 24 Jan. 2004; "Ai giovani Cattolici di Germania," 8 Aug. 1934, in Bertetto, *Discorsi di Pio XI,* 2:218.

67. Charles Pichon, *The Vatican and Its Role in World Affairs,* trans. Jean Misrahi (New York: E. P. Dutton, 1950), 147; Hachey, *Anglo-Vatican Relations, 1914–1939,* 274–79; ASV, SS, Rapporti con gli stati, AS, AAES, Germania, 1922–39, posizione 672, fascicolo 233, n. 3981/34; Orsenigo to Pacelli, 17 April 1935, ibid., posizione 650, fascicolo 199.

were passed against the Jews. The first deprived them of civil rights, while the second prohibited marriage between Aryans and Jews and ruled such marriages null and void.[68] Papal opposition was reflected in the revised condemnation of Nazi principles and practices presented to the Holy Office in 1936, which focused on racism, nationalism, Communism, and totalitarianism, and rejected the proposition that "the prime source and highest principle of all legal organization is the instinct of race."[69] It was one of several means of condemning Nazi philosophy and practice that Pius XI considered. Cardinal Francesco Marchetti Selvaggiani, secretary of the Holy Office, blocked the condemnation, for Selvaggiani, like Pacelli, opposed open conflict with Nazism. Pacelli and the Berlin nuncio, Orseni-go, remained committed to the concordat and counseled against steps that would compromise its future.[70]

The pope, on the other hand, believed that the dignity of the Holy See required that he denounce Nazi outrages, and he was confident that the Church would survive the resulting persecution. At the opening of January 1936, Pius spoke with the German ambassador at the New Year's reception for diplomats, and firmly denounced the outrages perpetrated by the Reich government, warning that the Church would endure while other entities would disappear.[71] Concerned primarily to defend the Church and its teaching, the pope still thought communism the greater threat in 1936.[72] But he was not prepared to join forces with either Fascism or Nazism in order to oppose it, and, like Father Rosa of the *Civiltà Cattolica*, he deemed the Nazi reaction against Communism destructive of Christian morals.

Pius complained that despite the concordat, Hitler's government continued to restrict the rights and activities of the institutional Church, imposing laws that contradicted its basic teachings. In February 1936, when Hitler sent Pius XI a congratulatory telegram on the anniversary of his coronation, the pope responded with criticism of developments in Ger-

68. Remak, *Nazi Years*, 148–50.

69. Godman, *Hitler and the Vatican*, appendix 2, 197.

70. Miccoli, "Santa Sede e Chiesa Italiana," 859; Orsenigno to Pacelli, 14 Feb. 1936, ASV, SS, Rapporti con gli stati, AS, AAES, Germania, 1922–39, posizione 643, fascicolo 162.

71. Godman, *Hitler and the Vatican*, 107–8.

72. "Siamo ancora sotto," 12 May 1936, *PP* 2:110; "Discorso inaugurale del Papa alla mostra stampa catolica," *CC* 87 (12 May 1936): 419.

many. Surprised by the pope's criticism, von Neurath, the foreign minister, sought to keep it from Hitler. The pope, however, insisted it be forwarded to the chancellor, and von Neurath reluctantly complied.[73] Following the remilitarization of the Rhineland, he confided to the French ambassador, "if you [French] had called forward 200,000 men you would have done an immense service to the entire world."[74] As the 1930s approached their end, relations between Berlin and the Vatican became increasingly tense.

Although Pacelli also decried Nazi outrages, he continued to advocate negotiation and diplomacy in order to preserve the concordat. He was distressed by the warning that Hitler had personally transmitted to Cardinal Michael von Faulhaber that if the Church did not abandon "its struggle against the racial laws . . . the clergy would be regarded as state-enemies,"[75] but he still counseled compromise. Meanwhile, the pope was dismayed by Mussolini's increasing emphasis on totalitarianism and racism as he moved closer to Hitler's Germany. Pius regretted that Mussolini had rejected the advice he had earlier offered Hitler—to eschew racism and anti-Semitism. German Church figures such as Cardinal Bertram concurred with the pope that the biological racism of Nazi anti-Semitism represented a threat to Christianity as well as to Judaism.[76] Pius XI's opposition to the doctrine of blood and race was also reflected in the critical articles that appeared in the *Osservatore Romano* and *Civiltà Cattolica*.[77] Throughout 1936–37, Vatican Radio invoked prayers for Jews persecuted by the Nazis. Thus, by the late 1930s, Pius XI had emerged as a powerful moral voice against Fascism and Nazism, which he denounced as fraudulent alternatives to Communism.[78]

The Nazi leaders recognized that while the Vatican shared their opposition to liberalism, modernity, and Communism, it refused to endorse their racism. The papal insistence that religious conviction rather than

73. Godman, *Hitler and the Vatican*, 108; ASV, SS, Rapporti con gli stati, AS, AAES, Germania, 1922–39, posizione 693–94, fascicolo 264, no. 226.

74. Charles-Roux, *Huit ans au Vatican*, 106.

75. Godman, *Hitler and the Vatican*, 82, 124.

76. Bernardini, "Origins and Development of Racial Anti-Semitism," 434; ASV, SS, Rapporti con gli stati, AS, AAES, Germania, 1922–39, posizione 641, fascicolo 158, no. 1060/33. See also Carroll, *Constantine's Sword*, 509.

77. "La questione giudaica," *CC* (1936), anno 87, vol. 4, 45.

78. Michael R. Marrus, "The Vatican on Racism and Antisemitism, 1938–39: A New Look at a Might-Have-Been," *Holocaust and Genocide Studies* 11 (winter 1997): 379; Lapide, *Three Popes and the Jews*, 96.

race defined Jewishness was one of many chasms separating the Church from the Third Reich.[79] In 1936, after three years of anti-Semitic policies, the Führer brushed aside the criticism of churchmen who deplored his mistreatment of the Jews. "Why do you complain?" he asked. "I am only following through on what you have taught for centuries."[80] Actually, the Nazi leader and racialists in the party loudly preached the difference between the long-standing Christian anti-Judaism and their own virulent anti-Semitism. As early as 1919 Hitler had warned that "Anti-Semitism as a political movement" had perforce to be based on the fact "that Judaism is a matter of race and not of religion."[81] Once in power, he continued to emphasize this distinction but occasionally found it convenient to blur the difference in an attempt to get the Church to back his program. Pius publicly repudiated such attempts to implicate the Church in the Nazi persecution of the Jews.

Pius, who had been considering a more explicit condemnation of Nazi philosophy and practice, was alarmed by Alois Hudal's *The Foundation of National Socialism,* which sought to reconcile Nazism with the Roman Catholic Church. Among other things, the volume undermined the Vatican's contention that clerical anti-Judaism had nothing to do with Nazi anti-Semitism. For this and other reasons, an angry pope pressed for its condemnation by the supreme tribunal. Pacelli, who feared the consequences of such a condemnation, once again intervened to propose a less confrontational course. As a result, the volume was disavowed in the 13 November 1936 issue of *L'Osservatore Romano,* which simply indicated that the book had been published without the permission of the Holy See.[82] Despite the stance of Pacelli and a coterie in the secretariat of state, Pius planned to do more to oppose Nazi policies.

The pope summoned the German bishops to Rome at the end of 1936. Early in the following year they met with Pacelli, who told them he did not expect the pope to live for more than two years.[83] Although they con-

79. See Carroll, *Constantine's Sword,* 509, 512.

80. Quoted in Franklin Hamlin Littell, "Inventing the Holocaust: A Christian Retrospect," *Holocaust and Genocide Studies* 9 (fall 1995): 182.

81. Quoted in Helmut Krausnick, "The Persecution of the Jews," in *Anatomy of the SS State,* ed. Helmut Krausnick et al. (New York: Walker and Co., 1968), 21.

82. Godman, *Hitler and the Vatican,* 126.

83. Included in the summons were the three German cardinals—Bertram, von Faulhaber, and Schulte—as well as Bishops Galen of Muenster and Preysing of Berlin. Ibid., 133.

curred that Catholicism was endangered by Nazi repression, Cardinal Faulhaber stressed the need to preserve the concordat, which provided the legal basis for the Church's activity in the Reich—precisely Pacelli's position. On 17 January, Pius met the German hierarchy from his sickbed. Disgusted by the many Nazi violations of the concordat, he nonetheless acknowledged its value as the legal basis for opposition. Still, Pius saw the need to do something about Nazi abuses and revealed his determination to issue a critical encyclical. Pacelli asked the German bishops whether such an encyclical might lead the Nazis to terminate the concordat. Von Faulhaber responded that this depended on its tone and suggested that it take a conciliatory rather than a condemnatory approach. Pacelli wrote a draft that the pope found weak and unfocused, and he substituted a more forthright and critical analysis of German developments—though it did not include the bold critique of racism and anti-Semitism found in the draft of the condemnation of the Holy Office. The general of the Jesuits, Ledochowski, nonetheless found it rather harsh. Clearly the resulting document, in the words of Pacelli, represented "a compromise between the Holy See's sense that 'it could not be silent' and its 'fears and worries.'"[84]

On 14 March 1937 the pope issued the encyclical *Mit brennender Sorge,* protesting the treatment of the Church in Germany and negating the principle of the division of humanity on a racial basis. It condemned the notions that "Religion and God are circumscribed by nation and race, by which they are worshipped," and that "Nothing has higher worth than the *Race* and the *People;* anything that is of value beyond them is to be measured by their standard." Pius railed against the attempts to discredit the Old Testament, charging that those who sought to banish it were guilty of blasphemy. He also exposed the fallacies of pantheism, denouncing attempts to alienate Catholics from the Church in favor of state loyalty, while rejecting state efforts to monopolize education. He urged the clergy to unmask and refute these errors, calling upon the faithful to remain true to Christ.[85]

See Pacelli's report on meeting with the German hierarchy, 15–16 Jan. 1937, ASV, SS, Rapporti con gli stati, AS, AAES, Germania, 1922–39, posizione 719, fascicolo 314, cited ibid., 134, 248.

84. See "The Holy Office's Comparison between Its Draft Condemnations and *Mit brennender Sorge* (1937)," Godman, *Hitler and the Vatican,* appendix 3, 200–225; ASV, SS, Rapporti con gli stati, AS, AAES, Germania, 1936–38, posizione, fascicolo 313, no. 43, cited ibid., 253n25; Pacelli quoted ibid., 147–48.

85. "Mit Brennender Sorge," 14 March 1937, *PE* 3:525–35; ASV, SS, Rapporti con gli stati,

The Nazis, who had brutally squashed most other critics, branded this encyclical a "call to battle against the Reich." Hitler was infuriated and vowed revenge against the Church.[86] "The National and racial formulas of the Reich do not square altogether with the dogmas of the Catholic Church," the Nazi periodical *Wille und Macht* pronounced in May 1937, criticizing the pope for addressing those in "prison cells and concentration camps." It parroted the party stance that racial issues had to be resolved by the folk and their state, without Vatican interference.[87] Pius vehemently disagreed, and was disturbed by Mussolini's September 1937 visit to Germany, fearing the spread of the Nazi contagion. He lamented that German Catholics in Rumania admired Hitler and considered the Nazi doctrines condemned in the recent papal encyclical compatible with the Catholic faith.[88] Pius XI's anti-Nazi policy failed to resonate in much of the German Church and part of the curia. Critics complained that *Mit brennender Sorge*, rather than tempering the Nazis, had enraged them, leading to a greater repression of German Catholics. These voices, including that of Pacelli and the secretariat of state, invoked diplomacy and the use of the concordat to redress grievances.[89] Such objections did not silence Pius XI's Vatican, which sanctioned a series of articles in the *Civiltà Cattolica* warning Catholics to eradicate all traces of anti-Semitism from their hearts, while another article in the Jesuit journal invoked coexistence between Catholics and Jews.[90]

In June 1937 the pope personally presided over a special session of the Congregation for Extraordinary Ecclesiastical Affairs to determine how to respond to Nazi racism. At the same time, Cardinal Ottaviani, the assessor of the Holy Office, brought Pius a decree placing Giulio Cogni's polemical book *Il razzismo,* which sought to spread anti-Semitism in Italy, on the Index. The pope readily approved the ban but felt more had to be done. "It is obviously necessary to do more and better; for ages they have been com-

---

AS, AAES, Germania, 1922–39, posizione 719, fascicoli 312–21; Godman, *Hitler and the Vatican,* appendix 3, 211–13.

86. *DGFP,* series D, vol. 1, no. 633; Amleto Cicongani to Pacelli, 24 April 1937, ASV, SS, Rapporti con gli stati, AS, AAES, Germania, 1922–39, posizione 720, fascicolo 329, no. 40, cited in Godman, *Hitler and the Vatican,* 149, 252n35.

87. *Persecution of the Catholic Church in the Third Reich,* 242.

88. ASV, SS, Rapporti con gli stati, AS, AAES, Germania, 1922–39, posizione 720, fascicolo 339; Godman, *Hitler and the Vatican,* 149.

89. Moro, *Chiesa e lo sterminio degli ebrei,* 105–6.

90. Miccoli, "Santa Sede e Chiesa Italiana," 857.

ing to me and saying such things [that racism and anti-Semitism had to be condemned], but they do nothing. Let them start to waffle less and *do* something."[91] Possibly the pope's frustration was provoked by the decision of the sacred tribunal on 2 June to postpone the condemnation of Nazism. Probably at the pope's directive, *Civiltà Cattolica,* which occasionally issued anti-Jewish pronouncements, declared that the Church condemned all forms of anti-Semitism.[92] Mussolini then announced that he shared the pope's position. "We are Catholics, proud of our faith and respectful of it," he told the Austrian chancellor, Schuschnigg, in 1937. "We do not accept the Nazi racial theories."[93] The following April, the Sacred Congregation of Seminaries, presided over by Pius XI, condemned the pernicious racism championed by Nazi Germany and charged Catholic academic institutions with combating these erroneous theories.[94]

Pius urged the rectors of Catholic universities to refute the "ridiculous" pronouncements of the Reich. These included (1) the notion that the "human races" are widely different from one another in their innate nature, (2) the call for strengthening the race and purity of blood by every means, (3) the claim that all intellectual and moral qualities stem from the blood, which determines the nature of the race, (4) the belief that the prime aim of education is to develop the character of the race, perceived as the highest good, (5) the conviction that religion is subject to the law of race and should be subordinate to it, (6) the notion that the standard of all legal organizations is the instinct of race, (7) the belief that nothing exists except the cosmos or universe, and (8) the claim that individuals do not exist except through the "state" and for the "state." The Catholic press concluded that these instructions constituted a "virtual encyclical against racism!"[95]

In July Pius stressed the absolute incompatibility between these errors and Catholicism, and reiterated his belief that Nazism opposed the spirit

91. Quoted in Godman, *Hitler and the Vatican,* 154.

92. "La questione giudaica e l'apostalto cattolico," *CC,* 23 June 1937.

93. Michaelis, *Mussolini and the Jews,* 35.

94. "Cronaca Contemporanea," *CC,* 9–22 June 1938; Patricia M. Keefe, "Popes Pius XI and Pius XII, the Catholic Church, and the Nazi Perseution of the Jews," *British Journal of Holocaust Education* 2 (summer 1993): 32.

95. "Pius XI's Instruction to the Rectors of Catholic Universities and Seminars to Refute 'Ridiculous Dogmas,'" in Godman, *Hitler and the Vatican,* appendix 4, 222–25; Passelecq and Suchecky, *Encyclique cachée de Pie XI,* 157.

of the creed and violated the teachings of the faith. His stance angered the Nazis and especially *Der Angriff*, the newspaper of Nazi Germany's Labor Front, which had long been critical of Pius XI's position on race. Among other things, it stigmatized the Vatican as the "Legal Defender of Racial Pollution."[96] Opponents of Nazi racism, on the other hand, were delighted by the Vatican's condemnation. Italian Jews were convinced that the Vatican stand against racial heresy had prevented the diffusion of racism in Italy. Pius declared that "a real religious persecution" prevailed in Germany and cited his need to provide a testament to the truth.[97]

Pius XI continued his denunciation of Nazi nationalism throughout 1938.[98] Appalled by its racial mythology and its flagrant breaches of morality, he deplored its extension to Austria following the *Anschluss.*[99] He was therefore outraged by the actions of Cardinal Theodor Innitzer, who indicated the episcopacy's support for the Nazi absorption of Austria, summoning him to Rome and demanding that he retract such support. Nazi persecutions in Germany and Austria saddened the pope not only as father of the faithful but as a simple man who saw human dignity betrayed.[100] He deplored the fact that the theological faculties of Salzburg and Innsbruck universities had been disbanded by the Nazis. In October 1938, during the Church's commemoration of the battle of Lepanto, young Catholics carried anti-Nazi placards, some boldly proclaiming that Christ was their Führer! The Nazis retaliated by accelerating their anti-Catholic campaign. Secretary of State Pacelli, more than anyone else, prevented a complete break with the regime the pontiff found so odious. When Cardinal Munderlein of Chicago referred to Hitler as "an Austrian paperhanger, and a poor one at that," and the German government protested to the Vatican, Pius XI refused to rebuke the cardinal; on the contrary, he praised him. Despite the growing tension between the Vatican and the Reich,

96. Bertetto, *Discorsi di Pio XI,* 3:770; Der Angriff, 1937–39, ASV, SS, Rapporti con gli stati, AS, AAES, Germania, 1922–39, posizione 730, fascicolo 345; *Persecution of the Catholic Church in the Third Reich,* 418.

97. Michaelis, *Mussolini and the Jews,* 243; "Al Sacro Collegio alla Prelatura Romana," 24 Dec. 1937, Bertetto, *Discorsi di Pio XI,* 3:678–80.

98. See "Il Santo Padre Ha Incominciato," 24 Dec. 1937, in Koenig, *Principles for Peace,* 539–40; "Le Missioni e il Nazionalismo," 21 Aug. 1938, ibid., 545; Hachey, *Anglo-Vatican Relations, 1914–1939,* 370, 379.

99. Charles-Roux, *Huit ans au Vatican,* 52.

100. "Anzituto Egli," 20 Oct. 1938, in Koenig, *Principles for Peace,* 548–49.

Pacelli assured the German ambassador that friendly relations would be restored. In fact, the German ambassador informed his government that Cardinal Pacelli sought to moderate the actions of this "difficult" pope.[101]

Papal anger increased when Mussolini's Italy moved closer to Hitler's Germany. Pius was especially pained to see Fascism adopt Nazism's brutality toward Jews. When Hitler visited Rome in May 1938, the pope left for Castel Gandolfo. *L'Osservatore Romano* ignored the Führer's presence, printing instead the pope's April condemnation of racism.[102] Furthermore, the Vatican museum was closed, and religious establishments were forbidden to display Nazi symbols. At the Vatican's "request," students of the German-speaking ecclesiastical college in Rome did not take part in the festivities surrounding Hitler's visit. The Romans also followed the pope's example, showing themselves less than gracious to the Nazi visitors, while the Archbishop of Florence, following the papal lead, closed the Duomo.[103]

From Castel Gandolfo Pius XI lamented the glorification of a "cross that was the enemy of Christianity." He repeated that "Catholic" meant universal and could be neither racial nor separatist.[104] Until the later 1930s, Il Duce had shown restraint on the racial issue so as to avoid a clash with Pius XI, recognizing that racism violated the teachings of the Church that had such a deep influence on Italians. The recently opened documents for the pontificate of Pius XI (1922–39) reveal that the *Anschluss,* which Mussolini opposed, proved a decisive turning point in Fascist Italy's relationship with Nazi Germany. Following the German absorption of Austria, which brought the Nazis to the Brenner frontier, Il Duce urged Pius XI to excommunicate Hitler. He apparently hoped that such a step would weaken Hitler's position in Catholic Austria and render him less dangerous to

101. William M. Harrigan, "Pius XII's Efforts to Effect a Détente in German-Vatican Relations, 1939," *CHR* 49 (July 1963): 177; George O. Kent, "Pope Pius XII and Germany: Some Aspects of German-Vatican Relations, 1933–1943," *AHR* 70 (Oct. 1964): 62; *DGFP,* series C, vol. 4, no. 482.

102. Hitler in Rome, 1938, ASV, SS, Rapporti con gli stati, AS, AAES, Germania, 1922–39, posizione 735, fascicolo 353; Lapide, *Three Popes and the Jews,* 113.

103. Alvarez, *Spies in the Vatican,* 202; William L. Shire, *Berlin Diary: The Journal of a Foreign Correspondent, 1934–1941* (New York: Knopf, 1941), 115.

104. Camille M. Cianfarra, *The War and the Vatican* (London: Oates and Washbourne, 1945), 122; Hachey, *Anglo-Vatican Relations, 1914–1939,* 389–94; Bernardini, "Origins and Development of Racial Anti-Semitism," 436.

Italy and Europe. When the Vatican did not comply, Mussolini decided to work with Hitler rather than against him, displaying solidarity with Nazi Germany by adopting its racist anti-Semitism.[105] Shortly thereafter, a Nazi commission ventured to Milan to assist the Italians in drafting their racial legislation.

In mid-July 1938 the Italian dictatorship released its "Fascist Manifesto on Race," which included ten "scientific" propositions on the racial issue and prepared the way for Fascist Italy's racial laws. The anti-Semitic manifesto was a slap in the face of the Church.[106] *L'Osservatore Romano* was cautious in its comments, but the pope was less prudent, branding it "a true form of apostasy" and urging Catholic Action associations to defy it. "We do not wish to separate anyone in the human family," the pope told the students of Propaganda Fide, "we clearly understand racism and exaggerated nationalism . . . as creating barriers between men and men, people and people, populations and populations."[107]

Once anti-Semitism became an official doctrine of the Fascist regime, the old pope made no secret of his compassion for the victims of persecution, while condemning "hatred" of the people once chosen by God.[108] To further develop his critique of the Nazi regime, Pius sought the assistance of the American Jesuit John La Farge, who over the years had rallied the Church against racism and whom the pope invited to meet with him on his way back from the International Eucharistic Congress at Budapest in April.[109] Pius had read and liked La Farge's *Interracial Justice,* published in 1937, which denounced the notion of "pure race" as a myth that could not serve as the basis for human relationships. La Farge reminded his readers that the teachings of Christ proclaimed the moral unity of the human

105. "Mussolini Asked Pope to Slam Hitler," *New York Daily News,* 23 Sept. 2003; Michaelis, *Mussolini and the Jews,* 146, 149, 173.

106. Meir Machaelis, "Fascism, Totalitarianism and the Holocaust: Reflections on Current Interpretations of National Socialist Anti-Semitism," *European History Quarterly* 19, no. 1 (1989): 93. For the text of the manifesto, see De Felice, *Storia degli ebrei sotto il fascismo,* 541–42.

107. "Agli Alunni dei Collegio di Propaganda Fide," 28 July 1938, in Bertetto, *Discorsi di Pio XI,* 3:780.

108. Michaelis, *Mussolini and the Jews,* 244; Dietrich, "Catholic Theologians in Hitler's Reich," 32.

109. For La Farge's account of his meeting with the pope, see John La Farge, S.J., *The Manner Is Ordinary* (New York: Harcourt, Brace, 1954), 253–72.

race, and that his Church offered salvation to all mankind. He warned that Christian social philosophy looked upon the deliberate fostering of racial prejudice as a sin that destroyed the creator's intended relationship of the individual to the rest of humanity.[110]

The eighty-one-year-old pontiff, exasperated by the fact that the racism and violation of human rights endemic to Nazi Germany were being brought to Italy, which had hitherto remained largely free of this contagion, commissioned La Farge to write an encyclical condemning these moral evils.[111]

This was not the first time Pius XI had relied on the Jesuits for a sensitive mission. In February 1926 he had summoned Michel d'Herbigny to the papal apartments, announcing that he had been selected for a secret mission to Moscow to establish a clandestine Church hierarchy there. Subsequently, in June 1926, he created a new Vatican Commission for Russia to deal with Soviet affairs, headed by the Jesuit bishop d'Herbigny. Later he relied on d'Herbigny to draft his 1930 statement denouncing the communist persecution of religion.[112] In the mid-1930s, the pope had again called upon the Jesuits to compose the condemnation of racism and anti-Semitism he hoped the Holy Office would launch, but he was blocked by tribunal members who feared the consequences. Now, with La Farge's help, Pius had the opportunity to issue this encyclical unimpeded. Aware that he would again encounter opposition if his intention became known, he swore the American Jesuit to secrecy, not even informing his secretary of state.[113]

Like La Farge, the pope saw the need for a spiritual and moral treat-

---

110. John La Farge, S.J., *Interracial Justice: A Study of the Catholic Doctrine of Race Relations* (New York: America Press, 1937), 12–15, 59–61, 75, 172–73. La Farge later published *The Race Question and the Negro: A Study of the Catholic Doctrine on Interracial Justice* (1943) and *The Catholic Viewpoint on Race Relations* (1956) among other volumes, as well as a series of articles in *America* and *Interracial Review*.

111. The reader will find the complete abridged French version of *Humanitas Generis Unitas* published for the first time in Georges Passelecq and Bernard Suchecky, *L'encyclique cachée de Pie XI . Une occasion manquée de l'Eglise face a l'antisémitisme*. The story of the encyclical is put into context in the preface, "Pie XI, les Juifs et l'antisemitisme," by Emile Poulat (Paris: Éditions La Découverte, 1995), 219–310. It was translated from the French by Steven Rendall, with an introduction by Garry Wills, and published as *The Hidden Encyclical of Pius XI* (New York: Harcourt, Brace, 1997).

112. Alvarez, *Spies in the Vatican*, 130–31, 138, 144.

113. Robert A. Hecht, *An Unordinary Man: A Life of Father John La Farge, S.J.* (Lanham, Md.: Scarecrow Press, 1996), 114–15.

ment of the defense of human rights. Pius XI outlined the topic and its method of treatment with the American Jesuit. "Simply say what you would say to the entire world if you were Pope," Pius told La Farge.[114] On 3 July 1938 La Farge dispatched a memorandum to the assistant to the New York provincial, describing his 22 June 1938 meeting with Pius and revealing that the pope had commissioned him to write an encyclical on what he deemed "the most burning issue of the day." La Farge reported that Pius XI believed that God had sent him, for he had been searching for someone to write on the topic. Given the pope's desire to have the encyclical quickly, Father Ledochowski, the General of the Jesuits, suggested that La Farge collaborate with two other Jesuits: the Frenchman Gustave Desbuquois of Action Populaire, a social action center in Paris, and the German Gustav Gundlach, a professor at the Gregorian University in Rome who had written previously against anti-Semitism. The three men feverishly outlined a draft over the summer of 1938, and in late September presented the projected encyclical, *Humani Generis Unitas* (the Unity of the Human Race), to Ledochowski for transmission to the pope.[115]

The document explicitly forbade Catholics "to remain silent in the presence of racism," noting that the struggle for racial purity "ends by being uniquely the struggle against the Jews." As a consequence, "millions of persons are deprived of the most elementary rights and privileges of citizens in the very land of their birth." Furthermore, anti-Semitism served as an excuse for attacking the sacred person of the Savior himself, and taken to its logical conclusion was an attack on Christianity. "It is the task and duty of the Church, the dignity and responsibility of the Chief Shepherd and of his brother Shepherds whom the Holy Ghost has placed to rule the Church of God, that they should point out to mankind the true course to be followed, the eternal divine order in the changing circumstances of the times." "The Redemption opened the doors of salvation to the entire human race," the encyclical continued, establishing a universal Kingdom without distinction between Jew and Gentile, Greek and barbarian.[116]

The draft did not renounce the Church's long history of anti-Judaism.

114. Ibid., 115; "Jesuit Says Pius XI Asked for Draft," *National Catholic Reporter,* 22 Dec. 1972, 3.

115. Hecht, *An Unordinary Man,* 115; Passelecq and Suchecky, *Encyclique cachée de Pie XI,* 115.

116. Galleys of La Farge's copy of *Humani Generis Unitas (HGU),* which was to be

Apparently the pope, and the Jesuit authors of the document, considered it distinct from anti-Semitism and ignored the possible relationship between the two. In fact, Gundlach, in his 1930 article on anti-Semitism in the *Lexicon für Theologie und Kirche,* focused on their differences, condemning the first while defending the latter.[117]

> The lofty concept which the Church has forever held relative to the vocation of the Jewish people even seen from their past history . . . do[es] not blind her to the spiritual dangers [to which contact with Jews can expose souls], nor make her unaware of need for safeguarding her children against spiritual contagion. Nor is this need diminished in our own time. Just as long as the unbelief of the Jewish people persists, just as long as there is active hostility to the Christian religion, just so long must the Church use every effort to see that the effects of this unbelief and hostility are not to redound to the ruin of the faith and morals of her own members. Where, moreover, she finds the hatred of the Christian religion has driven misguided souls, whether of the Jewish people or of other origin, to ally themselves with, or actively to promote revolutionary movements which aim to destroy society and to obliterate from the minds of men the knowledge, reverence, and [love] of God, she must warn her children against such movements, expose [the ruses and fallacies of their leaders], and find against them appropriate safeguards.[118]

These ends, the draft continued, could not be achieved by anti-Semitism, and in this it concurred with the conclusion of the 1928 decree that "the Apostolic See has protected this people against unjust oppression and just as every kind of envy and jealousy among the nations must be disapproved of, so in an especial manner must be that hatred which is generally termed anti-Semitism."[119]

While La Farge and his colleagues worked on the draft of the encyclical throughout the summer months, Pius XI made four speeches against racism between mid-July and mid-September 1938.[120] These speeches

---

published in the *Catholic Mind,* are preserved in the offices of the journal *America* and were transmitted to me by Professor Robert A. Hecht. The encyclical was supposed to appear in *Catholic Mind* of 1973 but somehow was never published. My quotations of the encyclical are taken from the galleys for the *Catholic Mind,* 31, par. 123; 33, pars. 131–32; 36b, par. 147; 38b, par. 154; and 34, par. 135. See also Passelecq and Suchecky, *Hidden Encyclical of Pius XI,* 283–96.

117. See Passelecq and Suchecky, *Hidden Encyclical of Pius XI,* 48.

118. Galleys of *HGU,* 35b, par. 142.

119. Ibid., 36, par. 144.

120. Speeches of 15 July, 28 July, 21 Aug., and 6 Sept. 1938, in Bertetto, *Discorsi di Pio XI,* 3:766–72, 777–90, 793–98, 869–72.

challenged the contentions made by Roberto Farinacci in *Il regime fascista* at the end of August, which traced the roots of anti-Semitism to Catholicism and charged that hatred of the Jews was central to Christianity. "We cannot in the course of a few weeks," Farinacci asserted, "renounce the anti-Semitic consciousness which the Church itself has formed over the millennia."[121] Pius was not silenced by these accusations, but continued to denounce Fascism and anti-Semitism. In Berlin Hitler decried the anti-Axis machinations of the Church of Pius XI, alarming conciliators in the curia.[122] Their concerns did not silence Pius, either.

Also in 1938 the pope selected the physicist Tullio Levi-Civita for membership in the Pontifical Academy of Science, the most prestigious scientific body under papal patronage, an expression of his contempt for Mussolini's Italian Academy, which had rejected Levi-Civita on racist grounds. In fact, he appointed this Jewish scientist chairman of the commission entrusted with awarding the papal prize, the "Premio Pio XI." Pius also admitted the Italian Jewish mathematician Vito Volterra into the Pontifical Academy of Science. "God is the Master of the sciences," the pope remarked as he named Volterra a member, adding, "All human beings are admitted equally, without distinction of race, to participate, to share, to study and to explore truth and science."[123]

Pius also kept a close watch on developments across the Atlantic, where the anti-Semitic radio priest Reverend Charles Coughlin found a wide audience in the United States, as millions were mesmerized by his broadcasts and read his column in the newspaper *Social Justice*. As early as 1930 the apostolic delegate, Archbishop Pietro Fumasoni-Biondi, attempted to curb the unruly cleric but found him protected by his superior, Bishop Michael Gallagher of Detroit. In 1935 Fumasoni-Biondi's successor as apostolic delegate, Amleto Cicognani, proved no more successful in moderating the tone and message of the popular radio priest. The Vatican likewise failed to have the American bishops issue some statement distancing the hierarchy from him. When the American bishops showed themselves reluctant to act, papal authority was invoked. In September 1936 *L'Osservatore Romano* denied Coughlin's claim that he had the approval of the

121. Quoted in Bernardini, "Origins and Development of Racial Anti-Semitism," 435.
122. Meir Michaelis, "Fascism, Totalitarianism and the Holocaust," 89.
123. Edward D. Kleinlerer, "Scholars at the Vatican," *Commonweal* 37 (4 Dec. 1942): 187–88.

Holy See. It was widely believed that the Vatican's refusal to make Detroit into an archdiocese, and the selection of Edward Mooney as Gallagher's successor as Bishop of Detroit, reflected Pius XI's dissatisfaction with Gallagher.[124]

Despite the papal denunciations of anti-Semitism, Archbishop Mooney allowed Coughlin to spew his lies about the Jews until the spring of 1942, when he was finally silenced. The archbishop did attempt to censor and control Couglin's publication *Social Justice* on the grounds that it was a Catholic newspaper. But the paper's attorneys resisted the archdiocesan efforts by noting that *Social Justice* "is not and never has been a Catholic publication," and that the corporation that owned it "will continue to edit and publish *Social Justice* without supervision of anyone except its own officers." Meanwhile, Cardinal Munderlain responded to Coughlin's anti-Semitic campaign on behalf of the Vatican, stating, "As an American citizen, Father Coughlin has the right to express his personal views on current events," but that he was "not authorized to speak for the Catholic Church, nor does he represent the doctrines and sentiments of the Church."[125] Pius XI objected to racism wherever it was found, whether in Germany, America, or at home in Italy. He rejected the notion that the Italian variety was homegrown and considered it a Nazi import. Although the Italian Foreign Office denied this, the pope would not be swayed in this belief.[126] Only at the end of his career did Mussolini acknowledge that the pope had gauged the situation accurately.[127] Il Duce's adoption of Hitler's anti-Semitism stirred the aged pope to express his wrath publicly. He complained that the Italian press censured his attack on racism, while it included Nazi commentary. Pius had his nuncio to Italy, Monsignor Borgongini Duca, denounce Italy's racist legislation.[128] Pius XI preferred the Latin term *gens Italica* and to speak of "peoples" rather than "races," not because he

124. Earl Boyea, "The Reverend Charles Coughlin and the Church: The Gallagher Years, 1930–1937," *CHR* 81 (April 1995): 211–13, 216, 218, 222–25.

125. Ronald Modras, "Father Coughlin and Anti-Semitism: Fifty Years Later," *JCS* 31 (spring 1989): 235, 239, 244; Norman Cohn, *Warrant for Genocide: The Myth of the Jewish World-Conspiracy and the Protocols of the Elders of Zion* (New York: Harper and Row, 1967), 235.

126. De Felice, in his *Storia degli ebrei italiani sotto il fascismo,* saw a clear connection between Fascist and Nazi racism.

127. Michaelis, *Mussolini and the Jews,* 155.

128. See *New York Times,* 6 Aug., 12 Aug., and 1 Sept. 1938.

shunned things German but because he considered the Latin terms more civil and less barbaric. Human dignity, he repeated, rested in a unified humanity.[129] Such papal statements guided the authors of the projected encyclical, and, not surprisingly, similar statements found their way into *Humani Generis Unitas.*[130]

During the long summer of 1938, Pius considered a revision of Vatican policy toward the German and Italian dictatorships, and was backed up by the Jesuit *Civiltà Cattolica,* which echoed the pope's sentiments, perceiving racism as fundamentally anti-Christian. But a good part of the clerical establishment continued to press for conciliation rather than conflict.[131] These moderates, hoping for a more diplomatic successor to Pius XI, were responsible for the little-known agreement concluded with the Fascist government in mid-August on the racial issue. Father Angelo Martini, granted access to the Vatican Archives for the pontificate of Pius XI (closed until very recently), wrote in 1978 that the "pact" of 16 August 1938 had three major provisions: racism and the Jewish issue, Catholic Action in Italy, and Church-state problems in Bergamo. It required concessions from both the Vatican and the Mussolini regime. In return for concessions to Catholic Action and changes in Bergamo, the Vatican had to leave the Jewish issue to the regime, which proposed to deal with it "politically." It thus called for total governmental freedom in racial matters, without Catholic interference. Under its provisions, only the Holy See could discuss such issues—but only privately with Mussolini. If accepted, the Church would have had to compromise its doctrines in order to safeguard Catholic Action groups. Clearly, this "pact" reflected Fascist priorities, with perhaps some ecclesiastical input by Father Pietro Tacchi-Venturi, an intermediary between Mussolini and the Holy See, and the nuncio, Monsignor Borgongini-Duca.[132]

It is inconceivable that the outspoken pope would have approved such

129. Bertetto, *Discorsi di Pio XI,* 3:782–83.

130. See sections 111 on race and racism, 112 on denial of human unity, and 116 denial of true religious and moral values, in the galleys of the encyclical *HGU,* preserved in the offices of *America,* 29b and 30, and in Passelecq and Suchecky, *Encyclique cachée de Pie XI,* 274–76.

131. *CC,* 10 Aug. 1938; Miccoli, "Santa Sede e Chiesa Italiana," 881.

132. Angelo Martini, S.J., "L'Ultima battaglia di Pio XI," in *Studi sulla questione romana e la conciliazione* (Rome: Cinque Lune, 1963), 186–87; Ariangiola Reineri, *Cattolici e fascismo a Torino, 1925–1943* (Milan: Feltrinelli, 1978), 192; Miccoli, "Santa Sede e Chiesa Italiana," 878.

an agreement, which violated his convictions, and he refused to follow its guidelines. In his talks of 21 August and 6 September he denounced the Fascist race manifesto as a "gross error" that violated Catholic doctrine. When he visited the College of the Propaganda Fide he warned the students to shun "exaggerated nationalism," which in his view was a real curse.[133] When Farinacci proclaimed the Jesuits allies of the regime against the Jews, the *Civiltà Cattolica* rejected the contention, noting that their attitude toward the Jews had never been based on racist principles. One journal described the pope's antiracist speech as initiating a *Kulturkampf* in reverse. Pius's position was strikingly similar to the one enunciated in the projected encyclical.[134]

The publication of these papal condemnations in the *Osservatore Romano* prompted Fascist and Nazi accusations that the pope had stepped beyond the bounds of religion. But the pope's attacks only grew stronger; he had to bear witness to the truth.[135] "No, it's not possible for us Christians to participate in anti-Semitism," the pope told a group of visiting Belgians on 6 September 1938. "Spiritually, we are Semites."[136] Nor was Vatican Radio silenced, but it continued to revile the attempt to introduce racism into Italy as "a gross error."[137] In mid-September Roberto Farinacci, a crusader for anti-Semitism, denounced the pope's position. "Religious questions may be the business of the pope, but political ones are the exclusive province of the *duce*," he wrote. "The pope is wrong in pretending that racialism is a religious problem." His paper *Il Regime Fascista* continued to oppose the "Judeophile" policies of Pius XI, castigating him as an ally of Jews, Communists, and Protestants. Mussolini, likewise, cautioned the Vatican to cease its Judeophile campaign.[138]

During the infamous Kristallnacht pogrom of 9–10 November 1938,

133. Moro, *Chiesa e lo sterminio degli ebrei*, 89; Agli Alunni di "Propaganda Fide," 21 Aug. 1938, in Bertetto, *Discorsi di Pio XI*, 3:784–86.

134. *CC*, 1 Oct. 1938; "Pio XI e un Appello," *OR*, 26 Jan. 1961. The similarities between Pius's pronouncements and the draft encyclical are apparent in sections 106–10 in the galleys of encyclical *HGU*, 28, 28b, 29, and in Passelecq and Suchecky, *Encyclique cachée de Pie XI*, 272–74.

135. *OR*, 30 July and 22–23 Aug. 1938; Ad Insegnanti di Azione Cattolica, 6 Sept. 1938, in Bertetto, *Discorsi di Pio XI*, 3:796.

136. Passelecq and Suchecky, *Encyclique cachée de Pie XI*, 181.

137. Quoted in Lapide, *Three Popes and the Jews*, 96.

138. Michaelis, *Mussolini and the Jews*, 240–41; 181.

Nazi thugs destroyed synagogues and vandalized Jewish businesses, killing more than ninety Jews throughout Germany. Some thirty thousand Jews were arrested and dispatched to concentration camps, and the Jewish community was required to pay $400 million for their support.[139] While Pius XI, possibly constrained by the secretariat of state,[140] did not personally denounce the barbarism, a number of high Church figures did, including the Cardinal Archbishop of Milan, the Cardinal Archbishop of Paris, the Primate of Belgium, the Patriarch of Lisbon, the Archbishop of San Francisco, and the rector of the Catholic cathedral in Berlin. Early in the same month, Mussolini issued a decree forbidding marriage between Italian Aryans and persons of "another race." It was followed by the decree of 17 November 1938, "Measures for the Defense of the Italian Race," which restricted Jewish marriage, employment, and schooling.[141] Pius complained that this represented a violation of the concordat. It was also denounced in the Vatican journal.[142] The pope wanted *L'Osservatore Romano* to publish his protest but Pacelli dissuaded him.[143] Nonetheless, outsiders such as the Roosevelt administration appreciated that Pius XI represented an important counterweight to the totalitarian dictatorships. In Italy, the Vatican's daily *Osservatore Romano* and its radio transmissions represented the only media outlet able to evade Fascist censorship.[144]

Papal reliance on the concordat does not necessarily mean that it defended only narrow ecclesiastical interests.[145] Pius believed it provided legal justification for protesting what the Fascists deemed "purely political issues," and in his Christmas allocution he again attacked the anti-Semitic measures as a violation of the concordat.[146] He did so despite Count Ciano's threat that such papal denunciations of Fascist racial policies

139. Saul Friedlander, *Nazi Germany and the Jews* (New York: HarperCollins, 1997), 269–77; Modras, "Father Coughlin and Anti-Semitism," 231.

140. Kristallnacht, 9–10 Nov. 1938, ASV, SS, Rapporti con gli stati, AS, AAES, Germania, 1922–39, posizione 742, fascicolo 356.

141. The text can be found in the *Raccolta ufficiale delle leggi e decreti del Regno d'Italia,* 1938, 4:2946–49.

142. "A proposito d'un decreto legge," *OR,* 14–15 Nov. 1938.

143. Martini, "L'Ultima battaglia di Pio XI," 219.

144. Alvarez, *Spies in the Vatican,* 240.

145. Giacomo Martina, "L'Ecclesiologia prevalente nel pontificato di Pio XI," in *Cattolici e fascisti in Umbria (1922–1945),* ed. Alberto Monticone (Bologna: Mulino, 1978), 233–34.

146. Con grande, 24 Dec. 1938, in Koenig, *Principles for Peace,* 549–51; *PP* 2:114; *New York Times,* 25 Dec. 1938.

made a clash with Mussolini's regime inevitable. In fact, during the last months of the pontificate, there was a marked deterioration in relations between the Vatican and the Fascist state. Papal critics derived some consolation from the conviction that the pope already "had one foot in the grave."[147] Age and illness curtailed but did not stop Pius XI's denunciations of the racism of the fascist regimes. Despite the concerted efforts of Pacelli and the nuncio to Italy to patch up relations between Il Duce and the pope, there was no healing this rift.[148] The strong stance that Pius XI assumed on the racial issue worried some in the Vatican. His comment that Catholics were spiritually Semites was deleted by the editors of *L'Osservatore Romano* under Pacelli's direction, and other Catholic papers in Italy followed suit. Knowing that his antiracist stance had critics in the Vatican, and fearing that his words might be censored, Pius apparently asked Monsignor Picard's *La Libre Belgique* to publish his remarks in their entirety. Thus the French press, followed by the Italian and finally by the world press, learned what the pope had said.[149]

For his condemnation of racism and defense of the Jews, the old pontiff was not only accused of being a Jew lover but of being Jewish himself. In fact, *Das Schwarze Korps,* in a poem published before his death, branded him the "Chief Rabbi of the Christian World."[150] His campaign against the racist policies of the dictators was frustrated not only by the hostility of the dictatorial regimes, his poor health, and his advanced age, but also by those in the Vatican seeking a more conciliatory successor. The Fascist regime even had some *monsignori* in its service, and they and others sought to isolate the old pontiff and create obstacles to his campaign against anti-Semitism. At the end of August 1938, when the Italian foreign minister warned the papal nuncio that a rupture between Church and state was inevitable if the pope continued to denounce racism, the nuncio responded, contrary to the pope's position, that he found nothing wrong with racism, asserting he was personally very "anti-Semitic."[151] Mussolini's

147. Galeazzo Giano, *Ciano's Hidden Diaries, 1937–1938* (New York: E. P. Dutton, 1953), 140–41; Michaelis, *Mussolini and the Jews,* 251; Shire, *Berlin Diary,* 88.

148. Richard A. Webster, *The Cross and the Fasces* (Stanford: Stanford University Press, 1960), 113–15.

149. Miccoli, "Santa Sede e Chiesa Italiana," 879–80.

150. *Persecution of the Catholic Church in the Third Reich,* 426–27.

151. Alvarez, *Spies in the Vatican,* 156, 159; Miccoli, "Santa Sede e Chiesa Italiana," 878; Webster, *Cross and the Fasces,* 114.

Italy, which intensified its espionage against the Vatican of Pius XI, knew of the divisions on the racial issue. "We know that on the racial issue the clergy is divided into two camps," Farinacci wrote in mid-September, adding that "the pope was in no position to do anything about it."[152]

Many in the Vatican saw godless communism as a greater evil and threat to the Church than racist fascism, noting that in 1924, the year of Lenin's death, there were some two hundred Catholic priests in the Soviet Union, whereas by 1938 there were only two![153] Soviet developments disturbed the pope, but he could not ignore the abuses of the fascist states. Consequently, the new year did not bring any improvement in relations between the Vatican and the fascist regimes, as an overworked and ailing Pius prepared a message on Church-state relations to be presented to the Italian bishops gathered in Rome for the tenth anniversary of the Lateran Pacts, 11 February 1939. In the interim the Vatican took steps to find positions for Jewish scholars and officials who had been dismissed, and in January, at the pope's insistence, a similar request was transmitted to the cardinals of North America, accompanied by a personal letter from Pius XI on behalf of the persecuted. Pius also spoke to the diplomatic corps accredited to the Holy See, seeking visas for the victims of racial persecution under Fascism and Nazism.[154] The British representative, who met with the pope at the end of the year, observed that since the Fascist program had adopted racialism, in violation of the fundamental tenets of the Church, he did not see "how the two systems can ever work in harmony together."[155]

In the meantime, what had happened to La Farge's encyclical, for which Pius had such high hopes? Pius XI was not informed that the antiracist encyclical he had commissioned had been delivered at the end of September but kept from him, until he heard from La Farge. Only when an angry pope demanded that it be delivered to him at once did the encyclical belatedly materialize.[156] Reportedly, he received the document on

152. Alvarez, *Spies in the Vatican*, 155; Martini, "L'Ultima battaglia di Pio XI," 189.

153. Alvarez, *Spies in the Vatican*, 142.

154. "Pio XI e un Appello," *OR*, Jan. 26, 1961; Keefe, "Popes Pius XI and Pius XII," 33.

155. Owen Chadwick, *Britain and the Vatican during the Second World War* (Cambridge: Cambridge University Press, 1986), 26.

156. It was only after Pius XI's death that Ledochowski informed La Farge that the encyclical had been delivered to the pope and was among his papers. Ledochowski added that since the new pope, Pacelli, had not yet had time to go over the "sundry papers left on his

21 January 1939, but is not certain whether he saw or read it before his death three weeks later. Most probably he did not, even though the failing pope was working on the draft of a new speech excoriating the Fascists. He died on 10 February 1939, before he could deliver it.[157] The draft of this speech, later published by John XXIII, regretted developments in Italy while insisting on the unity of the human family.[158] The draft of the La Farge encyclical was found on Pius XI's desk after his death, together with an attached note from Monsignor Domenico Tardini, indicating that Pius XI wanted the encyclical without delay![159] In light of Pius XI's condemnation of Italian anti-Semitism, it is not surprising that Mussolini was relieved by his death.[160]

Pius XI once said, in an address in 1929, that he would negotiate "with the devil himself" when it came to saving souls. Ten years later he had concluded that the Vatican could no longer coexist with Fascism and Nazism.[161] At his death, Pius was praised for his bravery in combating fascist racism. "More than once did we have occasion to be deeply grateful for the attitude which he took up against the persecution of racial minorities, and in particular for the deep concern which he expressed for the fate of the persecuted Jews of Central Europe," Bernard Joseph of the Jewish Agency wrote two days after his death. "His noble efforts on their behalf will ensure for him for all time a warm place in the memories of Jewish people wherever they live."[162] Rolf Hochhuth, critical of the "silence" of Pius XII, found it unfortunate that brave and resolute Pius XI died on the eve of World War II. After his death, a booklet published by the General Jewish Council, *Father Coughlin, His Facts and Arguments* (1939), quoted Pius XI to expose the fallacious arguments and anti-Semitic sentiments of the "radio priest."[163]

---

desk," it was "premature" to ask him what he planned to do with the draft. Jim Castelli, "Unpublished Encyclical Attacked anti-Semitism," *National Catholic Reporter*, 15 Dec. 1972, 8.

157. *AAS* 51 (1959): 129–35; *PP* 2:114.

158. Il Testo Inedito dell'ultimo discorso di Pio XI presentato da Sua Santità Giovanni XXIII, in Bertetto, *Discorsi di Pio XI*, 3:891–96.

159. "Jesuit Says Pius XI Asked for Draft," *National Catholic Reporter*, 22 Dec. 1972, 4.

160. Roger Aubert, *The Church in a Secularized Society* (New York: Paulist Press, 1978), 557.

161. Speech to the professors and students of the College of Mondragone, May 14, 1929, in Bertetto, *Discorsi di Pio XI*, 2:79; Alvarez, *Spies in the Vatican*, 169.

162. Quoted in Keefe, "Popes Pius XI and Pius XII," 33.

163. Patricia Marx Ellsberg, "An Interview with Rolf Hochhuth" (1964), in *The Papacy*

During the last years of his pontificate, Pius XI had publicly denounced racism as a religious heresy and a violation of natural law. The
encyclical he commissioned La Farge to write represented the logical culmination of this pope's attitude toward the persecution of the Jews. That
document professed Pius's incredulity that "there are still people who
maintain that the doctrine and practice of racism have nothing to do with
Catholic teaching as to faith and morals and nothing to do with philosophy, but are a purely political affair."[164] It seems certain that this pope
would have issued the encyclical, had he lived. His successor thought otherwise.

and Totalitarianism between the Two World Wars, ed. Charles Delzell (New York: John Wiley,
1974), 115; Modras, "Father Coughlin and Anti-Semitism," 233–34.

164. Galleys of encyclical *HGU,* 29b, and Passelecq and Suchecky, *Encyclique cachée de
Pie XI,* 275.

6

THE "SILENCE" OF PIUS XII AND HIS CRUSADE AGAINST COMMUNISM

The Pope at times cannot remain silent. Governments only consider political and military issues, intentionally disregarding moral and legal issues in which, on the other hand, the Pope is primarily interested and cannot ignore. His Holiness said. . . . How could the Pope, in these present circumstances, be guilty of such a serious omission as that of remaining a disinterested spectator of such heinous acts, while all the world was waiting for his words?*

TOWARD THE END OF PIUS XI'S PONTIFICATE, a dual specter haunted the Vatican. There was the fear that relations between Rome and the fascist dictators would deteriorate to the point that the concordats would collapse, and there was the fear that a new world war would erupt, with disastrous consequences for the Church. Those who sought to avert these plagues counted upon the leadership of the politically astute Eugenio Giovanni Pacelli, who had been nuncio in Munich and Berlin and knew Germany well. Expected to pursue a more diplomatic, less confrontational course than his

* *RDHSWW*, 423.

predecessor, Pacelli did not disappoint those who elected him.[1] Pacelli, by family background, training, and personality, seemed admirably suited to confront the emerging diplomatic crisis. Entering the Vatican secretariat of state in 1901, his career was from the first more diplomatic than pastoral. Even more than Pius XI, he preferred concordats to reliance on political parties.[2]

In 1915 Pacelli was dispatched by Benedict XV (1914–22) as envoy to Franz Josef, and two years later was transferred to Bavaria as nuncio and entrusted with the pope's peace effort in Germany.[3] During the Spartacist rising in Munich, communists led by Jews burst into the nunciature brandishing revolvers. Although these revolutionaries left without inflicting much physical damage, the incident left a psychological scar on Pacelli, and some believe it made him not only anticommunist but anti-Semitic.[4] A protégé of Cardinal Gasparri, Pacelli was named apostolic nuncio to the Weimar Republic in 1920 and dispatched to Berlin in 1925, remaining there until the end of 1929, when he was recalled to Rome and given the red hat. He left Germany with some regret and remained a staunch Germanophile throughout his life. In 1930 he replaced Gasparri as secretary of state, supporting Pius XI's policy of concordats by negotiating agreements with a number of German states.[5] His brother, Francesco, was one of the architects of the Lateran Accords, signed with Mussolini's Italy in 1929.

In the summer of 1933 Eugenio was instrumental in the conclusion of the controversial concordat with Hitler's Third Reich. Deemed an "ignoble bargain" by some, critics condemned Pacelli for negotiating with a monster for ecclesiastical advantage and for providing moral sanction to the

---

1. See Renato Moro, *Chiesa e lo sterminio degli ebrei,* 92–93.

2. Pacelli's great-grandfather had been minister of finance under Pope Gregory XVI (1831–46), while his grandfather held the post of undersecretary of the interior under Pius IX (1846–78). On Pacelli's diplomatic skills, see his letters to the Germans bishops (1934–39) in ASV, SS, Rapporti con gli stati, AS, AAES, Germania, 1922–29, posizione Scatole, 26; Phayer, *Catholic Church and the Holocaust,* 221.

3. See ASV, Archivio della Nunziatura Apostolica in Monaco, Mons, Eugenio Pacelli (1917–25, nunzio), buste 307–415; and SS, Rapporti con gli stati, AS, AAES, Baviera, posizione 190, 198, fascicoli 29, 40–53.

4. A number of communist leaders in post–World War I Germany were Jewish, including Rosa Luxemburg in Berlin, Eugene Levine in Munich, and Otto Bauer in Vienna. On the Spartacist rising and its effect on Pacelli, see John Cornwell, *Hitler's Pope: The Secret History of Pius XII* (New York: Viking, 1999), 74–75

5. Bavaria (1924), Prussia (1929), Baden (1932), and Austria (1933).

odious Nazi regime.[6] Neither Pope Pius XI nor Pacelli believed this was the case, but our actions do not always have the consequences we intend. Although Pius XI and Pacelli had markedly different personalities and temperaments, they collaborated in the pursuit of concordats. The two men complemented rather than mirrored each other, sharing the conviction that Catholic interests could best be assured by formal agreements that guaranteed the Church's freedom of action, even with regimes otherwise hostile to Christian principles. In fact, following the conclusion of the Reich concordat, both looked forward to the conclusion of an accord with Yugoslavia.[7] Divisions between the two arose on how best to respond to the flagrant violations of these "contracts" by the dictatorial regimes. The pope was inclined to protest every breach energetically, while his secretary of state proved more willing to hold his tongue and hope for the best.

Pius XI suspected that the Nazis, under the pretense of defending Western civilization, sought to subvert its Christian heritage, replacing it with a pagan philosophy. In March 1937 he issued *Mit brennender Sorge,* which condemned Nazism's racial myths and persecution of the Church.[8] Although Pacelli, under papal orders, played a part in drafting this critical encyclical, he sought to prevent a break between Berlin and the Vatican. "How can the Holy See continue to keep a Nuncio there? It conflicts with our honor!" Pius XI had complained to Pacelli. But the secretary of state had dissuaded the pope from breaking off relations, noting, "If we withdraw the Nuncio how can we maintain contacts with the German bishops?"[9] The overriding desire to preserve contacts between the Holy See and the German Church was a preoccupation that would persist during his own pontificate. It contributed to the momentary triumph of Pacelli's diplomacy over the pope's palpable disgust with Nazi policies during the prewar period.

When Pius XI secretly commissioned the American Jesuit John La

6. Cardinal Gasparri congratulated Cardinal Pacelli on the conclusion of the Reich concordat, 24 July 1933, ASV, SS, Rapporti con gli stati, AS, AAES, Germania, 1922–39, posizione 645, fascicolo 165; Blanshard, *Blanshard on Vatican II,* 144–45.

7. ASV, SS, Rapporti con gli Stati, AS, AAES, Germania, 1922–39, posizione 650, fascicolo 194, no. 305.

8. See the files on Vatican fears of neo-paganism in Nazi Germany (1934–40), ibid., posizione 670–73, fascicolo 233, no. 3884/34; *Mit Brennender Sorge,* 14 March 1937, ibid., posizione 719, fascicoli 312–21.

9. Quoted in Rhodes, *Vatican in the Age of Dictators,* 228–29.

Farge to draft the encyclical *Humani Generis Unitas,* he did so without consulting Pacelli. Gustav Gundlach, who collaborated with La Farge on the project, was convinced that Pacelli was never informed about it, and Pacelli later confessed as much.[10] Pacelli's exclusion is hardly surprising, given his attempt at every turn to frustrate Pius XI's harsher pronouncements on the Nazi regime for fear of provoking a diplomatic rupture with Hitler. It is also possible, conversely, that Pius XI did not wish to implicate a possible successor in an enterprise that might not succeed, thus limiting Pacelli's options.

Pacelli's supporters testified that Pius XI wanted to see Pacelli as the next pope, but this is far from certain. Few secretaries of state had assumed the tiara, and the Vatican's chamberlain is not usually considered for the papacy—and Pius appointed Pacelli to both posts! There is no evidence that the strong-willed Pius XI abandoned his confrontational approach to Nazi Germany at the eleventh hour, in favor of the conciliatory one of his secretary of state. It appears that the frailty of the aged pope weakened his control over Vatican affairs, undermining his ability to influence the course of the conclave that would convene after his death.

When the cardinals gathered in Rome to select a successor, the conciliatory faction was clearly in the ascendancy. On 2 March 1939, in a one-day conclave, a series of precedents were shattered as Pacelli was elected pope, taking the name Pius XII and opening a long and controversial pontificate (1939–58). The selection of this name, as well as his association with the former pope, led outsiders to suppose that he would continue Pius XI's policies. Perhaps this explains why part of the German press was less than enthusiastic about his election, although von Plessen of the German embassy at least preferred "a careful diplomat" to "an impulsive, irascible old man."[11] In a radio message the day after his election, the new pope called for a peace among families, rulers, and nations based on justice and charity.[12]

Pacelli donned the papal tiara at a troubled time, and would have to confront the ravages of World War II, the abuses of the Nazi, Fascist, and

10. Passelecq and Suchecky, *Encyclique cachée de Pie XI,* 124–26.

11. W. A. Purdy, *The Church on the Move: The Characters and Policies of Pius XII and John XXIII* (New York: John Day Co., 1966), 27.

12. *PP* 1:115.

Soviet regimes, the horror of the Holocaust, and the threats of communism and nuclear annihilation. His diplomatic skill and tact were attested to by the fact that the Germans as well as the French and English considered him the best candidate to succeed Pius XI.[13] Trained as a diplomat, Pius XII followed the path paved by Leo XIII and Benedict XV, rather than the more confrontational course of Pius IX, Pius X, and his immediate predecessor, Pius XI. Not surprisingly, soon after his accession the encyclical condemning racism and anti-Semitism was returned to its authors. Pius XI's critique of Fascist violations of the Lateran Accords was likewise scuttled. Pius XII had finally read *Humani Generis Unitas*, and he did incorporate sections of it in his first encyclical, *Summi Pontificatus*, of 20 October 1939, which acknowledged that his office obliged him to teach that in Christ there is neither Gentile nor Jew and to reject the claims of the absolute or totalitarian state. But the new pope rejected the explicit condemnation of anti-Semitism in Pius XI's draft.[14] Indeed, Pius XII never did condemn Fascist and Nazi anti-Semitism explicitly during his pontificate.

Following Pius XII's election, both conservative Catholics and critics of the papacy sought to blur the distinction between him and his predecessor by denying that the late pope had found fault with anti-Semitism, describing these claims as "exaggerated" or even false. Father Francescini Gemelli, the anti-Jewish rector of the Catholic University of Milan, claimed that the late pope was neither democratic, antitotalitarian, nor sympathetic toward the Jews. If the first assertion was true, the latter two were not. Still, others claim that the new pope's approach did not reflect a change in the Church's attitude but rather a change in tactics.[15] Many contemporaries disagreed. Jacques Maritain confided to Aryeh Kubovy, of the World Jewish Congress, that Pius XI would have issued a statement of the Church's position toward the Jews, but he doubted that Pius XII would do

---

13. Alvarez, *Spies in the Vatican*, 169.

14. Ethel Mary Tinnemann, "The Silence of Pope Pius XII," *JCS* 21 (spring 1979): 265; *AAS* 31 (1939): 413–53; Gordan C. Zahn, "The Unpublished Encyclical: An Opportunity Missed," *National Catholic Reporter*, 15 Dec. 1972, 9.

15. Daniel Carpi, "The Catholic Church and Italian Jewry under the Fascists," in *Yad Washem Studies on the European Jewish Catastrophe and Resistance*, ed. Shaul Esh (New York: KATV Publishing, 1975), 55; "Les grands themes des lettres," *Lettres de Pie XII aux Eveques Allemands, 1939–1944, ADSS*, 2:21.

so. Pius XII himself contradicted those who claimed there were no differences between himself and Pius XI, revealing that his predecessor had sought to terminate relations with the Reich but that he had restrained him.[16]

Three basic continuities determined Pius XII's diplomacy toward Nazi Germany: a deep affection for that nation and its people, a strong commitment to the Reich concordat of 1933, and an overriding fear of communism.[17] To this one might add the papal concern that expressing support for the Allies would at once undermine the Vatican's mediating role and weaken the Church in Germany. Pius XII feared that abandoning his impartiality would traumatize German Catholics, subject them to Nazi persecution, and jeopardize the unity of the universal Church. Perhaps he also shared the concern expressed by the nuncio in Berlin that if German Catholics were made to choose between their country and their faith, they might choose the former. Thus, although Pius selected the Francophile Cardinal Luigi Maglione, former nuncio to Paris, as secretary of state, his first priority was to conciliate Nazi Germany.[18]

Following Pacelli's accession, there was a relaxation of tensions between the Vatican and the Reich. One of Pacelli's first actions was to call together the German cardinals Michael Faulhaber of Munich, Adolf Bertram of Breslau, Karl Josef Sculte of Cologne, and Theodore Innitzer of Vienna, and inform them of his intention to send a personal letter to Hitler announcing his accession. This letter addressed the German leader as "Führer."[19] Hitler did not respond, and Germany was the only major power that did not dispatch a representative to the pope's coronation. Nonetheless, the pope was cordial and conciliatory when he met his old friend Diego von Bergen, German ambassador to the Holy See, a few days later.

16. Kubovy, "Silence of Pope Pius XII," 6:24; Rhodes, *Vatican in the Age of Dictators,* 229.

17. In this regard see the correspondence between Pacelli and Orsenigo in the ASV, SS, Rapport con gli stati, AS, AAES, Germania, 1922–39, as well as Michael Feldkamp, *Pius XII. und Deutschland* (Göttingen: Vandenhoeck and Ruprecht, 2000).

18. See the letters of 7 March 1933 and 2 May 1933 in which Orsenigo warns Pacelli that German Catholics should not be made to choose between the new regime and their Catholic faith, ASV, SS, Rappòrti con gli stati, AS, AAES, Germania, posizione 641–43, fascicolo 157, and posizione 643, fascicolo 159; *RDHSWW,* 4.

19. *DGFP,* series D, vol. 4, nos. 473, 475; Hansjakob Stehle, *Eastern Politics of the Vatican,* trans. Sandra Smith (Athens: Ohio University Press, 1981), 67.

By nature shy and gentle, the new pope lacked the fighting spirit of his predecessor, according to Monsignor Domenico Tardini, secretary of the Congregation of Extraordinary Ecclesiastical Affairs.[20] Others provided a more sinister interpretation, suspecting that Pacelli's Germanophile sentiments and anticommunism translated into support for Hitler and the Nazis. Criticism increased when Hitler violated the Munich Agreement and occupied Prague and what remained of Czech territory, without provoking a Vatican protest. Instead, the nuncio in Berlin, Cesare Orsenigo, attributed the invasion to the "nationalist fanaticism of the new generation." Pius also refused to intervene as the Nazis pressured the Poles for a series of concessions, maintaining a strict impartiality between aggressor and aggrieved.[21] Following Benedict XV, he insisted that the papal position was not one of neutrality—which implied indifference—but impartiality. It was a nicety and distinction understood by few, perhaps with the exception of Mussolini, who, following the outbreak of World War II, refused to classify Italy as neutral, insisting she be termed nonbelligerent.

Although Nazi Germany threatened the peace of Europe, the pope expressed his sympathy for the Reich and its people in April 1939. German diplomats were led to understand that Pius XII favored a public truce, so long as vital Church institutions and Catholic principles were not threatened.[22] As the war clouds thickened, he labored to preserve the impartiality of the Holy See, serving as a peacemaker and mediator. Critics complained of the pope's detachment and recourse to generalities in the face of the approaching whirlwind. The French believed that he was not doing enough to condemn the contemplated aggression by the Reich against Poland, and the French ambassador to the Vatican, François Charles-Roux, urged him to make it clear that the burden of guilt for provoking another war would fall on Nazi Germany.[23] This the pope refused to do; he did denounce the violation of treaties and preparation for war in his Easter message of 9 April 1939, but without blaming a particular nation.

The Holy Father seconded President Franklin Delano Roosevelt's nonpartisan initiatives for peace and asked the faithful in both camps to com-

20. Rhodes, *Vatican in the Age of Dictators*, 223.
21. *RDHSWW*, 93–96, 146; Koenig, *Principles for Peace*, 569–70.
22. Kent, "Pope Pius XII and Germany," 65; Harrigan, "Pius XII's Efforts to Effect a Détente," 184.
23. *RDHSWW*, 211.

mence a crusade of prayer for peace.[24] Despite these prayers, the European situation was aggravated by the conclusion of the military alliance between Fascist Italy and Nazi Germany on 22 May 1939, dubbed the Pact of Steel. Early in June, Pius, who sought solace in Scripture and prayer, issued an appeal for peace without referring to specific issues or territorial disputes, or differentiating aggressor from aggrieved. The nuncio to Paris, Cardinal Valerio Valeri, explained that while the Holy See endeavored to improve relations among nations, it could not compromise its impartiality, which would jeopardize its mediation efforts. While the papal position won support in the Axis camp, the French were furious with the "diplomatic dance" of the Vatican, which seemed shielded by the armor of indifference. Charles-Roux made it clear that the French were terribly disappointed, acknowledging that while everyone had expected some change from the course pursued by his predecessor, the difference seemed excessive.[25]

The papal nuncio defended Pius's position by asserting that, given the grave circumstances of international relations, the Holy See had to preserve its contacts with the two blocs, alienating neither. The French ambassador to the Holy See responded that the Holy See could fulfill its mission in one of two ways: by relying on politics and diplomacy, or by asserting and standing by the principles that the Church cherished. Pius chose to rely on his forty years of diplomatic experience. Thus he refused the request of Father Martin Gillet, master general of the Dominicans, that he plead with the totalitarian governments to renounce the use of violence in international relations.[26]

As the diplomatic situation deteriorated, the Holy See received identical communications from the Berlin and Rome embassies asking the pope to propose to the Allies a thirty-day truce for the purpose of organizing a conference of the foreign ministers of France, Great Britain, Italy, and Germany to resolve the Danzig question by mutual agreement, without Polish participation. Subsequently, the British government would submit the proposed solution for Polish acceptance. Neither London nor Paris was willing to coerce Warsaw into what seemed "a second Munich" certain to alienate public opinion at home.

24. Koenig, *Principles for Peace*, 565–66.   25. *RDHSWW*, 169.
26. Ibid., 169, 177.

Undaunted by the failure of diplomacy, Pius continued his efforts on behalf of peace. On 24 August, the day after the world was shocked by the news of the Nazi-Soviet Pact, he issued a radio appeal to politicians and public leaders to avert another catastrophe, proclaiming, "Nothing is lost with peace; all may be lost with war." On 31 August 1939 Pius again pleaded for peace.[27] The next day, when the German army invaded Poland, Pius refused to condemn the aggression.[28] His determination to preserve the Vatican's "impartiality" flowed from a number of factors, including the example set by Benedict XV during World War I, as well as his obligations under article 24 of the Treaty of the Lateran Accords, in which the Holy See pledged to remain apart from temporal disputes between states. Furthermore, the pope did not wish to offend the Catholic faithful who were found in both belligerent camps, and like the German hierarchy he dreaded the consequences that might follow a rupture with the Nazi regime.[29]

In his address to the Polish colony in Rome at the end of September, the pope offered consolation for the Poles' suffering but urged that their tribulation not promote rancor or hatred. Criticism of the pope's failure to denounce Nazi aggression against Poland prompted an unofficial Vatican explanation that the Holy See did not wish to provoke retaliation against the Poles, but that its silence did not suggest that the pope was indifferent to the Polish plight.[30] Skeptics were not convinced. Some deplored the fact that subsequently as many as 20 percent of Polish priests were murdered by the Nazis and that Pius XII failed to publicly protest this atrocity against his own clergy.[31] His "silence" on Nazi aggression toward Catholic Poland foreshadowed his silence during the larger genocide that ensued.

From the first, Pius XII relied upon oblique criticism rather than blunt public condemnation of Nazi aggression and brutality. This was manifest in his first encyclical to the universal Church, *Summi Pontificatus* (On the Limitations of the Authority of the State in the Modern World), in which he addressed the "fundamental errors" of the age that had led the world to

27. *RDHSWW*, 203, 183–84; *PP* 1:116; Koenig, *Principles for Peace*, 584–87.
28. Charles-Roux, *Huit ans au Vatican*, 343.
29. Moro, *Chiesa e lo sterminio degli ebrei*, 108–9, 116.
30. Koenig, *Principles for Peace*, 587–91; Roux, *Huit ans au Vatican*, 343; *New York Times*, 1 and 15 Oct. 1939.
31. See Carroll, *Constantine's Sword*, 684.

the present chaos. Among the causes of the malaise he listed the denial of a universal norm of morality for the individual, the society, and international relations, the rejection of God, the secularization of society, and the deification of the state. Pius borrowed two additional grave errors from Pius XI's unpublished *Humani Generis Unitas:* the forgetting of the law of human solidarity, and the equality of rational nature in all mankind. To consider the state an ultimate end to which everything else would be subordinate, the pope warned, was not only injurious to domestic life but destructive of international relations.[32]

While Pius XII's initial encyclical followed his predecessor's rejection in this respect, his "denunciation" of totalitarianism was general rather than specific, equally applicable to the Soviet Union, Nazi Germany, or Fascist Italy. At the end of the year, when he condemned the "calculated act of aggression against a small, industrious and peaceful nation" and complained about "the unlawful use of destructive weapons against non-combatants and refugees, against old men and women and children," the pope once again avoided naming any particular action or aggressor. Although Hitler and the Nazis suspected that the message was directed against them, Pius later explained that the small nation to which he had referred was Finland, the victim of Soviet aggression.[33]

Cautious in his condemnations, Pius had considerable sympathy for the Franco-British cause. Sir Francis d'Arcy Godolphin Osborne, the British ambassador to the Holy See since 1936, had substantial evidence of papal support for the Allied cause, but he hesitated to convey it to his government through insecure lines of communication.[34] In fact, in the closing days of the Polish campaign in October 1939, when senior officers of Germany's military intelligence secretly sought to overturn the Hitler regime and conclude a negotiated peace, they relied upon Pius XII to pave the way for talks. The pope assumed the task, compromising the neutrality of the papacy and placing himself at risk of retaliation for doing so.[35] The failure of the enterprise and the risks it entailed almost certainly made Pius much more cautious in his future actions. Nonetheless, in January 1940, this

32. Fremantle, *Papal Encyclicals in Their Historical Context*, 263–67; Jan Olav Smit, *Angelic Shepherd: The Life of Pope Pius XII* (New York: Dodd, Mead, 1950), 158–63.

33. Koenig, *Principles for Peace*, 634; Stehle, *Eastern Politics of the Vatican*, 197.

34. Alvarez, *Spies in the Vatican*, 239.

35. Ibid., 177; *RDHSWW*, 85.

pope secretly alerted the English of the impending Nazi invasion of the Low Countries, a step in the Nazi march westward.[36]

Pius revealed his inner sentiments in his correspondence with the new minister of Haiti in November 1939, proclaiming that the preservation of peace required the renunciation of the cult of might against right and the acceptance of the supreme authority of the Creator as the basis of individual and collective morality. He pleaded for the formation of an international organization to assure the reciprocal independence of nations while safeguarding their liberty and prosperity. The pope returned to the theme of a reorganization of international life and the construction of new juridical institutions in his Christmas message of 24 December 1939. During the early phase of the war he sought to keep Italy from entering, and he repeated this message during King Victor Emanuel III's visit to the Vatican.[37]

Papal peace efforts were supported by President Roosevelt, who shared the Vatican's desire to contain the conflict. At the end of December 1939 the American president dispatched Myron Taylor, a former president of United States Steel, as his personal representative to the Vatican, without formal title. Roosevelt appreciated the intricate network of international representation that had the Vatican as its focus and that he hoped could assist peace efforts. The Vatican appreciated the opening of relations with the United States, even unofficial ones.[38] "This is a Christmas Message which could not have been more welcome to Us," responded the pope to the American initiative, since it represents a "wider effort to alleviate the sufferings of the victims of war."[39] Pius was reassured by the presence of Roosevelt's representative. Perhaps this emboldened the pope to allow Vatican Radio in January 1940 to broadcast a detailed report on the persecution of the Poles.[40] During Taylor's first visit, the Vatican expressed its

---

36. Moro, *Chiesa e lo sterminio degli ebrei*, 110.

37. Koenig, *Principles for Peace*, 622–37.

38. At the time, the Holy See maintained diplomatic relations with thirty-seven governments to which it dispatched nuncios, while it sent apostolic delegates to another twenty-two states. The Americans, no less than the English, French, and Germans, believed that the Vatican had wider access to information worldwide than it actually enjoyed. Alvarez, *Spies in the Vatican*, 268–70, 243.

39. Quoted in Koenig, *Principles for Peace*, 640.

40. Myron C. Taylor, ed., *Wartime Correspondence between President Roosevelt and Pope Pius XII* (New York: Macmillan, 1947), 22–23, 33. Taylor arrived in Rome at the end of February, reserving a suite at the exclusive Excelsior Hotel in Rome and occupying a villa in Tuscany, but he spent little time in either residence, remaining mostly in the United States.

concern that Mussolini was preparing to abandon nonbelligerence and plunge Italy into the war on the Axis side. The United States and the Vatican worked jointly to dissuade Mussolini from entering the fray, but found him set on territorial expansion. Informing the American president that Italy's imprisonment in the Mediterranean had to end, Mussolini cited the need for a new geography. Both the pontiff and the president also worried about Romania, where the dictator Ion Antonescu was moving closer to the Axis powers.[41]

On 11 March 1940, the German foreign minister, Joachim von Ribbentrop, accompanied by the German ambassador to the Vatican, Diego von Bergen, presented a German peace proposal to the pontiff. Pius saw that the German initiative was a propaganda ploy and knew that it would be unacceptable to the allies. He took the opportunity, nonetheless, to privately catalogue Nazi abuses against the Church in the Reich and he read from reports he had received of the inhuman treatment of civilians in the occupied territories.[42] Distressed by the diplomatic, although obviously critical, position of the papacy, Hermann Wilhelm Göring, Reich minister of aviation, asked Alfieri, the Italian ambassador to the Vatican, how the Vatican would react should Italy enter the war. Alfieri made it clear that the reaction would be unfavorable. Göring worried that this negative attitude might affect public opinion in the United States, but he reassured the Italians that the war would be short.[43]

Mussolini worried about the opposition of both the Vatican and Italian public opinion to the prospect of Italy's entering the war. He had reason to be concerned about the Vatican, given its warning to the Allies of the impending Nazi attack on the Low Countries, which, it turned out, had been deciphered by Italian intelligence.[44] When German forces crossed the borders of the Netherlands, Belgium, and Luxembourg on 10 May 1940, and by mid-month pushed into France, Pius sent messages of

---

Between visits to Italy and the Vatican, he relied on his assistant, Harold Tittmann, who eventually found shelter in Vatican City.

41. Thomas B. Morgan, *The Listening Post: Eighteen Years on Vatican Hill* (New York: G. P. Putnam's Sons, 1944), 195; Koenig, *Principles for Peace*, 652; Dino Alfieri, *Dictators Face to Face*, trans. David Moore (Westport, Conn.: Greenwood Press, 1978), 9.

42. Smit, *Angelic Shepherd*, 215; Oscar Halecki, *Eugenio Pacelli: Pope of Peace* (New York: Ferrar, Straus and Young, 1951), 143–44; Alfieri, *Dictators Face to Face*, 9–11.

43. Alfieri, *Dictators Face to Face*, 26.

44. Alvarez, *Spies in the Vatican*, 177, 219.

condolence to the victims, expressing his regret to King Leopold that his people's homeland had been invaded and subjected to the cruelties of war. Similar regrets were dispatched to Queen Wilhelmina of Holland and Grand Duchess Charlotte of Luxembourg.[45]

The papal telegrams did not focus on the responsibility of the Nazis or their aggression, much to the chagrin of the French ambassador, François Charles-Roux, who reminded Rome that there were sins of omission as well as of commission. Charles-Roux noted that sympathy was one thing, condemnation of crime, another. Furthermore, Catholic circles in Paris were convinced that even these expressions of sympathy were virtually "wrenched" from a reluctant pope.[46] Still, they angered the Nazis and upset Mussolini, who was on the verge of joining the Nazis. Il Duce conveyed his displeasure to Pius, who found this criticism puzzling, since the unnamed aggressor had been Hitler, not Mussolini. Pius responded that he had only fulfilled his duty and could not remain silent when his conscience and apostolic ministry constrained him to speak. In 1940 the Holy Office condemned the sterilization policy and eugenic killings of the Nazi regime. Pius, informed of the brutal conditions in the "death house" of Dachau, later allowed Vatican radio to denounce the German atrocities there.[47] Some complained that this was too little, too late.

Perhaps Pius XII's moderation led Mussolini to see papal hostility to Fascist aims as more inconvenient than dangerous. It did not stop him, in any case, from entering the war on 10 June 1940, two weeks before the French sued for an armistice. Mussolini's intervention would prove disastrous for Italy, the Fascist regime, and the Vatican. In a letter of June 1940, Cardinal Eugene Tisserant, secretary of the Sacred Congregation for the Eastern Church, complained of the pope's silence on the pervasive German violence from the beginning of the war. Tisserant revealed that he had urged Pius XII to issue an encyclical reminding Catholics of the need to follow their consciences when confronted with evil, but that the pope had chosen not to do so.[48]

Still refusing to assign responsibility, Pius continued to decry the evils

45. Koenig, *Principles for Peace,* 668–69.   46. *RDHSWW,* 421, 431.

47. Alfieri, *Dictators Face to Face,* 16–17; *RDHSWW,* 75–77; Moro, *Chiesa e lo sterminio degli ebrei,* 111; "Memoirs of a Prisoner of Dachau Sent to the Vatican in 1940," ASV, SS, Rapporti con gli sati, AS, AAES, Germania, 1922–39, posizione 670–73, fascicolo 233, no. 1572/40.

48. Moro, *Chiesa e lo sterminio degli ebrei,* 118.

of war in general terms. In June he asked the belligerents to observe the principles of humanity in the occupied countries, urging France to find in her Christian faith the spiritual resources necessary to confront the current misfortune. During the course of 1940, the pope repeated many of the messages that Benedict XV had given during World War I, even though the two wars were vastly different, and the brutality of the Nazi regime differed in kind as well as in degree from that of imperial Germany. Like Benedict before him, Pius called for a day of prayer on 24 November 1940, and pleaded for harmony among nations. In his Christmas message of 24 December 1940, Pius prescribed universal prayer as the solution to the hatred that divided the world, the restoration of peace, and the emergence of an equitable order.[49]

Pius's approach to the two sides in the war was tinged by an uncompromising anticommunism, which influenced his reaction to the Nazi barbarism. He received disturbing reports of Nazi atrocities in the occupied territories, along with accounts of the persecution of the Church in Hitler's Germany, from Catholic clergy and lay people, and this presented him with a profound moral crisis. Pius lamented the widespread suffering on the battlefield and on the home front, and the evils affecting not only combatants but civilian populations, including the old, the young, the innocent and peace-loving, and those bereft of all defense. The first report the Vatican received of the genocide of Jews came from Monsignor Giuseppe Burzio, the chargé d'affaires in Slovakia, who alerted Pius on 27 October 1941. Drawing upon the information supplied by Catholic chaplains attached to the Slovakian army units supporting the German war effort on the eastern front, Burzio described the horrors of the first stage of the Holocaust.[50] This genocide presented the Vatican with a grave dilemma. How could it reconcile its determination to preserve "impartiality" with the moral imperative to condemn crimes against humanity and the scandalous violation of core Christian principles?

Although part of the Catholic clergy aided the Jews, the priest-historian Kevin Spicer has charged that the German Catholic Church as an institution was largely silent during the Holocaust.[51] In November 1942

49. Koenig, *Principles for Peace*, 670–79, 684–704.
50. Alvarez, *Spies in the Vatican*, 287.
51. In this regard see the letters of the bishop of Osnabruck on help provided the Jews,

Cardinal Faulhaber wrote Cardinal Bertram, president of the Fulda Bishops' Conference, that he was being implored by laypeople to have the bishops do something to halt the "brutal deportation of non-Aryans to Poland under inhuman conditions paralleled only in the African slave trade." Bertram responded that the Church had only limited ability to influence the regime and that the bishops must "concentrate on other concerns which are more important for the Church and more far-reaching," especially "how best to prevent anti-Christian and anti-Church influences on the education of Catholic youth."[52]

Pius was determined not to abandon his impartiality. In a note of 18 May 1943 Monsignor Domenico Tardini, the undersecretary of state, suggested that it would be inopportune for the Holy See to protest publicly against the many injustices the Nazis had perpetrated. First, this would be exploited for partisan purposes by one or the other camp, and second, the German government would only intensify its persecution of Catholics in Poland and further restrict the Holy See's contacts with the Polish hierarchy.[53] Consequently, Pius condemned egregious human rights violations and atrocities without referring to specific crimes. "To the powers occupying territories during the war, We say with all due consideration: let your conscience guide in dealing justly, humanely and providently with the peoples of occupied territories," the pope noted in his Easter message of 1941.[54] The Allies and many of the victims hoped the pope would say more, and Taylor and his assistant, Tittmann, warned the Vatican that it risked losing its moral leadership if it failed to denounce the Nazi crimes. Pius refused to go beyond these broad generalizations. Perhaps he feared that if he issued a call to arms against the Reich, German Catholics would not respond, revealing the weakness of Church authority in that "folkish" state.[55]

Not only Jews but Catholics criticized the pope for what they consid-

---

1934–41, AS, SS, AAES, Germania, 1922–39, posizione Scatole 48; Kevin Spicer, *Resisting the Third Reich: Catholic Clergy in Hitler's Berlin* (DeKalb: Northern Illinois University Press, 2004).

52. Rhonheimer, "Holocaust: What Was Not Said," 20–21.

53. Moro, *Chiesa e lo sterminio degli ebrei*, 119–20.

54. Koenig, *Principles for Peace*, 714; Smit, *Angelic Shepherd*, 224–25.

55. Kent, "Pope Pius XII and Germany," 71. See the warnings transmitted by Orsenigo, ASV, SS, Rapporti con gli stati, AS, AAES, Germania, 1922–39, posizione 643, fascicolo 159.

ered his vague statements. The Polish clergy implored him to denounce
Nazi barbarism in Poland and complained that the Nazis aimed to destroy
the Church as well as the Polish population. The Polish primate, Cardinal
August Hlond, asked Pius in 1941 if it was the will of God that Nazi iniqui-
ties be covered with a "veil of silence." The papal response that public
protest might make matters worse was less than convincing to some victims of the persecution. Monsignor Charles Radowski, forced from his
diocese in Worthegau, argued that speaking out could not make things
worse. "Silence gives consent," he maintained. His pleas were echoed by
Archbishop Adam Sapieha of Kraków, who told the Holy See that the entire Catholic world expected the Vatican to defend justice vigorously.[56] Despite these desperate pleas, Pius continued to work quietly through diplomatic channels to mitigate the plight of Catholic and Jewish Poles, and
refrained from denouncing the Germans. Might a more confrontational
response from the pope have curbed Nazi abuses and genocide? This question is still debated.

Many observers, both contemporaries and historians, have questioned
the motivation and effectiveness of the Pius XII's cautious approach, but it
is not the case that Pius XII did nothing to help the victims of Nazi brutality. The recently, albeit partially, opened wartime archives of the Vatican
reveal that Pius established the Vatican Information Service to provide information about thousands of war refugees and prisoners of war. His defenders argue that he probably instructed the churches to provide discreet
assistance to the Jews that quietly saved lives. Some churchmen, including
a number of cardinals, pressed him to do more. His "silence," they suggest,
created consternation among the faithful, sanctioned Nazi evil, and undermined the Church's spiritual viability.[57] Even Sister Pasqualina, the
pope's housekeeper, cook, and the closest thing he had to a companion
and confidant, claimed that she urged the pope to take a stronger stance
against Nazi atrocities. But this pope's personality, training, and diplomatic agenda pointed him in a different direction. "The Holy See must aid the
Jewish people to the best of our ability," he is alleged to have responded,
"but everything we do must be done with caution. Otherwise the Church

56. Tinnemann, "Silence of Pius XII," 267.
57. ASV, SS, Ufficio Informazioni Vaticano (prigionieri di guerra, 1939–47), 67; *DGFP*,
series C, vol. 1, no. 501.

and the Jews themselves will suffer great retaliation."[58] In fact, when Ambassador Taylor complained of Father Coughlin's anti-Semitism, Cardinal Maglione, in his reply, referred not to the actions of the reigning pope but to his predecessor's efforts on behalf of the Jews; Pius XI, in his view, was the only authoritative voice raised in Europe on their behalf.[59] To be sure, Maglione deplored the violations of the 1933 concordat and the Nazi attacks on divine, natural, and positive law, but the Vatican's protests were moderate and their focus restricted.[60] To many, the pope and curia seemed obsessed with the Communist menace, which led them to ignore Nazi atrocities, at least publicly. But this explanation fails to appreciate the complexity of the Vatican's motivation.

President Roosevelt likewise did not fully understand the personal and political factors behind Pius XII's moderation. He sought to convince the pope that the surest road to peace lay in supporting the Soviet Union and Great Britain against the Nazi menace, and he urged the Vatican to moderate its anticommunist stance. Meanwhile, Bernardo Attolico, Mussolini's representative to the Holy See, sought to convince the pope that the war against the Soviet Union was a crusade that warranted the Vatican's moral support. Pius XII was not prepared to follow either suggestion. On 9 September 1941 he received a letter from the American president that indicated among other things that the Soviets were on the brink of introducing some form of religious freedom in their territories, that the Soviet dictatorship was less dangerous than the Nazi, and that the survival of the U.S.S.R. would prove less dangerous to religious life than the survival of the Nazi dictatorship.[61] Pius disagreed but chose diplomatically not to focus on their differences, anxious not to alienate the Americans, on whom he increasingly relied. Although the pope despised Hitler, he was equally distressed by Stalin.[62]

During the war, Pius proved cautious in his approach toward both. If he held his tongue on Nazi atrocities, it must not be forgotten that he said nothing publicly against Soviet ones either. Furthermore, the Vatican

58. Quoted in Murphy, with Arlington, *La popessa* (New York: Warner Books, 1983), 197.
59. *RDHSWW,* 381.
60. Carlo Falconi, *The Silence of Pius XII,* trans. Bernard Wall (Boston: Little, Brown, 1970), 247.
61. Taylor, *Wartime Correspondence between Roosevelt and Pius XII,* 61.
62. Feldkamp, *Pius XII. und Deutschland,* 127.

steadfastly refused to support the Nazi invasion of the Soviet Union. The pope let Attolico know that if he had to denounce the Bolshevik violations he would feel constrained to denounce those of the Nazis as well, threatening that if he spoke out one day, he would say everything.[63] Monsignor Domenico Tardini retorted that although Communism was the worst enemy of the Church, the Nazis were a close second. The swastika was hardly a crusader's cross, Tardini said.

> I see the crusade, but not the crusaders. . . . If the Holy See were to call attention to the errors and horrors of Communism, it could not pass over the aberrations and persecutions of Nazism. . . . For that reason, I am at the present moment not making use of the crusade doctrine, but rather of the saying "Set a thief to catch a thief" (*un diavolo caccia l'altro*). All the better, if the other is the worse one.[64]

In its campaign against Communism, the Vatican refused to ally with its Fascist opponents, and did not support the right-wing rebellion against the Yugoslavian state. Even after the destruction of Yugoslavia in 1941, Pius refused to extend diplomatic recognition to the new Oustachi state. Furthermore, the Holy See continued to combat the forced conversions of the Serbs in Croatia. "According to the principles of Catholic doctrine," read the Vatican pronouncement, "conversion should not be the result of external coercion but of the soul's adherence to the truths taught by the Catholic Church."[65] Although Mussolini's disciple, Ante Pavelic, who founded the Croatian Fascist Party, or Oustachi, remained a practicing Catholic, the Vatican viewed his regime with skepticism, while Monsignor Felici, the papal legate in Belgrade, urged that clerics be forbidden to take part in his movement. Pavelic's repeated pleas for Vatican recognition were rejected. Meanwhile, the secretary of state instructed the de facto nuncio in Croatia to assure the chief rabbi of Zagreb that the Holy See, in order to alleviate suffering, had prudently involved itself on behalf of the wives and children of the deported Jews.[66]

During the Nazi genocide, the Vatican used diplomatic means to get

63. Attolico to Ciano, 16 Sept. 1941, *DDI*, 9th series, 7:580–81.
64. Quoted in Stehle, *Eastern Politics of the Vatican*, 209.
65. Falconi, *Silence of Pius XII*, 304.
66. Rhodes, *Vatican in the Age of Dictators*, 325; Kevin Madigan, "What the Vatican Knew about the Holocaust, and When," *Commentary* (Oct. 2001): 49.

Slovakia and Hungary to halt their brutalization of the Jews.[67] When the newly formed government of Catholic Slovakia adopted a Jewish code, the Slovak bishops, in October 1941, dispatched a protest to President Tiso. When this priest replied that he perceived no conflict between Nazi principles and Catholic social doctrine, the papal undersecretary of state retorted that he might have to remove Tiso's name from the list of monsignori.[68] Although more than forty thousand of the roughly ninety thousand Slovak Jews were deported in 1942, Eichmann grudgingly conceded that instead of deporting only Jews capable of labor, "in the spirit of Christianity" families would be deported together![69] Some have argued that Pius did not assume a critical stance toward the racist course pursued by the Vichy regime; others have disputed this contention.[70]

Somewhat more was done to assist the Jews of Romania. Following the promulgation of its racial laws in July 1940, the nuncio, Andrea Cassulo, objected immediately, winning concessions for baptized Jews from the Antonescu government. Subsequently the nuncio broadened his efforts, and in October of that year he appealed on behalf of nonconverted Jews. When his pleas went unanswered and plans were introduced to deport Romanian Jews, additional Vatican protests were launched in August and September 1942. For this and other reasons, the Romanian government did not carry out the threatened deportations. "For two long years, when the deportation of Romanian Jewry was already decided and about to be carried out," wrote the chief rabbi of Romania, "the high moral authority of the Nuncio saved us."[71] Again in 1942, Monsignor Valeri protested the persecution of the Jews of Vichy France, condemning the deportations as a gross violation of the religious beliefs Marshall Pétain had professed when he assumed office. The available archival documents also reveal that the

67. John T. Pawlikowski, "The Papacy of Pius XII: The Known and the Unknown," in *Pope Pius XII and the Holocaust,* ed. Carol Rittner and John K. Roth (London: Leicester University Press, 2002), 58.

68. Lapide, *Three Popes and the Jews,* 138; Richard J. Wolff, "The Catholic Church and the Dictatorships in Slovakia and Croatia, 1939–1945," *Records of the American Catholic Historical Society of Philadelphia* (1978): 10–12.

69. Madigan, "What the Vatican Knew about the Holocaust," 43.

70. Robert O. Paxton, "France: The Church, the Republic, and the Fascist Temptation, 1922–1945," in Wolff and Hoensch, *Catholics, the State, and the European Right,* 84.

71. Quoted in John F. Morley, *Vatican Diplomacy and the Jews during the Holocaust, 1939–1943* (New York: KTAV Publishing, 1980), 45–46.

Vatican used diplomatic means with countries such as Spain and Portugal to grant exit visas to Jews.[72]

The Holy See adopted a more cautious approach when confronting Hitler, whose power posed a greater threat to the Church and the millions subject to his will and whim. In a speech at the end of January 1942, shortly after the conference at Wannsee (20 January), where the "final solution" had been mapped out, Hitler vowed that the Jews of Europe would be eliminated for at least one thousand years. His threatening remarks were noted by the papal secretary of state, Maglione.[73] News of mass executions of Jews reached the Vatican by March 1942. In the fall, the Holy See received more information that the Germans were systematically killing Jews. At the end of August, Andrzey Szeptyckyi, the Greek Catholic metropolitan of Lvov, wrote Pius of the atrocities against the Jews.[74] Despite Diego von Bergen's assurances that Pius was preparing a more forthright and open condemnation of the Nazi regime, this did not materialize. Since Pius XII's correspondence was regularly intercepted and read, he had recourse to circumlocution, hoping that the true meaning of his message would eventually be deciphered.[75] The obstinate refusal of the Nazis to respond to the Holy See's private appeals led Pius to fear that matters would be made worse by public denunciations.

In radio addresses, Pius sought to understand why Divine Providence permitted such indescribable suffering. His answer was that man must trust in God, who permits at times "the violation of law, the tormenting of innocent, peaceful, undefended, helpless men." In this atmosphere of terror, Pius pointed to the example of the early Christians and their conviction of ultimate victory. He confided that he had agonized over whether to denounce Nazi atrocities and especially the extermination of the Jews, but after long prayers and many tears he had concluded that such pronouncements would do more harm than good.[76] He also expressed his concern that public condemnation would create a dangerous rift between German

72. Pawlikowski, "Papacy of Pius XII," 58.

73. Moro, *Chiesa e lo sterminio degli ebrei*, 130.

74. Tinnemann, "Silence of Pius XII," 271–72; Bernauer, "Holocaust and the Catholic Church's Search for Forgiveness."

75. Leonidas E. Hill III, "The Vatican Embassy of Ernst von Weizsacker, 1943–1945," *JMH* 39 (March 1967): 143; Alvarez, *Spies in the Vatican*, 26.

76. Koenig, *Principles for Peace*, 734–35, 770; Moro, *Chiesa e lo sterminio degli ebrei*, 157.

Catholics and their countrymen. In his "silence," Pius XII followed the German hierarchy, which made no collective remonstrance on the evils inflicted upon the Jews. Thus Cardinal Maglione reported that the Holy See had been careful not to give the German people the impression that it had done anything against Germany. For all these reasons Pius was unwilling to go beyond general condemnations of violence and brutality. He was unwilling to excommunicate individuals, to abrogate concordats, to recall nuncios, or to make broad appeals to the Catholic public. He apparently feared putting Catholics to the test, concerned that the German bishops and laity might not accede to his requests. The Vatican, he said, had done what it could.[77]

In his Christmas message of 1942, Pius XII expressed sympathy for those "who without fault on their part, sometimes only because of race or nationality, have been consigned to death or to a slow decline."[78] The metropolitan, Szeptyckyi, warned the pope that the German regime, perhaps to a greater degree than the Bolshevist one, was diabolical, committing the most horrible crimes against the Jews and others. In May 1942 Pius was also informed of the mass extermination (*uccisioni in massa*) of Jews from Germany, Poland, and the Ukraine. By this time the undersecretary of State, Montini, who later became Paul VI, had concluded that the massacre of Jews had assumed atrocious and frightening proportions. Meanwhile, the military chaplain stationed with Italian troops in the east, Father Pirro Scavizzi, personally informed Pius that the elimination of Jews through mass murder was almost total, without regard for children or even infants.[79] Although it had precise information, how much the Vatican fully understood and grasped is another matter, and it was not alone in its incomprehension. As late as August 1943 the American administration contested the reports of Jewish groups on the exterminations, asserting that these claims could not be confirmed and insisting that the Jews in the camps were working![80]

Pius's overriding priority apparently remained the preservation of Vatican impartiality. He thus avoided any action that might endanger Ger-

---

77. Tinnemann, "Silence of Pius XII," 278–284.
78. Koenig, *Principles for Peace*, 804.
79. Stehle, *Eastern Politics of the Vatican*, 214–20; Alvarez, *Spies in the Vatican*, 289–90.
80. Moro, *Chiesa e lo sterminio degli ebrei*, 134, 144.

man Catholics or the unity of the universal Church. He refused to condemn the Holocaust publicly, fearing the results for those subject to the Nazi occupation, the well-being of the organizational Church, the weakening of the Nazi regime to the advantage of the equally odious Bolshevist one, and perhaps his own personal security. Vatican officials defended this stance. "There is constant pressure on the Holy See from the Axis powers to denounce alleged Allied atrocities and, because of its silence, the Holy See is very often accused of being pro-ally. The Holy See could not very well, therefore, condemn Nazi atrocities on the one hand without saying something, for instance, about Russian cruelties on the other."[81]

In the last years of the war, the pope continued publicly to avoid many of the issues provoked by the brutal Nazi war, occupation, atrocities, and genocide of Jews and Roma (gypsies). According to German reports, the Vatican's principal preoccupation was the Bolsehivization of Europe. Thus Monsignor Tardini suggested to Roosevelt and Churchill that they help the Russians—but only within limits, hoping that a stalemate between the Nazis and the Soviets would weaken both. Adhering to this course, the Vatican did not obstruct American military aid to the Soviet Union, which was criticized by Catholics in the United States until Monsignor Tardini explained to the American bishops that Pius XI's encyclical against atheistic Communism (*Divini Redemptoris* of 1937) condemned the ideology but not the Russian people.[82] While the Holy See had few illusions about National Socialism, which had kept church doors open, it had absolutely none about Bolshevism, which had earlier closed them and was therefore deemed a greater evil. For this among other reasons, Pius XII was reluctant to speak out against Germany's brutal conduct in Poland even though its president in exile pleaded, "may the voice of the Holy Father . . . finally break [through] the silence of death." His voice was no more heeded than that of Pius's old friend Bishop Konrad Preysing of Berlin, who asked the pope to denounce the Holocaust publicly. Again, Pius responded that he could not do anything that would undermine the unity of the universal Church.[83] Besides, he believed he had already addressed these abuses.

81. Quoted in Kent, "Pope Pius XII and Germany," 71.

82. Kent, "Pope Pius XII and Germany," 76; Stehle, *Eastern Politics of the Vatican*, 211.

83. John Lukacs, "The Diplomacy of the Holy See during World War II," *CHR* 60 (July 1974): 277; Phayer, *Catholic Church and the Holocaust*, 64–65.

Pius always believed that he said more than others heard. He told Preysing that his Christmas message of December 1942 had denounced the treatment of non-Aryans under German occupation. It is true that he did not mention the Jews specifically, there or elsewhere, during the war or in its aftermath. However, one of Pius's defenders has noted that he used the Italian word *stirpe*, which he insists was used for centuries as an explicit reference to the Jews. Obviously most of the Nazis and their victims did not know this. "We have spoken briefly but we have been well understood," wrote the pope. His assessment was seconded by a report in the British Public Records Office (FO 371/3436359337 of 5 January 1943), which noted that "the pope's condemnation of the treatment of the Jews and the Poles is quite unmistakable, and the message is perhaps more forceful in tone than any of his recent statements."[84] Whether this was wishful thinking on the part of the British or an accurate assessment of the papal note remains questionable. Others have noted that the "forcefulness" of this papal message reveals more about the weakness of prior ones than it does about the strength of the 1942 Christmas message.

Confronted with the Nazis' mass murder of European Jews, Pius appreciated the Jews' plight but insisted that "as the situation is at present we are unfortunately not able to help them effectively in other ways than our prayers."[85] He promised to raise his voice on their behalf again, if this became necessary and circumstances permitted. The argument that his reticence sprang from his fear of greater evil, should he speak out, has been championed most recently by Marc-Andre Chargueraud in *Les Papes et la Shoah, 1932–1945* (2002). Nonetheless, others in the Church and even the curia continued to urge the pope to follow the example of Pius XI and openly denounce the persecution and atrocities, warning of the danger to papal moral leadership should he fail to do so. "I am afraid history will reproach the Holy See for following a policy of convenience for itself, and not much more," said Cardinal Eugene Tisserant, prefect of the Congregation of the Eastern Church, adding that this was "extremely sad, above all for those who lived under Pius XI."[86]

84. See Ronald J. Rychlak, "Goldhagen v. Pius XII," *First Things* (June–July 2002): 38–41.

85. Karl Otmar von Aretin, *The Papacy and the Modern World*, trans. Roland Hill (New York: McGraw-Hill, 1970), 213.

86. Quoted in Stehle, *Eastern Politics of the Vatican*, 215.

Some even suggested that Pius excommunicate the Führer. Pius XII knew that Hitler was not a practicing Catholic and doubted the efficacy of such a step. And he feared that Hitler's reaction and revenge would prove catastrophic, and so preferred not to provoke him. Such considerations had not prevented Pope Pius IX (1846–78) from issuing a series of condemnations of the Risorgimento or from indirectly excommunicating the men who had united Italy and seized Rome. But Pius XII shunned such a confrontational course.

Unquestionably, prudent considerations reinforced the pope's policy of accommodation. There were reports that the Vatican's public protest against the Nazi execution of Polish clergy in 1939 had made matters worse. Responding to the pleas of the German bishops, Pius suspended Vatican radio broadcasts condemning anti-Catholic measures, the concentration camps, and the abuses of civilians. Then, too, the bishop's protest against the Nazi program of euthanasia did not stop the killing of the "unproductive," which was expanded when it was extended to the east.[87] Furthermore, public protests might well have aroused Hitler to take punitive actions against the organizational Church in the vast stretches of Europe where his will was law. Monsignor Montini insisted that "Every word against Germany and Russia would be bitterly paid for by the Catholics who are subject to the regimes in these countries." One A. Wolfsson, who managed to escape from Rome because of the Vatican's quiet intervention, appreciated the Holy See's public silence.[88]

Privately, Pius XII himself had reservations about his conciliatory approach and the failure to speak out more forcefully and openly against the atrocities, for he feared that such caution might be perceived as anti-Semitism. In fact, Angelo Roncalli, later Pope John XXIII, noted in his diary that during a meeting with Pius XII on 11 October 1941, the pope inquired whether his silence regarding Nazi behavior would be judged badly.[89] These doubts were also expressed to Alfieri, the Italian ambassador, according to notes taken by Monsignor Montini.

---

87. Lapide, *Three Popes and the Jews,* 245; Robert A. Graham, "The 'Right to Kill' in the Third Reich: Prelude to Genocide," *CHR* 62 (Jan. 1976): 72.

88. Stehle, *Eastern Politics of the Vatican,* 195; Lapide, *Three Popes and the Jews,* 263.

89. Murphy, with Arlington, *La popessa,* 197; Bernauer, "Holocaust and the Catholic Church's Search for Forgiveness," 3.

The Pope at times cannot remain silent. Governments only consider political and military issues, intentionally disregarding moral and legal issues in which, on the other hand, the Pope is primarily interested and cannot ignore. His Holiness said, regarding this point, that he had had occasion of late to read St. Catherine's letters, who writing to the Pope, admonishes him that God would subject him to the most stringent judgment if he did not react to evil or did not do what he thought was his duty. How could the Pope, in these present circumstances, be guilty of such a serious omission as that of remaining a disinterested spectator of such heinous acts, while all the world was waiting for his words?[90]

In retrospect, it appears that Pius XII's musings on his moral imperative to speak out did not suggest any real intention to do so. Instead, the pope sought refuge in prayer. Although he remained appreciative of German culture, he finally recognized that "Germany, by abandoning every human mode of behavior, has aroused total mistrust on the other side." He also seemed to realize the danger to the Church posed by a Nazi victory in the war, apparently confiding to the Spanish foreign minister, Serrano Suner, that this would be followed by "the greatest period of persecution" Christians had ever confronted. Anxious for a "speedy conclusion of the war" and "a permanent peace," Pius reluctantly concluded that so long as the Germans continued their inhuman tendencies the Church could not mediate the conflict among the combatants.[91] Interestingly enough, he implied that it was the Allies rather than the papacy that would not, and could not, negotiate with Nazi Germany because of its inhuman and un-Christian policies. Although no other institution opposed the deification of the state and race as clearly as the Catholic Church, some suggest that the condemnation of racism was not intended to benefit the Jews.[92] In the eyes of Christian and Jewish critics, this represented a moral failure.

Throughout 1943, as the brutality increased, Pius took refuge in Church affairs, outlining general conditions of peace that angered even the Germans, who accused the Vatican of being steeped in a "moral-political fog."[93] Publicly ignoring the genocide, Pius XII had much to say on other

---

90. *RDHSWW*, 423.
91. Moro, *Chiesa e lo sterminio degli ebrei*, 112; Kent, "Pope Pius XII and Germany," 78; Stehle, *Eastern Politics of the Vatican*, 215, 236.
92. Rhonheimer, "Holocaust: What Was Not Said," 11.
93. Stehle, *Eastern Politics of the Vatican*, 240.

issues. He spoke on the uses of atomic energy in February 1943, while drafting encyclicals on the Mystical Body of Christ (June 1943), and the promotion of biblical studies (September 1943), while deploring the continuing international strife.[94] His condemnation of the euthanasia of the mentally deficient did not specifically cite the Nazi programs and policies. In his encyclical on Holy Scripture, *Divino Afflante Spiritu* (1943), Pius XII did note the special preeminence of the people of Israel—a dangerous assertion while the anti-Semitic Nazis still controlled much of Europe.[95] Perhaps Pius was emboldened by the fact that the tide of battle was turning, as the German forces surrendered at Stalingrad in early February 1943, while Italian and German forces ceased fighting in North Africa in May 1943. The Vatican was disturbed by the Allied call for unconditional surrender at the Casablanca conference in January 1943, believing it would lengthen the conflict and bring the Soviets into central Europe. Nor did Pius relish the proposed Allied invasion of Italy, praying that Italy would not be further ravaged and making his concerns clear to the Allies.

On 18 May 1943 the pope wrote President Roosevelt, reminding him of Taylor's promise that the Italian people would be treated with consideration and shielded from further pain and devastation, and that the precious heritage of Christian civilization would be saved from irreparable ruin. Promising to concentrate on military targets, the Americans indicated that Allied aviators would scrupulously avoid the bombardment of Vatican City. Sensing the centrality of the Vatican in Italian and European events, Hitler that summer appointed one of the most experienced diplomats in Germany, Ernst von Weizsacker, who had served as state secretary from 1938 to 1943, as the German ambassador to the Vatican, replacing von Bergen. The Allied invasion of Sicily in July 1943 served as prelude to the massive bombardment of Rome's railroad yards on 18 July. The pope hastened to write President Roosevelt, restating his prayer that "as far as humanly possible, the civil population be spared the horrors of war."[96] The invasion finally nudged the pope from his impartiality, and the Vatican ex-

---

94. *PP* 1:121; Eucardio Momigliano, ed., *Tutte le encicliche dei sommi Pontefici* (Milan: Dall'Oglio Editore, 1959), 1162–1223; *Selected Documents of His Holiness Pope Pius XII: 1939–1958* (Washington, D.C.: National Catholic Welfare Conference, n.d.), 3–49.

95. Moro, *Chiesa e lo sterminio degli ebrei*, 161; Oesterreicher, *New Encounter between Christians and Jews*, 51.

96. Taylor, *Wartime Correspondence between Roosevelt and Pius XII*, 90–91, 95.

pressed its desire for regime change in Italy and the opening of peace negotiations.[97] Toward the end of July, the Fascist Grand Council called for
Mussolini's resignation, which was followed by his dismissal and arrest by
the king, as Marshal Pietro Badoglio took charge of an interim government. Italy surrendered on 8 September 1943, prompting a German invasion and occupation of Rome on 10 September. Several days later a daring
Nazi rescue of Mussolini led to the eventual establishment of a Nazi satellite state in Salò in northern Italy, under the nominal leadership of Il
Duce.

Italians and the pope were now confronted with the prospect of a brutal occupation, as the Nazis stormed into the peninsula to check the Allies'
advance. While the king, the Badoglio government, and the general staff
fled Rome, Pius remained. Some believed that this confirmed Hitler's earlier conclusion that the pope was more resilient than either Mussolini or
the king.[98] Pius XII's behavior during the occupation led many to challenge this assessment. Fear gripped Vatican City as German paratroopers
patrolled its perimeter. Vatican archivists sought to hide sensitive documents, while Allied diplomats on its borders burned their ciphers and
confidential files. Rumor spread that the Nazis might push into Vatican
City and seize the pope, as the French had done during the revolutionary
and Napoleonic periods. Documents released by the Vatican in 2005 reveal
that Hitler had in fact planned to kidnap the pope.[99] Pius XII and clerical
circles were alarmed by the prospect. On 7 October 1943 the German foreign minister, von Ribbentrop, officially informed the Holy See that the
sovereignty and territorial integrity of Vatican City would be respected.[100]

Although the Germans decided not to occupy the papal territory, they
ordered the arrest of the Jews in the Eternal City, despite the fact that its
Jews had provided the ransom earlier demanded. On 16 October 1943, the
Nazis rounded up some one thousand Jews under the pope's very windows and began to transport them to concentration camps. In response,
the pope instructed Monsignor Alois Hudal, the rector of Santa Maria del-

97. Martin Clark, *Modern Italy, 1871–1982* (London: Longman, 1984), 298.
98. Lukacs, "Diplomacy of the Holy See during World War II," 277–78.
99. Alvarez, *Spies in the Vatican*, 187; "Hitler Wanted to Kidnap Pope," *New York Daily News*, 16 Jan. 2005, 33.
100. Moro, *Chiesa e lo sterminio degli ebrei*, 174.

l'Anima, to complain to the German commander, General Stahel, while his secretary of state, Cardinal Maglione, privately protested the deportation, asserting that if it continued this might put the pope in the difficult position of having to denounce the Nazi action publicly. However, Maglione added that Weizsacker was free to report their conversation to his superiors, or not.[101] The pope thus merely threatened, but did not in fact publicly protest this crime against humanity and the sanctity of the Eternal City.[102] To further arouse critics, the Vatican issued a communiqué later in October, at the instigation of Weizsacker, asserting that the German military forces in Rome were behaving to the Vatican's complete satisfaction. Although it is true that the SS was responsible for the seizure of the city's Jews and that it was the police who raided a number of buildings protected by the Lateran Accords, they would not have been able to do so without the support of the German military the pope praised. No wonder the Germans preferred the approach of Pius XII to that of his predecessor.[103]

Despite the Nazi atrocities, Pius steadfastly refused to abandon his neutrality and denounce the Germans explicitly. Critics complained that the Bishop of Rome had remained silent in the face of the Nazi brutalization of the Jews of his city, unlike many of the bishops in France, who had spoken out against similar outrages. Even the German ambassador noted the pope's moderation in his communications with the German Foreign Office. "The Pope, although reportedly beseeched by various sides, has not allowed himself to be drawn into any demonstrative statement against the deportation of the Jews of Rome," the ambassador reported. "Even though he has to calculate that this attitude will be held against him by our opponents and taken advantage of by Protestant circles in Anglo-Saxon countries, he has also in this touchy matter done everything in order not to burden relations with the German government and German agencies in Rome." He found the papal course "too wise, too prudent, and too diplomatic." Others have observed that Ernst von Weizsacker, the new German

101. The Holy See had offered the Jews of the city a loan to help them meet the German demand. Ibid., 174–76.

102. Kent, "Pope Pius XII and Germany," 78.

103. Hill, "Vatican Embassy of von Weizsacker," 147; Alvarez, *Spies in the Vatican*, 208; Morley, *Vatican Diplomacy and the Jews*, 180–81; Guenter Lewy, "Pius XII, the Jews, and the German Catholic Church," *Commentary* 37 (Feb. 1964): 32.

ambassador to the Holy See, distorted the Vatican position in his report to Berlin in order to avoid further Nazi retaliation, which he deemed counterproductive.[104] While the pope did not speak publicly, he was not inactive. There were numerous discreet and diplomatic protests, whose impact remains uncertain.[105]

Defenders of Pius XII's diplomatic strategy note that several thousand antifascist politicians and Jews were accorded refuge in church buildings during the occupation. Furthermore, while the Vatican intervened on behalf of baptized Jews far more often than it did on behalf of the nonconverted, this followed the provisions of the concordat of 1933. Nonetheless, "the Vatican's championing of the rights of baptized Jews implicitly denied the premises of all racial legislation," in the words of one critic.[106] Furthermore, the German ambassador warned the Vatican that a public outburst would probably provoke stronger action against the Jews and even endanger the person of the pope. Some observers are convinced that the pope's "subtle benevolence" avoided a massive massacre of Roman Jewry. Others discount the papal role in saving Rome's Jews.[107]

Interestingly enough, Pius XII continued to debate whether he was pursuing the right course. In March 1944 he confided to the Archbishop of Cologne that it was "painfully difficult to decide whether reticence and cautious silence are called for, or frank speech and strong action."[108] Despite his moderation, there were tensions between the Vatican and the German occupiers and even veiled threats of the pope's possible deportation. Both pope and curia discounted the Nazi assurances that the sovereignty of Vatican City would be respected, and worried about the personal security of the pontiff. Pius let it be known that he would not leave Rome under any circumstances, and that he would protest any violence against the Vicar of Christ. Secretary of State Maglione convened a special meeting of the Congregation for Extraordinary Ecclesiastical Affairs to consid-

104. Weizsacker quoted in Hilberg, *Destruction of the European Jews,* 430. See also Moro, *Chiesa e lo sterminio degli ebrei,* 160; Alvarez, *Spies in the Vatican,* 191.

105. Moro, *Chiesa e lo sterminio degli ebrei,* 169.

106. Morley, *Vatican Diplomacy and the Jews,* 196.

107. Hill, "Vatican Embassy of von Weizsacker," 151. For arguments that minimize the pope's effectiveness in helping Jews, see the work of Susan Zuccotti, especially *Italians and the Holocaust* and *Under His Very Windows: The Vatican and the Holocaust in Italy* (New Haven: Yale University Press, 2000).

108. Quoted in Stehle, *Eastern Politics of the Vatican,* 213.

er conferring special ecclesiastical responsibilities on a number of nuncios, should the Vatican prove unable to communicate freely with its representatives abroad. According to Monsignor Charles Burns, former archivist of the Vatican Archives, there is evidence therein to suggest that Pius XII left instructions that were he to be arrested by the Nazis, "the College of Cardinals was to consider him resigned and elect a new pope."[109]

Meanwhile, the advance of the Allied forces in the peninsula, the breaching of the Gustav line in May, followed by the fall of Cassino on 18 May 1944 and the piercing of the German line in the Alban hills, paved the way for an advance on Rome. The German commander, General Albert Kesselring, proposed that Rome be considered an open city and withdrew his forces as Pius issued an address to the cardinals reviewing the present afflictions.[110] On 4 June 1944 the Allies entered Rome, the first of the European capitals to be liberated, facing only sporadic resistance. Persisting in his impartiality, the pope addressed a crowd in St. Peter's Square and praised God that the capital had been spared. "Today we rejoice," he told the assembled Romans, "because, thanks to the mutual collaboration of both contending parties, the Eternal City has been preserved."[111] Continuing his even-handed course, Pius thanked both the Nazis and the Allies for sparing Rome further anguish.

As the collapse of Nazi Germany became certain, the Vatican assumed a more interventionist position on the continuing genocide in the Axis satellite states. In a letter to the papal nuncio in Hungary, Angelo Rotta, Pius described its policies as unworthy of a country with a long Catholic tradition. In June 1944 he dispatched a telegram to Admiral Horthy of Hungary on behalf of the persecuted.

> Supplications have been addressed to us from different sources that we should exert all our influence to shorten and mitigate the sufferings that have for so long been peacefully endured on account of their national or racial origin by a great number of unfortunate people belonging to this noble and chivalrous nation. In accordance with our service of love, which embraces every human being, our fatherly heart could not remain insensible to these urgent demands. For this reason we apply to your Serene Highness appealing

109. Smit, *Angelic Shepherd*, 234; Alvarez, *Spies in the Vatican*, 187; John Thavis, "Talk of Pope's Resignation Is No Longer Taboo," *Brooklyn Tablet* 95 (8 June 2002): 11.
110. *PP* 1:121.
111. Halecki, *Eugenio Pacelli: Pope of Peace*, 205–6.

to your noble feelings in the full trust that your Serene Highness will do everything in your power to save many unfortunate people from further pain and suffering.[112]

Still, during the war and its aftermath, Pius XII quietly opposed the establishment of a Jewish home in the Holy Land as well as Soviet expansion in Europe. Monsignor Tardini explained that the Holy See, then as in the past, disapproved of making Palestine a Jewish homeland. Even Roncalli, the future John XXIII, who had helped to rescue Jews during the war, opposed Jewish emigration to Palestine.[113]

Some suspected that Pius XII wanted to speak out more forcefully against Soviet atrocities but was constrained from doing so because this might alienate the American Allies. Following Rome's liberation, the pope and his secretary of state were increasingly concerned about the expansionism of the Soviet Union. Monsignor Tardini warned that the war might lead to a rapid diffusion of communism and predicted the onset of the cold war, where a precarious peace would rest on mutual fear.[114] Some complained that the papacy's "moral powers seem to have been unduly dulled" by its obsessive concern with the communist threat and its reluctance to antagonize the Third Reich, charging that this realism was achieved at the expense of the highest principles of the Church.[115] Pius personally, though prudently, contributed to the campaign against the "communist menace" in September 1944, calling for the reconstruction of the world on a Christian foundation. In a radio address he railed against any social order that rendered impossible the possession of private property. He returned to many of these themes in his Christmas message of 24 December 1944, which called for a halt to the bloodletting, without regard to war guilt, reparations, or balance of forces.[116]

Following the death of Cardinal Maglione in 1944, Pius did not name a

---

112. Quoted in Rychlak, "Goldhagen v. Pius XII," 49–50.

113. Silvio Ferari, "La S. Sede e la questione di Gerusalemme (1943–1948)," *Storia Contemporanea* 16 (Feb. 1985): 139–40; Moro, *Chiesa e lo sterminio degli ebrei*, 198–99. The papers of the Archivio della Delegazione Apostolica in Gerusalemme e Palestina in the ASV still remain largely closed.

114. Stehle, *Eastern Politics of the Vatican*, 238–39.

115. Hill, "Vatican Embassy of von Weizsacker," 158.

116. "Oggi, al compiersi," *PP* 1:121; Stehle, *Eastern Politics of the Vatican*, 243; *PP* 1:122; *Selected Documents of His Holiness Pope Pius XII: 1939–1958*, 1–15.

successor but personally assumed the direction of foreign affairs, assisted by Tardini, who headed the Congregation of Extraordinary Ecclesiastical Affairs, and Monsignor Montini, the head of the Congregation of Ordinary Affairs. Pius disagreed with Roosevelt's optimism vis-à-vis Stalin and the Soviet Union, harbored serious reservations about the terms of the Yalta agreement, and opposed the key role assigned the Soviet Union in the postwar period.[117]

In May 1945 an unconditional surrender was signed at General Eisenhower's headquarters. Perhaps this encouraged Pius finally to speak out against the "santanic spectre" of National Socialism and the horror of Dachau and the other camps. Following years of diplomatic neutrality, the pope finally called Nazism "the arrogant apostasy from Jesus Christ, the denial of His doctrine and of His work of redemption, the cult of violence, the idolatry of race and blood, the overthrow of human liberty and dignity."[118] In his speech of 12 June he deplored the killing of thousands of priests, religious, and laypeople, but still said nothing specifically about the Jewish genocide. Even later, *L'Osservatore Romano* and *La Civiltà Cattolica* had little to say about the revelations emerging from the Nuremberg trials.[119] What was said many deemed too little, too late. The pope, in many people's eyes, did not seem to grasp the moral threat posed to the Church by his cautious response to the genocide and his immersion in curial minutiae. Pius XII had assured the preservation of the Church in Germany, but at the expense of its universal moral mission, in the view of his critics. Some have even charged that the Vatican facilitated the escape of Nazis from Europe and their settlement in Peron's Argentina after the war.[120]

Jacques Maritain, named French ambassador to the Holy See after the war, was troubled by the anti-Semitic current in Western society and urged Pius XII to condemn both anti-Judaism and anti-Semitism. He be-

117. Carlo Falconi, *The Popes in the Twentieth Century: From Pius X to John XXIII*, trans. Muriel Grindrod (Boston: Little, Brown, 1967), 265.

118. John S. Conway, *The Nazi Persecution of the Churches, 1933–1945* (London: Weidenfeld and Nicolson, 1968), 326.

119. Rhonheimer, "Holocaust: What Was Not Said," 11; Moro, *Chiesa e lo sterminio degli ebrei*, 199–200.

120. See Uki Goni, *The Real Odessa: Smuggling the Nazis to Perón's Argentina* (New York: Granta Books, 2002).

lieved that Church teaching and theology had contributed to the hatred that led to the extermination of 6 million Jews, and in July 1946 he wrote a letter to his friend and admirer, Giovanni Montini, undersecretary of state, asking him to plead with the pope to address this serious issue. Maritain acknowledged the quiet papal wartime efforts on behalf of the Jews, but saw the need for the pope to address the tragedy more directly and openly.[121] The ambassador said that he appreciated the pope's reluctance to speak out during the horrific events "in order not to make the persecution even worse and not to create insurmountable obstacles in the way of the rescue he was pursuing." Now that Nazism had been vanquished, however, he joined the call of so many anguished souls to beg Pius "to make his voice heard."

Maritain's letter was dispatched on 12 July, and four days later Pius XII granted him an audience. The pope, as he had during the war and the genocide, remained convinced that he had addressed the problem. He made reference to his comments to a Jewish delegation and reminded Maritain that his remarks of 29 November 1945 had been published on 30 November in *L'Osservatore Romano*. Pius had told the seventy refugees:

> Your presence, Gentlemen, seems to us an eloquent testimony to the psychological transformations and the new orientations that the world conflict has, in its different aspects, created in the world. . . . The abyss of discord, the hatred and folly of persecution which, under the influence of erroneous and intolerant doctrines, in opposition to the noble human and authentic Christian spirit, have engulfed incomparable numbers of innocent victims, even among those who took no active part in the war. . . . The Apostolic See remains faithful to the eternal principles of the law, written by God in the heart of every man, which shines forth in the divine revelation of Sinai and which found its perfection in the Sermon on the Mount and has never, even it the most critical moments, left any doubt as to its maxims and applicability. . . . Your presence here is an intimate testimony of the gratitude on the part of men and women, who in an agonizing time, and often under the threat of imminent death, experienced how the Catholic Church and its true disciples know how, in the exercise of charity, to rise above the narrow and arbitrary limits created

121. See Robert Royal, ed., *Jacques Maritain and the Jews*, (Notre Dame: University of Notre Dame Press, 1994). Much of the material presented here is drawn from a lecture by Michael Marrus of the University of Toronto. It was then used by Gregory Baum in his "Essay on Jacques Maritain and the Vatican's Judaism and the Jews," published in *The Ecumenist* 39 (spring 2002): 1–3, and reprinted in *Newsletter of the Association of Contemporary Church Historians* 8 (Sept. 2002): 1–4.

by human egoism and racial passions. . . . You have experienced yourselves the injuries and the wounds of hatred; but in the midst of your agonies, you have also felt the benefit and sweetness of love, not the love that nourishes itself from terrestrial motives, but rather with a profound faith in the heavenly father, whose light shines on all men, whatever their language and their race, and whose grace is open to all who seek the Lord in a spirit of truth.[122]

Jacques Maritain was deeply disappointed by the reaction of the pope, and deeply disturbed by the evasive tone of his remarks. Although he had spoken to the pope about the Jews and anti-Semitism, Pius referred to neither in his response. Maritain, who understood the pope's caution during the war, could not comprehend his reluctance to do so afterward. Nor did he understand why the pope refused to acknowledge the relationship of anti-Semitism to the Christian theological heritage. The Frenchman deemed Pius XII's postwar attitude much more damning than his silence during the war. Most of Pius XII's defenders have failed to address this issue. Writing later to a friend, Maritain discerned "an absence of papal leadership on the Jewish question." Maritain resigned his post as French ambassador to the Holy See in disgust.[123] But he kept his feelings about Pius XII to himself, in contrast to Hochhuth, who issued a public condemnation of the pope's conduct with respect to the Nazi genocide.

The record reveals that during the postwar period Pius XII did not endorse efforts for Catholic-Jewish reconciliation, and despite the enormity of the Holocaust saw no reason for such a reconciliation. It is true that in the mid-1950s Pius directed that in the prayer for the Jews, *perfideles* no longer be translated as "perfidious" but rather as "unbelievers" or "unfaithful."[124] He did little more. Indeed, a postwar document, discovered only at the close of 2004, instructed French Church authorities that Jewish children baptized during the Holocaust should remain within the Church—even at the cost of keeping them from their own families! Dated Paris, 23 October 1946, the one-page memo allegedly summarized the stance of the Holy Office and was supposedly approved by Pius XII.[125] Whether Pius XII actually saw or approved the memo is unknown. What

122. Quoted in Baum, "Jacques Maritain and the Vatican's Judaism," 2–3.
123. Ibid.; Pawlikowski, "Papacy of Pius XII," 63.
124. Phayer, *Catholic Church and the Holocaust,* 217; Cardinal William Keeler, "The Catholic Church and the Jewish People," http://www.bc.edu/research/cjl/meta-elements/texts/articles/keeler_ICCJ_2003.htm, accessed 2 Feb. 2004.
125. The document was printed in Milan's *Corriere della Sera* at the end of December

we do know is that this pope did not foresee or initiate any substantial changes in Catholic-Jewish relations.

Why was Pius XII unable to address the Jews as Jews or acknowledge the Church's anti-Judaism? Gregory Baum believes that he was inhibited by the "traditional orthodoxy" and lacked a theology that would have permitted him to repudiate anti-Semitism in Christian terms. Had Pius issued the public condemnation of anti-Semitism in 1946 that Maritain urged, and recognized the unfortunate role played by Christian anti-Judaism in the Holocaust, his legacy would probably have been different. He adhered to tradition on other issues as well, telling a group of Italian jurists in 1953 that in principle the Church could not approve a complete separation of Church and state. He did acknowledge, however, that sometimes it is better to tolerate error than to try to eliminate it.[126] Pius would elaborate no further on Church-state relations, religious liberty, or Catholic-Jewish relations.

The pope's position during and after the war allowed some of the German clergy to stress their own suffering under Nazism rather than examine their shortcomings. Not all the bishops chose this evasive tactic, however, and at the behest of Bishop Preysing, an apology was included in the first pastoral letter of the bishops after the war. It deplored the fact that they had remained "indifferent to the crimes against human freedom and human dignity." Even more specific was the 1948 statement of the Mainz Katholientag, which contritely acknowledged "crimes against the people of Jewish stock."[127] Some lay Catholics in Germany continued their criticism of the hierarchy and those who supported them. Noting that the German people and their bishops and priests had cooperated with the Nazis, Konrad Adenauer expressed his conviction "that if the bishops had altogether on a given day spoken out from their pulpits in opposition, much could have been avoided."[128] His criticism was largely ignored. Only

2004 and transmitted worldwide by the Associated Press. "Found Memo Renews Flap over Vatican's WW II Role," *New York Daily News*, 1 Jan. 2005, 14.

126. *Newsletter of the Association of Contemporary Church Historians* 8 (Sept. 2002): 3–4; Blanshard, *Blanshard on Vatican II*, 179; Robert McAfee Brown, *The Ecumenical Revolution* (New York: Doubleday, 1969), 248.

127. Pastoral of the German Bishops at Fulda (23 Aug. 1945), in *The Catholic Mind* 43 (Nov. 1945), and cited in Bernauer, "Holocaust and the Catholic Church's Search for Forgiveness," 3; *Die Kirchen und das Judentum. Dokumente von 1945 bis 1985*, ed. Rolf Rendtoff and Hans Henrix (Paderborn: Verlag, 1989), cited ibid.

128. Adenauer quoted in George Kenzler and Vokder Fabricus, eds., *Die Kirchen im drit-*

following the death of Pius XII was there a profound transformation of the German episcopacy's attitude toward the Holocaust.

In the remaining years of the 1940s, the pope dedicated himself to the reconstruction of Europe and the reconstitution of the Church structure worldwide. He also pleaded for the banishment of atheism in the struggle against Communism. As Stalin consolidated his hold on Eastern Europe, Pius protested the condemnations and the false accusations hurled against the Church, which suggested to some that he was selective rather than timid in his response to persecution. Deploring the crude Soviet attempts to prohibit religion, the pope launched a counterattack on the unbelievers who sought to subvert the faith. At this juncture, Pius cast off the diplomatic restraint he had earlier displayed toward the Nazis and spoke out publicly against Communism.

In the summer of 1949 Pius had the Holy Office prescribe excommunication for those who voted for, joined, or even collaborated with the godless Communists or their allies. In 1951 he urged the persecuted Catholics of Czechoslovakia to stand firm in their faith, praising them for their constancy in the face of brutal persecution. In 1952 he expressed his consolation and provided encouragement to the clergy and people of China, urging Catholics there to continue to trust in Christ. The same year, he supported the Romanians, who were experiencing a similar persecution, reminding them of past trials and assuring them of ultimate victory. Pius XII's "crusade" against Communism and his vocal opposition to the Soviet Union led some to question his earlier reluctance to condemn the Nazi genocide. Was the moral dilemma posed by Communism greater than that of Nazism, or were political, chronological, and organizational factors responsible for the pope's postwar transformation and his willingness to speak out against Soviet abuses? The evidence available to date is inconclusive, as is the documentation of the selectively opened wartime archives of the Vatican.

The pope's concern for the situation in Italy, and in Rome in particular, remained constant. He feared the prospect of a communist takeover of the country and worked actively to prevent it. Initially opposed to the establishment of an Italian Christian Democratic Party, at war's end he accepted it and encouraged Catholic Action groups to participate in parlia-

---

ten Reich, (Frankfurt: Fischer, 1984), cited in Bernauer, "Holocaust and the Catholic Church's Search for Forgiveness," 3.

mentary politics. Under his guidance the Vatican openly intervened in the Italian elections of 1948, appealing to the parish clergy and to 3 million members of Catholic Action organizations. Clerical intrusion in Italian public life reached a high point in 1952, when Luigi Gedda, fearing that the left might win the municipal elections in Rome, proposed a Christian Democratic coalition with the parties of the right—a move opposed by De Gasperi but apparently approved by Pius XII. The pope's fear of Communism and the left encouraged an accommodation with the neofascist and authoritarian right.

Pius XII remained a cold and distant personality for many, and was remembered for the concordat with Nazi Germany, which he continued to defend after the war. "Although the Church had few illusions about National Socialism," he told the cardinals, "it must be recognized that the Concordat in the years that followed brought some advantages, or at least prevented worse evils." He insisted on its preservation, and in March 1957 the West German constitutional court ruled that it remained binding on Germany.[129] Critics considered his diplomacy of compromise a moral liability, even when it brought tangible political advantages. He continued to favor concordats with repressive as well as democratic regimes, signing one with Franco's Spain in 1953 and another with Trujillo's Dominican Republic in 1954. The negative assessment of Pius XII was reinforced by the appearance of Rolf Hochhuth's *The Deputy* in 1963, which portrayed Pius as insensitive to the Holocaust and preoccupied with the narrow clerical interests of the institutional Church.

In failing health, Pius XII died on 11 October 1958 at the age of eighty-two. In death, even more than during his life, controversy surrounded his papacy. Praised effusively by world leaders and Jewish groups at his death, within five years he was depicted as indifferent to the genocide. It was charged that he did little to cleanse the atmosphere of racial hatred that had not only led to the destruction of European Jewry but had undermined basic Christian principles. In this respect, his "silence" was seen to be doubly damnable. Being historians rather than prophets, we cannot know what would have been the impact and consequences of a more public and pronounced opposition to the Holocaust. We can only survey what

---

129. Rhodes, *Vatican in the Age of Dictators,* 183; Blanshard, *Blanshard on Vatican II,* 146.

Pius XII did and explore why, rather than speculate on the consequences of a different policy. Some have recently suggested that Pius XII's "silence" was the result of his alleged anti-Judaism, while others claim that he was unfairly stigmatized him as anti-Semitic and as "Hitler's pope." One author has depicted him as a key player in "the rise of Adolf Hitler," charging that his desire to retain the Kirchensteuer or "church tax" led him to ignore "the atrocities against the Jews."[130] The campaign to beatify Pius XII alongside John XXIII provoked a storm of controversy that may have contributed to the Vatican decision to postpone his beatification and advance the cause of the conservative Pius IX (1846–78) instead, alongside the more liberal John XXIII (1958–63), in 2000. This has been denied repeatedly by the Reverend Peter Gumpel, the chief judge in the beatification process of Pius XII, who insists that "the process is moving ahead normally and swiftly."[131] Partially in response to the charges against Pius XII, John Paul II opened the Vatican Archives on papal relations with Germany for the years 1922–39, following the selective opening of wartime documents that reveal the pope's assistance to prisoners of war.[132] The availability of millions of new documents has failed to convert either the critics or the champions of this pope, who remain polarized.[133]

The debate is reflected in the literature on Pius XII, perhaps the most extensive for any successor of Peter. Confusion flows from the controversy surrounding his reaction to the Holocaust, the work created by admirers and detractors, and the fact that the Vatican Archives remain partially closed for the period. Following the publication of Rolf Hochhuth's play *The Deputy* (in German in 1963 and English in 1964), which presented a critical, ahistorical picture of Pius XII, Pope Paul VI allowed four Jesuits access to the Vatican Archives for the war years. They published twelve volumes of the *Actes et documents du Saint Siège relatifs à la seconde guerre mondiale* (Vatican City, 1965–81). The publication did not stem the controversy, and the historiographical debate between denigrators and defenders of Pius XII continues. In 1999 John Cornwell published *Hitler's Pope: The*

130. Paul L. Williams, *The Vatican Exposed: Money, Murder and the Mafia* (New York: Prometheus Books, 2003), 41, 48.

131. "Rome Goes Forward to Honor Pius," *New York Daily News*, 15 Jan. 2005, 8.

132. Jason Horowitz, "Vatican Opens Files to Rebut War Criticism of Pius XII," *New York Times*, 14 Feb. 2003.

133. Pawlikowski, "Papacy of Pius XII," 57.

Secret History of Pope Pius XII, which claims that Pius exerted an unfortunate influence on developments. More scholarly and balanced, though still critical of Pius, are the monographs by Susan Zuccotti, *Under His Very Windows: The Vatican and the Holocaust in Italy* (2000), and Michael Phayer, *The Catholic Church and the Holocaust, 1930–1965* (2000).

These critical accounts have been countered by the favorable volumes of Sister Margherita Marchione, *Yours Is a Precious Witness: Memoirs of Jews and Catholics in Wartime Italy* (1997), *Pope Pius XII: Architect for Peace* (2000); and *Consensus and Controversy: Defending Pope Pius XII* (2002). The historical and moral reputation of Pius has also been upheld by Pierre Blet (one of the Jesuits allowed to catalogue the wartime documents), in *Pius XII and the Second World War According to the Archives of the Vatican,* trans. L. J. Johnson (1999), and, more recently, by Ronald J. Rychlak, *Hitler, the War and the Pope* (2000); Ralph McInerny, *The Defamation of Pius XII* (2001); and Marc-Andre Chargueraud, *Les Papes et la Shoah, 1932–1945* (2002). A less polemical, more subtle defense of Pius XII is provided by Justus George Lawler in his *Popes and Politics: Reform, Resentment and the Holocaust* (2002).

A more balanced historiography on the papacy and the Holocaust has begun to emerge. Without judging whether the Vatican could or should have done more, Martin Gilbert, in *The Righteous: The Unsung Heroes of the Holocaust* (2003), disputes the contention that the Catholic Church was inactive and silent during the genocide. In an edited volume on *Pope Pius XII and the Holocaust* (2002), Carol Rittner and John K. Roth present articles by sixteen scholars expressing a wide range of views on the subject. José Sanchez's *Pius XII and the Holocaust: Understanding the Controversy* (2002) provides a well-balanced survey of the historiography on this pope's role during the Holocaust.

7

JOHN XXIII, PAUL VI, AND VATICAN II

Aggiornamento and the New Relationship

between Catholics and Jews

Also among man's rights is that of being able to worship
God in accordance with the right dictates of his own con-
science, and to profess his religion both in private and in
public. *

PIUS XII'S DEATH IN EARLY OCTOBER 1958 led to the conclave of 25 October. Although the full complement of cardinals then numbered seventy, only
fifty-three were present, and when two died prior to the conclave their
number was reduced to fifty-one. The Italians, who constituted eighteen
out of the fifty-one, represented the largest and most important bloc, followed by the French cardinals, who formed the second-largest group after
the Italians.[1] This solidified the candidacy of the seventy-six-year-old Angelo Giuseppe Roncalli, who was well known and admired by both
groups. His advanced age likewise proved advantageous, for many of the
cardinals favored a short, transitional papacy that would not substantially

---

* *Pacem in Terris,* Pope John XXIII's encyclical of 11 April 1963, on establishing universal
peace in truth, justice, and charity. *PE* 5:108.

1. Some, citing unnamed FBI sources, have claimed that the conservative Cardinal
Giuseppe Siri had been elected pope but that the French cardinals "annulled" his election.
See Williams, *Vatican Exposed,* 92.

transform the institution. On 28 October Roncalli was elected pope as a compromise candidate, assuming the name John XXIII. The name he chose, as well as his ambitious goals for the faith, led some to suspect that he viewed himself as another John the Baptist. In many ways this assessment proved prophetic.

Although a product of the Tridentine Church and in many respects a traditionalist, the new pope's genial personality was radically different from that of his aloof, introverted, aristocratic predecessor. Almost immediately the gregarious John made it clear that, unlike Pius XII, he did not intend to take his meals alone. One Saturday morning he stopped to bless the Jews of Rome as they were coming out of their temple after prayers—the first pope ever to do so. It was an early indication that John would seek the Catholic-Jewish reconciliation that Pius XII had not pursued. These and other actions served to highlight the differences between the two men.[2] Unlike Pius, who stemmed from the black nobility of Rome, Angelo Giuseppe Roncalli was the third of thirteen children of a poor sharecropper family of Sotto il Monte, outside Bergamo. Acclaimed by some as a breath of fresh air, he was derided by others as a peasant. Roncalli's background and education were branded "inferior" to those of Pacelli, his aristocratic predecessor. In 1901 he enrolled in the Roman Seminary of the Apolinare, where he studied theology and history. Called for compulsory Italian military service in 1901, he returned to his studies at the end of 1902. At the Apolinare he won the prize for Hebrew, a language he studied with great interest. He became a deacon in 1903 and the following year was ordained a priest. Early in 1905, when the socially minded Giacomo Radini-Tedeschi was made Bishop of Bergamo, Angelo, who shared his social concerns, was appointed his secretary. When Italy entered World War I in 1915, Angelo was recalled to the military and remained in the army until the end of 1918, rising to the rank of lieutenant in the chaplains' corps. In 1920 he was called to Rome to serve as the director of the Italian section of Propaganda Fide and was named a monsignor in 1921.

Unlike the well-connected Pacelli, Roncalli had few significant connections or powerful patrons to advance his ecclesiastical career, but even his detractors acknowledged his talent for interpersonal relations. His first

2. See Paul Hofmann, *O Vatican! A Slightly Wicked View of the Holy See* (New York: Congdon and Weed, 1984), 27.

diplomatic assignment came in 1925, when he was selected as apostolic visitor to Bulgaria, with a residence in Sofia, far from a choice assignment.[3] Roncalli felt isolated and lonely during his decade in this Eastern Orthodox country, but he fulfilled his assignment with tact and talent. His stay there instilled in him respect for the religious convictions of others. Most of the difficulties he confronted in Eastern Europe, he confessed, were caused not so much by the Bulgarians but by the cumbersome central organs of ecclesiastical administration, an experience that led him to favor reform. In 1931 he was named the first apostolic delegate to Bulgaria, where he continued to concern himself with the problems of the Eastern churches.[4] In 1935 he was dispatched as apostolic delegate to Turkey and Greece, two other non-Catholic countries, where he remained until 1944, establishing an office in Istanbul for locating prisoners of war, and assisting Jewish refugees in German-controlled territories during World War II.[5]

His experiences in Bulgaria, Greece, and Turkey brought him into contact with Orthodox Christians, Muslims, and Jews, which deepened his respect for the religious beliefs of non-Catholics.[6] Eyewitnesses report that he was deeply moved by the wartime reports he received of the persecution and plight of the Jews, and sought to help by every means at his disposal, including providing counterfeit baptismal certificates to those in flight from the Nazis.[7] He personally supervised their assistance and succeeded in preventing many deportations from Slovakia, Hungary, and Bulgaria. Cardinal Franz Koenig believed that his later determination to seek reconciliation with the Jews was influenced by his reaction against the Nazi atrocities and the abuse of Christian anti-Judaism to justify their genocide. "As Apostolic Delegate in the Near East, John XXIII had come to know the distress and mortal anguish of the Jews fleeing from their persecutors," Cardinal Koenig wrote, adding that subsequently "he felt an ur-

3. Pope John XXIII, *Journal of a Soul*, ed. Loris Capovilla, trans. Dorothy White (New York: McGraw-Hill, 1965), 205–6.

4. The papers of the Archivio della Delegazione Apostolica in Bulgaria of the ASV remain closed for the modern period, so one must rely on memoir material and printed documents for an examinations of events during Roncalli's tenure there.

5. See the Ufficio Informazioni Vaticano (Prigionieri di Guerra, 1939–47) in the ASV.

6. Patrick Granfield, "John XXIII (1958–63): The Father of the Second Vatican Council," in Coppa, *Great Popes through History*, 2:516.

7. Carroll, *Constantine's Sword*, 37.

gent desire to set against the immeasurable and bottomless hate of those days, a lasting word of love."[8]

At the end of 1944, when General de Gaulle, the new French head of state, deemed Valerio Valeri, who had served as nuncio since 1936 both in Paris and Vichy, persona non grata and a Vichy collaborator, Pius XII called upon Roncalli to replace him. Although some in the curia were surprised by the appointment of this "peasant," the amiable Roncalli served Rome well in Paris, resisting French attempts to expel thirty-three French bishops from their sees. As nuncio he developed good relations with both French politicians and bishops. He succeeded beyond all expectations in assuaging Gallic anger and was duly rewarded by Pius XII, who found that most people underestimated the rotund Roncalli. In 1951 Pius appointed him Vatican observer to UNESCO,[9] in 1952 made him a cardinal, and in 1953 named him Patriarch of Venice, where the seventy-one-year-old cardinal expected to spend the rest of his life. Circumstances determined otherwise, however, and in October 1958 he left for Rome to take part in the conclave that elected him pope. A more complex personality than his genial appearance suggested, he was a man who knew what he wanted and how to get it.[10]

Once pope, John devoted himself and his office to reconciliation with the modern world, quickly embracing people of other religious persuasions and championing ecumenism. Aware of the tremendous transformation wrought by World War II and the postwar settlement, as well as the profound impact of the scientific and technological revolutions, he believed that the Church had to break out of its self-imposed ghetto and engage the contemporary world. In his first public address, given on 29 October 1958, John outlined his aims, which included seeking unity between Catholics and Orthodox Christians and achieving reconciliation with other religious groups. Departing from the thunderous denunciations of his predecessors, he stressed the need for unity in the Church and the world, and sought peace and harmony in the secular as well as the religious order.

---

8. Quoted in Oesterreicher, *New Encounter between Christians and Jews*, 114.

9. The papers of the Archivio della Nunziatura Apostolica in Parigi of the ASV are opened only selectively up to January 1922, and are at present closed for the subsequent period. The papers of the Archivio della Missione della Santa Sede Presso l'UNESCO of the ASV remain closed.

10. See Fesquet, *Drama of Vatican II*, 5.

He noted in his journal that it was his "duty not only to shun evil but also to do good." Here and elsewhere he spoke about the unity of mankind, the title and theme of Pius XI's never released encyclical against racism and anti-Semitism.[11]

In his first encyclical, "On Truth, Unity and Peace," John stressed that God created all men as brothers, not as foes.[12] He urged humanity to reject all that separates and divides it, and to join in mutual and just regard to shared opinion and fraternal unity. John welcomed religious leaders from the Eastern Orthodox, Anglican, and Protestant churches, while also reaching out to Jews and other non-Christians. This pope saw Jews not as enemies of the faith but as close relatives. In fact, it was reported that when he administered the sacrament of confirmation to a young Jewish boy, he encouraged him to remain a good Jew, to go to synagogue and support the Jewish school, telling the boy, "by being a Catholic, you do not become any less a Jew."[13] As word spread of the "liberal" sentiments and "good heart" of the new pope, Jews joined liberal Catholics in applauding his efforts. They, too, had heard that John perceived the Church as the mother of all people.

When a Jewish group visited John to thank him for his efforts on behalf of Jews when he was apostolic delegate to Turkey during World War II, he welcomed them warmly, saying, "I am Joseph your brother!" Unlike his immediate predecessor, John XXIII recognized that a reordering of the ties between the Church and the Jews was long overdue. He deplored the genocide that the Jews of Europe had endured, and he seemed to realize, as a number of previous popes had not, that the anti-Judaism so prevalent in the Christian community might have facilitated the massacre of millions of Jews. Consequently, he quickly called for the removal of derogatory passages from the liturgy. On Good Friday, when Cardinal Augustin Bea was to conduct the service and chant the intercessory prayer on behalf of the Jewish people, John sent him word to delete the phrase "perfidia Judaica." Initially it seemed that the elimination of the reference to the "per-

---

11. Pope John XXIII, *Journal of a Soul*, 37; "Votre visite," 11 June 1959, *PP* 1:225.
12. "Ad Petri Cathedram," 29 June 1959, *PP* 1:226.
13. Robert Blair Kaiser, *Pope, Council and World: The Story of Vatican II* (New York: Macmillan, 1963), 49, quoted in Thomas G. Lederer, "2000 Years: Relations between Catholics and Jews before and after Vatican II," http://www.Arthurstreet.com/2000 YEARS, p. 10, accessed 18 Oct. 2002.

fidious Jews" had reference only to the churches of Rome, but on 5 July 1959 an instruction from the Sacred Congregation of Rites, at the pope's direction, extended the papal decision to the entire Church.[14] Today the Catholic prayer for the Jews reads:

Let us pray also for the Jews,
to whom God spoke first.
May He grant that they advance
in the understanding of His world and love. . . .
In Your loving kindness
hear the prayers of Your Church
so that the people You made Your own in olden days
Attain the fullness of salvation
Through Christ our Lord.[15]

Although the new pope selected the conservative Domenico Tardini, who had been Pius XII's undersecretary for external affairs, as his secretary of state, he planned changes that transcended the expectation of those who thought he would remain a transitional pope. Early on, he saw the need for some updating, or *aggiornamento,* of the Church, as well as its *aperturismo,* or opening up. In fact, he was the first pope since the Reformation to frankly acknowledge that the Church required substantial reform. When questioned about his *aggiornamento* and *aperturismo,* he allegedly went to one of the windows of his apartments and thrust it open to let in fresh air. He had invoked *aggiornamento* as early as 1957, perceiving synods and councils as the constitutional way to effect this ecclesiastical renewal. This led to his decision to convene the twenty-first council of the Church to implement the *aggiornamento* he deemed necessary.[16] Among other things, he was determined to reexamine the relationship of the Church to the Jews, selecting Father Augustin Bea of the Society of Jesus, the former confessor of Pius XII, to provide leadership and direction on three issues: first, the Church's declaration on its relationship to non-

---

14. Oesterreicher, *New Encounter between Christians and Jews,* 53, 109.
15. Ibid., 110.
16. Peter Hebblethwaite, *Pope John XXIII: Shepherd of the Modern World* (New York: Doubleday, 1985), 264. Although the papers of John XXIII and Paul VI, the two popes who presided over the Second Vatican Council, remain closed, many of the council papers have been opened. See index no. 1198 of the Concilio Vaticano II in the ASV.

Christian religions; second, its stance on ecumenism; and third, a declaration on religious liberty.[17]

Soon after donning the tiara in January 1959, John announced his decision to call a Church council.[18] Familiar with the clerical establishment and aware of the sentiments of those addicted to tradition, John realized that the task ahead would be daunting, but he was not discouraged by the many obstacles he knew would emerge. He probably realized that his age and health would not allow him to see the council to its conclusion, but this did not deter him either.

Paradoxically, the need for a council was shared by conservatives, among them Cardinal Alfredo Ottaviani and Cardinal Ernesto Ruffini, who assumed that the Second Vatican Council would reinforce the First Vatican Council (1869–70) by refuting contemporary errors, liberal illusions, and misguided opinions. They did not foresee it as a pastoral one ushering in a "little holy madness," as did the pope, who refused to play the part of a simple caretaker. They mirrored an entrenched attitude in the curia, which looked backward rather than forward. Fortunately, John's reformism found resonance among other members of the clergy and received the support of Cardinal Giovanni Montini of Milan, who also envisioned the council as a force for reform rather than reaction. Both he and Pope John expected that the forthcoming council would provide the Church's long-postponed response to modernity.[19] Among other things, Montini foresaw the need to revise the Church's relationship to the Jews. John's reformism found critics as well as champions, creating controversy and clouding the perspective on his pontificate, and that of his successor, Montini, who brought the council to a conclusion after John's death.

In light of John's progressive agenda, it is surprising, indeed strange, that he selected the traditionalist Archbishop Pericle Felici as secretary of the preparatory commission of the council. John probably selected Felici to appease the conservatives, while relying on Montini to prepare a more progressive program. This represented one of the many compromises that John was constrained to make before the opening and during the first session of the council, revealing his ability to maneuver between conflicting

17. Oesterreicher, *New Encounter between Christians and Jews,* 19.

18. "Questa festiva," 25 Jan. 1959, *PP* 1:216; "The Tender Emotion," 28 Oct. 1959, ibid., 229.

19. "Tender Emotion," 229, 232, 234; Peter Hebblethewaite, *Paul VI: The First Modern Pope* (New York: Paulist Press, 1993), 1.

factions. A reformist course was outlined in Giovanni Montini's Lenten pastoral of 1962, *Pensiamo al Concilio* (Let Us Think about the Council), and in Pope John's September 1962 broadcast on Vatican Radio. In the interim, in 1960, John established ten commissions to examine particular questions for conciliar consideration and created a special secretariat for promoting Christian unity, authorizing it to take part in the preparatory work of the council. This preliminary planning proved massive, and Montini's role was impressive. The commissions drafted some seventy decrees to be debated, which were eventually whittled down to seventeen.

Discussion on the Jews commenced with John's suggestion that the council should say something special about the Jews to express Christian indebtedness to them. A number of Arab states were alarmed by the prospect, and their diplomats immediately lobbied against any official Catholic statement on the Jews, warning that doing so might jeopardize the status of their Catholic subjects. Some believe that had John initially understood the problems inherent in tackling the Jewish question, including the sensitivity of Jews, Muslims, and Eastern-rite Catholics on the issue, he might have issued a white paper on the subject rather than bring it before the council.[20] In retrospect, his decision to bring the Jewish question before the council was the right one, for it brought it to public attention and assured that it would have the greatest impact both inside and outside the Church.

Following three years of laborious preparation, the council officially opened on 11 October 1962. Cardinal Montini outlined the program. He foresaw that one session would focus on the nature of the Church, another would explore its mission, and a third would examine the Church's relationships with other groups. Throughout, Montini stressed the council's work as renewal and *aggiornamento*. It was to be a positive rather than a punitive council. To enhance its message and render it truly "catholic," Montini cited the need to reach out to the entire world and all civil society.[21] John said as much in his opening address in St. Peter's Basilica, where he invoked the unity of the human family and portrayed the Church as the loving mother of all. This was not necessarily the goal of the Roman

20. Blanshard, *Blanshard on Vatican II*, 123, 129.
21. Hebblethwaite, *Pope John XXIII*, 326, 373, 409, 422, 442–43; Hebblethwaite, *Paul VI*, 284.

curia or "Italian machine," whose twelve congregations, six offices, and three tribunals often championed traditionalism and appeared addicted to past practice. They were bolstered by a conservative clique who shared their sentiments and sought among other things to obstruct any reconsideration of the Church's long-standing relationship to the Jews and Judaism.

John, whose vision from the first was ecumenical and who perceived himself as a reconciler, did not share their apprehension, nor was he restrained by an anti-Judaic theology. As early as 1900 he wrote that since all mankind was crafted in the image of God, "should I not love them all, why should I despise them?"[22] He reiterated this theme in a letter to the president of Turkey in 1959, in which he again spoke of the unity of humanity. From the first, John sought to emphasize everything that unites, and to remove anything that unduly divides, believers in God. Regarding humanity as one family, he saw the need for human welfare to assume a global dimension. For this and other reasons, he applauded the efforts of the United Nations on behalf of the displaced and refugees. He encouraged Catholics to leave their ghetto and to recognize that they had more important things to do than hurl stones at the Communists. Early on he committed himself to work for the glory of God, the Church, and the salvation of souls.[23] He saw the council as a means of achieving these ends. His ambitious plans were more easily imagined than implemented, but his convictions set the agenda for discussion.

Inspired by Pope John's reformism, Rome's Biblical Institute petitioned the central preparatory commission of the council in April 1960 to examine relations between Catholics and Jews, and to abandon both anti-Judaism and anti-Semitism. John commissioned Cardinal Bea to prepared a draft on the relationship between the Church and the people of Israel. In addition to promoting unity within the Christian camp, the secretariat for promoting Christian unity sought reconciliation with the Jewish brethren by condemning the long history of discrimination against Jews.[24] Among other things, Cardinal Bea perceived a link between the need for a new

---

22. Quoted in Hebblethwaite, *Pope John XXIII*, 66.

23. *PP* 1:212, 214, 225, 230, 243, 251; Pope John XXIII, *Journal of a Soul*, 299, 13; Fesquet, *Drama of Vatican II*, 27.

24. Oesterreicher, *New Encounter between Christians and Jews*, 114–15; Fesquet, *Drama of*

Christian relationship with the Jewish people and the Nazi genocide. His call for reconciliation was seconded by the German bishops, whose pastoral letter, released on the eve of the opening of the council, advocated atonement. Meanwhile, John met with the representatives of non-Catholic communities, receiving the Archbishop of Canterbury and ordering the change in the Easter liturgy that referred to the "perfidious Jews," mentioned above. The council's eventual message on the Church's bonds to the Jewish people, the core of its "Declaration on the Relationship of the Church to Non-Christian Relations," owes its existence to John's mandate.[25]

On 13 June 1960 John met with Jules Isaac, an important advocate of Jewish concerns, whose book *Jesus and Israel* (1948) focused on the link between Christian anti-Judaism and the anti-Semitism that culminated in the Holocaust. Isaac had been received by Pius XII in 1949, but his view of Christian anti-Judaism had apparently aroused the suspicions of that pontiff.[26] He found John more receptive to his pleas and presented the pontiff with a copy of his work. During the audience, Pope John expressed his reverence for the Old Testament, especially for the Prophets, the Psalms, and the Book of Wisdom. Isaac told the pope that he had raised Jewish hopes, and he revealed the things Jews hoped the council would correct, including correction of the false and unjust statements about Jews in Church texts and repudiation of the notion that the Jewish Diaspora was a punishment inflicted by God. Referring to the decrees of the Council of Trent, Isaac asked John to emphasize that the fundamental cause of Christ's death was the guilt of all sinners, rather than place the burden primarily upon the Jews.

John was sympathetic to these requests, and when Isaac asked him if he and his people had reason to hope, John responded, "You have reason for more than a little hope."[27] When Isaac asked the pope to appoint a committee to review the Church's relations with the Jews, Pope John al-

---

Vatican II, 181. See also the printed works of Cardinal Augustin Bea in the Carte Bea of the ASV.

25. Stjepan Schmidt, *Augustin Bea, the Cardinal of Unity* (New Rochelle: New City Press, 1992), 505–6; Wilton Wynn, *Keepers of the Keys: John XXIII, Paul VI, and John Paul II: Three Who Changed the Church* (New York: Random House, 1988), 217; Oesterreicher, *New Encounter between Christians and Jews*, 103–5.

26. Phayer, *Catholic Church and the Holocaust*, 204.

27. Oesterreicher, *New Encounter between Christians and Jews*, 105, 108.

legedly responded that he had been thinking about it, and sent Isaac to see Cardinal Bea with this request.[28] Isaac noted in his diary that Pope John's response to his pleas on behalf of the Jews was positive and warm.[29] Later in the year, John elaborated further on his position toward the Jews. "There is a great difference between the one who accepts only the Old Testament and the one who joins to the Old the New as the highest law and teaching," he told a group of visiting Jews. "These differences, however, do not extinguish the brotherhood that springs from a common origin [of Christians and Jews]."[30]

Now John had to bring the flock around to his point of view on reconciliation with Jews and other non-Christians—no small task. He confessed as much to Jules Isaac, reminding him that although he was the head of the Church, he could not effect meaningful change without the support of others. "What you see here is not an absolute monarchy," he told Isaac.[31] Cardinal Bea, whose secretariat was assigned the responsibility for elaborating a statement on the Church's relations with the Jews, was assisted by Father Gregory Baum, who outlined a short exposition. It affirmed three things: first, the affinity of the Christian Church with Israel and the fulfillment, not the invalidation, of the Old Testament by the New; second, that a holy remnant of the Jewish people accepted Jesus as Savior, and that God had not rejected the Jewish people; and third, that the Church hoped for Israel's final reconciliation with Jesus, but that meanwhile Christians should treat Jews with love and respect rather than disdain and contempt.[32]

These points were taken into consideration by the "Subcommittee to Deal with the Problems of the Church's Relationship to the Jewish People," composed of Abbot Leo Rudloff, Father Gregory Baum, and Monsignor John M. Oesterreicher. Rumors that this subcommittee, and possibly the council itself, would issue a positive statement on the kinship of Christians and Jews further alarmed some Arab governments, which commenced a concerted diplomatic campaign to derail it, causing a number of frightened Vatican officials to waver in their resolve. Indeed, opposition

28. Phayer, *Catholic Church and the Holocaust*, 208.
29. Carroll, *Constantine's Sword*, 38.
30. Quoted in Oesterreicher, *New Encounter between Christians and Jews*, 112.
31. Ibid., 108.
32. Ibid., 129.

came not only from Arab governments but from Catholic theologians who were not prepared for such a statement, which they found in conflict with their traditional reading of Scripture. Despite such opposition, the subcommittee pressed forward and prepared the first draft of the *Decretum de Iudaeis* in the week of 27 November to 2 December 1961. It read:

> The Church, the Bride of Christ, acknowledges with a heart full of gratitude that. . . . the beginnings of her faith and election go as far back as to the Israel of the Patriarchs and Prophets. . . . Similarly, her salvation is prefigured in the deliverance of the Chosen People out of Egypt, as in a sacramental sign.
>
> The Church in fact believes that Christ, who "is our peace," embraces Jews and Gentiles with one and the same love and that He made the two one.
>
> Furthermore, the Church believes in the union of the Jewish people with herself as an integral part of Christian hope. With unshaken faith and deep longing the Church awaits union with this people.
>
> As the Church, like a mother, condemns most severely injustices committed against innocent people everywhere, so she raises her voice in loud protest against all wrongs done to Jews, whether in the past or in our times. Whoever despises or persecutes this people does injury to the Catholic Church.[33]

This statement provided a belated and indirect condemnation of the Holocaust, but these words were not universally appreciated in the Church. There were those who looked askance at this and other proposed innovations. To overcome their reservations, Pope John, in his speech of 25 December 1961 convoking the Second Vatican Council, expressed the need to address the problems of the modern age.[34] This would not be easily accomplished, he said, for the council confronted a series of impediments, not least the insistence of many clergy on the use of Latin, which few laypeople had mastered. In February of the new year, John announced that the council would open on 11 October 1962.[35] The month before its scheduled convocation, the doctors informed the eighty-year-old pope that he was suffering from stomach cancer, which made it unlikely that he would personally bring the council to its conclusion. Undaunted, John determined to press forward, donned his steel-rimmed eyeglasses, and presided over the council's opening session. In attendance were more than

---

33. Ibid., 158–59.
34. "Humanae salutis," 25 Dec. 1961, *PP* 1:270.
35. "Consilium. diu Nostra," 2 Feb. 1962, *PP* 1:271.

2,600 priests—it was the greatest gathering of any Church council and some considered it the greatest religious event of the twentieth century. It generated great interest both within and outside the Church.[36] Not surprisingly, divisions soon emerged, as some assumed a more "conservative" stance and others called for a more "liberal" approach.

From the first, the council's projected statement on the Jews provoked the greatest interest and controversy. The council planners had originally expected that the first draft of the *Decretum de Iudaeis* would be presented during the first session of the council, read and digested by its members, and discussed during the second session. This expectation was scuttled in June, four months before the council convened, following the announcement that Dr. Nahum Goldmann, president of the World Jewish Congress, would send Dr. Chaim Wardi, an official of Israel's Ministry of Religious Affairs, as its representative in Rome. Both Catholic conservatives and Arab diplomats used this as a pretext to prevent the council's consideration of *Decretum de Iudaeis,* denouncing the flagrant Israeli interference in the work of the council. Hoping to defuse the situation, the central preparatory commission, during their last session in June, removed the draft decree on the Jews from the council's agenda and postponed its consideration.

Cardinal Montini's position on the delay is not known. What is certain is that he consistently defended the diplomatic course pursued by Pius XII during the Holocaust of not inciting further Nazi retribution by speaking out against the genocide. Indeed, at the height of the controversy unleashed by Hochhuth's play, *The Deputy,* he wrote the editor of the British Catholic weekly the London *Tablet,* praising Pius XII and denying that his conduct was inspired by a political calculations. "As for his omitting to take up a position of violent opposition to Hitler in order to save the lives of those millions of Jews slaughtered by the Nazis," Montini wrote, "an attitude of protest and condemnation such as this young man [Hochhuth] blames the Pope for not having adopted would have been not only futile but harmful."[37] Thus, while Montini was willing to reform Catholic-Jewish relations, he was not prepared to rebuke his patron for his position

36. "Cancer Didn't Stop Council," *New York Newsday,* 12 Oct. 1992; James Breig, "Gregory the Great Named Top Pope by Scholars," *Brooklyn Tablet,* 17 April 1999, 5; David Van Biema, "A Church Transformed," *Time* magazine, 21 March 2003, A36.

37. *Tablet* (London), 29 June 1963, 714.

on the Jews, which he apparently shared. His stance was reform yes, rebuke no. Others in the curia wanted neither one nor the other.

Conservative and curial opposition led some to fear that the Jewish issue would be ignored and the decree on Christian-Jewish relations quietly shelved in the Vatican Archives next to Pius XI's *Humani Generis Unitas*. But, unlike Pius XI's encyclical, the question had already entered public debate and could not be swept under the rug. To keep the matter alive, Cardinal Bea drafted an article entitled "Are the Jews Guilty of Deicide and Are They Forever Damned?" for publication in the *Civiltà Cattolica*. His response to both queries was a resounding no, and he provided the theological arguments to bolster his position. Apparently for political reasons, including the anticipated Arab reaction, Cardinal Tardini requested its withdrawal. However, Bea—perhaps with papal encouragement— published it under a pen name in the German Jesuit journal *Stimmen der Zeit*, and it was soon translated and distributed to the council priests. Its appearance and distribution brought the declaration on the Jews to the forefront, as did Bea's direct appeal to Pope John. Bea reminded John of his secretariat's mandate to shed light on the Church's relations with the Jews and indicated that, although it had been removed from the agenda for reasons of political expediency, the council should consider it. Some found it interesting, others ironic, that Cardinal Bea, Pius XII's confessor, considered reconciliation with the Jews central to the renewal of the Church.

Pope John responded in a personal note on 13 December 1962 assuring Bea of his full support.[38] His support for the declaration on the Jews was shared by a number of bishops, who anxiously awaited conciliar action. On 7 December 1962, as the first session neared its end, Bishop Mendez Arceo of Cuernavaca, Mexico, asked whether "Catholic pastors and faithful show these sons of our common father Abraham a real love after the example of the Sovereign Pontiff, or whether on the contrary they display a subconscious Anti-Semitism."[39] Opinion within the council and the Church was divided on this question, but Cardinal Bea, deeply committed to the declaration, introduced some modifications to the first draft, and

38. Phayer, *Catholic Church and the Holocaust*, 209–10.
39. Fesquet, *Drama of Vatican II*, 96.

also revised the draft of the broad "Schema on Ecumenism," in the hope of securing its approval.[40]

When John closed the first session of the Second Vatican Council with a mass on 8 December 1962, the great expectations it had aroused remained unfulfilled. During its first two months, no decrees had been approved, the Jewish issue had been temporarily shelved, and there was dissension on this and a number of other matters. Nonetheless, John appreciated the council's impact on the world, including non-Catholics.[41] Although in failing health, in April 1963 he issued the encyclical "Pacem in Terris" (On Establishing Universal Peace in Truth, Justice, Charity, and Liberty), which insisted on freedom of conscience and freedom of worship. Among other things, the encyclical specified that "Also among man's rights is that of being able to worship God in accordance with the right dictates of his own conscience, and to profess his religion in private and in public."[42] It represented an important departure from the prevailing papal position, which had for centuries remained suspicious of religious liberty. Some perceived "Pacem in Terris" as a directive to the council.

Recognizing the great tasks still confronting the council, John appointed a commission to continue its work during the recess. Thus the modified statement on the Jews was incorporated into chapter 4 of the "Schema on Ecumenism" and approved by the secretariat for Christian unity in its session of 25 February to 2 March 1963. How it would be received was still very much in question, especially since John's health was deteriorating rapidly. Before his death, John XXIII had allegedly read *The Deputy,* which renewed his determination to proceed with the transformation of Christian-Jewish relations.[43] John's failing health encouraged the entrenched opposition to resort to Byzantine intrigues, first to stall and then to quash the statements on the Jews and religious liberty. John apparently suspected as much and feared that the next session would undermine much he had sought to achieve. John hoped that Montini, who shared much of his vision, would succeed him as pope. Montini's long association with Pius XII and his diplomatic experience as secretary of state made him far less spon-

40. Oesterreicher, *New Encounter between Christians and Jews,* 159–68.
41. See "Mirabilis ille Episcoporum," 6 Jan. 1963, *PP* 1:287.
42. "Pacem in Terris," 11 April 1963, *PP* 1:290–91.
43. Carroll, *Constantine's Sword,* 45.

taneous and much more cautious on most issues, including Christian-Jewish relations, which may have enabled him to garner conservative as well as liberal support on divisive issues.[44]

Christians, Jews, and others of good faith mourned John's death on 3 June 1963. In fact, the night preceding his death, the chief rabbi of Rome, accompanied by a group of Jewish pilgrims, ventured to St. Peter's Square to pray for the ailing pope. Earlier the rabbi had petitioned the council to follow "the shining example given by Pope John." Jews as well as Christians considered the death of John "a death in the family." Undeniably, John had captured the imagination and earned the affection of much of the Christian and non-Christian world.[45] Although his pontificate lasted only four and a half years, it had a major impact on the Church and the relationship between Catholics and Jews. According to Hans Küng, in less than five years John had breathed more new life into the Church than his predecessors had done in five centuries.[46] Some critics concurred but differed in their evaluation of the changes. Among those dissatisfied with the proposed changes was the ultraconservative Cardinal Ottaviani, who reportedly prayed that he would die before the end of the council so that he would die a Catholic.

Vatican II introduced many innovations in both liturgy and dogma. Among other things, priests were no longer to turn their backs on the congregation while sanctifying the Host and were to begin saying the Mass in the vernacular rather than in Latin. Judaism was no longer to be considered superseded by Christianity. More than a million people signed a petition for John XXIII's beatification, encouraging Paul VI to initiate proceedings for his canonization as a saint. It is widely believed that if the ancient custom of popular canonization had remained in effect in 1963, John would have been immediately proclaimed a saint by the huge crowd in St. Peter's Square that gathered to mourn his death. Early in 2000, Pope John Paul II recognized a miracle performed by John XXIII in curing a nun of a dangerous disease, paving the way for his beatification.[47]

44. Sandro Magister, *La politica vaticana e l'Italia, 1943–1978* (Rome: Reuniti, 1979), 294; Phayer, *Catholic Church and the Holocaust,* 211.

45. Oesterreicher, *New Encounter between Christians and Jews,* 161; McAfee Brown, *Ecumenical Revolution,* 59.

46. Carroll, *Constantine's Sword,* 550.

47. *New York Times,* 28 Jan. 2000, A6.

Despite the popular outpouring of love for John XXIII, conservatives complained that he had unwisely unleashed liberal reforms in the Church that had sparked calls for further ill-conceived ecclesiastical changes. The liberals who called for these further changes applauded his innovations. The conclave that assembled in June 1963 quickly divided into two camps, one supporting the election of the "liberal" Montini, Archbishop of Milan and widely acknowledged as the choice of John XXIII, the other favoring the conservative Giuseppe Siri, Archbishop of Genoa. Opponents of Montini noted that he had not favored Luigi Gedda's interventionism in Italian political life, had followed the philosophical precepts of Jacques Maritain, had drafted and worked for the reformist agenda of Vatican II, and was thought to support the priest worker movement in France. Some of them argued that Pius XII, the champion of the traditionalists, had had serious enough doubts about Montini to decline naming him a cardinal and had "exiled" him to Milan. But the "liberal" faction outnumbered the conservatives, and on 21 June the sixty-five-year-old Montini was elected pope, taking the name Paul and announcing his determination to reach out to the world.[48] His election seemed to signal that the College of Cardinals, if not the curia, recognized that it could not and should not attempt to undo the work of John or abort the process of the Church's conciliation with the modern world.

The son of a wealthy bourgeois family active in Catholic political life, Montini was ordained a priest in 1920 and attended the Gregorian University, the University of Rome, and the Accademia dei Nobili Ecclesiastici, where he studied diplomacy. Following a brief tenure at the nunciature in Warsaw (1923), he returned to Rome and entered the secretariat of state, serving as ecclesiastical assistant or chaplain to the Italian association of Catholic university students in Rome (Federazione Universitaria Cattolica Italiana). Cardinal Eugenio Pacelli made him undersecretary for ordinary affairs and furthered his diplomatic and ecclesiastical career.[49] When Pacelli became pope in 1939, Montini functioned as pro-secretary of state. During World War II, Montini was entrusted with organizing and supervising the Vatican's extensive relief efforts and coordinated Pius XII's

48. Hebblethewaite, *Paul VI*, 319, 326–31.
49. For the early life and career of Giovanni Montini, see Richard J. Wolff, "Giovanni Battiosta Montini and Italian Politics, 1897–1933," *CHR* 81 (April 1985): 228–47.

Office of Information for Prisoners of War. Pius XII appreciated Montini's "balance" and "self-control," but there were differences between the two. Among other things, Pius had serious reservations about mixing politics and religion, while Montini ardently supported political Catholicism.

Although Montini served Pius XII loyally, Pius refused to make Montini a cardinal, banishing him instead to the archbishopric of Milan in 1954 after his seventeen years of service in the secretariat of state. Montini was thus ineligible for election to the papal throne when Pius XII died in 1958. Pius intimated that he had attempted to name Montini a cardinal but that Montini had refused the offer. This seems unlikely, in that Montini expressed no reservations about accepting the honor when it was conferred by his successor. Pope John XXIII had a long and close friendship with Montini, who was one of the first people he wrote to following his election, and among the first archbishops named cardinal by the new pope. John arranged matters so that Montini would play an important role in the council, and early on believed that Montini would succeed him, according him special rooms in the Vatican during the first session of the council.[50] It was recognized that Montini had played a key role in shaping the direction of the council and shared much of John's vision. His appointment of the progressive Cardinal Bea to the Holy Office in October 1963 was seen as an attempt to balance its more conservative members.[51] It also provided papal support for the conciliar statements on the Jews and religious liberty, which Bea openly and ardently championed.

Soon after his election, in his first public address, Paul VI announced that the council would reopen on 29 September 1963. *Aggiornamento* remained Paul's goal, as he called for the completion and implementation of the council's reforms. Paul made it clear that he would follow John's course and directives. "As far as understanding the modern world and drawing close to it," he wrote, "I think I am on the same lines as Pope John."[52] This confession pleased liberals but alarmed traditionalists. Very probably to reassure the latter, Paul confirmed the conservative Amleto Cigognani as his secretary of state; he held the office until 1969. As 29 September drew near, Paul invited non-Catholic observers to attend and em-

---

50. Hebblethwaite, *Pope John XXIII*, 345; *PP* 1:211.
51. Fesquet, *Drama of Vatican II*, 138–39.
52. Hebblethwaite, *Paul VI*, 12.

phasized the council's reform agenda. At the solemn opening of the second session he recalled the council's four goals: Church awareness, renewal, Christian unity, and dialogue with the modern world.[53]

The second session lasted from 29 September to 4 December 1963 and witnessed more than forty working sessions and some six hundred speeches. There was considerable bickering between liberal and conservative factions behind the scenes, which Paul had reluctantly to mediate. The Roman curia and the council often disagreed on the pressing issue of ecumenical encounters with non-Catholics. In fact, Cardinal Cicognani spearheaded an attempt to reduce the statement on the Jews to a minor passage in the chapter on the Church.[54] Controversy also surrounded the proposed declaration on religious liberty, which likewise provoked dissension and a barrage of criticism. It was defended on 20 November 1963 by Bishop Emile de Smedt of Bruges, who denounced the "Machiavellianism" of Catholics who invoked freedom of religion when Catholics were in a minority but refused to concede it when they constituted a majority. To those who cited the numerous nineteenth-century papal condemnations of religious liberty, the Belgian bishop responded that they had to be interpreted within the "historical and doctrinal context" that spawned them.[55] Conservatives remained unconvinced, alarmed by what they denounced as the historicist and relativist approach of the proponents of religious liberty, which they branded religious license bordering on indifferentism.

Although a majority favored some statement supporting religious liberty, a minority obstinately opposed it. Opponents continued to point to the pronouncements of a series of nineteenth- and twentieth-century popes right down to Pius XII, who either opposed or had grave reservations about religious liberty and condemned religious equality. Cardinal Alfredo Ottaviani deemed it a "very serious matter" to allow every religion to propagate itself, while Cardinal Ernesto Ruffini of Palermo proclaimed that Catholicism, as the one true faith, was entitled to receive governmental support. He insisted that the illusion of "religious liberty" be replaced

---

53. *PP* 1:295, 300–302.
54. Blanshard, *Blanshard on Vatican II*, 130.
55. The account in the following three paragraphs relies on Fesquet, *Drama of Vatican II.* See especially 243, 78, 253, 343, 219.

by the pragmatic reality of "religious toleration." Father de Broglie-Revel, a Jesuit professor of dogmatic theology at the Gregorian University, denounced the text on religious liberty as incoherent, claiming that it equivocated and sought an impossible compromise between the principles of liberalism and those enunciated by Pope Pius IX. Bishop Antonio de Castro of Brazil believed that such "religious freedom" conflicted with the doctrines of Popes Leo XIII and Pius XII, which pronounced that error had no rights but might be accorded some concessions to avert greater evil. He joined them in deeming "absurd" the notion of honoring those in error by granting them equality.

The statement on the Jews also produced tensions and demanded a number of compromises. Brought to the floor as part of the "Schema on Ecumenism," it was delivered only on 8 November 1963. The next day Dr. Nahum Goldmann, president of the World Jewish Congress, issued a statement applauding the fact that the council was considering eliminating religious teachings that provoked contempt, persecution, and hatred of Jews. His sentiments were shared by a number of bishops in the hall, who urged that that the statement on the Church and the Jews be debated and approved. However, they had to contend with the conservative and Arab charge that organized Jewry was attempting to dictate to the council. On this and a number of other occasions Jewish intervention unintentionally worked to undermine the efforts of Catholic allies. The American Rabbi Marc Tannenbaum even declared that if the council approved the declaration on the Jews it would do so "in spite of the Jews, not because of them."[56]

Cardinal Bea sought to remain above the fray, a difficult if not impossible feat. In his report to the general congregation, he defended chapters four and five of the draft decree on ecumenism, which dealt respectively with the attitude of the Church toward Jews and religious liberty and were both controversial. On 18 November the leaders of the Eastern Church spoke out against issuing a chapter on the Jews. They objected to it on several grounds—first and foremost in response to the pressure of the Arab states, which feared its political consequences and implicit support for Zionism. To allay their concerns, Cardinal Bea stressed the religious char-

56. Quoted in John Jay Hughes, "Review of Thomas Brechenmacher and Hardy Ostry, Rom und Jerusalem," *CHR* 88 (Oct. 2002): 800.

acter of the schema, noting that Christ, the apostles, and the Virgin Mary were Jews and that Saint Paul considered Christians the sons of Israel. For these and other reasons he said, the Church could not countenance anti-Semitic sermons and teachings. If some Jews put Christ to death, he continued, it was no less true that Christ asked his Father to forgive them, and Bea said that the followers of Christ would do well to follow his example.[57]

Others argued that the statement on the Jews did not belong in the "Schema on Ecumenism," while still others resented the "presumption" of Dr. Israel Benzeev, president of the Association for the Propagation of Judaism, who suggested that Catholics should recognize Saturday as the day of the Lord.[58] The Latin patriarch of Jerusalem, Alberto Gori, opposed the statement on Jews, protesting that it accorded Jews special treatment over other faiths.[59] Although the council's secretary general, Archbishop Felici, promised an early discussion of the chapter on Jews, this did not take place. Because of the vocal opposition of a minority, the statement on the Jews was once again postponed in the closing days of the second session. Indeed, the council closed on 4 December 1963 without even a procedural vote on whether to accept or reject the transmitted draft as a basis for discussion. Cardinal Bea was disappointed. "Since the Church in this Council is striving to renew itself by 'seeking again the features of its most fervent youth' as John XXIII of venerable memory said," Bea concluded, "it seems imperative to take up this question."[60] Despite its broad support, some still feared the statement on Jews would never reach the floor.

To reassure the majority, who were frustrated by the postponement, Cardinal Bea promised that eventually the chapters on religious liberty and the Jews would be discussed and approved.

Everything will be done without haste. These chapters will be seriously treated in the next session. "What is put off is not put away." Let us continue to work, and I urge you to send me your observations before January 31, 1964. We will then be able to provide you with better texts. What John XXIII said at the end of the first session, I say to you now: the second session has been very fruitful because of the ecumenical dialogue it began. This dialogue is not merely a written text, a charter; it is a living dialogue in our hearts. Like Saint

57. Fesquet, *Drama of Vatican II*, 243.
58. Ibid., 229.
59. Blanshard, *Blanshard on Vatican II*, 128.
60. Oesterreicher, *New Encounter between Christians and Jews*, 170–78.

John resting his head on Christ's breast, we now feel the pulsations of Christ's heart better and have a much clearer understanding that we are realizing his will: *ut unum sint.*[61]

The American bishops were particularly interested in the question of the Church's relations to the Jews, the issue of racism, and the statement on religious liberty. Bishop Robert E. Tracy of Baton Rouge, on behalf of the 147 American bishops, urged the council to issue a solemn declaration against racism "which would have worldwide scope and would be a consolation for all who are deprived of their liberty."[62] During the second session Bishop Emile Josef De Smedt had opened the general debate on the issue of religious liberty, citing four major arguments on its behalf: the truth of the claim, its utility in defending the faith against atheism, the recognition that men must live together in peace, and the advancement of ecumenism.[63] His report was applauded by "liberals" but deemed irrelevant by "conservatives," who pressed for postponing this issue as well.

At the close of the second session, Paul realized that much remained to be done. He introduced the agenda for the third session in December while announcing a pilgrimage to the Holy Land early the next year, one of sixteen trips abroad to six continents during his pontificate. His projected trip to the Holy Land, at a time when the Holy See did not enjoy diplomatic relations with Jordan, which then controlled east Jerusalem, or with Israel, which had incorporated the rest of the city, aroused curiosity and provoked astonishment.[64] The first pope to fly in an airplane and the first to visit the Holy Land, Paul met Athenagoras II, the ecumenical Patriarch of Constantinople, as well as the Armenian Patriarch and the Anglican Archbishop of Jerusalem. During his visit of 4–6 January 1964, Paul also met with both King Hussein of Jordan and President Zalman Shazar of Israel, invoking peace and unity. Some believed that Paul's trip to the Holy Land was a sign of his respect for the Jewish people undertaken to expedite and facilitate the conciliar declaration on the Jews.[65] Although this declaration was overwhelmingly supported by the Americans and by a

---

61. Quoted in Fesquet, *Drama of Vatican II*, 272.
62. Ibid., 189.
63. Blanshard, *Blanshard on Vatican II*, 75.
64. Hughes, "Thomas Brechenmacher and Hardy Ostry," 799.
65. Ibid.

majority of the council members, determined opposition from conservatives once again succeeded in delaying action.

In August 1964 Paul issued his first encyclical, *Ecclesiam suam*, which emphasized his willingness to continue the dialogue with non-Catholic Christians, with non-Christians, and even with nonbelievers. "The aim of this encyclical," Paul wrote, "will be to demonstrate with increasing clarity how vital it is for the world, and how greatly desired by the Catholic Church, that the two should meet together, and get to know and love one another."[66] It represented a radical departure from Pio Nono's encyclical *Qunata cura* and the attached "Syllabus of Errors" of a century earlier. Following the lead of Pope John, Paul addressed Jews, Muslims, and the followers of the Afro-Asian religions. "We will not deny to these religious affirmations the respect that their spiritual and moral values demand," he vowed, "and we wish to join them in promoting and defending common ideals of religious liberty, human solidarity, culture, societal welfare and order."[67] Some saw even more in this message than another statement of Paul's support for the Jews and religious liberty, speculating that Rome might emerge as a center for the study of comparative religions.

During the course of the third session, which opened in September and closed on 21 November 1964, Pope Paul indicated that the Church was prepared to participate in ecumenical dialogue. Meanwhile, Cardinal Richard James Cushing of Boston, expressing the sentiments of the American contingent, called for a strong declaration on the Jews. "Catholics have not conducted themselves properly towards the Jews," he said. "They have been guilty of indifference, and sometimes of crimes. We must ask them pardon for our faults." Similar sentiments were expressed by the coadjutor, Bishop Elchinger of Strasbourg. "They [the Jews] have been the victims of grave injustices in the past: torture, forced baptisms, various humiliations," he confessed, adding, "let us be honest enough to recognize and repudiate these."[68]

The shadow of the Holocaust loomed over Catholics as well as Jews, exerting unspoken pressure to reform the traditional approach, which had failed to prevent and perhaps had contributed to the Nazi genocide. The

66. "Ecclesiam suam," 6 Aug. 1964, *PE* 5:135.
67. Quoted in Oesterreicher, *New Encounter between Christians and Jews*, 222.
68. Quoted in Fesquet, *Drama of Vatican II*, 360, 364.

fresh memory of that genocide also mitigated the intolerance of some, encouraging them to favor religious liberty. Bishop de Smedt's text on the matter read in part: "The state must recognize and defend freedom of religion for all its citizens. . . . It must neither direct nor hinder religion."[69] In the words of another, modernity's central protagonist was freedom.

Once again a counterattack was led by conservative bishops and the Oriental patriarchs.[70] The always outspoken Cardinal Ernesto Ruffini of Palermo insisted that the Jews should admit they unjustly condemned Christ and repent for their own transgressions against the Christians. Meanwhile, a scurrilous pamphlet was circulated in Rome charging that an unholy Judeo-Masonic alliance had taken control of the council. Cardinal Tappouni, Patriarch of Antioch, opposed the declaration on the Jews for other reasons: "I urgently request that this totally unsuitable declaration be abandoned immediately. It is not that we are against the Jewish religion or for discrimination. Moreover, we are nearly all Semites. We do not want this declaration because it would cause very serious pastoral difficulties. It is said back home that the Council is pro-Jewish, and this does us much harm."[71]

Tappouni's words influenced priests who feared for the future of the Church in the Middle East or had other concerns about the consequences of reversing Church policy. Nonetheless, the majority remained steadfast in their support of the statements on religious liberty and the Jews. "Once again the Church of yesterday plotted against the Church of today," Henri Fesquet noted in his diary. "But they are too weak—and they know it—to do more than delay an inevitable result for a few months."[72]

Proponents of religious liberty and reconciliation with Jews were forced to make some concessions to conservatives and the curia. The chapter on the Jews was transformed—some claimed demoted—into a declaration by the secretariat for Christian unity and, along with the declaration on religious liberty, was virtually banished to an appendix of the draft on ecumenism. The document on the Jews was incorporated into

69. Ibid., 541.

70. For a detailed account of this counterattack, see Hardy Ostry and Thomas Brechenmacher, *Rom und Jerusalem. Konzil, Pilgerfahrt, Dialog der Religionen* (Trier: Paulinus Verlag, 2000).

71. Fesquet, *Drama of Vatican II*, 358–59.

72. Ibid., 548.

a broader statement entitled "On the Relation of the Church to Non-Christian Religions." Despite these revisions, the coordinating commission still found the documents wanting, so that yet another draft was prepared and introduced by Cardinal Bea on 25 September. Unquestionably, the attempt to make it acceptable to "conservatives" and allay Arab concerns weakened its impact and distressed the champions of a radical transformation of Catholic-Jewish relations. In the debate that followed on 28 September, many bishops called for a stronger, more explicit condemnation of anti-Judaism and anti-Semitism as well as a clearer statement of the intrinsic bond between Judaism and Christianity.[73] In response to their outcry, the declaration was revised yet again.

As the divisions of the third session deepened, word spread that the curia was planning to delay and possibly block the two controversial declarations, on Jews and religious liberty. There was some substance to the rumor, for on 9 October, during a meeting of the secretariat for unity, Cardinal Bea introduced two letters dispatched by Archbishop Felici, the secretary general of the council. He stated he was writing on behalf of higher authority—hinting that this was at the suggestion of the pope himself. These letters seemed to indicate that there was considerable dissatisfaction with the two declarations the secretariat had amended and elaborated. One letter indicated that the provision on religious liberty had to be examined by a mixed commission, a majority of whose members were known to be vocal opponents. The second insisted that the declaration on the Jews also had to be examined by a commission of six. Suspicion spread that Pope Paul tolerated and perhaps was even behind the attempt to torpedo these measures. This caused consternation among the liberals in the council and undermined Paul's popularity among them.[74] Others suspected that the plan to derail the declarations was the work of the Eastern patriarchs. Whatever their origin, the letters were immediately perceived as a maneuver to circumvent the rules of the council, defy the authority of the bishops, and emasculate the work of the secretariat for Christian unity.

Sixteen cardinals wrote the pope, protesting the boycott of the two declarations and their removal from the jurisdiction of the secretariat for religious unity. A hastily drawn petition calling for a vote on both was

---

73. Oesterreicher, *New Encounter between Christians and Jews*, 184–203.
74. Blanshard, *Blanshard on Vatican II*, 50.

signed by almost five hundred members of the council. The extraordinary appeal had an impact on Pope Paul, who assured them that the secretariat for unity would remain responsible for both declarations.[75] Nonetheless, Paul refused the request for an immediate vote, so that the vote on religious liberty, originally set for 19 November, was postponed. However, *Lumen Gentium*, the dogmatic constitution on the Church of 21 November 1964, noted that the Jews were a people most dear to God and concluded that they and other non-Christians could not be blamed for their ignorance of Christ and His Church.[76] Some conservatives balked at such language. Cardinal Ruffini found it one-sided and therefore unfair, complaining that while Christians were being urged to love Jews, the Jews were not being told to love Christians. He claimed that the Talmud taught the Jews to despise all other people as wild animals and hinted that the Freemasons' conspiracy against the Church was fueled by Jews.[77] Despite conservative opposition, during his visit to Bombay in early December Pope Paul reiterated his desire and determination to narrow the gap between the world's Christians and non-Christians and to continue the dialogue with all the people of the globe.[78] At the same time he assured conservatives that their views would be aired, and made no effort to silence those who departed from the majority position of the council. In February 1965 when Bishop Luigi Carli of Segni wrote in his diocesan magazine that the Jews of Christ's time, and their descendants down to the present, bore the collective guilt for Christ's death, he received no papal reprimand.[79]

Although Paul favored reform on theological and philosophical grounds, he apparently still clung viscerally to long-entrenched Church convictions regarding Jews. These sentiments were revealed in his Passion Sunday sermon at Santa Maria della Guadalupe, in which he expressed regret that the Jewish people had not recognized their Messiah and had finally killed him. This sermon confused and dismayed many of the pope's supporters. "How could the pope accuse the Jewish people of killing Christ," the chief Rabbi of Rome Elio Toaff asked, "just when the Council

---

75. Ibid., 215–18.

76. Austin Flannery, ed., *Vatican Council II: The Conciliar and Post Conciliar Documents* (Grand Rapids: Eerdmans, 1992), I, 367.

77. Oesterreicher, *New Encounter between Christians and Jews*, 211–12.

78. *PP* 1:329–31.

79. Poncins, *Judaism and the Vatican*, 171.

seemed to be prepared to abrogate this curse?"[80] Rabbi Toaff and Dr. Sergio Piperno, president of the union of Italian Jewish communities, sent a telegram to the Vatican that read: "Italian Jews express their sorrowful amazement at charge Hebrew people in death of Jesus contained in Sovereign Pontiff's homily, delivered shortly before Easter Roman parish Our Lady of Guadalupe and reported official Vatican Press, thus renewing deicide accusation, secular source tragic injustices towards Jews, to which solemn affirmations Vatican Council seemed to terminate for ever."[81] Some believed the pope's words revealed the depth of the ingrained anti-Judaism within the Church and its leadership, whose eradication could be commenced but not completed by the council. Others complained that Paul VI's message contradicted his Easter message of 1964, in which he had proclaimed that "every religion raises us toward the transcendent Being, the sole Ground of all existence and all thought, of all responsible action and all authentic hope."[82] In fact, the two sermons were not completely in conflict, for in the 1965 sermon Paul stressed that "Christ did not curse His crucifiers, but prayed the Father to forgive them, for they did not know what they were doing," adding, "And in our own time, too, opposition to God is more than anything else a sign of ignorance, of a lack of knowledge of Christ and His teaching."[83] In fact, such ignorance reached the upper echelons of the Church hierarchy, providing an unfortunate example for the laity. The hierarchy and curia also remained deeply divided, and the debate over the declaration on religious liberty, which had reached its seventh draft, raged on.

Many Italian and Spanish prelates warned that the adoption of religious liberty would result in "indifferentism, laicism, and the eventual collapse of the Church in Catholic countries."[84] This fear echoed in the hearts and minds of countless others and found strong resonance in the curia. Archbishop Marcel Lefebvre, superior general of the Holy Spirit Fathers, denounced the declaration on religious liberty as a "Trojan horse" directed against the traditional magisterium of the Church. The declaration was also opposed by the newly formed International Assembly of Fathers, sup-

80. Phayer, *Catholic Church and the Holocaust*, 213.
81. Quoted in Poncins, *Judaism and the Vatican*, 143.
82. Quoted in Oesterreicher, *New Encounter between Christians and Jews*, 221.
83. Ibid., 256.
84. Blanshard, *Blanshard on Vatican II*, 94.

ported by Cardinals Ruffini, Siri, and Santos, among others. Bishop Belasco of Amoy, China, repeated many of their accusations against the declaration on religious liberty. "It is infected with juridical legalism and contradicts the traditional doctrine of the Church," he warned. He feared it would "breed pragmatism, indifferentism, and neutralism."[85] Some perceived a dangerous liaison between the declaration on religious liberty and that on the Jews, convinced that the one reinforced the other to the detriment of the institutional Church. Others saw the connection but considered it a positive and natural development that would bring long-range benefits to the faithful. Thus the German episcopate welcomed the council's pronouncement on the Jews, acknowledging, "We are aware of the awful injustices that were perpetrated against the Jews in the name of our people."[86] They were joined by a chorus of other priests and bishops who decried the silence of many Christians during the Holocaust, the long history of injustices perpetrated by Christians against Jews, and the unjust condemnation of an entire people. Clearly, a majority urged, indeed demanded, a statement of rectification.

The committees examining the proposal sought to delay the vote that most conservatives believed would go against them, but Pope Paul, sensing the mood of the majority, opposed any further delay and called for a vote. When the council stalled on the question of religious liberty, Paul summoned both sides to his study. After listening patiently to advocates and opponents of postponement, he determined that there would be a vote on Cardinal Bea's formulation. Whatever his own belief, Pope Paul was not prepared to flagrantly disregard the majority opinion of the council on a matter clearly within its jurisdiction. Brought to the floor at last in September 1965, the declaration on religious liberty was approved in a preliminary vote of 1,997 in favor and 224 opposed.[87] On 4 October, as Paul, dubbed the "Pilgrim Pope," left for New York to address the United Nations, the work of the council continued, with Arab diplomats and conservative Catholics expressing serious reservations about the declaration on the Jews. The Arabs felt that it would further legitimize the state of Israel. The conservative Catholics hesitated, admitting that previous leaders of the Church hierarchy had made mistakes in their reaction to and treat-

85. Fesquet, *Drama of Vatican II*, 569, 599.
86. Phayer, *Catholic Church and the Holocaust*, 214.
87. Blanshard, *Blanshard on Vatican II*, 95.

ment of the Jews while at the same time arguing that the council should defend everything that came down from the past! Some in both groups welcomed the issuance of a counterdeclaration charging that the declaration on the Jews was one only an "anti-pope" could approve. "The Fathers who have been so interested during Vatican II in freeing the Jews from their part in the death of Christ actually want to force the church implicitly to condemn and contradict herself before the whole world," it warned. "It is obvious that only an anti-pope or a secret conspiracy could approve a declaration of this kind."[88] This proclamation against the Jewish declaration was endorsed by more than twenty-five Catholic movements in the United States, Europe, and the Middle East.

At the same time, ad hominem attacks were unleashed against the proponents of the declarations on the Jews and religious liberty. Thus the charge of simony was made against Cardinal Bea, who was primarily responsible for the text on the Jews, accusing him of accepting Jewish money for the work of his secretariat.[89] Many of these charges reeked of the anti-Judaism of the preconciliar Church and the anti-Semitism of the prewar period. Few had foreseen or predicted at the opening of the council such bitter discussion and great divisions on the matter of the Church's relationship to the Jews. On 28 October 1965, Paul promulgated five council documents, including the declaration "Nostra aetate" (In Our Time) on the Church's attitude toward non-Christian religions.[90]

Although the question of the Church's relationship to the Jews was placed within the broader context of the "Declaration on the Relationship of the Church to Non-Christian Religions," the passage on the Jews, approved by more than 2,300 members of the council, received more attention around the world than any other issued by Vatican II. Among other things, this passage proclaimed that the Church reproved every form of persecution and deplored "all hatreds, persecutions, displays of anti-Semitism leveled at any time or from any source against the Jews."[91] Some saw it as the beginning of a process to reverse almost two thousand years of hatred and vilification. In fact, it did prove an important turning point

88. Fesquet, *Drama of Vatican II*, 712.

89. Poncins, *Judaism and the Vatican*, 138–39.

90. Flannery, *Vatican Council II*, 1:738–42; "Declaration on the Relation of the Church to Non-Christian Religions," "Nostra aetate," proclaimed by His Holiness Pope Paul VI on 28 Oct. 1965.

91. Quoted ibid., 741.

in Catholic-Jewish relations. Critics as well as champions of the declaration acknowledged that it opened a new dialogue.

"Nostra aetate" broke new ground and was immediately hailed as the Magna Carta of Christian-Jewish relations, but some still harbored serious doubts about it. On the one hand, some conservatives claimed that it went too far and would ultimately prove detrimental to Christian practice and undermine traditional theology. Paradoxically, a number of these critics concurred with the conclusions of the Jewish convert F. Fejto, who declared, "If the Jew is right, Christianity is only an illusion," reflecting precisely the fears of conservative opponents. The second part of his conclusion was much more to their liking. "If Christianity is right, the Jew is, in the most favourable hypothesis, an anachronism—the image of something which ought no longer to exist.[92] Unwilling, perhaps unable, to concede the first, they to had to confront the reality of a Judaism that survived—but they had little desire to do so and even less to assist in its survival. These opponents feared that the dialogue and reconciliation of Christian and Jews would elevate Jews while diminishing Christians, reversing the traditional Catholic attitude toward Judaism that had persisted for fifteen centuries. "For people of the Jewish faith, steeped in the Talmud, reconciliation . . . means nothing less than the abandonment by Christianity in its entirety of everything that constitutes the essence of its doctrine, and its integral return to Judaism, which for its part intends to yield nothing, and firmly maintains its position of intransigence.[93]

Liberals within the Church, and certain Jewish groups from the outside, on the other hand, complained that the document did not go far enough and were distressed that the stronger language in the original had been substantially watered down to accommodate the opponents. For one thing, the declaration chose not to investigate the main sources of Christian hatred and persecution. For another, there were no references to the state of Israel or the Holocaust and no apology for past transgressions, while the Jewish heritage of Jesus was virtually ignored.[94] Finally, there was no explicit retraction of the charge of deicide.

Although the word "deicide" itself was removed from the final draft, it noted:

92. Quoted in Poncins, *Judaism and the Vatican*, 114.
93. Ibid., 120.
94. Carroll, *Constantine's Sword*, 553; Lederer, "2000 Years," 16.

Since Christians and Jews have such a common spiritual heritage, this sacred Council wishes to encourage and further mutual understanding and appreciation. This can be obtained, especially, by way of biblical and theological inquiry and through friendly discussions.

Even though the Jewish authorities and those who followed their lead pressed for the death of Christ (cf. John 19:6), neither all Jews indiscriminately at that time, nor Jews today, can be charged with the crimes committed during his passion. It is true that the Church is the new people of God, yet the Jews should not be spoken of as rejected or accursed as if this followed from Holy Scripture. Consequently, all must take care, lest in catechizing or in preaching the Word of God, they teach anything which is not in accord with the truth of the Gospel message or the spirit of Christ.[95]

"Nostra aetate" thus reinforced the teaching of the Council of Trent that Jesus died because of the sins of humanity and that his death should not be pinned on the Jews alone. The passage of these measures suggested to many observers that the Church had finally renewed an authentic dialogue with Judaism and the Jews, though many acknowledged that it represented only a beginning.

Hoping to allay Arab fears, both Cardinal Bea and Pope Paul emphasized that no political connotations should be ascribed to the council's approval of the declarations. "As regards the Jewish people, it must again and again be made clear that the question is in no sense political, but is purely religious," Cardinal Bea explained. "We are not talking about Zionism or the political state of Israel, but about the followers of the Mosaic religion, wherever in the world they may dwell."[96] Bea's explanation was criticized as a poorly contrived excuse and denounced as an artificial division rejected by many Jews and their opponents alike. Bea's words notwithstanding, the council's action had clear political consequences, for many assumed that the earlier repudiation of Israeli statehood had been reversed and that a new political climate between Israel and the Vatican would now take shape. Recognizing that the Israelis controlled a large part of the territory of the former mandate of Palestine, Paul's Vatican did in fact seek pragmatically to speak a common language with the Israeli government.[97]

On 7 December the declaration *Dignitatis humanae* on religious liber-

---

95. Quoted in Flannery, *Vatican Council II*, 1:741.
96. Quoted in Kreutz, *Vatican Policy on the Palestinian-Israeli Conflict*, 119.
97. Ibid.

ty was promulgated, whereby Catholics were no longer to associate freedom of conscience with Luther, the Masons, or the evils of indifferentism.
It would not have materialized without the combined efforts of John XXI-
II, Paul VI, Cardinal Bea, and the support of the progressive majority of
the council. The declaration made clear that every individual has the right
to religious freedom without coercion, which is based on the dignity of
the human person as revealed by the word of God.[98] In this manner the fathers of Vatican II seemed to renounce the notion of indifferentism outlined by Gregory XVI in the *Mirari vos* of 1832 and Pius IX's "Syllabus of
Errors" of 1864. In order to mollify the conservative opposition, the declaration on religious freedom stipulated that the freedom it proclaimed
dealt with immunity from civil action but left "untouched traditional
Catholic doctrine on the moral duty of men and societies toward the true
religion and toward one Church of Christ."[99] The conservatives would
have none of it. The relationship between religious liberty and the proclamation of Catholicism as the one true faith continues to create debate and
controversy to this day. "The Second Vatican Council taught us that the
Announcement of Christ as the only Savior of the world does not forbid,
but on the contrary calls for, the peaceful relations with the believers of
other religions," noted Pope John Paul II, representing one side of the debate.[100] Others disagree.

On 8 December 1965, Pope Paul declared the council, which had approved sixteen documents in its four sessions, closed. Even the most severe
critics of the Church understood its impact and recognized that in its
wake the Church could no longer be described as "a monolithic glacier of
reactionary thought" in conflict with the modern world.[101] In fact, the
council left intact the traditional Catholic doctrine on the moral duty to
pursue the true faith. Nonetheless, many saw Vatican II as an important
point of departure in its abolition of the religious justification for anti-
Semitism.

The decade that followed witnessed considerable discussion of the issues raised by the Second Vatican Council and the desirability of imple-

98. Flannery, *Vatican Council II*, 1:800.
99. *Dignitatis humanae*, declaration on religious freedom proclaimed by His Holiness,
Pope Paul VI, on 7 Dec. 1965, http://www.chrisusrev.org/www1, and ibid., 1:799–812.
100. *The Pope Speaks: The Church Documents Bimonthly* 46 (Nov.–Dec. 2001): 323.
101. Blanshard, *Blanshard on Vatican II*, x.

menting its decrees. The difficulties of the *dopoconcilio,* or postconciliar age, were every bit as troubling as those confronted by the council itself. Early on, Cardinal Bea stressed that the declaration on the Jews should lead to effective action, and Pope Paul created commissions to continue its work. In his directives to the postconciliar central commission at the end of January, the pope provided guidelines for coordinating postconciliar activities and interpreting the council's decrees, while noting the additional tasks needed to be done. In 1969 the secretariat for promoting Christian unity put forward a model for a Christian spiritual exegesis via a Jewish perspective.[102] In October 1974 Paul created a commission for religious relations with Jews joined to the secretariat for promoting Christian unity. Its function was to foster relations between Catholics and Jews and eventually to do so in collaboration with other Christians.[103]

At the beginning of 1975 the Vatican Commission for Religious Relations with the Jews issued guidelines and suggestions for the implementation of the conciliar declaration "Nostra aetate." The introduction restated the conviction that the "spiritual bonds and historical links binding the Church to Judaism condemn all forms of anti-Semitism and discrimination, which in any case the dignity of the human person alone would suffice to condemn." It then proposed some practical applications in different areas of Church life to improve Catholic-Jewish relations, calling first of all for the establishment of real dialogue between the two faiths. Such dialogue, it indicated, presupposes that each side wishes to know the other better and requires mutual respect. Second, it emphasized the key links between Christian and Jewish liturgy, recalling the continuity of the Christian faith with that of the earlier covenant. In the realm of teaching and education, the guidelines insisted that the Old Testament should not be set against the New but that the two complement rather than simply supplement each other. Regarding the trial and death of Jesus, it recalled the conciliar statement that Christ's death did not rest with the Jews. It concluded that Christian-Jewish collaboration to date had done much for mutual understanding, but that "there is still a long road ahead."[104]

102. Lederer, "2000 Years," 16.

103. Flannery, *Vatican Council II,* 1:748–49.

104. "Guidelines and Suggestions for Implementing the Conciliar Declaration Nostra Aetate (n.4), by the Vatican Commission for Religious Relations with the Jews," Jan. 1975, http://www.jcrelations.net/stmnts/vatican1-75.htm, accessed 18 Oct. 2002.

"As far as we are concerned, it is our firm intention to hold fast to its perspectives and to put them into practice untiringly, day after day in our pastoral activity and service for the whole Church," Pope Paul promised, adding, "nor shall we permit ourselves to be influenced by certain unwanted pressures, perhaps motivated by lack of knowledge."[105] But there was a wrong and right way to go about this. In Paul's words, the Church was in the world, not of the world but for the world.[106] This distinction created some confusion. Presiding over a divided Church, Paul ensured that most conciliar reforms were implemented while moderating the alienation of the conservatives who vehemently opposed this modernization and modification of Catholic-Jewish relations.

Relations with the Jewish state, as well as with Jews, were in flux. The Vatican could not ignore the stunning Israeli victory in the six-day war of June 1967, which forced it to reconsider its stance on the internationalization of Jerusalem, as the Knesset united Jerusalem into a single city under Israeli rule on 27 June 1967. More than ever the Vatican understood the need for improving relations with the government that controlled all of the Holy City and most of the territory of Palestine. Thus talks commenced early in July between the Israeli prime minister, Levi Eskhol, and Monsignor Angelo Felici, the Vatican undersecretary for extraordinary affairs.[107] Recognizing the changed situation, the Vatican gradually abandoned its insistence on the creation of an international regime for Jerusalem, calling instead for the recognition of its special status under international guarantees. In his address to the College of Cardinals on 22 December 1967, Pope Paul VI outlined his solution to the status of Jerusalem:

> There are two essential aspects that are impossible to evade. The first concerns the Holy Places properly so called and considered as such by the three great monotheistic religions, Judaism, Christianity, and Islam. It is a matter of guaranteeing freedom of worship, respect for, preservation of and access to the Holy Places, protected by special immunities thanks to a special status, whose observation would be guaranteed by an institution international in

---

105. *The Teachings of Pope Paul VI* (1970) (Washington, D.C.: United States Catholic Conference, 1971), 194.

106. "Uno dei risultati," of 12 July 1967 and "Noi divevamo," of 19 July 1967, *PP* 1:404.

107. Kreutz, *Vatican Policy on the Palestinian-Israeli Conflict,* 126–29.

character, taking particular account of the historic and religious personality of Jerusalem. The second aspect of the question refers to the free enjoyment of the legitimate civil and religious rights of persons, residences, and activities of all communities present on the territory of Palestine.[108]

Paul VI's call for international guarantees of the Holy Places in Jerusalem was supported by a number of other Christian groups, including the World Council of Churches. It was resisted and rejected by the Israeli government, which regarded it as check by the international community on its sovereignty. The Holy See's continued opposition to any exclusive control—religious or political—by any one party led to tensions between the papacy and the Israelis. Thus Pope Paul confronted friction and misunderstanding outside the Church with Israelis and others, and inside the Church from "liberals" and "conservatives."

Nonetheless, this pope supported efforts to implement the teachings of Vatican II and sought to further the reconciliation of Catholics and Jews. Nineteen-seventy-seven witnessed the appearance of a study paper, "Mission and Witness of the Church," produced for the meeting of the International Catholic-Jewish Liaison Committee in Venice that year. In the paper, Tommaso Federici emphasized the "irreversible" nature of the Church's new understanding of its relationship to the Jewish people, while insisting that the Old Covenant had not been superseded or nullified. "The Church recognizes that in God's revealed plan, Israel plays a fundamental role of her own: the sanctification of the Name in the world. The Church is clear too that the honor of the Name is never unrelated to the salvation of the Jewish people who are the original nucleus of God's plan of salvation. . . . Christ did not nullify God's plan but rather (serves) as the living and efficacious synthesis of divine promise."[109]

Although Paul supported Federici's stance, he was willing to listen to conservative opposition and concerns as well. This led some critics to charge that this pope, seeking a balance between extremes in the Church, was indecisive. They rejected his attempts to support the majority while respecting the minority. Paul in turn felt he had been misunderstood in

108. Quoted in George Emile Irani, *The Papacy and the Middle East: The Role of the Holy See in the Arab-Israeli Conflict, 1962–1984* (Notre Dame: University of Notre Dame Press, 1986), 80.

109. Keeler, "Catholic Church and the Jewish People."

his search for a *via media* between reform and revolution. Paul VI died at Castel Gandolfo on 6 August 1978, and an assessment of his pontificate began immediately. Unquestionably, he brought John XXIII's council to a successful conclusion and continued his program of *aggiornamento* with the contemporary world. He did so without undermining papal authority, while avoiding a schism in the Church. He helped to internationalize the Vatican, visited the Holy Land, and continued the reconciliation between Catholics and Jews. Nonetheless, there was criticism of his person and pontificate, as conservatives complained he had gone too far and liberals that he had not gone far enough. Unquestionably, however, along with John, he had brought about a radical change—and many believed one for the better—in Catholic-Jewish relations, and had helped to open a new era for the Roman Catholic Church.

8

APOLOGY AND RECONCILIATION

John Paul II Confronts the Church's Anti-Judaic

Past and the Holocaust

I am pleased that my ministry in the See of Saint Peter

has taken place during the period following the Second

Vatican Council when the insights which inspired the

Declaration "Nostra Aetate" are finding concrete expres-

sions in various ways. Thus the way two great moments

of divine election—the Old and the New Covenants—

*are drawing closer together.** *

FOLLOWING PAUL VI'S DEATH IN 1978, the Church remained deeply divided over the consequences of the Second Vatican Council. Some warned that Rome confronted its most serious crisis since the French Revolution. Conservatives, led by Marcel Lefebvre, denounced conciliar innovations, regretted the reconciliation with Judaism and the abandonment of the Latin mass, and pined for the traditionalism of the pre–Vatican II period. To complicate matters, liberals who decried Rome's conservative stance on sexual and administrative issues as well as the limitations on the laity, were like-

---

* Pope John Paul II, *Crossing the Threshold of Hope*, ed. Vittorio Messori (New York: Knopf, 1994), 99–100.

wise dissatisfied, complaining that John's *aggiornamento* had been abort-ed. Some believed that the Church and papacy were at a crossroads and had either to embrace reform and modernity or reject them and seek refuge in traditionalism. This conflict was compounded by national rival-ries. The Italians, the largest bloc, expecting the practice of almost half a millennium to continue, demanded another Italian pope. Others dis-agreed, convinced that the time had come to end the Italian monopoly of the papacy.

On 25 August, the first day of the conclave, the cardinals listened to a reading of Paul's apostolic constitution on the election of the pope. The next day, on the fourth ballot, Cardinal Albino Luciani, the Patriarch of Venice, was elected the 262d successor to Peter. By choosing a double name, John Paul was understood to convey his approval of the council ini-tiated by John XXIII and brought to its conclusion by Paul VI and his ap-parent determination to continue the work of his two predecessors.[1] In his inaugural message, he revealed his desire to develop the pastoral plan of Paul, whose pontificate drew from his predecessor, "the great-hearted pas-tor, Pope John XXIII." At the same time, he pledged his commitment to the teaching of the Second Vatican Council, championing reconciliation with the modern world, religious liberty, and improved relations with Ju-daism. Recognizing that he had neither John's "wisdom of heart" nor Paul's "preparation and learning," John Paul shared their vision of serving the Church.[2] Like them, he favored implementing the decrees of Vatican II and pledged his ministry to its heritage.[3] Disdaining ostentation and shar-ing his namesakes' humility, John Paul preached that the Church existed to assist others while remaining open to the whole of humanity.[4] These goals were more easily announced than fulfilled.

The new pope faced a host of problems, and realized to his dismay that his largely pastoral experience had not prepared him for his enormous pa-

1. Peter Hebblethwaite, *The Year of Three Popes* (New York: Collins, 1979), 44–46, 71; Gordon Thomas and Max Morgan-Witts, *Pontiff* (Garden City, N.Y.: Doubleday, 1983), 119, 128, 156–57; Hofmann, *O Vatican!* 33.

2. *PP* 2:843.

3. John Paul I to the cardinals and the world, 27 Aug. 1978, in Albino Luciani, *The Mes-sage of John Paul I* (Boston: Daughters of St. Paul, 1978), 25–40.

4. *PP* 2:844–45; Angelus message of 3 Sept. 1978, in Luciani, *Message of John Paul I,* 65–66.

pal responsibilities. He found it necessary to rely on the curial cardinals, many of whom did not share his reformist goals, to administer the departments of the Vatican.[5] Nonetheless, his grave responsibilities taxed his health, which had never been robust. He had endured a tubercular condition early in life, complicated by several heart ailments and a painful circulatory disease. Since he had long remained silent about his poor health, some suspected foul play when he died after only thirty-three days in office.[6] John Paul did introduce a new simplicity and humility to the papal office, but these changes were more stylistic than substantive, and the brevity of his pontificate prevented more meaningful innovations.

In the second conclave of 1978, the Italians split along conservative-liberal lines. The contest was between the ultraconservative Archbishop of Genoa, Giuseppe Siri, who reportedly had not grasped the fact that there had been a Second Vatican Council, and the more progressive Archbishop of Florence, Giovanni Benelli, who aroused conservative concerns. Many saw the election as a referendum on Vatican II, including its declarations on religious liberty and reconciliation with the Jews. These differences contributed to the election of the fifty-eight-year-old Cardinal Karol Wojtyla, Archbishop of Krakow, on 16 October, the first Polish pope. His election was heralded not only in Poland but in Latvia and Lithuania as well. Like John Paul I, his background was more pastoral than diplomatic, although his position in Communist Poland had required a degree of diplomatic finesse.

Speculation arose concerning his choice of the name John Paul II and what it revealed about his commitment to the Second Vatican Council. This was not easily discerned, for the Polish pope sent mixed messages. On the one hand, his assumption of the name John Paul seemed to indicate a commitment to the council. This notion was reinforced by the fact that, as auxiliary bishop of Krakow, and later as archbishop, Wojtyla had played a part in the four sessions of the council and had advocated that the Church assume a more biblical, less clerical tone. He had supported the religious freedom proclaimed in the council's declaration on religious liberty and

5. *PP* 2:843–44; John Paul I to Cardinal Villot, 27 Aug. 1978, in Luciani, *Message of John Paul I*, 43–47.

6. In this regard see David Yallop, *In God's Name: An Investigation into the Murder of Pope John Paul I* (New York: Bentham Books, 1984), and Williams, *Vatican Exposed*.

had approved of "Nostra aetate" and the reconciliation it promoted between Catholics and Jews. Early on he concluded that Judaism, the religion of the Old Testament, had a special relationship to Catholicism, and that the origins of its faith and election were found in the patriarchs, Moses, and the prophets. He therefore appreciated the efforts of the Second Vatican Council, which stressed the Jewish roots of Christianity, and seconded its call for mutual understanding and respect between the two faiths.[7] In his words, "the Second Vatican Council taught us that the announcement of Christ as the Holy Savior of the World does not forbid, but on the contrary calls for, the pursuit of peaceful relations with the believers of other religions."[8]

At the same time, he shared much of the traditionalist agenda of those who railed against the innovations of the council and was a staunch opponent of Communism, having experienced it firsthand in Poland. But he did not embrace the anti-Judaism that some conservatives wished to preserve. At home, he maintained close contact with the city's Jewish community and cordial relations with its head.[9] Wojtyla appreciated the council's advocacy of reconciliation between Catholics and Jews, which reflected his experience in his native Wadowice. Until he was eighteen, Karol had lived in a town of ten thousand inhabitants, three thousand of whom were Jewish. He reported that before the outbreak of World War II, Jews and Christians lived harmoniously side by side. In fact, the owner of the home in which the Wojytla family lived was Jewish, as were many of his friends.[10] At least one-quarter of his elementary school classmates were Jewish, and he had a number of Jewish friends, including Jerzy Kluger, with whom he forged a lifelong friendship. Indeed, one writer has claimed that Wojtyla's friendship with Kluger influenced his commitment, as pope, to Catholic-Jewish reconciliation.[11] The prewar harmony he remembered—not necessarily shared by the Jews of Wadowice—was shat-

7. John Paul II, *Crossing the Threshold of Hope*, 95–96.

8. John Paul II's homily at the mass closing the extraordinary consistory (24 May 2001), *The Pope Speaks: The Church Documents Bimonthly* 46 (Nov.–Dec. 2001): 323.

9. John Paul II, *Crossing the Threshold of Hope*, 98.

10. Gian Franco Svidercoschi, "The Jewish 'Roots' of Karol Wojtyla," http://www.vatican.va/jubilee_2000...zine/ju_mago11119997, accessed 6 April 2001.

11. See Darcy O'Brien, *The Hidden Pope: The Untold Story of a Lifelong Friendship That Is Changing the Relationship between Catholics and Jews; The Personal Journey of John Paul II and Jerzy Kluger* (New York: Daybreak Books, 1998).

tered by the war and the Nazi occupation, which, Christians and Jews alike agreed, made things far worse for both.

The persecution of Catholics and Jews in Nazi-occupied Poland distressed Wojtyla, who was appalled by the systematic elimination of Jews simply because they were Jews. At the time of his birth, Poland was home to more Jews than any country in the world, but only a small number survived the Nazi genocide. He perceived Auschwitz as a symbol of the Jewish Holocaust, revealing the evil of a system constructed on racial hatred and greed for power. "To this day, Auschwitz does not cease to admonish us," he wrote later, "reminding us that anti-Semitism is a great sin against humanity, that all racial hatred inevitably leads to the trampling of human dignity." He shared the sentiments of Cardinal Adam Sapieha, in whose underground seminary he studied for the priesthood and who issued false baptismal certificates to Jews while organizing networks to feed and conceal those who could not be sent to freedom.[12]

Wojtyla, like John XXIII before him, recognized early on the need to expunge the anti-Judaism of the Church, which nourished anti-Semitism. In fact, he followed John Paul I in declaring total support for Vatican II and promised to implement its teachings and renew the Church according to its mandates.[13] This delighted the liberals, while conservatives took solace in his commitment to other forms of traditionalism and his defense of papal prerogatives. His systematic restructuring of the curia along conservative lines and his appointment of traditionalists in the hierarchy unsettled those disturbed by his "authoritarianism." From the first, this pope proved difficult to classify. Recognizing that he could not do everything, he assumed as his first task to gather the people of God in unity. His investiture homily revealed his intention of serving humanity and called for the opening of state frontiers as well as political and economic systems.[14]

12. John Paul II, *Crossing the Threshold of Hope,* 97; Malachi Martin, *The Keys of This Blood: The Struggle for World Dominion between Pope John Paul II, Mikail Gorbachev, and the Capitalist West* (New York: Simon and Schuster, 1990), 550–51.

13. Mieczyslaw Malinski, *Pope John Paul II: The Life of Karol Wojtyla,* trans. P. S. Fall (New York: Seabury Press, 1979), 23.

14. *Messages of John Paul II,* ed. Daughters of St. Paul (Boston: St. Paul Editions, 1979), 2:28–28; "The Pope: A See Change," *The Economist,* 29 April 1995; Malinski, *Pope John Paul II,* 82, 118; Andre Frossard, ed., *Be Not Afraid: Pope John Speaks Out of His Life, His Beliefs, and His Inspiring Vision for Humanity,* trans. J. R. Foster (New York: St. Martin's Press, 1984), 28.

Observers soon learned that he was less willing than Paul VI to tolerate criticism, whether from liberals or conservatives.

Toward the end of January 1979, on his first trip outside Italy, the pope went to Mexico, stopping in Santo Domingo 25–26 January, where he revealed liberal sentiments in invoking a more humane international order. Subsequently, in opening the Latin American bishops' conference in Puebla, he expressed his conservative convictions in warning against the Marxist-inspired liberation theology expounded by Latin American Jesuits. At Monterry, he sympathized with the plight of workers and peasants, but he would not sanction a purely economic and political liberation, which ignored spiritual liberation from sin.[15] He ordered the Jesuit father Tom Drinan to resign his seat in the U.S. Congress, and seconded the conclusion of the Congregation of the Doctrine of the Faith that Hans Küng could no longer be deemed a Catholic theologian. Liberal Catholics in the United States and Western Europe were disappointed and troubled by this conservative course.

John Paul's traditionalism found a more receptive audience in Poland, where he traveled on his second trip outside Italy and implicitly expressed his support for the Solidarity movement.[16] During his triumphant tour of his homeland, he made clear that his conservative stance on birth control, abortion, and clerical celibacy did not extend to the Church's traditional position on Judaism, enthusiastically endorsing Vatican II's mandate for dialogue and reconciliation between Catholics and Jews. During his visit to Auschwitz on 7 June 1979, he prayed for the victims of the Holocaust. Pausing before the memorial stone with its Hebrew inscription, he expressed his inner thoughts: "This inscription stirs the memory of the People whose sons and daughters were destined to total extermination. This People has its origins in Abraham, who is our father in faith as Paul of Tarsus expressed it. Precisely this People, which received from God the commandment: 'Thou shalt not kill,' has experienced in itself to a particular degree what killing means. Before this inscription it is not possible for anyone to pass by with indifference."[17]

15. Daughters of St. Paul, *Messages of John Paul II*, 2:212–18, 274–81; Malinski, *Pope John Paul II*, 241.
16. Alexiev, "The Kremlin and the Vatican," *Orbis* (fall 1983): 556.
17. See http://www.vatican.va/jubilee_2000...ine/ju_mag_01111997, accessed 6 April 2001.

These heartfelt sentiments were not shared by all in the Church and were challenged in no uncertain terms by those who questioned the validity of the Second Vatican Council, which they denounced as an "anti-council." Some extremists even branded John Paul II an antipope! He summoned Marcel Lefebvre, a critic of the Second Vatican Council, to Rome, and ordered him to cease his public attacks on Vatican innovations. Lefebvre refused to obey, and consecrated the bishops who shared his opposition to religious liberty, for which John Paul II, in return, excommunicated him.

Perhaps to placate moderate conservatives and preserve an even-handed policy, he proved equally vigorous in his opposition to liberal critics within the Church. During his October 1979 visit to the United States and the United Nations, the pope called for obedience and was uncompromising in his position on birth control, clerical celibacy, abortion, and the role of women in the Church. Critics complained that on these issues he followed in the footsteps of Pius XII, whose contributions he praised and whose actions during the Holocaust he staunchly defended.[18] Similar sentiments were expressed in New York, where he addressed the United Nations, and in Washington, where he met with Church officials at the Catholic University of America.[19] Nonetheless, John Paul continued to pursue a reformist course on interfaith questions. Early in February 1981 he met with Rome's chief rabbi, Elio Toaff, and once again outlined his progressive position on relations between the two faiths. Dissatisfied with the progress to date, the following year he announced that much more had to be done to foster Catholic-Jewish discourse, citing, especially, the need to sow the seeds of a "flowering of Jewish-Catholic dialogue" among the young.[20]

During his numerous pastoral visits abroad and before audiences at home, John Paul II made a point of meeting representatives of the Jewish community. He promised Jewish groups that he would build upon the foundation provided by "Nostra aetate," the Second Vatican Council, the Vatican Commission for Religious Relations with the Jews, and the work of his predecessors—and he honored this commitment. In 1980 he ad-

18. "Pius XII's Contributions Hailed," *Brooklyn Tablet*, 5 April 1979.
19. An official schedule of the papal visit can be found in *U.S. News and World Report*, 8 Oct. 1979.
20. Lederer, "2000 Years," 17.

dressed Jewish groups from Paris and Sao Paulo and met with Jews from Mainz. He spoke to Jewish representatives from Manchester, England, in 1982 and Warsaw in 1987. Throughout his pontificate he dispatched cordial messages to leaders of the Jewish community—of Madrid (1982), Switzerland (1984), the United States (1985), Lyons (1986), Buenos Aires (1987), Cologne (1987), Vienna (1988), Strasbourg (1988), and Mexico (1990), among others.[21]

John Paul's concerted effort to create close and amicable relations with the "elder brothers" of the faith formed part of his broader program of *aggiornamento*—making the Church better attuned to the modern world, the process begun by John XXIII. In his initial encyclical, "The Redeemer of Man" (March 1979), the new pope focused on the role of the Church in the contemporary world and sought to prepare it for the new millennium. His campaign to eradicate both anti-Judaism and anti-Semitism from the Church and the broader society was part of this effort. "Auschwitz opened our eyes," he said in his encounter with representatives of the Episcopal Council in March 1982, as he stressed the urgent need to keep that memory alive.[22] He repeatedly made the point that the Jewish religion was not extrinsic but intrinsic to Catholicism, and that the policy of contempt and the notion of supersession had no place within the postconciliar Church.

In his quest for a solution to the conflict in the Middle East, he met with Yasser Arafat in September 1982, renewing his appeal for peace in Lebanon after the murder of President-elect Bechir Gemayel. The papal invocation for Lebanon was repeated in his apostolic letter "Les Grands Mysteres" (1984) on the problems of that war-torn country and the suffering of its people. John Paul's position on Jerusalem remained the one he had enunciated in his apostolic letter "Redemptionis anno" of 20 April 1984, which saw the Holy City as the sacred patrimony of all believers, and the crossroads of peace for the people of the Middle East. In his attempt to resolve the problems of the Holy Land, he met with King Hassan II of Morocco in Casablanca in the summer of 1985, President Amin Gemayel of Lebanon in February 1986, and Jordan's King Hussein in the summer of

---

21. For relations with Judaism, see http://www.vatican.va/roman_curia/...hrstyni_doc _220511992, accessed 20 April 1998.

22. Remi Hoeckman, "Auschwitz: The Triumph of Evil in a Society without God," http://www.vatican.va/jubilee_2000...zine/ju_mag_0111197, accessed 20 April 1998.

1987. The Middle East in general, and Israel in particular, remained papal concerns throughout his pontificate.

John Paul had to confront problems in the western Mediterranean as well as on its eastern shore, as Italians expressed discontent with the concordat of the Lateran Accords of 1929, concluded during the pontificate of Pius XI and the dictatorship of Benito Mussolini. After more than a century of committed opposition to the separation of Church and state in Catholic countries, John Paul's Vatican finally recognized it in Italy. Article 1 of the concordat signed on 18 February 1984 stipulated that "the Italian Republic and the Holy See reaffirm that the State and the Catholic Church, each in its own order, are independent and sovereign, and . . . to mutually cooperate for the promotion of mankind and the welfare of the Nation."[23] Although John Paul sought to keep the Church out of the political arena, he assumed political and global commitments, and, following the banning of Solidarity in Poland, he opened a dialogue with Warsaw and the Kremlin. His fluency in Polish, Italian, German, French, English, Spanish, and Portuguese facilitated his role as Rome's roving ambassador. This papal form of shuttle diplomacy was temporarily suspended, but not halted, by the attempt made on his life by the Turkish terrorist Mehemet Ali Agca on 13 May 1981.

In June 1982 John Paul II met with U.S. president Ronald Reagan, who had also survived an assassination attempt, and discussed the Soviet domination of Eastern Europe and the need for peace and justice worldwide. Richard Allen, Reagan's national security advisor, claimed that the pope and president were plotting to "hasten the dissolution of the communist empire."[24] This exaggeration contained a germ of truth, for the two men did conspire about how best to counter Soviet control over Eastern Europe. Appreciative of the advantages derived from their collaboration, Allen's successor, William Clark, proposed that the United States regularize relations with the Holy See. In January 1984 full diplomatic relations were established at the level of apostolic nunciature and embassy between the Holy See and the United States, more than a century after the disruption of this relationship. In 1984 President Reagan named William A. Wil-

23. Quoted in Maria Elisabetta de Franciscis, *Italy and the Vatican: The 1984 Concordat between Church and State* (New York: Peter Lang, 1989), 225.

24. Quoted in Carl Bernstein, "The Holy Alliance," *Time* magazine, 24 Feb. 1992, 28.

son of California ambassador to the Holy See. In 1985, the year Mikhail Gorbachev became secretary general of the Communist Party in the Soviet Union, the pope announced the opening of the Secret Vatican Archives for the pontificates of Pius X (1903–14) and Benedict XV (1914–22). Subsequently, he partially opened them for the pontificate of Pius XI (1922–39). Foreseeing the demise of the Soviet imperium in Eastern Europe and the end of the cold war, John Paul II issued an encyclical calling for a European unity with Christianity as its spiritual core.[25]

Papal participation in the diplomatic arena never overshadowed John Paul's religious mission. Among other things, John Paul remained dedicated to the full implementation of the decrees of the Second Vatican Council. At the end of 1985 he convoked an extraordinary meeting of the World Synod of Bishops to mark the twentieth anniversary of the council. The same year, the Holy See, through its Commission for Religious Relations with the Jews, published "Notes on the Correct Way to Present the Jews and Judaism in Preaching and Catechesis in the Roman Catholic Church." Providing detailed practical instruction on assessing the relationship of Jesus and Judaism in the New Testament, this document called on clergy to present a positive image of the Jews, in keeping with the strictures of the Second Vatican Council. Unlike the earlier documents published by the Holy See on Catholics and Jews, this one finally took note of Israel. Among other things, it declared that "the State of Israel should be seen in a historic context and ultimately interpreted within God's design."[26] Although this did not quite amount to diplomatic recognition, it signaled religious recognition. Subsequently, in an address to Australian Jewish leaders in 1986, John Paul pronounced clearly and unequivocally that there was no theological justification for the persecution of Jews and branded such discrimination "sinful."[27] In this he echoed the sentiments of Pope Pius XI and the "secret encyclical" he had commissioned.

John Paul II further demonstrated his commitment to Catholic-Jewish harmony by an unprecedented visit to Rome's main synagogue on 13 April 1986, where he prayed with Rabbi Elio Toaff and with Giacomo Saban,

25. See ASV, SS, Rapportini con gli Stati, AS, AAES, Germania, 1922–39; "The Pope: A See Change," *The Economist,* 29 April 1995, 24.

26. Lederer, "2000 Years," 18.

27. Eugene J. Fisher and Leon Klenicki, eds., *Pope John Paul II on Jews and Judaism* (Washington, D.C.: United States Catholic Conference, 1987), 96–97.

president of Rome's Jewish community. He spoke on that occasion of the need to keep the memory of Auschwitz alive so as to ensure that such evil would never again prevail over good. Recognizing that the general acceptance of legitimate pluralism in the social, civil, and religious spheres had been long in coming, he acknowledged that the discrimination and unjustified limitation of religious freedom practiced against the Jews were deplorable, and he especially condemned the genocide of millions of innocent victims, quoting three points from Vatican II's "Nostra aetate."

> The first is that the Church of Christ discovers her "bond" with Judaism by "searching into her own mystery." The Jewish religion is not "extrinsic" to us, but in a certain way is "intrinsic" to our own religion. With Judaism therefore we have a relationship which we do not have with any other religion. You are our dearly beloved brothers and, in a certain way, it could be said that you are our elder brothers.

> The second point noted by the Council is that no ancestral or collective blame can be imputed to the Jews as a people for "what happened in Christ's passion." So any alleged theological justification for discriminatory measures or, worse still, for acts of persecution, is unfounded. The Lord will judge each one "according to his own works," Jews and Christians alike.

> The third point that I would like to emphasize in the Council's Declaration is a consequence of the second. Notwithstanding the Church's awareness of her own identity, it is not lawful to say that the Jews are "repudiated or cursed," as if this were taught or could be deduced from the Sacred Scriptures of the Old or the New Testament.[28]

Much of the goodwill engendered by the pope's moving discourse in Rome's synagogue was squandered by his decision to receive Kurt Waldheim, the president of Austria, in June 1987. Waldheim was accused of collaborating with the Nazis, and Jews worldwide were outraged. Even in the United States the Vatican was criticized for its insensitivity. During the pope's visit to Miami in 1987, Rabbi Mordecai Waxman, speaking on behalf of organized American Jewry, confronted the pope on anti-Judaism, anti-Semitism, the Vatican's failure to recognize Israel, and the pope's decision to meet with Waldheim. The pope did not seem to take offense. He addressed the Jewish audience as "dear brothers and sisters," noted their

28. John Paul II's discourse during his visit to Rome's Synagogue, 13 April 1986, available at http://www.vatican.va/jubilee, accessed 20 April 1998.

common heritage, and again condemned the crimes of the Shoah. He praised the Catholic-Jewish dialogue in the United States and supported the decision by U.S. Catholic schools to introduce a formal curriculum on the Holocaust.[29] He pledged to work for the resolution of the tensions that remained between the Vatican and the Jewish community. Apparently John Paul appreciated Waxman's honesty, for in 1998 he named him Knight Commander of St. Gregory the Great, the fifth Jew and first rabbi so honored.[30] Liberal critics charged that the pope was less tolerant of dissent within the Church, and that while he sought to mend relations with the Jews, he did little else to please reformist Catholics. Indeed, some charged that John Paul II sought reconciliation with those outside the Church but was increasingly intolerant of dissent within.

John Paul's external program of mending fences with the Eastern bloc called for both religious and political reconciliation. By 1989 the Vatican and Warsaw had agreed to establish diplomatic relations. Catholic Poland was the first communist-bloc nation to do so, provoking dramatic changes there and in the rest of Eastern Europe. In December 1989 Gorbachev, in a historic visit—the first between the head of the Soviet government and a pope—met in Rome. Lech Walesa became president of Poland at the end of 1990, marking the beginning of the end of Soviet control of Eastern Europe. The following year the Communist system in the Soviet Union itself collapsed, as the various republics refused to follow Moscow's directives. At the end of 1991, when President Boris N. Yelstin of Russia visited the pope in Rome, the Soviet Union had collapsed. Although the papal role in this process has been variously assessed, Gorbachev concluded that Pope John Paul II had played "a major political role" in undermining communism in Eastern Europe.[31] Certainly it was with the Vatican's support that the Soviet Union, in the early fall of 1991, recognized the independence of the Baltic republics of Latvia, Lithuania, and Estonia, whose incorporation into the Soviet Union the Vatican had never recognized.

In November 1991 Pope John Paul II had a long talk with President George H. W. Bush, with whom he had disagreed on the need for war in

29. See Keeler, "Catholic Church and the Jewish People."

30. Ari L. Goldman, "Mordecai Waxman, Rabbi Who Chided Pope, Dies at 85," *New York Times*, 15 Aug. 2002, C11.

31. Thomas Patrick Melady, *The Ambassador's Story: The United States and the Vatican in World Affairs* (Huntington, Ind.: Our Sunday Visitor, 1994), 18, 25.

the Persian Gulf. In fact, the pope had written to both Bush and President Saddam Hussein of Iraq, urging them to do all within their means to avoid a conflagration. His efforts proved futile. Relations between the Holy See and the United States improved after the signing of the peace. To be sure, differences remained—including their attitude toward Israel, which the Vatican still did not officially recognize in the early 1990s, even after it had established diplomatic relations with Albania in September 1991. It is true that as early as September 1987, when the pope met with members of the International Liaison Committee of Catholics and Jews, he revealed that he understood that the Jewish people saw in Israel a fulfillment of ancient prophecy.[32] Nonetheless, problems persisted that prevented the Vatican's recognition of Israel. For one thing, the Holy See still feared that either Arab or Jewish domination of Palestine would prove detrimental to Christian interests. Rome had outlined a policy toward Palestine that it could not immediately or easily jettison. After Vatican II, the major obstacles in Jewish-Vatican relations were political rather than religious, with the Holy See playing a major role in the campaign against racism and anti-Semitism even as it delayed the regularization of relations with Israel. Its diplomatic position did not adversely affect the papal efforts at religious reconciliation with Judaism, however. The pope, who had helped protect Jews in his native Poland during the German occupation, denounced the renewed outbursts of xenophobia and anti-Semitism in Europe and again expressed his solidarity with the Jews.[33]

The Vatican sought unsuccessfully to separate Catholic-Jewish religious relations from political questions involving the recognition of the state of Israel and its claims on Jerusalem. In 1948, following the Israeli declaration of independence and proclamation of Jerusalem as its capital, the Holy See refused to recognize either development. Originally Rome sought international status for Jerusalem, later modifying this to international guarantees for access to the holy places. It wanted more than the unilateral guarantee of the Israeli government, and it adopted a stance strikingly similar to the one it had assumed on the Roman question, when it stubbornly refused to accept the terms of the Italian Law of Papal Guarantees (1871) proposed by Catholic Italy. Once the Church's theological

32. Keeler, "Catholic Church and the Jewish People."
33. "Pope Rips Xenophobia," *New York Newsday,* 29 Oct. 1992.

understanding of Judaism changed, the earlier opposition to Zionist goals, based on the Jews' denial of Jesus' divinity, disappeared. Despite the charges of continuing anti-Judaism or anti-Semitism in Vatican circles, Rome's major concerns vis-à-vis relations with Israel were now political and diplomatic rather than religious or racist. The Vatican also expressed concern about the technical state of war between Israel and many of its neighbors.

Following the Madrid conference of 1991, which foreshadowed an improvement in Arab-Israeli relations, the Holy See viewed more favorably the prospect of opening full diplomatic relations with the government of Israel. It was strongly encouraged to do so by the administration of the first George Bush. In fact, his secretary of state, James Baker, instructed the new ambassador to the Holy See, Thomas Patrick Melady, to urge the Holy See to recognize the state of Israel. The issue had also been raised during Melady's confirmation hearing before the Senate. For this and other reasons, Melady made the opening of diplomatic relations between the Vatican and Israel a top priority, and this goal was achieved shortly after his tenure as ambassador ended.

According to Melady, a conference on the Middle East held in Madrid in October 1991 was what seemed to break the logjam. Cardinal Angelo Sadano, the papal secretary of state, agreed that the Madrid conference had provided new impetus in the process. John Paul personally informed President Bush during their November 1991 meeting that he was pleased with the progress of the Middle East peace negotiations, and the president expressed his hope that these negotiations would lead to the normalization of Vatican-Israeli relations. The prospect of such a development was advanced by a visit to the Middle East by Cardinal John O'Connor, who met with Egyptian president Hosni Mubarak, Israeli prime minister Yitzak Shamir, Jordan's King Hussein, and Lebanese prime minister Karame. O'-Connor met with the pope early in January 1992, encouraged the Holy See to take steps to establish diplomatic relations with Israel, and proposed the creation of a bilateral commission to study the matter. This commission was formed the following summer.

The meeting of Israeli foreign minister Shimon Peres with the pope in October 1992 provided additional momentum for the establishment of Vatican-Israeli relations. During the course of their friendly forty-five-minute meeting, Peres invited the pope to visit Israel, and John Paul responded that it had long been his desire to visit the Holy Land. Despite the goodwill emanating from Rome and Jerusalem and the encouragement of Washington, many issues remained unresolved, and both the Israeli ambassador to Italy, Avi Pazner, and the American ambassador to the Vatican, Thomas Melady, were frustrated by the pace of progress. Melady's staff suggested that he recommend that the outgoing president, Bush, who was highly regarded in Vatican circles, appeal directly to the pope to establish diplomatic relations with Israel. The American president followed their advice and on 28 December 1992 wrote the Holy Father: "At this holy season when people of many faiths turn their eyes towards Bethlehem, I encourage you to move ahead toward the establishment of diplomatic relations with Israel. I believe that such a courageous and generous reaction would be appreciated by the friends of peace around the world and would make a significant contribution to the historic process now begun in building peace and reconciliation in the Middle East."[34] Although the papal response was cautious, the Holy See was clearly moving toward establishing diplomatic relations with Israel. This was finally accomplished, in March 1993, in a fifteen-article agreement signed in Jerusalem by Monsignor Claudio Celli, Vatican assistant secretary of state, and Yossi Beilen, Israeli deputy minister.

Article 1 of the agreement provided that both the state of Israel and the Holy See would uphold and defend human rights and freedom of religion. Article 2 committed the signatories to cooperation in opposing all forms of anti-Semitism, racism, and religious intolerance. For its part, the Holy See reiterated its condemnation of persecution and hatred directed against the Jewish people, especially the desecration of Jewish synagogues and cemeteries. In the third article the two parties recognized their freedom of action in their own areas of competence, although they pledged cooperation in matters affecting both. The fourth article dealt with sensitive issues for the Vatican and Israel. Among other things, it assured Israel's continuing commitment to respect and maintain the status quo in the Christian holy places and the Christian communities in Israel. The Israeli government also pledged respect for, and protection of, sacred places such as churches, monasteries, cemeteries, and the like.

34. The account of efforts to establish diplomatic relations between Rome and Israel is taken from Melady, *Ambassador's Story*, 124–35. Bush's letter to the pope is quoted at 34–35.

Article 5 declared the parties' mutual interest in promoting Christian pilgrimages to the Holy Land, in the hope that such ventures would assure a better understanding between the people and religions of Israel. The sixth article safeguarded the right of the Catholic Church to establish and maintain schools and institutes of study in Israel, conforming to the rights of the state in education. Articles 7, 8, and 9 encouraged cultural exchange, recognized the right of expression of the Catholic Church through its own communications media, and provided protection for the charitable functions of the Church in Israel, respectively. Article 10 reaffirmed the right of the Church and Holy See to own property; in article 11 the Church promised that, while maintaining the right to exercise its moral and spiritual teaching, it would remain apart from all strictly temporal conflicts. The final three articles focused on administrative and technical issues and the mechanisms for the implementation of the prior articles and the exchange of representatives.[35] Pope John Paul was delighted that full diplomatic relations between the Holy See and Israel were at long last established, writing later that he never doubted this would occur.[36] On 29 September 1994 the pope received the first Israeli ambassador to the Holy See.

John Paul's support of religious liberty and reconciliation with the Jews and Israel, which won liberal acclaim, was balanced by his conservative actions, which liberals found less pleasing. In March 1992 the German Catholic theologian Eugen Drewerman was suspended for challenging the Vatican's stance on clerical celibacy and contraception and for questioning the physical resurrection of Jesus and the literal virginity of Mary. Drewerman's suspension should have provided an example for other dissenting clergy, but it did not deter the Bishop of Evreux, Jacques Gaillot, from advancing similar views. Gaillot, who endorsed the controversial French-made abortion pill, advocated the use of condoms, and favored the marriage of priests, was allowed to retain his title, but all churches were removed from his jurisdiction. Archbishop Raymond G. Gunthausn of Seattle, chastised by the Vatican for his liberal policies involving marriage annulments, liturgical innovations, sterilizations at Catholic hospitals, matters involving homosexual groups, and clerical education, found his

---

35. "Fundamental Agreement between the Holy See and the State of Israel," 30 Dec. 1993, available at http://listserv.american.edu/catholic/church/vatican/vatisr.txt, accessed 6 April 1999.

36. John Paul II, *Crossing the Threshold of Hope*, 100.

authority in these areas transferred to his auxiliary, Bishop Wuerl.[37] John Paul also prohibited political activity by ordained priests, and ordered the four Nicaraguan priests participating in the Marxist Sandinista government to withdraw from their order.

The pope was supported in this conservative course by Cardinal Joseph Ratzinger, prefect of the Congregation of the Doctrine of the Faith, and the equally traditional Jean Jerome Hamer, prefect of the Congregation for Religious. Returning to the United States in 1993, John Paul resolutely condemned abortion rights, which President Clinton supported. In his private talks with the president, the pope urged the United States to assume a greater initiative in bringing peace to the Balkans in general and Bosnia in particular, as well as in easing tensions in the Middle East.[38] The unsettled conditions in the Middle East continued to haunt the Vatican, as did its position on such issues as birth control. The media, John Paul complained, conditioned society to hear only what it wanted to hear. The Church, he insisted, could not court popularity but had to teach what humanity must do to gain eternal life.[39] His message was heard, but not always followed, by the people in the pews.

On Catholic-Jewish relations, by contrast, John Paul II continued to pursue the progressive path outlined by Vatican II. Throughout his pontificate he remained committed to opposing anti-Judaism and improving relations with the Church's elder brothers—although a degree of sibling rivalry continued. On 7 April 1994 there was a Vatican concert for the commemoration of the Shoah attended by the pope and the chief rabbi of Rome, Elio Toaff. Some perceived the concert as another gesture toward healing the wounds of the millennia-old rift between Christianity and Judaism. Hearing the Kaddish, the traditional Jewish prayer for the dead, in-

37. "French Bishop Removed for Challenging Vatican," *New York Times,* 14 Jan. 1995; "The Pope: A See Change," *The Economist,* 29 April 1995, 24; Ari L. Goldman, "Censured Archbishop Quietly Departs for Seattle," *New York Times,* 14 Nov. 1986.

38. "Vatican Hits Clinton Decrees on Abortion," *New York Newsday,* 24 Jan. 1993; Susan Page, "A Sermon for Clinton," *New York Newsday,* 13 Aug. 1993; Alain L. Sanders, "John Paul Superstar," *Time* magazine, 22 Aug. 1993; Bob Keeler and Susan Page, "Papal Plea for Life," *New York Newsday,* 13 Aug. 1993, 2.

39. John Paul II, *Crossing the Threshold of Hope,* 172–73; Joe Nicholson, "Pope Levels New Blast at 'Evil' Birth Control," *New York Post,* 23 Sept. 1993; Peter Steinfels, "Papal Encyclical Says Church Must Enforce Basic Morality," *New York Times,* 3 Oct. 1993; Richard N. Ostling, "A Refinement of Evil," *Time* magazine, 4 Oct. 1993; Richard N. Ostlin, "Till Annulment Do Us Part," *Time* magazine, 16 Aug. 1993.

toned here, dramatically revealed John Paul II's determination to continue his efforts to narrow the gap between the two faiths.[40]

Meanwhile, the political and religious rapprochement between the Holy See and Israel accelerated the Vatican's attempt to secure a negotiated solution of the long-simmering, often volatile Middle East conflict. In the fall of 1993 John Paul met with Elias Hrawi, president of Lebanon, to explore prospects for peace in his troubled country and the larger region. In the spring of the following year he discussed these matters with the Israeli prime minister, Yitzak Rabin, as the Vatican established working contacts of a permanent and official character between the Holy See and the Palestinian Liberation Organization, with a PLO office of representation to the Holy See and contacts with the organization through the nuncio in Tunisia. In September 1995 John Paul II met with Yasser Arafat in his search for peace in the region. He was deeply troubled by the assassination of Rabin and sent a message of condolence to the government on 4 November 1995. In mid-December he met Rabin's widow, Leah Rabin.

When the peace talks stalled in the aftermath of Rabin's assassination, John Paul wrote to Prime Minister Benjamin Netanyahu and Yasser Arafat in June 1997, encouraging both to pursue a peaceful resolution of their differences. "The Israeli and Palestinian Peoples are already shouldering a burden of suffering which is too heavy: this burden must not be increased; instead it deserves the utmost commitment to finding the paths of necessary and courageous compromise," he wrote Netanyahu. Anticipating the close of the century and the millennium, he predicted that "only a Holy Land at peace will be able to welcome in a worthy manner the thousands of pilgrims who during the Great Jubilee of the Year 2000 will wish to come to pray there." He expressed similar sentiments in his letter to Arafat. "In the name of God I appeal to the Palestinian and Israeli leaders to consider above all the good of their peoples and the younger generation," he wrote the president of the Palestinian authority. "These generations must not continue to experience the already excessive suffering which has affected these two peoples."[41]

John Paul personally expressed his desire for peace in the Middle East

40. "Coming Together: A Historic Vatican Ceremony Helps to Heal the Division between Christians and Jews," *New York Newsday*, 11 April 1994.

41. Santo Padre to Signor Benjamin Netanyahu and Yasser Arafat, http://www.vatican.va.news_services/bulletin/news/879.html, accessed 20 April 1998.

to the new Israeli ambassador, Aharon Lopez, in March 1998. He feared that the tentative progress that had been achieved would be imperiled by a host of difficulties and expressed grave concern that the increasingly volatile situation threatened the prospect of "release from the seemingly endless spiral of action, reaction, and counter-reaction." He foresaw no resolution "unless all parties act with genuine goodwill and solidarity."[42] Neither side heeded his words, resorting instead to a seemingly endless cycle of violence and revenge. Nonetheless, the pope's effort for peace worldwide, his role in the collapse of Communism, and his spirited defense of the rights of the downtrodden of the "third world" made John Paul an international celebrity. "Let Pope John Paul II be a mediator, whether it be in Jerusalem, the Gaza strip, the Hague, the United Nations," noted one observer. "Nobody, Christian, Jew or Muslim would ever doubt his moral authority."[43] It was an optimistic appraisal.

In December 1994 *Time* magazine named John Paul II its man of the year, an award that had been bestowed on Pope John XIII in 1962. John Paul did not rest on his laurels but continued to press his convictions, exercising his authority through public pronouncements and decrees. Contraception, he held, was manifestly wrong, and the Church had no authority to permit priestly ordination for women. During his talk to the synod on religious life, the pope specified that the synod should not discuss the issue of female ordination, which he deemed absolutely impermissible. Abortion he branded a grave sin, stipulating that even rape could not justify what was intrinsically evil. Sex outside marriage was also wrong, and the pope pledged that the Church would continue to uphold that prohibition despite "deviations" among couples.[44] He stressed the universal values and mission of the Church, calling for "inculturation" that would blend non-Catholic and non-European values with Vatican dogma without diluting its central moral strictures.[45] "Catholicism will be more universal-

42. Discorso del Santo Padre all Ambasciatore di Israele presso la Santa Sede in occasione della presentatzione delle lettere credenziali, 20 April 1998, http://www.vatican.va/news_services/bulletin/news/481.html, , accessed 20 April 1998.

43. Steve Dunleavy, op-ed, "This Conflict Could Use a Papal Referee," New York Post, 6 Jan. 2003, 4.

44. "Pontiff's Letter Calls for Equality," New York Newsday, 11 July 1995; "Pope Opens Synod on Religious Life," New York Times, 3 Oct. 1994; "The Pope: A See Change," The Economist, 29 April 1995, 24; "Pope: Nonmarital Sex Is Wrong," Brooklyn Tablet, 9 July 1994.

45. Bob Keeler, "Pope Urges Peace in Rwanda, Opens Talks on Africa," New York News-

ized, with a different approach to the ancient cultures of non-European peoples," the pope promised, adding, "it must be de-westernized."[46] The pope's global mission was also reflected in the consistory of 1994, which appointed thirty new cardinals from twenty-four countries, reducing the Italians to twenty out of 120 cardinals.[47] In January 1995 the pope departed for an eleven-day Asian tour that took him to New Guinea, Australia, and Sri Lanka. In his final mass in the Philippines, some 4 to 5 million people gathered to greet the pope, who was joined in prayer by members of China's state-sponsored supervised church, the Chinese Patriotic Association, which since 1949 had elected its own bishops without the approval of the Vatican. In a mid-January message, broadcast to the estimated 10 million Roman Catholics in China, John Paul called for reconciliation and unity in the Chinese Catholic Church.[48]

In the spring of 1995 the pope issued his eleventh encyclical letter, "The Gospel of Life," addressed to the human family that shared the modern world. Defending life in vigorous language, he restated the Church's opposition to contraception, abortion, euthanasia, and capital punishment. Noting that the passage of unjust laws created problems of conscience for morally upright people who have a right not to be implicated in evil actions, the pope warned that "each individual in fact has moral responsibility for the acts which he personally performs; no one can be exempted from this responsibility, and on the basis of it everyone will be judged by God himself."[49] Some Jewish, Muslim, and also Catholic leaders applauded the pope's courage in denouncing the "culture of death" and defending the sanctity of life for the whole of mankind.

In an apostolic letter issued on the occasion of the fiftieth anniversary of the outbreak of World War II, John Paul again denounced the "planned barbarism" against the Jewish people, which he perceived as the greatest shame of humanity. He wrote:

day, 11 April 1994; Alan Cowell, "Vatican Ponders Church Role in Africa," *New York Times*, 1 May 1994.

46. Quoted in Malinski, *Pope John Paul II*, 189.

47. Alan Cowell, "Pope Appoints 30 Cardinals, 2 from U.S.," *New York Times*, 31 Oct. 1994.

48. "Pope Arrives in Manila Amid Bomb Threats," *New York Post*, 13 Jan. 1995; "Chinese to See Pope," *Tampa Tribune*, 9 Jan. 1995.

49. "Pope's Letter: A Sinister World Has Led to Crimes against Life," *New York Times*, 31 March 1995.

The object of this "final solution," designed by a deviant ideology, the Jews, were subjected to indescribable privations and brutality. Initiated by vexatious and discriminatory measures, it ended with millions being transported to extermination camps.

The Jews of Poland, more than others, were subject to these tribulations: the images of the siege of the ghetto of Warsaw, as well as the pictures and news from the concentration camps of Auschwitz, Majdanek or Treblinka are greater than any horror that human beings can imagine.[50]

In the meantime, word spread that Pius XI had planned to issue an encyclical condemning racism and anti-Semitism in 1938 but had died before he could do so. This encouraged the American Jewish Committee, in the spring of 1996, to petition John Paul II to issue an encyclical denouncing anti-Semitism and thus help to guard future generations from the evil flowing from this hatred.[51] In fact, the pope did intend to have the Holy See say something more on the subject of the Shoah and the anti-Semitism that fostered it. Early in 1997 reports emerged that the Vatican was preparing a commission to explore the historical roots of anti-Semitism among Catholics. John Paul II's numerous denunciations of anti-Judaism, anti-Semitism, and the Holocaust unwittingly brought into sharper focus Pius XII's cautious, often coded language on these issues. In part, chronology and circumstances explain the stark contrast of these divergent papal responses, but some believe that differences in character and conviction also played a part.

In the fall of 1997 John Paul acknowledged that by blaming the Jews for the death of Jesus, certain Christian teachings might have helped fuel anti-Semitism.[52] At the same time, the Vatican disclosed plans for a three-day symposium at the end of October and early November that would explore the Christian roots of anti-Semitism. In attendance were cardinals, Church officials, and sixty Roman Catholic scholars. Jews were not invited, much to their disappointment. Tullia Zevi, president of the Union of Italian Jewish Communities, hoped that Jews might at least attend as observers but

50. Lettera Apostolica in occasione del cinquantesimo anniversario dell'inizio della II Guerra Mondiale, 27 Aug. 1989, http://www.vatican.va/holy_father..._-of-the-iiworld-war_italian.shtml, accessed 20 April 1998.

51. Press Release of the American Jewish Committee, 18 April 1996, http://ajc.org/press_release/pope, accessed 4 Nov. 1998.

52. Lederer, "2000 Years," 20.

was told otherwise. Vatican officials explained that the symposium was an internal Church matter, at once an exercise in Christian theology and an examination of conscience for Christians. For this reason, Jewish participation was not deemed appropriate.[53] Father Georges Cottier, O.P., secretary of the theological commission hosting the meeting, revealed that the symposium aimed to "isolate erroneous teachings on the New Testament" that could serve as "a pretext" against the Jews and the Jewish people. He was encouraged that John Paul opened the meeting with the statement that the object of the symposium was "the correct theological interpretation of the relations between the Church of Christ and the Jewish people." While the pope unequivocally condemned anti-Semitism, he drew a clear distinction between this odious movement, which drew its inspiration from pagan ideology, and the teachings of the Catholic Church. Nonetheless, John Paul acknowledged that, "in the Christian world"—he did not say the Church itself—"erroneous and unjust interpretations of the New Testament regarding the Jewish people and their alleged culpability have circulated for too long, engendering sentiments of hostility towards this people."[54] The clear implication was that the anti-Judaic current in the Church had contributed to anti-Semitic hatred and thereby facilitated its foul deeds—words that Pius XII had never uttered. Father Cottier was more explicit, noting:

> There are some readings which are theologically incorrect or wrong in the New Testament, and which have served as a pretext of a hostility which was diffused in large portions of the Christian populations, in which the Jewish population found itself scattered. Too many unjustifiable attitudes found their justification; and from there is born in many Christians a passivity and an absence of reaction when Europe was in the throes of the violent Hitlerian wave.[55]

This was the clearest apology and sign of repentance issued by the Vatican on the Catholic reaction to the Holocaust. It was one of a series of mostly indirect apologies and admissions of wrongdoing. More than a

53. Ruth E. Gruber, "Anti-Semitism Forum at Vatican Bars Jews," http://www.jewishsf. com/bk971031/iforum.jtm, accessed 18 Oct. 2002.

54. "Searching for the Roots of Anti Semitism," http://www.catholic.net/RCC/Periodicals/Igpress/CRW/CRW1297/Vatican.html, accessed 7 April 1999.

55. Georges Cottier, "The Meaning of a Symposium," http://www.vatican.va/jubilee_2000...zine/ju_mago1111997_p-22_en.shtml, accessed 20 April 1998.

decade earlier, the Vatican had sanctioned a new initiative in Catholic-Jewish relations. In the summer of 1987, during a meeting of representatives of the Holy See's Commission for Religious Relations with the Jews and the International Jewish Committee on Inter-Religious Consultations, Cardinal Johannes Willebrands, president of the Catholic group, announced that his commission would draft an official Catholic document on the Shoah. On 1 September 1987, the members of the commission met with John Paul II, who emphasized the importance of their work for the Church and the world. John Paul recounted his personal experience and view of the horror that had led to the annihilation of a large part of the Jewish population in Poland. Repeating what he earlier had said to the Jewish community of Warsaw, he noted that the genocide of Jews was a warning, a witness, and a silent cry for the whole of humanity. The Jewish group, and Jews throughout the world, welcomed the drafting of such a document, hoping it would combat attempts to revise or deny the reality of the Holocaust or to trivialize its religious significance for Christians, Jews, and all humanity.[56] It was more than a decade in the making.

In 1994 John Paul urged Catholics to repent for their failings to protest the brutalization of Jews, and the bishops of Germany, France, and Poland did so. In 1995, on the fiftieth anniversary of the liberation of Auschwitz, a document issued by the German bishops placed considerable responsibility for the Holocaust on the Church.[57] Then, in the fall of 1997, the Catholic Church in France issued its own apology to the Jews for its silence before the events of the Holocaust in France. Their "Declaration of Repentance" criticized their anti-Semitism and their conformity and obedience to the secular power, which led them to acquiesce and collaborate with "a murderous process." Archbishop Olivier de Berranger also repented for the history and influence of the centuries-old anti-Judaism of the Catholic Church, which contributed to its indifference to the plight of the victims. The bishop's statement, issued at the end of September 1997, noted:

56. "Conferenza stampa di presentatzione del documento della Commissione della Santa Sede per i Rapporti religiosi con l'Ebraismo: Noi Ricordiamo: Una Reflessione sulla Shoah," http://www.vatican.va/new_services/bulletin/news.2571.html, accessed 20 April 1998.

57. Eric J. Greenberg, "Will Pope Bail Out Flawed Vatican Text?" *Jewish Week*, 14 Aug. 1998.

The vast majority of church officials, bound up in loyalism and docility that went far beyond traditional obedience to the established powers, stuck to an attitude of conformism, caution and abstention, dictated in part by fear of reprisals against charitable works and Catholic youth movements. They did not realize that they had considerable power and influence, and that given the silence of other institutions, their statements could through its echo have formed a barrier to the irreparable.

In the face of the persecution of Jews, especially the multi-faceted anti-Semitic laws passed by Vichy, silence was the rule, and words in favor of the victims the exception.

Today we confess that silence was a mistake. We beg for the pardon of God, and we ask the Jewish people to hear this word of repentance.[58]

Later, the Polish Roman Church, led by the Primate Jozef Glemp, apologized for those Poles who killed their Jewish neighbors in Jedwane and elsewhere.[59] These extraordinary admissions of responsibility raised the expectations of what the Vatican would say in its pending declaration on the Church and the Shoah.

Upon receiving the statement on the Holocaust drafted for the Vatican in the spring of 1998, John Paul thanked the new president of the Commission for Religious Relations with the Jews, Cardinal Edward Cassidy, and expressed the hope that the document "We Remember: A Reflection on the *Shoah*," drafted under his direction and published on 16 March 1998, would help to heal the wounds of past misunderstandings and injustices. In his letter presenting the apology for publication, John Paul said that the Holocaust remained an indelible stain on the twentieth century. The magnitude of the crime raised many issues, the document read, as it called for "a 'moral and religious memory' and particularly among Christians, a very serious reflection on what gave rise to it." At the same time, the document insisted on the need to differentiate "between anti-Semitism, based on theories contrary to the constant teaching of the church on the unity of the human race and on the equal dignity of all races and peoples, and the long standing sentiments of mistrust and hostility that we call anti-Judaism, of which, unfortunately Christians also have been guilty."[60] "We Remember" condemned them both.

58. Roger Cohen, "French Church Issues Apology to Jews on War," *New York Times*, 1 Oct. 1997, A8.

59. "Catholic Apology to Jews," *New York Times*, 25 May 2001, A4.

60. Commission for Religious Relations with the Jews, "We Remember: A Reflection on

The Vatican statement did not address clearly the question of whether the Nazi persecution of the Jews was facilitated by the anti-Jewish prejudices embedded in some Christian minds and hearts. Had Christians provided all possible assistance to the persecuted? Many had, even at the risk of their own safety, the document said, and it paid tribute to them; but others had not. Perhaps in response to the charge of Pius XII's silence, Pius was commended for personally or through his representatives helping to save hundreds of thousands of Jewish lives. As for the silence of other Christians, the document noted, "We cannot know how many Christians in countries occupied or ruled by the Nazi power or their allies were horrified at the disappearance of their Jewish neighbors and yet were not strong enough to raise their voices in protest." It did not probe why they lacked this strength or assume responsibility for their inaction, but advised that "for Christians this heavy burden of conscience of their brothers and sisters during the Second World War must be a call to penitence." "We Remember" concluded on the note that the Church at the end of the millennium sought to "express her deep sorrow for the failures of her sons and daughters in every age," which it presented as an "act of repentance or *teshuva*." It also expressed hope for a new Catholic-Jewish relationship and looked forward to a future "in which there will be no more anti-Judaism among Christians or anti-Christian sentiment among Jews, but rather a shared mutual respect."[61]

Reaction to the document was generally favorable, but some observers were disappointed that, although the document credited Pius XII with saving hundreds of thousands of lives, it did not explain why this pope never took sides during the war or publicly and clearly denounced the slaughter. Word also circulated that issuance of the document had been delayed owing to divisions in the Vatican over what to say on the issue of how anti-Judaism in the Church had contributed to the anti-Semitism of the Nazi regime. Rabbi David Rosen, presiding over the Israeli office of the Anti-Defamation League and serving as its co-liaison for the Vatican, had a mixed reaction. "It is a very important statement, but it is disappointing in certain respects," he observed. In his view, the "Catholic bishops' confer-

---

the Shoah," available at http://www.vatican.va/roman_curia/pontiofical_councils.chrstuni/ documents.rc_pc_chrstun, accessed 16 Oct. 2002.

61. Ibid.

ences in France, Germany, Hungary, Poland and other countries have gone further in acknowledging a deeper responsibility for the moral climate that allowed Nazism to dominate much of Catholic Europe." Elan Steinberg, executive director of the World Jewish Congress, agreed that the Vatican statement did "not compare favourably with the French Catholic Bishops' Conference or the German Catholic Bishops' Conference." [62] Others in the Jewish community were even more critical. "We are very sad, very disappointed," responded Rabbi Leon Klenicki, director of the department of interfaith affairs of the Anti-Defamation League, who charged that "the document falls short of the mark, it's taking a step backward."

Although many of the faithful defended the text of "We Remember," the document also had Catholic critics, who complained that it, like other Vatican apologies, once again failed to indict official Church statements as well as its actions and inaction for provoking hatred of the Jews. Like prior Vatican pronouncements, wrote Garry Wills, it distinguished between "the indefectible fidelity of the church" whose extraordinary magisterium never condemned the Jews, and "the weakness of her members."[63] Father Richard P. McBrien, speaking at the American Jewish Committee's headquarters in New York City, described "We Remember" as coming twenty years too late. Nor was McBrien surprised by its ringing defense of Pius XII or by official Catholic support for that defense, observing that a Vatican official would be no more likely to criticize such a document than a cabinet officer in Washington would be to criticize a policy of the president. Father McBrien revealed that he had heard that this was a watered-down version of the original draft, and he quoted Father Remi Hoeckman, who reportedly complained that "he had presented the Vatican with a race horse, but what came back was a camel." Nonetheless, McBrien noted that the document had been issued by a Vatican commission rather than the pope, who had an extraordinary record of mending fences with Jews. "There remains an opportunity for him as the earthly head of the church

62. Rosen quoted in Celestine Bohlen, "Vatican Repents Failure to Curb Killing of Jews," *New York Times*, 17 March 1998; Steinberg quoted in BBC News On-Line, "Vatican Apologizes over Holocaust," httpl://news.bbc.co.uk/1/low/world/europe/65889.stm, accessed 18 Oct. 2002.

63. Garry Wills, "The Vatican Regrets," http://www.nybooks.com/nyrev/archdisplay.cgi?20000525029R@p2, accessed 24 March 2004.

finally to step beyond this 'holding action,'" the liberal Catholic theologian noted, "and to make the kind of straightforward statement for the universal church."[64] And in fact, John Paul did intend to do more. Cardinal Cassidy acknowledged as much when he announced that the exploration of Catholic-Jewish relations was not complete and promised that "nothing is closed with this document."[65]

John Paul expressed his intention to continue his dialogue and reconciliation with the Jewish people in his apostolic letter of 1994 on "The Coming of the Third Millennium." Meanwhile, an in-depth theological and historical assessment was commenced. At the end of 1999 the International Theological Commission headed by Cardinal Ratzinger issued a thirty-one-page study entitled "Memory and Reconciliation: The Church and the Faults of the Past," as a preliminary to John Paul's projected apology of the New Year and new millennium.[66] Among other things, "Memory and Reconciliation" denounced anti-Jewish prejudice and declared that the relationship between Christians and Jews required a special examination of conscience, while deploring the hostility of many Christians toward Jews.[67] It failed to explore how this hostility was nourished, however, and studiously avoided the responsibility of the papacy in the process.

Two weeks later, at a special mass of pardon held on the first Sunday of Lent, 12 March 2000, John Paul offered an unprecedented apology for Catholic transgressions of the past two thousand years. Despite the reservations and resistance of some in the Vatican, the pope pushed for a program of "purification of memory" during the Jubilee year 2000, to include a critical examination of Christian conduct during the Crusades, the Inquisition, and World War II.[68] To emphasize the religious significance of the apology, seven cardinals participated with the pope in drawing attention to a number of lapses, past and present, including religious intolerance and injustice toward Jews, women, indigenous peoples, immigrants,

---

64. Quoted in Greenberg, "Will Pope Bail Out Flawed Vatican Text?" 14.

65. Quoted in Bohlen, "Vatican Repents Failure to Curb Killing of Jews."

66. Alessandra Stanley, "Vatican Outline Issued on Apology for Historical Failings," *New York Times*, 2 March 2000.

67. "Memory and Reconciliation: The Church and the Faults of the Past," Dec. 1999, http://www.vatican.va/roman_curia/congregations/cfaith/documents/rc_con_cfaith, accessed 22 July 2002.

68. "Pope Says Historical Wrongs Justify Reconciliation," Brooklyn *Tablet*, 8 Nov. 2003, 10.

and the poor. Cardinal Edward Cassidy confessed sins against the people of Israel and asked worshippers to "pray that, in recalling the sufferings endured by the people of Israel throughout history, Christians will acknowledge the sins committed by not a few of their number against the people of the Covenant." To this prayer John Paul II answered: "God of our fathers, you chose Abraham and his descendants to bring your name to the nations: We are deeply saddened by the behavior of those who in the course of history have caused these children of yours to suffer, and asking your forgiveness we wish to commit ourselves to genuine brotherhood with the people of the Covenant. We ask this through Christ our Lord." [69]

Some perceived the Lenten mea culpa as another bold interfaith initiative, significant for the Church as well as for the descendants of those abused. Others were not as optimistic in their appraisal and voiced their disappointment that the apology was offered on behalf of the Church's "sons and daughters"—implicitly, its wayward sons and daughters—rather than the Church itself. The Reverend Thomas Reese, editor of the Jesuit magazine *America,* argued that the apology skirted the issue of whether past Church leaders, as well as lay Catholics, were responsible for Catholic sins. "The document should have put it in bold print that 'children of the church' includes popes, cardinals and clergy, and not just people in the pews," Reese wrote. "The pope had a great idea that some in the Vatican are obscuring with a fog machine." The apology also received a mixed reaction from Jews. The dean of the Simon Wiesenthal Center, Rabbi Marvin Hier, hailed it as an "important step forward" but regretted that it had not specifically addressed the Holocaust. [70] Saul Klausner, a Holocaust survivor, called the pope's effort noble but was saddened that it did not delve into the actions of Pius XII during the war. There was a consensus among Jews in New York that this was a good start—but that more had to follow. [71]

In a sense, John Paul II agreed, and he made clear in the months following that he intended to say more. In March 2000, during his trip to Is-

---

69. "Excerpts from the Apology by the Pope and Cardinals," *New York Times,* 13 March 2000, A10.

70. Reese and Hier quoted in Alessandra Stanley, "Pope Asks Forgiveness for Errors of the Church Over 2000 Years," *New York Times,* 13 March 2000, A10.

71. Tracey Tully, "Jews in N.Y.: It's a Start, but Too Much Left Unsaid," *New York Daily News,* 13 March 2000.

rael, John Paul visited Yad Vashem, which commemorates the unidentified victims of the Holocaust. The aged and ailing pontiff remained silent before the memorial, later explaining that words could not encompass the tragedy of the Holocaust. In many ways this visit represented the culmination of John Paul's determination to effect the reconciliation between Catholics and Jews begun by the Second Vatican Council. The pope's pilgrimage was broadcast live to an Israeli audience, who viewed it as a historic journey of healing and a crucial turning point in Jewish-Christian relations. To be sure, some were disappointed that the pope was silent on those Church leaders, especially Pius XII, who had not publicly condemned the genocide.[72] The pope did say:

> As Bishop of Rome and successor of the Apostle Peter, I assure the Jewish people that the Catholic Church, motivated by the Gospel law of truth and love and by no political considerations, is deeply saddened by the hatred, acts of persecution and displays of anti-Semitism directed against the Jews by Christians at any time and in any place. The Church rejects racism in any form as a denial of the image of the Creator inherent in every human being.
>
> In this place of solemn remembrance, I fervently pray that our sorrow for the tragedy which the Jewish people suffered in the 20th century will lead to a new relationship between Christians and Jews. Let us build a new future in which there will be no more anti-Jewish feeling among Christians or anti-Christian feeling among Jews, but rather the mutual respect required of those who adore the one Creator and Lord, and look to Abraham as our common father in faith.
>
> The world must heed the warning that comes to us from the victims of the Holocaust and from the testimony of survivors. Here at Yad Vashem the memory lives on, and burns itself into our souls. It makes us cry out.[73]

John Paul was convinced that his pilgrimage to the Holy Land helped to strengthen the special bonds that link the Catholic and the Jewish faiths.[74] In fact, the pope's words and his dramatic visit did have a pro-

72. Alessandra Stanley, "At Yad Vashem, Pope Tries to Salve History's Scars," *New York Times*, 24 March 2000, A6.

73. "Speech of John Paul II: Visit to the Yad Vashem Museum," 23 March 2000, http://www.vatican.va/holy_father/john_paul_ii/travels/documents/hf_jf_spe2000323_ yad-vashem, accessed 27 March 2001; "In the Pope's Words: 'The Echo of Heart-Rending Laments,'" *New York Times*, 24 March 2000, A1, A6.

74. "Pope John Paul II's Homily at the Mass Closing the Extraordinary Consistory (24 May 2001)," in *The Pope Speaks: The Church Documents Bimonthly* 46 (Nov.–Dec. 2001): 323.

found impact on Israelis and Jews worldwide. Cabinet minister Haim Ramon, expressing the sentiments of his government, termed the papal speech at Yad Vashem "another milestone" in the reconstruction of relations between the Vatican and Israel. The prime minister, Ehud Barak, who lost two grandparents at Treblinka, called the visit to Yad Vashem the climax of a "historic journey of healing."[75] The pope met with the chief rabbis at Hechal Shlomo, where he confessed that he had always sought to overcome old prejudices and to highlight the spiritual patrimony shared by Jews and Christians, and that he looked forward to an era of mutual respect and cooperation.

A few days later, John Paul continued his mission of reconciliation by visiting the Western Wall, where, following Jewish custom, he tucked a note to God into a crevice of that structure. His message again reflected his heartfelt desire for harmony between the two faiths. "God of our fathers, you chose Abraham and his descendants to bring your name to the nations," John Paul wrote. "We are deeply saddened by the behavior of those who in the course of history have caused these children of yours to suffer." In Jerusalem the pope also met with the mufti sheik Ikrima Sabri, who read a speech in Arabic, proclaiming that Jerusalem was "eternally bonded to Islam." The pope diplomatically responded that from his perspective Jerusalem was "part of the common patrimony" of Christianity, Islam, and Judaism.[76]

Although some old wounds remained, relations between Jews and Catholics unquestionably improved following John Paul II's visit to the Holy Land at the dawn of the new millennium. Following the trip, a large group of influential rabbis and other Jews, some 170 in all, signed a statement called "Dabru Emet" (Speak the Truth), which called upon their brethren to modify their distrust of Christians and recognize the strides they had made since Vatican II in revising Christian teaching about Jews and Judaism. Like many of the statements of the post–Vatican II Church, "Dabru Emet," drafted by Dr. Tikva Frymer-Kensky, Dr. David Novak, Dr. Peter Ochs, and Dr. Michael Signer, stressed the commonalties between

75. Rod Dreher, "Dramatic Words Reflect His Entire Papacy," *New York Post,* 24 March 2000, 2; Uri Dan, "Pope Airs Christian Regrets in Holocaust-Memorial Tour," ibid., 24 March 2000, 2.

76. Quoted in Deborah Sontag and Alessandra Stanley, "Ending Pilgrimage, the Pope Asks God for Brotherhood," *New York Times,* 27 March 2000, A1, A10.

the two faiths, including the worship of the same God, respect for the authority of the Old Testament, and shared moral principles. David Novak argued that since major Christian groups had rethought their beliefs about Jews and Judaism, it behooved "Jewish thinkers to respond accordingly."[77]

> The humanly irreconcilable difference between Jews and Christians will not be settled until God redeems the entire world as promised in Scripture. Christians know and serve God through Jesus Christ and the Christian tradition. Jews know and serve God through Torah and the Jewish tradition. That difference will not be settled by one community insisting that it has interpreted Scripture more accurately than the other; nor by exercising political power over the other. Jews can respect Christians' faithfulness to their revelation just as we expect Christians to respect our faithfulness to our revelation. Neither Jew nor Christian should be pressed into affirming the teaching of the other community.
>
> A new relationship between Jews and Christians will not weaken Jewish practice. An improved relationship will not accelerate the cultural and religious assimilation that Jews rightly fear. It will not change traditional Jewish forms of worship, nor increase intermarriage between Jews and non-Jews, nor persuade more Jews to convert to Christianity, nor create a false blending of Judaism and Christianity. We respect Christianity as a faith that originated within Judaism and that still has significant contacts with it. We do not see it as an extension of Judaism. Only if we cherish our own traditions can we pursue this relationship with integrity.[78]

The praise for this statement was balanced by concern on the part of some Jewish leaders, who found within the seven-point document a dangerous blurring of distinctions between the "two irreconcilable faiths."[79] Their criticism was echoed by some conservative Catholics, whose concern was in part reflected in the almost simultaneous publication of a document entitled "Dominus Iesus," on the "Unicity and Salvific Universality of Jesus Christ and the Church," released by Cardinal Ratzinger, prefect of the Congregation for the Doctrine of the Faith. How could this Vatican statement, which declared that "the Roman Catholic Church is the only

77. Quoted in Laurie Goodstein, "Influential Jewish Group Extends a Hand to Christians," *New York Times,* 8 Sept. 2000, A22.

78. "Dabru Emet: A Jewish Statement on Christians and Christianity," *New York Times,* 10 Sept. 2000, 37.

79. Goodstein, "Influential Jewish Group Extends a Hand."

way to salvation, rejecting alternate paths" and advocated the "missioniz-
ing of non-Catholics," sit with the pope's profession of tolerance and respect for Judaism? critics asked.[80] The document seemed to denigrate the
convictions of others. Point 22, for example, read: "With the coming of the
Savior Jesus Christ, God has willed that the Church founded by him be the
instrument for the salvation of all of humanity." Although "Dominus
Iesus" indicated that the Church had a sincere respect for the religions of
the world, "at the same time," one critic charged, "it rules out in a radical
way that mentality of indifferentism characterized by a religious relativism
which leads to the belief that 'one religion is as good as another.'"[81] "Dominus Iesus" appeared to revert to the conservative condemnations of indifferentism found in Gregory XVI's "Mirari vos" of 1832 and in Pius IX's
"Quanta cura" and "Syllabus of Errors" of 1864.

Cardinal Ratzinger expressed competing interpretations of Catholicism's relations to Judaism following the publication of "Dominus Iesus."
In an interview published in mid-October 2000, the seventy-three-year-
old German cardinal said, "We're waiting for the moment when Israel will
say yes to Christ," but added, "we also know that, throughout the course of
history, precisely in the position of standing before the door, it (Israel) has
had a special mission which has been of significance for the world."[82]

These conflicting positions reflected divisions within the Church and
curia as well as the institutional need to harmonize the present stance toward the Jews with past practice and Scripture. This proved no easy task.
Although essentially an internal Church debate, it necessarily had external
repercussions and cast a shadow over Catholic-Jewish relations. One immediate casualty was the Vatican-sponsored "day of Jewish-Christian
dialogue," which had to be postponed when Rome's Jewish community
opted to boycott the meeting. Rabbis Elio Toaff and Abramo Piatelli, both
scheduled to participate, canceled following the September publication
of "Dominus Iesus," claiming that the unfortunate climate it created was
not conducive to dialogue. Other Italian Jews likewise refused to take
part on the grounds that "the Vatican had changed its tone in recent

80. Eric J. Greenberg, "One Step Forward, Two Steps Back," *Jewish Week*, 15 Sept. 2000.
81. "Dominus Iesus: On the Unicity and Salvific Universality of Jesus Christ and the
Church," *Brooklyn Tablet*, 20 Sept. 2000, 4A.
82. Quoted in Michael Lawton, "Church Is Waiting for Israel to Accept Jesus," ibid., 21
Oct. 2000.

months."[83] Jews resented both the claim that salvation came from Jesus alone and the beatification of Pius IX (1846–78), whom they condemned for his role in the Mortara affair and for his alleged anti-Judaic, if not anti-Semitic, slurs. These developments seemed to counter the conciliatory gestures of John Paul II, including his trip to Israel and the apologies he had issued there and earlier. Tullia Zevi, director of interreligious relations for the European Jewish Congress, was surprised and saddened by the postponement but saw it as inevitable. "It's difficult to talk when you say your religion in a first-class religion and all the others are second rate."[84] These supremacist views were harbored not only by Catholics but by a number of other Christians, Jews, Muslims, and Hindus. Steinberg, of the World Jewish Congress, found such sentiments in the Catholic camp appalling and expressed his support for the boycott of the Christian-Jewish encounter.[85]

Catholic circles sought to minimize the damage to Judeo-Catholic relations by blaming the media for misconstruing "Dominus Iesus" by taking quotations out of context. This was the message of Cardinal William Keeler of Baltimore, who spoke before a Jewish audience. Keeler also defended the beatification of Pius IX, noting that his actions in the Mortara affair were wrong by today's standards but should be assessed in historical perspective. Citing the different cultural context in which the Jewish child was seized and then raised as a Christian, Keeler concluded that Pius "acted in accord with his conscience as shaped in the times in which he lived."[86] This relativism, which alarmed some conservative Catholics, also failed to mollify many Jews. Some Catholics tried to defend "Dominus Iesus" by observing that by proclaiming Christianity "as the only true religion, it does not claim all others are false, or even that Christianity is perfect as it is lived today." But this line of thought seemed to defy logic and was rejected by both conservative and liberal Catholics, as well as by Jews. *La Civiltà Cattolica,* the Jesuit journal with close links to the Vatican, assumed a more defiant tone. "Even at the cost of causing non-benevolent,

83. Cindy Wooden, "Jews Walk Out on Dialogue," ibid., 30 Sept. 2000, 1.

84. Ibid. In the ASV, see Congregazione dei Vescovi e Regolari, Cause e Processi.

85. Victor L. Simpson, "Jews Boycott Vatican Meeting to Protest Document on Catholic Primacy," 23 Sept. 2000, http://www.naplesnews.com/oo/o9/religion/d4995637a.htm, accessed 18 Oct. 2002.

86. Frank Callaham, "Cardinal Keeler Addresses Jewish Audience: Says Media Missed Point of Salvation Document," *Brooklyn Tablet,* 21 Oct. 2000.

even harshly contrary reactions," it editorialized, "Christianity feels an obligation to affirm that is not just one true religion among others, but the
true religion."[87]

Cardinal Ratzinger, head of the doctrinal congregation that drafted
and released "Dominus Iesus," was distressed by the public reaction, which
he said "completely ignored the true theme of the declaration."[88] Although
Ratzinger claimed that the document had been misrepresented and taken
out of context, he failed satisfactorily to explain its true meaning, the inspiration behind it, and its ultimate aims. Neither liberal Catholics nor
Jews would admit that they had erred in their interpretation simply because Ratzinger said so. Cardinal Edward Cassidy, president of the Pontifical Council for Promoting Christian Unity, reportedly found neither the
timing nor the language of the document opportune. It was likewise criticized by the German bishop Walter Kasper, secretary of the Pontifical
Council presided over by Cassidy, who noted that "it lacked the necessary
sensitivity." Meanwhile, Oblate Father Tissa Balasuriya, director of the
Center for Society and Religion in Colombo, Sri Lanka, found "Dominus
Iesus" to be in stark contrast to a document recently published by the Pontifical Council for Inter-religious Dialogue.[89] Tensions and misunderstanding between Catholics and Jews increased when a committee of three
Catholic and three Jewish scholars, established in 1999 to review the twelve
volumes published by the Vatican on its wartime activities, dissolved itself
after the Vatican refused to open its archives for the war years, as the committee had requested. In the meantime, Father Peter Gumpel, head of the
team exploring the beatification of Pius XII, complained that the recent
statements of the Jewish side represented a "defamatory campaign" against
the Catholic Church. Noting that many documents in the archives for the
period after 1922 numbered more than 3 million pages and were still not
catalogued, Father Gumpel promised that those for the wartime period
would be opened "as soon as possible." In February 2002 the Vatican announced that it would release Vatican documents of the pontificate of
Pius XI (1922–39), and some of those of Pius XII, in 2003, and those of the

87. Cindy Wooden, "Church Does Not Teach Other Religions Are False," ibid., 14 Oct.
2000, 12.

88. "Card. Ratzinger Saddened by Reaction to Document," ibid., 14 Oct. 2000, 11.

89. "Germans, Asians Question Vatican Document," ibid., 23 Sept. 2000, 7.

entire pontificate of Pius XII afterward. This was heralded by the World Jewish Congress as a positive step.[90]

During the pontificate of John Paul II relations between Catholics and Jews improved, although they were subject to periodic fluctuations of this kind. Tension arose following the canonization of Edith Stein in 1998, some Jews noting that Stein had died because she was a Jew and resenting the Church's alleged "claim to her martyrdom." Writing for the Anti-Defamation League, Abraham H. Foxman, its national director, and Rabbi Leon Klenicki, its director of interfaith affairs, argued that Stein's canonization represented another attempt on the part of Church figures "to appropriate the symbols of Jewish suffering to minimize the significance of Catholic anti-Semitism and, by focusing on its own victimization, to deflect examination of the church's role in creating an environment that made possible the Holocaust."[91] In their view, this strategy had commenced with the establishment of a Carmelite monastery in Auschwitz in the 1980s, erected there for the purpose of prayer for the victims of the genocide. This "appropriation" of Jewish suffering was also seen in the canonization of Maximilian Kolbe, who sacrificed his life to save that of another prisoner. The canonization of Kolbe and Stein, and the establishment of the Carmelite monastery, conveyed the impression that Auschwitz was a place of Christian martyrdom rather than Jewish extermination, according to Foxman and Klenicki. Even Jewish groups' presentation of a menorah to the Vatican in 1999 engendered controversy. Representatives of other Jewish organizations, including the World Jewish Congress and the Anti-Defamation League, upset over the plans to beatify Pius XII, questioned the presentation of the menorah in light of the "inadequate apologies" of the Vatican.[92]

90. Philip Pullella, "Vatican Accuses Jews of 'Defamatory Campaign,'" 8 Aug. 2001, http://www.rense.com/general12/vaticanaccuses.htm, accessed 18 Oct. 2002; "Vatican to Open Pius XII Records," *New York Newsday,* 17 Feb. 2002.

91. "Canonization Prompts Call for New Vatican Apology to Jews," 11 Oct. 1998, http://www.news-star.com/101198/new_vatican.shtrml, accessed 18 Oct. 2002; statement of Abraham H. Foxman and Rabbi Leon Klenicki, "The Canonization of Edith Stein: An Unnecessary Problem," Position Paper of Anti-Defamation League, Sept. 1997, 2, available through the ADL, 823 UN Plaza, New York, NY, 10017.

92. Alessandra Stanley, "Vatican Acquires a Large Menorah and a Dispute," *New York Times,* 14 April 1999. In the course of his twenty-seven-year pontificate, John Paul II canonized more saints than any of his predecessors. Some aroused greater controversy than others.

The beatification of Pope Pius IX also caused friction. And some complained that John Paul had not done enough to silence the anti-Semitism spewed by some of his clergy.[93] Vatican policy in the Middle East also created tension between members of the two faiths, provoking considerable resentment on the part of some Israelis and other Jews. Early in 2000 an agreement between the Vatican and the PLO specified that "unilateral decisions and actions altering the specific character and status of Jerusalem are morally and legally unacceptable." The Israeli government summoned the papal nuncio, protesting the Vatican's interference in the sensitive negotiations with the Palestinians. The Vatican responded that the Vatican-PLO agreement had "nothing to do with the [Mideast] peace process." Subsequently, Monsignor Francis Chullikatt of the Vatican mission to the United Nations endorsed the U.S.-inspired "road map" for peace in the Middle East and called for the establishment of two independent and sovereign states in the region "living side by side in peace and security."[94]

In the spring of 2001 Jews were dismayed by John Paul II's conduct during a visit to Syria. At his meeting with its leader, Bashar Assad engaged in an anti-Jewish tirade in which he accused the Jews of betraying Christ and urged Christians and Muslims to make common cause against the Jews. The pope said nothing to refute these anti-Judaic and anti-Semitic slurs, prompting anger and disappointment among Jews worldwide. Nor did John Paul challenge the grand mufti of Syria, Sheik Ahmad Kuftaro, who asked the pope to stop Israel's "atrocious aggression."[95] Abraham Foxman of the Anti-Defamation League described the pope's failure to respond as "unacceptable and irresponsible" and as "coming close to being guilty of the sin of silence."[96] Vatican spokesmen responded that Assad's remarks were mere political rhetoric and that the pope never responded to such statements while a guest abroad. There was little criticism of the pope's visit to Babi Yar, in the Ukraine, the site of the massacre of some one hundred thousand Jews in September 1941.

93. Peter S. Green, "Jewish Museum in Poland: More Than a Memorial," New York Times, 9 Jan. 2003, A4.

94. Niles Lathem and Uri Dan, "Furor as Pope Sides with PLO on Jerusalem," New York Post, 16 Feb. 2000, 4; Tracy Early, "The Vatican Offers Map for Peace," Brooklyn Tablet, 8 Nov. 2003, 1.

95. "A Vexed Mission of Reconciliation," New York Times, 8 May 2001, A26.

96. Eric J. Greenberg, "Open Season on Jews," Jewish Week, 11 May 2001.

During this time there was considerable Jewish and Israeli questioning and resentment of the Vatican's attempt to pursue "an even-handed policy" in the Middle East. The Vatican, for its part, expressed grave concern during the Israeli siege of the Church of the Nativity in Bethlehem, believed to be built over the site of the birthplace of Jesus, into which Palestinian gunmen had fled in early April 2002. Although Israeli president Moshe Katsay reassured John Paul that they would neither damage the church nor harm the religious in its compound, both pope and curia remained concerned. John Paul denounced the "indiscriminate acts of terrorism against Israel," but he also criticized the Jewish state for imposing "unjust conditions and humiliations" upon the Palestinians." "The tragic conflict highlights the very urgency of the dialogue between the three Abrahamitic religions: Judaism, Christianity, and Islam," said Cardinal Walter Kasper, president of the Commission for Religious Relations with the Jews. He added that "there cannot be peace in the world without peace between the world religions."[97] Dialogue did not immediately resolve differences. In seeking a negotiated solution to the Palestinian problem, Pope John Paul publicly criticized the Israeli building of a wall to separate Jews and Palestinians, which he saw as another obstacle to "peaceful coexistence."[98] Many Jews resented the Vatican's call for Israeli restraint as unfair and unfortunate.

At the same time, there were positive developments in Catholic-Jewish relations, and Jews generally appreciated Cardinal Kasper's statement commemorating the thirty-sixth anniversary of the publication of "Nostra aetate," the historic Vatican document that paved the way for improved relations between Christians and Jews. Yosef Lamdan, the Israeli ambassador to the Holy See, described "Nostra aetate" as "an enormous step forward in Catholic-Jewish relations."[99] In Rome, the annual day for Christian-Jewish dialogue in 2002 led to a frank exchange of views. "When

97. Judith Sudilovsky, "Israel Tells Pope that Church in Bethlehem Is Safe," *Brooklyn Tablet*, 13 April 2002; Judith Sudilovsky, "Church of the Nativity Damaged by War in Bethlehem," ibid., 13 April 2002; "Pope Blasts 'Unjust' Israeli," *New York Post*, 2 April 2002, 6; Cardinal Walter Kasper's talk at Boston College, 6 Nov. 2002, available at http://www.bc.edu/research/cjl/meta-elements/trexts/articles/Kasper_6Nov02.htm, accessed 2 Feb. 2004.

98. "Pope Criticizes Israeli Wall, Deplores Terrorist Attacks," *Brooklyn Tablet,* 22 Nov. 2003, 11.

99. "Cardinal Recalls Vatican II Document on Relations with Jews," http://www.cwnews.com/Browse/2001/10/16718.htm, accessed 18 Oct. 2002.

the Catholic Church says it believes God remains faithful to his covenant with the people of Israel," the new chief rabbi of Rome, Riccardo Di Segni, said, "it must admit the possibility that Jews can be saved without believing in Jesus Christ."[100] Di Segni's view seemed to be supported by the release of the Pontifical Biblical Commission's document, written at the end of 2001 and released in 2002, entitled "The Jewish People and their Sacred Scriptures in the Christian Bible." Among other things, it said, "The Jewish Messianic wait is not in vain." It noted, "We, like them, live in expectation," adding, "the difference is in the fact that for us, he who will come will have the traits of that Jesus who has already come and is already active and present among us." The document underscored that Christianity and its Scriptures were "inescapably related to Judaism and its Bible," noting some of the pastoral implications of the close relationship. Some saw this document as a counterweight to "Dominus Iesus," which had earlier provoked such controversy.[101]

Soon thereafter, in August 2002, the United States Bishops Committee on Ecumenical and Inter-religious Affairs issued a joint Catholic-Jewish statement entitled "Reflections on Covenant and Mission." The statement proclaimed that "Campaigns that target Jews for conversion to Christianity are no longer theologically acceptable in the Catholic Church." Cardinal Keeler of Baltimore, the U.S. Bishops' moderator for Jewish relations, affirmed "the continuing validity of the covenant of God with the Jewish people, citing St. Paul's statement that "the gifts and call of God are irrevocable."[102] Pointing to the "unique spiritual linkage with the Jews," the statement quoted Cardinal Kasper's remarks of May 2001.

> The term mission, in its proper sense, refers to conversion from false gods and idols to the true and one God, who revealed himself in the salvation history with his elected people. Thus mission, in this strict sense, cannot be used

100. "Rome Rabbi Says Christians Must Accept Jews' Salvation," *Brooklyn Tablet*, 26 Jan. 2002.

101. "Vatican: Jews Do Not Wait in Vain for Messiah," 5 Aug. 2002, http://www.christianitytoday.com/ct/2002/009/18.24.html; Donald Senior, "Rome Has Spoken: A New Catholic Approach to Judaism," http://www.bc.edu/research/cjl/meta-elements/trexts/articles/senior.htm, accessed 2 Feb. 2004; "Vatican Document on Judaism Praised by Jews," http://www.ananova.com/news/story/sm_498944.html, accessed 18 Oct. 2002.

102. "Catholic Mission to Jews Ends," 8 Aug. 2002, available at http://www.freerepublic.com/focus/news/735234/posts, accessed 18 Oct. 2002; Jerry Filteau, "Catholic-Jewish Statement Stirs Conversion Debate," *Brooklyn Tablet*, 31 Aug. 2002.

with regard to Jews, who believe in the true and one God. Therefore, and this is characteristic, there exists dialogue, but there does not exist any Catholic missionary organization for Jews. . . . The Church believes that Judaism, i.e., the faithful response of the Jewish people to God's irrevocable covenant, is salvific for them, because God is faithful to his promises.[103]

While Cardinal Keeler hoped that the joint statement would facilitate reconciliation and mark a significant step forward in Jewish-Catholic dialogue, it created new problems as it sought to resolve older ones. Paradoxically, it led the Southern Baptist Convention to accuse the Roman Catholic Church of anti-Semitism for excluding Jews from evangelization.[104] Conservative Catholic theologians such as Father John Echert, in turn, found parts of the statement "contrary to divine revelation" and feared that it approached "apostasy." In his view, "precisely because Jews share an expectation of the coming of the Messiah, they should be targeted and the primary focus of our efforts for converts to Christ."[105] This had been the Church's past practice right up to the Second Vatican Council. Stunned by the critical conservative reaction to the revised stance, Cardinal Keeler sought to conciliate conservatives by clarifying that the statement did "not represent a formal position taken by the United States Conference of Catholic Bishops or the Bishops' Committee for Ecumenical and Inter-religious Affairs."[106]

One Jewish leader believed that the cardinal was forced to backtrack in the face of criticism from "the Church's right wing." Another Jewish leader and interfaith expert pointed to the difficulties facing those within the Church who wanted to foster theological change. "The Church has not yet fully come to terms with the existence of a viable Judaism," said Rabbi James Rudin, adding, "it's very tortured for them because the origin of their faith came out of Judaism."[107] However, the Church did make progress, as the Catholic bishops joined Lutheran and Anglican bishops in asserting that Jews should not be singled out for evangelization. "We see no conflict between a dialogue based on mutual respect for the sacredness

---

103. Filteau, "Catholic-Jewish Statement Stirs Conversion Debate."

104. Eric J. Greenberg, "Conversion Controversy Continues," *Jewish Week*, Aug. 30, 2002, 5.

105. Filteau, "Catholic-Jewish Statement Stirs Conversion Debate."

106. Greenberg, "Conversion Controversy Continues," 5.

107. Ibid.

of the other and the Christian mission to preach the Gospel," they said. "An aggressive direct effort to convert the Jewish people would break the bond of trust built up for over 30 years and recreate enmity between our 'elder brothers and sisters' and ourselves."[108] This interdenominational Christian response to Judaism and evangelization reflected the spirit of Vatican II and the commitment of John Paul II to improving relations between the two faiths.

In 2003, as the prospect of an Anglo-American preemptive strike against Iraq loomed, John Paul took steps to avoid another conflagration. A peace emissary was dispatched by the Vatican to President George W. Bush, and Cardinal Pio Laghi urged the American president to make "every effort" to avoid the outbreak of war in this volatile region. The threat of war also led the pope to meet with Rome's chief rabbi, Riccardo Di Segni, as he called for Christians and Jews to pray to preserve the fragile gift of peace—*shalom.* "In these days the dangerous rumbling of war can be heard," the pope told the Roman Jewish delegation. "We, Jews and Catholics, feel the urgent mission of imploring peace from God, the creator and eternal, and of being peacemakers ourselves."[109] The invocation of prayer for a common goal was one of the many ways in which John Paul reached out to the Jewish community, which generally responded warmly. At the end of 2003 the Simon Wiesenthal Center presented another menorah to John Paul II and gave him its Humanitarian Award "for his 'lifelong friendship' with the Jewish people and his efforts to promote Catholic-Jewish understanding."[110]

In January 2005 John Paul II selected the Jewish-born French cardinal Jean Marie (formerly Aaron) Lustiger of Paris to represent the Holy See at the commemoration of the sixtieth anniversary of the liberation of Auschwitz.[111] The reaction in the Jewish community was mixed. However, in late March 2005, as the pope's fragile health deteriorated and he was administered the last rites, Jews joined Christians in praying for John Paul II,

108. Filteau, "Catholic-Jewish Statement Stirs Conversion Debate."

109. Elisabeth Bumiller, "Peace Envoy from Vatican in U.S. for Talks with Bush," *New York Times,* 4 March 2003, A12; "Pope and Rome Rabbi Talk about the Need for Prayer," *Brooklyn Tablet,* 22 Feb. 2003, 6.

110. "Menorah for the Pope," *Brooklyn Tablet,* 6 Dec. 2003, 12.

111. "Jewish-Born French Cardinal Will Represent the Holy See at Auschwitz," ibid., 15 Jan. 2005, 11.

who died in early April. The election of Cardinal Joseph Ratzinger as Pope Benedict XVI soon thereafter led Jews to hope that this collaborator of John Paul would continue his predecessor's policy of reconciliation.

John Paul II's contribution to the reconciliation of Catholics and Jews has still to be fully assessed in historical perspective. It seems safe to say, however, that most observers concur that he continued the momentum of the Second Vatican Council in improving these relations, helped to move Catholics further away from old misconceptions about the Jews and Judaism, and opened the door for future dialogue.

CONCLUSION

The Papacy and the Jews, Past and Present

By bending in prayer at the Western Wall, the Kotel, the

pope symbolically created a new future. The Church was

honoring the Temple it had denigrated. It was affirming

the presence of the Jewish people at home in Jerusalem.

The pope reversed an ancient current of Jew hatred with

that act, and the Church's relationship to Israel, present

as well as past, would never be the same. Referring to the

sight of the stooped man in white with his trembling

hand on the sacred stones of the wall, a senior Israeli offi-

cial said, "This is a picture that will appear in the history

books—both Catholic and Jewish.*

THE OFTEN TORTURED RELATIONSHIP BETWEEN CATHOLICS AND JEWS stretching over millennia has undergone dramatic and substantial changes during the latter half of the twentieth century and the first decade of the twenty-first. Two events played a key role in this transformation, which some have described as an evolution and others as a revolution: the Holocaust and the Second Vatican Council. The tragedy of the former played a part in ushering in the reforms of the latter, two decades after the genocide of the Jews. In a sense, the fifteen lengthy sentences of the "Nostra aetate" of Vatican II, conceived by John XXIII and advanced and implemented by Popes Paul VI and John Paul II, represented the Church's belated response to the

* Carroll, *Constantine's Sword*, 600.

Holocaust. Together, they have played a key role in transforming the dialogue between Catholics and Jews. As a consequence, many Jews no longer think of the Church and papacy only in terms of the Crusades and the Inquisition but also in terms of Vatican II and "Nostra aetate."

The provisions of "Nostra aetate" and its subsequent implementation have been deemed groundbreaking, reversing a long period of clerical hatred, papal oppression, and Catholic persecution of Jews, while affirming the continuing validity of Judaism. The popes and bishops in council have issued official "magisterial" teaching against anti-Semitism, while affirming the importance of healing Catholic-Jewish relations. In the words of Cardinal Johannes Willebrands, who served as president of the Pontifical Council for Religious Relations with Jews, "Never before has a systematic, positive, comprehensive, careful, and daring presentation of Jews and Judaism been made in the Church."[1] Substantial cooperation between members of the two faiths has followed in the decades since the Holocaust and Vatican II. For some twenty years, leaders of the Roman Catholic and Jewish communities have met semiannually to discuss various aspects of Catholic-Jewish relations. The participants in these consultations are delegates of the Bishops Committee for Ecumenical and Interreligious Affairs of the United States Conference of Catholic Bishops (BCEIA) and the National Council of Synagogues (NCS), representing the Central Conference of American Rabbis, the Rabbinical Assembly of Conservative Judaism, the Union of American Hebrew Congregations, and the United Synagogues of Conservative Judaism. In August 2002 the two umbrella groups offered their "Reflections on Covenant and Mission." The Catholic reflections recognized the growing appreciation of the eternal covenant between God and the Jewish people, concluding that campaigns to convert Jews to Christianity are no longer theologically acceptable in the Catholic Church. The Jewish reflections focused on the mission of the Jews and the perfection of the world.[2]

Since 1969 the Christian Scholars Group, which includes Roman Catholic and Protestant scholars, has been working on a revision of the

---

1. Eugene J. Fisher and Leon Klenicki, eds., *In Our Time: The Flowering of Jewish-Catholic Dialogue* (Mahwah, N.J.: Paulist Press, 1990), 4, quoted in Lederer, "2000 Years," 2.

2. The National Council of Synagogues and the Bishops Committee for Ecumenical and Interreligious Affairs, "Reflections on Covenant and Mission," 12 Aug. 2002, http://www.bc.edu/bc_org/research/cjl/Documents/ncs_usccb120802,html, accessed 6 Oct. 2003.

Christian relationship to Judaism and the Jewish people, and has welcomed the cooperation of Jewish groups. The group applauded the September 2000 publication of "Dabru Emet: A Jewish Statement on Christians and Christianity," a Jewish reexamination of Christianity. Early in 2004 the two chief rabbis of Israel, the chief Ashkenazi and chief Sephardic rabbis, visited the pope in Rome, calling for continued reconciliation and brotherhood between the two faiths. In turn, the pope praised the official dialogue commenced in 2002 between the Vatican and the chief rabbinate of Israel. "In the twenty-five years of my pontificate," he told the rabbis, "I have striven to promote Jewish-Catholic dialogue and to foster ever greater understanding, respect and cooperation between us. . . . We must spare no effort in working together to build a world of justice, peace and reconciliation of all peoples."[3] The rabbis, who appreciated the pope's efforts for reconciliation, appealed to him to continue his public condemnations of anti-Semitism.

Meanwhile, across the Atlantic in New York City, cardinals from Europe, Asia, and North America met with an international group of Jewish religious leaders at Yeshiva University with the aim of strengthening Catholic-Jewish ties. Catholic participants in the New York dialogue, initiated by Cardinal Jean-Marie Lustiger of Paris and hosted by the World Jewish Congress, were pleased with the results—although they stipulated that additional issues had to be addressed. They therefore planned a series of follow-up conferences to "address the challenges of general religious peace and confront the rise of hate and anti-Semitism."[4] Despite the attempts of some to separate religious, diplomatic, and political issues, this proved difficult, if not impossible, to do.

In fact, the religious reconciliation has been such that political and diplomatic factors rather than religious ones have increasingly influenced the attitude of many Europeans toward Jews. Some have suggested that in liberal Western circles antagonism toward the Israeli "occupation" of the Palestinian territories and people has generated a new "anti-Semitism." Thus, at Easter 2001, a leading French newspaper ran a cartoon that

3. Quoted in Cindy Wooden, "The Chief Rabbis of Israel Make First Visit to Vatican," *Brooklyn Tablet*, 24 Jan. 2004, 7.
4. Daniel J. Walkin and Laurie Goodstein, "In Upper Manhattan, Talmudic Scholars Look Up and Find Cardinals Among the Rabbis," *New York Times*, 20 Jan. 2004, B5; "Catholic and Jewish Leaders will Maintain Dialogue," *Brooklyn Tablet*, 31 Jan. 2004, 13.

showed Ariel Sharon nailing Yasser Arafat to a cross, reviving the imagery of deicide. The following year, again during the Easter season, an Italian journal published a cartoon depicting the infant Jesus menaced by an Is-raeli tank, the child asking, "What, are they here to kill me again?"[5]

The old portrayal of Jews as killers of Christ persists, even though the Church and the papacy have clearly abandoned it. In 2003 and early 2004 Mel Gibson's controversial film *The Passion of the Christ,* with its alleged depiction of Jews as "bloodthirsty rabble," provoked angry protests and fears that it would revive anti-Judaism and anti-Semitism. The actor-director, a Catholic traditionalist who rejects the reforms of Vatican II, aroused the suspicions of liberal Catholics as well as Jews.[6] Rabbi Eugene Korn of the Anti-Defamation League was among many who complained that the film presented Jews as responsible for the crucifixion of Jesus; he warned that it "could turn back the clock on decades of positive progress in interfaith relations."[7]

Fuel was added to the fire when the press reported that John Paul II had previewed the film and had approved its message. Archbishop Stanis-law Dziwisz, the pope's personal secretary and an ultraconservative Cath-olic, allegedly conveyed the pope's approval to Gibson's co-producer, who released it to the media. Soon the press in America and abroad was repeat-ing the pope's alleged five-word assessment of the film: "It is as it was."[8] News that the pope had given his seal of approval to a film that many peo-ple suspected was anti-Semitic sent shock waves through the interfaith community. Jewish and liberal Catholic leaders predicted that Jewish-Catholic relations would suffer as a consequence and that the film could inspire a new wave of anti-Semitism. Archbishop Dziwisz, trying to defuse the situation, confirmed that the pope had seen the film but had not shared his thoughts on it publicly. Gibson, for his part, evidently cut the

5. See Emanuele Ottolenghi, "Anti-Semitism in Europe Is All about Denial," *Newsday,* 24 Feb. 2003.

6. "Mel's Passion Put to the Test," *New York Post,* 17 Nov. 2003, 22–23; Laurie Goodstein, "Months before Debut, Movie on Death of Jesus Causes Stir," *New York Times,* 2 Aug. 2003, 1, 10.

7. Eric J. Greenberg, "Jews Horrified by Gibson's Jewish Film," *Jewish Week,* 15 Aug. 2003, 1, 10.

8. Randy Kennedy, "'Passion' Film is Incendiary, 2 Jewish Leaders Report," *New York Times,* 23 Jan. 2004, A12; Eric J. Greenberg, "Questioning Pope's Nod to 'Passion,'" *Jewish Week,* 26 Dec. 2003, 12; Frank Rich, "The Pope's Thumbs Up for Gibson's 'Passion,'" *New York Times,* 18 Jan. 2004, 1.

footage in which the Jewish high priest says to the crowd, "His blood be on us and on our children." Gibson also made it clear that he opposes anti-Semitism, which he called a "sin."[9]

The acrimonious debate over the film and John Paul's alleged approval of it was short-lived, however, and has not halted overall progress in Christian-Jewish relations. In September 2002 the Christian Scholars Group issued a ten-point guide to Christian relations with the Jews. It specified that (1) God's Covenant with the Jewish people endures; their covenant with God has not been superseded; (2) Jesus of Nazareth lived and died as a faithful Jew; Christians worship the God of Israel in and through Jesus; (3) ancient rivalries must not define Christian-Jewish relations today; (4) Judaism is a living faith, enriched by many centuries of development; (5) the Bible both connects and separates Jews and Christians, for although both draw from the same biblical texts of ancient Israel, they have developed different traditions of interpretation; (6) although Christians for centuries taught that salvation comes only through Jesus Christ, Christians now recognize God's redemptive power in the Jewish tradition; (7) Christians should not target Jews for conversion since they have an eternal covenant with God; (8) Christian worship that teaches contempt for Judaism dishonors God, and Church leaders should search their teachings, Scripture, prayers, and sermons for distorted images of Judaism; (9) the special relationship between the land of Israel and the Jewish people should be affirmed; (10) Christians should work with Jews for healing the problems that plague the world.[10]

These and similar cooperative efforts have led Jewish as well as Christian circles to recognize that the declarations of Vatican II and their implementation have fundamentally altered the Catholic-Jewish dialogue and have provided the foundation for increased mutual understanding and appreciation. "Like the 'Magna Carta,' the Declaration of Independence, the United States Constitution, 'Nostra aetate' broke new ground and pro-

9. Frank Brun I, "Pope Has Not Endorsed Gibson Film, Report Says," *New York Times*, 20 Jan. 2004, E1; "Gibson Deletes Scene from 'Passion,'" *New York Daily News*, 5 Feb. 2004; Tracy Connor, "Mel's 'Passion' for Gore Extreme, He Admits," *New York Daily News*, 15 Feb. 2004, 13.

10. Christian Scholars Group on Christian-Jewish Relations, "A Sacred Obligation: Rethinking Christian Faith in Relation to Judaism and the Jewish People," 11 Sept. 2002, http://www.bc.edu/bc_org/research/cjl/Christian_Scholars_Group/Sacred_Obligation.htm, accessed 2 Feb. 2004.

vided the mandate for constructive change," noted Rabbi A. James Rudin of the American Jewish Committee.[11] There has been less agreement on other aspects of papal policy toward Jews, however, because "Nostra aetate" did not offer an apology and made no reference to the state of Israel. These perceived shortcomings were addressed in the aftermath of Vatican II, but other difficulties still remained between Catholics and Jews and between "liberal" and "conservative" Catholics.

One complaint, as we saw in the last chapter, has been that the Church has apologized for the silence, and therefore the complicity in the Nazi genocide, of its lay members, but to date has tended to absolve the Church structure of responsibility. Unlike the French and German Church hierarchies, which have openly recognized their own shortcomings in this respect, the papal hierarchy has steadfastly refused to do so. In the words of one critic, the Church attributes fallibility to its "sinful children" but not to itself.[12] Others have complained of a Church leadership enveloped in secrecy and stubbornly unwilling to recognize or accept responsibility for its sins of omission and commission. It is within this framework that the "silence" of Pius XII—the two volumes of published correspondence between the Vatican and Polish bishops contain only two references to the extermination of the Jews—assumes such a central role.[13] For this and other reasons, the efforts to beatify and eventually canonize Eugenio Pacelli have provoked bitter opposition and ongoing controversy. But Pius XII's failure to assume a determined public stance against the Nazi genocide does not make him an anti-Semite or an enemy of Judaism, nor does it necessarily reflect a centuries-old papal crusade against the Jews. Pius XII's position toward the Jews, like that of his predecessors, was far more complex and nuanced than many of his critics will allow. Although Pope John Paul II did not criticize Pius's conduct during the Holocaust, his own actions have departed from the discreet diplomacy of this earlier pope. In fact, John Paul publicly denounced the massacres and deportations in Kosovo in 1998–99, the massacres in Rwanda, and many other episodes of bloodshed and injustice worldwide, many of them involving racial, ethnic,

11. Eugene J. Fisher, A. James Rudin, and Marc H. Tannenbaum, eds., *Twenty Years of Jewish-Catholic Relations* (Mahwah, N.J.: Paulist Press, 1986), 2–3, quoted in Lederer, "2000 Years," 19.

12. Carroll, *Constantine's Sword*, 448.

13. Tinnemann, "Silence of Pius XII," 279.

and tribal hatred. Furthermore, during a conference of Church scholars in 2003 commemorating the pontificate of Leo XIII (1878–1903), John Paul II acknowledged that there have been shortcomings and mistakes in the two-thousand-year history of the Church. In his words, these historical wrongs had to be recognized before true reconciliation could occur.[14]

John Paul's recognition of Church errors, his outspoken condemnation of genocide and ethnic cleansing, and his calls for the prompt persecution of crimes against humanity have not ended criticism of the papacy or blunted denunciations of its anti-Judaic past practices. This opposition is reflected in the massive, growing, and increasingly controversial historical literature on the papacy and the Jews. The hostile attitude of the papacy toward the Jews over the millennia has been explored in James Carroll's *Constantine Sword: The Church and the Jews* (2001), while David I. Kertzer's *The Popes against the Jews: The Vatican's Role in the Rise of Modern Anti-Semitism* and Garry Wills's *Papal Sin: Structures of Deceit* (2000) focus on the more recent period.

Daniel Goldhagen, author of *Hitler's Willing Executioners: Ordinary Germans and the Holocaust* (1996), raises the question of how the Church's precepts and practices contributed to the genocidal anti-Semitism that animated the Nazi regime. "Anti-Semitism led to the Holocaust. Anti-Semitism has been integral to the Catholic Church," Goldhagen writes, adding, "Surely the question of what the relationship is between the Church's Anti-Semitism and the Holocaust should be at the center of any general treatment of these subjects." Goldhagen quotes with approval a passage from James Carroll, who claims in *Constantine's Sword* that "an inquiry into the origins of the Holocaust in the tortured past of Western civilization is necessarily an inquiry into the history of Catholicism." Both concur that "the main responsibility for producing this all-time leading Western hatred lies with Christianity. More specifically, with the Catholic Church."[15] Goldhagen's most recent book on the subject, *A Moral Reckoning: The Catholic Church during the Holocaust and Today* (2002), carries this argument further. But even some who acknowledge the interrelation-

14. John Thavis, "John Paul II Puts His 'Bully Pulpit' to Good Use," *Brooklyn Tablet*, 17 April 1999, 1; "Pope Says Historical Wrongs Justify Reconsideration," *Brooklyn Tablet*, 8 Nov. 2003, 10.
15. Goldhagen, "What Would Jesus Have Done?" 22.

ship between anti-Judaism and anti-Semitism are critical of Goldhagen's methodology and obvious bias against the Church. Georg Denzler, for example, who has deplored the Catholic hierarchy's timidity in confronting Nazi abuses, finds Goldhagen's polemical account, based on contentious secondary sources, wanting.[16]

There are Catholic, Protestant, and Jewish critics of the papacy's policies and practices toward Jews over the course of two millennia. Indeed, in certain quarters it has become fashionable to demonize the papacy and the Church for their role in the Holocaust. Pinchas Lapide claims that the Church's long history of anti-Judaism paved the way for anti-Semitic racism at the turn of the century. These contentions are supported by David Kertzer, Hans Küng, and Richard Steigmann-Gall.[17] Steigmann-Gall claims that all too many German Christians, both Catholic and Protestant, allowed their religious antipathies toward Jews (anti-Judaism) to parallel and in some cases to support the Nazi persecution of the Jews (anti-Semitism). Steigmann-Gall's work is serious and scholarly, but unfortunately much of the literature on the papacy and the Jews is polemical rather than historical, seeking to condemn rather than to explore impartially. Furthermore, a number of these writers virtually ignore the persistent reality that hostility between Jews and Christians was often mutual, and that some Jews have been guilty of anti-Christian sentiment and conduct.[18]

The anti-Judaic aspects of papal and ecclesiastical policy over the centuries have been real enough, but they is not the whole story, and to gloss over the Church's protective measures toward the Jews is historically irresponsible. A number of historians and other writers have argued that we must get beyond the assumption that the entire scope of Christian-Jewish relations must be viewed through the lens of a one-sided intolerance and persecution.[19] They see the history of papal-Jewish relations not as an inexorable pattern but as a series of ups and downs. To be sure, there have been shameful periods and unfortunate incidents over the centuries, but

16. See Georg Denzler, *Widerstand ist nicht das richtige Word. Katholische Priester, Bischoefe under Theologen im Dritten Reich* (Zurich: Pendo Verlag, 2003).

17. Lapide, *Three Popes and the Jews*, 87; Kertzer, *Popes against the Jews*, 5; Küng, "From Anti-Semitism to Theological Dialogue," 11–12; Richard Steigmann-Gall, *The Holy Reich: Nazi Conceptions of Christianity, 1919–1945* (Cambridge: Cambridge University Press, 2003).

18. Corky Siemaszko, "Sharon Sticking to Map," *New York Daily News*, 10 June 2003, 19.

19. See Roth, "Bishops and Jews in the Middle Ages," 17.

these have often been followed by more positive developments—and neither should be arbitrarily ignored or minimized.

In examining the papacy and the Jews in the contemporary era, some have even been dismissive of the far-reaching changes in Catholic-Jewish relations ushered in by the Second Vatican Council. It is true that the council commenced rather than completed the process of reconciliation. "Nostra aetate" of 1965, the Vatican's "Guidelines and Suggestions for Implementing the Conciliar Declaration" of 1975, and "Notes on the Correct Way to Present the Jews and Judaism in Preaching and Catechesis in the Roman Catholic Church" of 1985 have made a strong start in this process, but for many Jews these steps have not been sufficient.[20] One continuing point of contention is the relationship between anti-Judaism, or opposition to the Jews because of their religious beliefs, and anti-Semitism, based on "race." Students of both history and theology have differentiated the older anti-Judaic and newer anti-Semitic forms of prejudice against the Jews. While both engaged in discrimination, segregation, and other forms of persecution, papal anti-Judaism did not seek the systematic elimination of Jews that Nazi anti-Semitism did.[21]

John Rousmaniere writes that the older form of prejudice is often termed theological anti-Judaism because it is founded on theological rather than racial grounds. In his words, anti-Judaists "believe that Jews are to be held in contempt, because of their disbelief in Jesus Christ as Messiah and savior. Even more important, Jews are to be punished collectively because they killed Jesus." By contrast, "anti-Semitism is often called 'racial anti-Semitism' because it is founded on a conviction that Semites—a term for Jews that is derived from Noah's son Shem—are genetically inferior to non-Jews."[22] Anti-Semites preach that Jews must be segregated or even eradicated less they pollute the Gentiles.

Some, like Steigmann-Gall, find this distinction academic and irrelevant, observing that anti-Judaism and anti-Semitism share many characteristics and claiming that the former contributed to the latter. These critics maintain that political or racial anti-Semitism rested upon centuries of cultural anti-Semitism, which in turn was seen to be grounded in

20. Lederer, "2000 Years," 19.
21. Katz, *From Prejudice to Destruction*, 323.
22. Rousmaniere, *Bridge to Dialogue*, 6–7.

theological anti-Semitism or anti-Judaism. Thus members of the World Jewish Congress, among others, have traced the breeding ground of anti-Semitism to Christian dogma.[23] The Church and the papacy have been willing to acknowledge that some of its members succumbed to anti-Judaism but somewhat more reluctant to recognize any racial bias within its ranks, deeming such views contrary to the tenets of the faith. Racist anti-Semites, the Vatican had steadfastly maintained, sin by violating Catholic principles and Church teaching. Unfortunately, critics complain, the Holy See has never fully confronted the question of the relationship between clerical anti-Judaism and virulent anti-Semitism.

It is true that, although anti-Judaism has a clear religious basis, many in the Church who espoused anti-Judaic sentiments did so in language strikingly similar to the racial slurs uttered by anti-Semites. Part of the Christian laity, as well as the Catholic clergy, joined in a de facto "unholy alliance" with racists and bigots, whose sins were all too often overlooked by a Vatican that couched its protests in a nebulous language that was often little understood and largely ignored. This was true of individual clergy as well as of the press that was subject to its influence—most notably the semiofficial *Osservatore Romano* and the Jesuit *Civiltà Cattolica*. Regardless of the fine distinctions so important to the Vatican, it is not difficult to conclude that anti-Judaism and anti-Semitism had something in common, for both conversion and genocide led to the disappearance of the Jews. In the eyes of some, they were merely different means to the same end.

Furthermore, some churchmen called for segregation rather than conversion. This program found substantial support in segments of the Jewish community. Some Jews, noting that the Torah regards the Jewish people as innately different from all others, affirmed an impassable gulf between themselves and others. In fact, some believed that the Talmudic literature depicted Christianity as one of the heretical sects to be controlled and Israel alone as the true servant of God. Nor should it be forgotten that this Talmudic tradition included a body of precepts and prohibitions that regulated the contact of Jews with Gentiles, and these were not simply guidelines but binding regulations.[24] Initially, then, Jews as well as

---

23. Littell, "Uprooting Antisemitism," 16; Kubovy, "Silence of Pope Pius XII," 18.
24. Katz, *Exclusiveness and Tolerance,* 146–48, 24–25.

Christians favored segregation, which was supported by the early Talmud, the exposition of Jewish Scripture, rabbinic tradition, and folk stories that sought to restrict Jewish contact with non-Jews.[25] In fact, Jacob Katz sees the social segregation of the Middle Ages a logical consequence of Jewish religious separation.[26]

Reciprocal enmity of a kind between Jews and Christians has endured for some two millennia. Some even view the "Judeo-Christian tradition" as a myth that masks continuing opposition between theological enemies.[27] From this perspective, the Jews who did not acknowledge Jesus actually persecuted the Christians who did. As Christianity spread and Jews became a minority in an increasingly Christian world, the hardships imposed by the anti-Judaic program of the Church and papacy caused greater suffering than that flowing from Jewish hostility toward Christians, contributing to the formulation of the popular negative image of the Jew. Hence the argument for a link between religiously inspired anti-Judaism and secular anti-Semitism.

Many theorists of anti-Semitism trace its origins not to the medieval Church but to the late eighteenth-century Enlightenment. Writers from Karl Marx to Hannah Arendt have perceived animosity toward Jews as a by-product of the march toward modernization. These writers see a complex relationship between modernity and anti-Semitism in which anti-Semitism is understood as a reaction to modern social and political conditions. Theodor Adorno and Max Horkheimer, like Arendt, trace anti-Semitism to the Enlightenment and the failure of modernity, but seek its roots much further back; in their view it is a mixture of "modern" and "archaic" modes of domination. They conclude that modern animosity toward Jews points to deeper problems inherent in modernity itself. For Adorno and Horkheimer, anti-Semitism represents a crisis of the Western tradition that transcends Jewish-Gentile relations and is just one aspect of the negative resolution of the dialectic of the Enlightenment.[28]

Hannah Arendt was one of the first thinkers to address in a thorough

---

25. Kertzer, *Popes against the Jews,* 140.
26. Katz, *Exclusiveness and Tolerance,* 43.
27. See Cohen, *Myth of the Judeo-Christian Tradition.*
28. See David Seymour, "Adorno and Horkheimer: Enlightenment and Antisemitism," *Journal of Jewish Studies* 51 (autumn 2000): 299–307.

and systematic way the question of whether the anti-Semitism that led to the Holocaust was the logical culmination of centuries of Christian anti-Judaism. She concluded that it was not. "The notion of an unbroken continuity of persecutions, expulsions, and massacres from the end of the Roman Empire to the Middle Ages, the modern era, and down to our times, frequently embellished by the idea that modern anti-Semitism is no more than a secularized version of popular medieval superstitions," she wrote, "is no less fallacious (though of course less mischievous) than the corresponding antisemitic notion of a Jewish secret society that has ruled, or aspired to rule, the world since antiquity."[29]

Arendt posited a radical discontinuity between historical Christian anti-Judaism and Nazism, locating the transition in the Enlightenment's march to modernity. She perceived anti-Semitism as a secular nineteenth-century ideology, quite distinct from the earlier religious conflict between Catholics and Jews. At the end of World War II, Arendt, following Jacob Katz, rejected the notion of an eternal, ubiquitous anti-Semitism, always and everywhere determining the relationship between Jews and Gentiles.

> Needless to add, it was Jewish historiography, with a strong polemical and apologetical bias, that undertook to trace the record of Jew-hatred in Christian history, while it was left to the antisemites to trace an intellectually not too dissimilar record from ancient Jewish authorities. When this Jewish tradition of an often violent antagonism to Christians and Gentiles came to light, "the general Jewish public was not only outraged but genuinely astonished," so well had its spokesmen succeeded in convincing themselves and everybody else of the non-fact that Jewish separateness was due exclusively to Gentile hostility and lack of enlightenment. Judaism, it was now maintained chiefly by Jewish historians, had always been superior to other religions in that it believed in human equality and tolerance. That this self-deceiving theory, accompanied by the belief that the Jewish people had always been the passive, suffering object of Christian persecutions, actually amounted to a prolongation and modernization of the old myth of chosenness . . . is perhaps one of those ironies which seem to be in store for those who, for whatever reasons, try to manipulate political facts and historical records.[30]

29. Hannah Arendt, *Antisemitism*, part 1 of *The Origins of Totalitarianism* (New York: Harcourt, Brace and World, 1968), vii.

30. Arendt, *Antisemitism*, viii–ix. See also Katz, *Exclusiveness and Tolerance*, chapter 12, which Arendt quotes in this passage.

Arendt's thesis has been supported most recently by Norman G. Finkelstein, the son of Holocaust survivors, among others.[31]

Both the Fascists and the Nazis at one time or another informed the Church that their anti-Semitic program simply continued the prevailing anti-Judaism sanctioned by the papacy and long practiced by the Church. However, the future Führer, in a letter of 16 September 1919, indicated otherwise. "Anti-Semitism as a political movement," he wrote, "must be based on a matter of race and not of religion," a position maintained also in *Mein Kampf*.[32] Convinced that Jews were members of a race rather than a religion, he warned they could not be sufficiently combated on a religious basis, for "a splash of baptismal water could always save the business and the Jews at the same time."[33] The Nazi periodical *Wille und Macht* resented Pius XI's interference regarding the Reich's policy toward the Jews, and it made the same argument—that this was a matter of race rather than religion, so that the state rather than the Church had authority. Indeed, *Der Angriff*, the newspaper of the German Labor front, charged that this pope's unwarranted defense of the Jews rendered him the "legal defender of racial pollution."[34] Likewise, the "Fascist Manifesto on Race," published in the *Giornale d'Italia* on 15 July 1938, claimed that Italian anti-Semitism was purely biological, without philosophical or religious foundation. In Il Duce's view, the Jewish problem had "to be placed not on the political or religious, but squarely on the racial plane."[35]

The precise relationship between the papal policy of disparagement and partial protection of Jews and the Nazi genocide remains uncertain. Many who were raised in the anti-Judaic heritage and were contemptuous of Jews never became anti-Semites. Some have assumed that the peasants of southern Italy, steeped in Catholicism's anti-Judaism, were ripe for recruitment to the Fascist program. This is disputed by Arturo Carlo Jemolo, who tells of a Jewish friend of his, exiled to a southern Ital-

31. Norman G. Finkelstein, "Reflections on the Goldhagen Phenomenon," in Norman G. Finkelstein and Ruth Bettina Birn, *A Nation on Trial: The Goldhagen Thesis and Historical Truth* (New York: Henry Holt, 1998), 92–93.

32. Quoted in Krausnick, "Persecution of the Jews," 21.

33. Adolf Hitler, *Mein Kampf* (Boston: Houghton Mifflin, 1943), 120.

34. *Persecution of the Catholic Church in the Third Reich*, 242, 418.

35. "Marcello Ricci: una testimonianza sulle origini del razzismo fascista," ed. Mario Toscano, *Storia Contemporanea* 27 (Oct. 1996): 895–96; Bernardini, "Origins and Development of Racial Anti-Semitism," 442.

ian village for antifascist activities, who aroused the curiosity of his peasant hostess by never attending mass. When he explained that he was a Jew, she responded, quite dumbfounded, "Nonsense, you're just as white as I am!" In fact, Andrew Canepa credits the influence of Catholicism, among other things, for the lack of xenophobia and anti-Semitism in Italy.[36] Even some of Rome's most severe critics do not blame the Church for the Holocaust. In *Hitler's Willing Executioners,* Goldhagen, who charges that the disparagement of Jews was central to Christianity, concludes that the Church wished not to kill but to convert the Jews. In a later work he acknowledges that the relationship between anti-Semitic belief and anti-Jewish action is complex and open to interpretation, and that, at the very least, anti-Judaism was refracted through the lens of each national culture.[37]

Indeed, one author has found that religious Poles, who were steeped in the "teaching of contempt" toward Jews, were no more likely either to attack or to rescue Jews than were their secular or atheistic compatriots.[38] Likewise, David Kertzer, although critical of the papal attitude toward Jews, acknowledges that European anti-Semitism cannot be attributed wholesale to the papacy and the Church, and he notes that many of the Church's mortal enemies were virulently anti-Semitic. Hans Küng reports that what the Nazis added to anti-Judaism was the racial element, whose theoretical foundation was prepared by the Frenchman Count Arthur Gobineau and the Anglo-German Houston Stewart Chamberlain and executed by the Nazis in their death camps.[39] Very often these writers depict the Church as monolithic, instead of probing the words and works of "individual popes, theologians, bishops or of legal texts or canons of council." We might add that one cannot probe or assess the Catholic attitude toward relations with the Jews by studying papal documents alone.[40] Indeed, toward the end of John Paul II's pontificate, as in the last years of that of

---

36. Canepa, "Reflections on Antisemitism," 107–8.

37. Daniel Jonah Goldhagen, *Hitler's Willing Executioners: Ordinary Germans and the Holocaust* (New York: Knopf, 1996), 53; Goldhagen, "What Would Jesus Have Done?" 22, 33.

38. See Nechama Tec, *When Light Pierced the Darkness: Christian Rescue of Jews in Nazi-Occupied Poland* (New York: Oxford University Press, 1986).

39. Kertzer, *Popes against the Jews,* 16–17; Küng, "From Anti-Semitism to Theological Dialogue," 12.

40. Roth, "Bishops and Jews in the Middle Ages," 1–2.

Pius XI, some have questioned whether the pope's pronouncements were his own or those of the men surrounding him.[41]

The extent to which anti-Judaism facilitated anti-Semitism is difficult if not impossible to assess. That the former had some impact upon the latter even the papacy and the hierarchy agree, and recognition of the relationship between the two unquestionably played a part in the determined efforts of the Second Vatican Council to eradicate anti-Judaic convictions from its teaching following the horror of the Holocaust. John Paul II called on Catholics throughout the world to accept some responsibility for the religious pretenses used by Nazi hatemongers, acknowledging that it was easier for Christians to ignore the brutality of the death camps in light of their mistaken belief in the responsibility of the Jews for Christ's death. "In the Christian world . . . the wrong and unjust interpretations of the New Testament relating to the Jewish people," he said, "contributed to soothing consciences to the point that when a wave of persecutions swept Europe fueled by pagan anti-Semitism . . . the spiritual resistance of many was not that which humanity expected from the Disciples of Christ."[42] John Paul II stopped short of criticizing his vicar, and continuously and ardently defended Pope Pius XII. In the modern era, few popes have openly criticized their predecessors. Nonetheless, John Paul II recognized the Holocaust as a Christian, if not a papal, problem.

In 1998, at the request of the bishops of Poland, John Paul composed a prayer for the Jews, which is now read annually on Poland's day of reflection on the Jews and Judaism, providing a broader model worldwide on how Catholics should pray for Jews. It reads:

God of Abraham, the prophets, Jesus Christ, in you everything is em-
    braced, toward you everything moves, you are the end of all things.
Hear the prayers we extend for the Jewish people
Which, thanks to its forefathers, is still very dear to you.
Instill within them a constant, ever livelier desire to deepen your truth
    and love.
Help them, as they yearn for peace and justice, that they may reveal to the
    world the might of your blessing.

41. John Thavis, "At Vatican, It's Not Always Clear Who Speaks for Pope," *Brooklyn Tablet*, 24 Jan. 2004, 9.
42. Quoted in Lederer, "2000 Years," 2.

Succor them, that they may obtain respect and love from those who do
not yet understand the greatness of suffering they have borne, and
those who, in solidarity and a sense of mutual care, experience together the pain of wounds inflicted upon them.

Remember the new generations of youth and children, that they may, un-
changeably faithful to you, uphold what remains the particular mystery of their vocation.

Strengthen all generations so that, thanks to their testimony, humanity
will understand that your salvific intention extends over all the human family, and that you, God, are for all nations the beginning and
the final end.[43]

In "We Remember," the papacy called for universal Catholic repentance for the direct sins of Catholics involved in the Holocaust as well as
repentance for the indirect, malevolent effects of Christian polemics
against Jews that arose from the misinterpretation of Scripture.

The popes since Vatican II—John XXIII, Paul VI, John Paul I, John
Paul II, and Benedict XVI—have done a considerable amount to rectify
mistaken notions regarding the Catholic attitude toward the Jews and
have abandoned attempts at proselytism. Thus today there exists not one
Church-sanctioned organization for the conversion of Jews.[44] Although
Church officials have repeatedly denounced earlier "mistaken" teaching
and practices regarding the Jews, the ultimate institutional responsibility
for the failures has not been sufficiently explored. The Vatican's apparent
support for the beatification of Sister Anne Catherine Emmerich, who has
been accused of drafting anti-Semitic reflections on the Passion of Christ,
has caused confusion and consternation among some Catholics and Jews.
Despite these and other shortcomings, a real reconciliation between
Christians and Jews has commenced, and a considerable literature has
emerged to shed light on its implications for both faiths.[45] There is also a

---

43. Quoted in Keeler, "Catholic Church and the Jewish People."

44. Eugene Fisher, "The New Agenda of Catholic-Jewish Relations," July 2001,
http://www.bc.edu/research/cjl/meta-elements/texts/articles/Fisher_New Agenda.htm, accessed 2 Feb. 2004.

45. Among the useful volumes in this regard one should mention *The Holocaust. Never
to Be Forgotten: Reflections on the Holy See's Document "We Remember"* (Mahwah, N.J.:
Paulist Press, 2001) which includes the text of the document, commentaries by Cardinal Avery Dulles and Rabbi Leon Klenicki, as well as an address by Cardinal Edward Cassidy,

broad consensus, although not total agreement, that the popes following the Second Vatican Council, and most notably Pope John Paul II, have helped the Church come to terms with two important events in Christian and Jewish history, the Holocaust and a restored Israel.[46]

---

ex-president of the Holy See's Commission for Religious Relations with the Jews. *Humanity at the Limit: The Impact of the Holocaust Experience on Jews and Christians,* ed. Rabbi Michael A. Signer (Bloomington: Indiana University Press, 2000), contains thirty-two essays by Jewish and Christian scholars that dwell on the consequences for both faiths.

    46. Littell, "Uprooting Antisemitism," 24.

SELECT BIBLIOGRAPHY

Primary Sources

Abbott, Walter M., ed. *The Documents of Vatican II.* New York: America Press, 1966.

Acta Nuniature Polanae: Achille Ratti (1918–1921). Rome: Rome Institutum Historicum Polonicum, 1995.

Acta Pio IX. Pontificis Maximi. Pars prima acta exhibens quae ad Ecclesiam universam spectant (1846–1854). Rome: Artium, 1855.

Acta Romana Societatis Iesu, vol. 7 (1932–34); vol. 9 (1935–40). Rome, 1935, 1941.

Acta Summi Pontificis Joannis XXIII. 2 vols. Vatican City: Typis Polyglottis, 1960, 1964.

Acta Synodalia Concilii Vaticani Secundi. Vatican City: Editrice Vaticana, 1965.

Actes et documents du Saint Siège relatifs à la second guerre mondiale. Ed. Pierre Blett, Robert A. Graham, Angelo Martini, and Burkhard Schneider. Rome: Libreria Editrice Vaticana, 1965–81.

Actes de Benoit XV: Encycliques, motu proprio, brefs, allocutions, actes des dicastres. Paris: Bonne Presse, 1926–34.

Actes de Leon XIII: Encycliques, motu proprio, brefs, allocutions, actes des dicastres. Paris: Bonne Presse, 1931–37.

Actes di S.S. Pie XI: Encycliques, motu proprio, brefs, allocutions, actes des dicastres. Paris: Bonne Presse, 1932–36.

Akten deuschen Bischofe uber die Loge der Kirche, 1933–1945. Mainz: Grünwold, 1976–79.

Akten Kardinal Michael von Faulhabers, 1917–1945. 2 vols. Ed. Ludwig Volk, S.J. Mainz: Grunwald, 1978.

Alfieri, Dino. *Dictators Face to Face.* Trans. David Moore. Westport, Conn.: Greenwood Press, 1978.

Althaus, Friedrich, ed. *The Roman Journals of Ferdinand Gregorovius, 1852–1874.* London: George Bell and Sons, 1906.

Anderson, Floyd, ed. *Council Daybook: Vatican II, Sessions 1 and 2.* Washington, D.C.: National Catholic Welfare Conference, 1965.

Appeals for Peace of Pope Benedict XV and Pope Pius XI. Washington, D.C.: Catholic Association for International Peace, 1931.

Atti del Sommo Pontefice Pio IX, Felicemente Regnante. Parte seconda che comprende I Motu-proprii, chirografi editti, notificazioni, ec. per lo stato pontificio. Rome: Tipografia delle Belle Arti, 1857.

Augustine. *City of God.* Ed. David Knowles. Trans. Henry Bettenson. Baltimore: Penguin, 1972.

Berenbaum, Michael, ed. *Witness to the Holocaust.* New York: HarperCollins, 1997.

Bertetto, Domenico, ed. *Discorsi di Pio XI.* 3 vols. Turin: Società Editrice Internazionale, 1959.

Beyer, Jean, S.J., ed. *John Paul II Speaks to Religious.* Baltimore: Little Sisters of the Poor, 1988.

Beyrens, Eugene. *Quatre ans à Rome.* Paris: Plon, 1934.

Blakiston, Noel, ed. *The Roman Question: Extracts from the Despatches of Odo Russell from Rome, 1815–1870.* London: Chapman and Hall, 1962.

Bland, Joan. *The Pastoral Vision of John Paul II.* Chicago: Franciscan-Herald Press, 1982–86.

Blet, Pierre. *Pius XII and the Second World War According to the Archives of the Vatican.* Trans. L. J. Johnson. New York: Paulist Press, 1999.

Boff, Leonardo. *Faith on the Edge: Religion and Marginalized Existence.* New York: Harper and Row, 1989.

Bonaparte, Napoleon. *Correspondance de Napoleon Ier.* Paris: Imprimere Imperiale, 1859.

———. *The Corsican: A Diary of Napoleon's Life in His Own Words.* Ed. R. M. Johnson. Boston: Houghton Mifflin, 1910.

Brady, W. Maziere, ed. *Anglo-Roman Papers.* Vol. 3, *Memoirs of Cardinal Erskine, Papal Envoy to the Court of George III.* London: Alexander Gardner, 1890.

Braham, Randolph L., ed. *The Vatican and the Holocaust: The Catholic Church and the Jews during the Nazi Era.* New York: Columbia University Press, 2000.

Bressan, Edoardo. "L'Osservatore Romano e le relazioni internazionali della Santa Sede (1917–1922)." In *Benedetto XV e la Pace—1918,* ed. Giorgio Rumi, 233–53. Brescia: Morcelliana, 1990.

Brunacci, A. *Ebrei in Assisi duante la guerra. Ricordi di un protagonista.* Assisi, n.d.

Bullarii Romani Continuatio. Ed. Andreas Barberi. Rome: Camerae Apostolicae, 1835–55.

Butler, Cuthbert. *The Vatican Council: The Story Told from Inside in Bishop Ullathorne's Letters.* New York: Longmans, Green, 1930.

Cani, A., and F. Vitozzi, eds. *Processo Romana per la causa di Beatificazione . . . del Servo di Dio, Papa Pio IX.* Torre del Greco: Palomba, 1908.

Capovilla, Loris F., ed. *Giovanni XXIII. Quindici Letture.* Rome: Edizioni di Storia e Letteratura, 1970.

Caprara, Jean. *Concordat, et recueil des bulles et brefs de N.S.P., le Pape Pie VII, sur les affaires actuelles de l'Église de France.* Liege: Lemarie, 1802.

Caprile, Giovanni, ed. *Il Concilio Vaticano II.* 5 vols. Rome: Civiltà Cattolica, 1965.

———. *(Paul VI) Il Sinodo dei vescovi. Interventi e documentazione.* Rome: Edizione Studium, 1992.

———. *Karol Wojtyla e il Sinodo dei Vescovi.* Vatican City: Vatican Press, 1980.

Carlen, Claudia, ed. *A Guide to the Encyclicals of Roman Pontiffs from Leo XIII to the Present Day, 1878–1937.* New York: H. W. Wilson Co., 1939.

———. *Papal Pronouncements: A Guide, 1740–1978.* Vol. 1, *Benedict XIV to Paul VI;* vol. 2, *Paul VI to John Paul I.* Ann Arbor: Pierian Press, 1990.

———. *The Papal Encyclicals.* Vol. 1, *1740–1878;* vol. 2, *1878–1903;* vol. 3, *1903–1939;* vol. 4, *1939–1958;* vol. 5, *1958–1981.* Raleigh, N.C.: McGrath Publishing, 1981.

Casella, Mario. "La crisi del 1938 fra Stato e Chiesa nella documentazione dell'Archivio Storico Diplomatic degli Affari Esteri." In *Rivista di Storia della Chiesa in Italia* 54 (January–June 2000): 91–186.

Castelli, Michelangelo. *Ricordi di Michelangelo Castelli.* Turin: Roux e Favale, 1888.

Catechism of the Catholic Church. Mahwah, N.J.: Paulist Press, 1994.

Catholics Remember the Holocaust. Washington, D.C.: National Conference of Catholic Bishops, 1998.

Cattaneo, Carlo. *Ricerche economiche sulle interdizioni imposte dalla legge civile agli Israeliti.* Milan, 1835.

Cavagna, A. M., ed. *Pio XI e l'Azione Catolica. Documenti relativi a l'A.C.I.* Rome: Ferrari, 1929.

Cavalleri, Ottavio, and Germano Gualdo, eds. *L'Archivio de Mons. Achille Ratti visitatore apostolico e nunzio a Varsavia (1918–1921).* Vatican City: Archivio Vaticano, 1990.

Cavour, Camillo di. *Diari (1833–1856).* Ed. Alfonso Bogge. Rome: Ministero Beni Culturali, 1991.

Cerio, F. Diaz de, and M. F. Nunex y Monez, eds. *Instrucciones secretas a los nuncios de Espana en el siglio XIX (1847–1907).* Rome: Editrice Pontificia Univesità Gregoriana, 1989.

Charles-Roux, François. *Huit ans au Vatican.* Paris: Flammarion, 1947.

Chassin, C. L., ed. *Les elections et les Cahiers de Paris en 1789.* Paris: Maison Quantin, 1888.

Ciano, Galeazzo. *Ciano's Hidden Diaries, 1937–1938.* New York: E. P. Dutton, 1953.

———. *Diario.* Milan: Rizzoli, 1950.

———. *L'Europa vers la Catasrofe.* Verona: Mondadori, 1948.

Cianfarra, Camille M. *The War and the Vatican.* London: Oates and Washbourne, 1945.

Codex Iuris Canonici Pii X. Rome: Typis Polyglottis Vaticanis, 1947.

Colalpietra, Rafaele. "Il Diario del Conclave del 1829." *Critica Storica* 1 (1962): 517–41.

———. "Il Diario Brunelli del Conclave del 1823." *Archivio Storico Italiano* 120 (1962): 76–146.

Collecion de Enciclicas y Otras Cartas de los Papas Gregory XVI, Leon XIII, Pio X, Bededicto XV y Pio XI. Madrid: Saes Hermanos, 1935.

Collins, Joseph B., ed. *Chatechetical Documents of Pope Pius X.* New York: Saint Anthony Guild Press, 1946.

Commission for Religious Relations with the Jews. "Guidelines and Suggestions for Implementing the Conciliar Declaration Nostra Aetate." 1 December 1974. In *The Vatican and the Holocaust: The Catholic Church and the Jews during the Nazi Era,* ed. Randolph L. Braham, 113–21. New York: Columbia University Press, 2000.

———. "Notes on the Correct Way to Present the Jews and Judaism in Preaching and Catechesis in the Roman Catholic Church." 24 June 1985. In *The Vatican and the Holocaust: The Catholic Church and the Jews during the Nazi Era,* ed. Randolph L. Braham, 123–36. New York: Columbia University Press, 2000.

Commissione per la pubblicazione dei Documenti diplomatici. *I Documenti Diplomatici Italiani.* 8th series, vol. 13; 9th series, vol. 3. Rome: Libreria dello Stato, 1953, 1959.

Consalvi, Ercole. *Memorie del Cardinale Ercole Consalvi.* Ed. Mario Nassali Rocca. Rome: Signorelli, 1950.

Consular Relations between the United States and the Papal States: Instructions and Despatches. Ed. Leo Francis Stock. Washington, D.C.: Catholic University of America Press, 1945.

Correspondence between President Roosevelt and Pope Pius XII. New York: Macmillan, 1947.

Correspondence between President Truman and Pope Pius XII. New York, 1952.

Crétineau Joly, J., ed. *Mémoires du Cardinal Consalvi, secrétario d'état de Pape Pie VII.* 2 vols. Paris: Plon, 1864.

Crispolti, Filippo. *Pio IX, Leone XIII, Pio X, Benedetto XV. Ricordi personali.* Milan: Treves, 1932.

Dalla Torre, Giuseppe. *Azione Cattolica e fascismo.* Rome, 1945.

Dalla Torre, Paolo. *Pio IX e Vittorio Emanuele II. Dal loro carteggio privato negli anni del licaceramento (1865–1878).* Rome: Istituto di Studi Romani Editore, 1972.

De Ecclesia: The Constitution of the Church of Vatican II Proclaimed by Pope Paul VI. Glen Rock, N.J.: Paulist Press, 1965.

De Gasperi, Alcide. *Lettere sul Concordato.* Brescia: Morcellinana, 1979.

Discorsi e Radio Messagi di Sua Santità Pio XII. 2 vols. Milan: Società Editrice "Vita e Pensiero," 1941.

Discorsi, messaggi, colloqui del Santo Padre Giovanni XXIII. 5 vols. Vatican City: Tipografia Poliglotta, 1961–67.

Discorsi Parlamentari di Giovanni Giolitti. 4 vols. Rome: Tipografia della Camera dei Deputati, 1953–56.

Discourses of the Popes from Pius XI to John Paul II to the Pontifical Academy of Sciences, 1936–1986. Vatican City: Pontificia Academia Scientiarum, 1986.

Documents on British Foreign Policy, 1919–1939. 2d series. Vol. 5. London: H. M. Stationery Office, 1956.

Documents on German Foreign Policy, 1918–1945. Ed. Paul R. Sweet. London: H. M. Stationery Office, 1937–57.

Documents sur la négociation du concordat e sur les autres rapports de la France avec le Saint-Siège en 1800 et a 1801. Ed. A. H. Boulay de la Meurte. 6 vols. Paris: Leroux, 1891–1905.

Doing the Truth in Charity: Statements of Pope Paul VI, John Paul I, and John Paul II. Ed. John B. Sheerin. New York: Paulist Press, 1982.

Duerm, Charles van, ed. *Correspondance du Cardinal Hercule Consalvi avec le Prince Clément de Metternich.* Louvain: Polleunlis and Ceuterick, 1899.

———. *Un peu plus de lumiere sur le conclave de Venise et sur le commencements du pontificat de Pie VII, 1799–1800.* Louvain: University Press, 1896.

Ecumenical Council, Vatican II. "Declaration on the Relationship of the Church to Non-Christian Religions" ("Nostra aetate," 28 October 1965). In *The Vatican and the Holocaust: The Catholic Church and the Jews during the Nazi Era,* ed. Randolph L. Braham, 111–12. New York: Columbia University Press, 2000.

Ellis, John Tracy, ed. *Documents of American Catholic History.* Chicago: Henry Regnery Co., 1967.

Fappani, Antonio, and Franco Molinari, eds. *Giovanni Battista Montini Giovane. Documenti inediti e tesitomonianze.* Turin: Marietti, 1979.

Farini, Luigi Carlo. *Lo stato romano dall'anno 1815 al 1850.* Florence: Le Monnier, 1853.

Farinacci, Roberto. *La Chiesa e gli ebrei.* Rome: Tevere, 1938.

Federzoni, Luigi. 1927. *Diario di un ministro del fascismo.* Ed. Adriana Macchi. Florence: Pasigli Editori, 1993.

Ferrajoli, Alessandro, ed. *Lettere inedite di Antonio Canova al Cardinale Ercole Consalvi.* Rome: Forzani, 1888.

Filipuzzi, Angelo. *Pio IX e la politica Austriaca in Italia dal 1815 al 1848*. Florence: Felice Le Monnier, 1958.

Fisher, Eugene, et al. *Twenty Years of Jewish-Catholic Relations*. Mahwah, N.J.: Paulist Press, 1986.

Flannery, Austin, ed. *Vatican Council II: The Conciliar and Post Conciliar Documents*. 2 vols. Grand Rapids: Eerdmans, 1992.

Fleury, Comte. *Mémoirs of the Empress Eugenie*. New York: Appleton and Co., 1920.

Franciscis, Pasquale de, ed. *Discorsi del Sommo Pontefice Pio IX Pronunziati in Vaticano ai fedeli di Roma e dell'orbe dal principio della sua prigionia fino al presente*. 4 vols. Rome: G. Aurelj, 1872.

Foundations for Peace: Letters of Pope Pius XII and President Roosevelt. London: Catholic Truth Society, 1941.

Franco, Giovanni Giuseppe. *Appunti storici sopra il Concilio Vaticana*. Ed. Giacomo Martina. Rome: Università Gregoriana Editrice, 1972.

Fremantle, Anne, ed. *The Papal Encyclicals in Their Historical Context*. New York: G. P. Putnam's Sons, 1956.

Frossard, Andre. *"Be Not Afraid": Pope John Paul Speaks Out on His Life, His Beliefs, and His Inspiring Vision for Humanity*. Trans. J. R. Foster. New York: St. Martin's Press, 1984.

Gabriele, Mariano, ed. *Il Carteggio Antonelli-Sacconi (1850–1860)*. Rome: Istituto per la Storia del Risorgimento Italiano, 1962.

Gasquet, Cardial. *A Memoir*. New York: P. J. Kenedy and Sons, 1953.

Gilson, Étiene, ed. *The Church Speaks to the Modern World: The Social Teachings of Leo XIII*. New York: Image Books, 1954.

Giolitti, Giovanni. *Memoirs of My Life*. Trans. Edward Storer. New York: Howard Fertig, 1973.

Giorani. Igino. *Encicliche sociali dei papi*. Rome: Editrice Studium, 1942.

Giovanni XXIII. *Lettere, 1958–1963*. Ed. Loris Capovilla. Rome: Edizioni di storia e letteratura, 1978.

Goodich, Michael. *Other Middle Ages: Witnesses at the Margins of Medieval Society*. Philadelphia: University of Pennsylvania Press, 1998.

Great Britain, Foreign Office. *British and Foreign State Papers*. Vol. 36 (1847-48); vol. 37 (1848–49). London: H. M. Stationery Office, n.d.

———. *British Documents on the Origins of the War, 1898–1914*. Ed. George P. Gooch and Harold Temperly. London: H. M. Stationery Office, 1926.

Gregorovius, Ferdinand. *The Ghetto and the Jews of Rome*. Trans. Moses Hadas. New York: Schocken Books, 1966.

Grissell, Hartwell de La Garde. *Sede Vacante, Being a Diary Written during the Conclave of 1903*. London: James Parker, 1903.

Guitton, Jean. *Dialogues avec Paul VI*. Paris: Fayard, 1967.

Hachey, Thomas E., ed. *Anglo-Vatican Relations, 1914–1939: Confidential Reports of the British Minister to the Holy See*. Boston: G. K. Hall, 1972.

Haffner, Paul, ed. *Discourses of the Pope from Pius XI to John Paul II to the Pontifical Academy of Sciences*. Vatican City: Pontificia Academia, 1986.

Herzl, Theodor. *Diaries*. Trans. Marvin Lowenthal. New York: Dial Press, 1956.

Hill, L. E., ed. *Die Wiezsacker Papiere 1933–1950*. Frankfurt: Allstein, 1974.

Hitler, Adolf. *Mein Kampf*. Boston: Houghton Mifflin, 1943.

Hitler's Secret Conversations. 1941–1944. New York: Farrar, Straus and Cudahy, 1953.

Holy See's Commission for Religious Relations with the Jews. "We Remember: A Reflection on the Shoah" (March 1998). In *The Vatican and the Holocaust: The Catholic Church and the Jews during the Nazi Era*, ed. Randolph L. Braham, 100–109. New York: Columbia University Press, 2000.

House, Edward Mandell, and Charles Seymour. *What Really Happened at Paris*. New York: Scribner's, 1921.

Hughes, Michael, and Mitchell Allen, eds. *German Parliamentary Debates, 1848–1933*. New York: Peter Lang, 2003.

Il Congresso di Vienna del 1815 e la Precedenza dei Rappresentati pontificii nel corpo diplomatico. Relazione del Cardinale Ercole Consalvi, Segret. di Stato e Ministro Plenipotenziario del Sommo Pontifice Pio VII al Cardinale B. Pacca, Camerlengo di S.R.C. Pro Secrtari di Stato. Rome: Tipografia vaticana, 1899.

Insegnamenti di Paolo VI. 16 vols. Vatican City: Libreria Editrice Vaticana, 1963–77.

"Inter Arma Caritas": The Vatican Office of Information for Prisoners of War, Instituted by Pius XII (1939–1947). Vatican City: Vatican Archives, 2004.

Intervento dell'Italia nei documenti segreti dell'Intesa. Rome: Casa Editrice Rassegna Internazionale, 1923.

Italia, Commissione per la publicazione dei Documenti Diplomatici. *I Documenti Dipoltatici Italiani. Prime Serie (1861–70)*. Rome: Libreria dello Stato, 1952.

Jabalot, Ferdinando. *Degli ebrei nei loro rapporti colle nazioni cristiane*. Rome: Poggioli, 1825.

John XXIII. *Journal of a Soul*. Ed. Loris Capovilla. Trans. Dorothy White. New York: McGraw-Hill, 1965.

———. *Letters to his Family*. Ed. Loris Capovilla. Trans. Dorothy White. New York: McGraw-Hill, 1970.

John Paul II. *Crossing the Threshold of Hope*. Ed. Vittorio Messori. New York: Knopf, 1994.

———. *Person and Community: Selected Essays by Karol Wojtyla*. Trans. Theresa Sandok, O.S.M. New York: Peter Lang, 1993.

———. *Pilgrim of Peace: Homilies and Addresses*. New York: Harmony Books, 1987.

———. *Speeches and Selections*. Warsaw: Warszawa Instyhut, 1991.

———. *Spiritual Pilgrimage: Texts on Jews and Judaism, 1979–1995*. Ed. Eugene J. Fisher and Leon Klenicki. New York: Crossroad, 1995.

———. *The Poetry of John Paul II. Roman Triptych: Meditations*. Washington, D.C.: USCCB Publishing, 2003.

———. *Toward a Philosophy of Praxis*. New York: Crossroad, 1981.

Keeler, Cardinal William H. "The Catholic Church and the Jewish People." Available at http://www.bc.edu/research/cjl/meta-elements/texts/articles/keeler_ICCJ_2003.htm.

Kenzler, George, and Vokder Fabricus, eds. *Die Kirchen im dritten Reich*. Frankfurt: Fischer, 1984.

Kertesz, G. A., ed. *Documents in the Political History of the European Continent, 1815–1939*. Oxford: Clarendon Press, 1968.

Koenig, Harry C., ed. *Principles for Peace: Selections from Papal Documents from Leo XIII to Pius XII*. Washington, D.C.: National Catholic Welfare Conference, 1943.

La Briere, Yves de. *La Patrie et la Paix: Textes pontificaux traduits et commentes.* Paris: Desclee, 1938.

Lansang, Robert. *The Big Four and Others of the Peace Conference.* Boston: Houghton Mifflin, 1921.

L'archivio di Monsignor Achille Ratti visitatore apostolico e nunzio a Varsavia (1918–1921). Ed. Ottavio Cavalleri. Vatican City: Archivio Vaticano, 1990.

Leonis XIII Pontificis Maximi Acta. 23 vols. Rome: Ex Typographia Vaticana, 1881–1905.

Lehnert, Pascalina. *Pio XII. Il prilegio di servivlo.* Milan: Rusconi, 1984.

Leiber, Robert, S.J. "Pius as I Knew Him." *The Catholic Mind* 57 (1959): 292–304.

Leroy, Pierre S.J., ed. *Letters from My Friend Teilhard de Chardin.* Trans. Mary Lukas. New York: Paulist Press, 1976.

Lettres apostoliques de S.S. Pie X. Encycliques, motu proprio, brefs, allocutions, actes des dicastres. 8 vols. Paris: Bonne Press, 1930–36.

Levy, Richard S., ed. *Antisemitism in the Modern World: An Anthology of Texts.* Lexington, Mass.: D. C. Heath, 1991.

Littell, Franklin Hamlin. "Reaction of a Protestant Theologian to the Vatican's We Remember Document." In *The Vatican and the Holocaust: The Catholic Church and the Jews during the Nazi Era,* ed. Randolph L. Braham, 71–87. New York: Columbia University Press, 2000.

Lloyd George, David. War Memoirs. Vol. 4. Boston: Little, Brown, 1937.

Loisy, Alfred. *Mémoires pour servir à l'histoire religieuse de notre tesmps.* Paris: E. Mourry Editeur, 1931.

L'Opera della Santa Sede nella Guerra Europea. Raccolta dei documenti (Agosto 1914–Luglio 1916). Rome: Tipografia Poliglotta Vaticana, 1916.

Luciani, Albino. *Illustrisimi: Letters from Pope John Paul I.* Trans. William Weaver. Boston: Little, Brown, 1976.

———. *The Message of John Paul I.* Boston: Daughters of St. Paul, 1978.

Ludwig, Emil. *Talks with Mussolini.* Boston: Little, Brown, 1933.

Lukacs, Lajos. *The Vatican and Hungary, 1846–1878: Reports and Correspondence on Hungary of the Apostolic Nuncios in Vienna.* Trans. Zsofia Kormos. Budapest: Akademiai Kiado, 1981.

Macmillan, Harold. *The Blast of War, 1939–1945.* New York: Harper and Row, 1968.

Madges, William, and Micael J. Daley, eds. *Vatican II: Forty Personal Stories.* Mystic, Conn.: Twenty-Third Publications, 2003.

Malgeri, F. ed. *Gli atti dei congressi del partito popolare italiano.* Brescia: Morcelliana, 1969.

Maffi, Pietro. *Lettere, omelie, e discorsi.* Turin: Società Editrice Internazionale, 1931.

Maioli, Giovanni, ed. *Pio IX da Vescovo a Pontifice. Lettere al Card Luigi Amat, Agosto 1839–Luglio 1848.* Modena: Società Tipografico Modonese, 1943.

Marx, Karl. *The Communist Manifesto.* Ed. Frederic L. Bender. New York: W. W. Norton, 1988.

Massari, Giuseppe. *Diario delle cento voci.* Bologna: Cappelli, 1959.

Mazzini, Joseph. *Italy, Austria, and the Pope.* London: Albonesi, 1845.

McCormick, Anne O'Hare. *Vatican Journal, 1921–1954.* New York: Ferrar, Straus and Cudahy, 1957.

Melady, Thomas Patrick. *The Ambassador's Story: The United States and the Vatican in World Affairs*. Huntington, Ind.: Our Sunday Visitor, 1994.

Melzi d'Eril, Francesco. *I carteggi di Francesco Melzi d'Eril*. Ed. Carlo Zoghi. 5 vols. Milan: Museo del Risorgimento, 1958–61.

Mercier, Cardinal. *Per Crucem ad Lucem. Lettres Pastorales*. Paris: Bloud et Gay, 1916.

Messages of John Paul II. Ed. the Daughters of St. Paul. Boston: St. Paul Editions, 1979.

Metternich, Klemens von. *Mémoires, Documents écrits divers laissés par le prince de Metternich*. Ed. Prince Richard Mettternich. 8 vols. Paris: Plon, 1880–84.

Metternich-Winneburg, Richard, ed. *Memoirs of Prince Mettenich, 1773–1815*. Trans. Mrs. Alexander Napier. New York: Howard Fertig, 1970.

Miller, J. Michael, ed. *The Encyclicals of John Paul II*. Huntington, Ind.: Our Sunday Visitor, 1999.

Minghetti, Marco. *Miei Ricordi*. 3d ed. Turin: Roux, 1888.

Momigliano, Eucardio, ed. *Tutte le encicliche dei sommi Pontefici*. Milan: Dall'Oglio Editore, 1959.

Monti, Antonio. *Pio IX nel Risorgimento Italiano con documenti inediti*. Bari: Laterza, 1928.

Montini, Giovanni Battista. *Pensiamo al Concilio*. Milan: Archdiocesen Press, 1962.

———. "Pius XII and the Jews." *Tablet* (London), 29 June 1963.

Morgan, Thomas B. *A Reporter at the Papal Court: A Narrative of the Reign of Pope Pius XI*. New York: Longmans, Green, 1937.

———. *The Listening Post: Eighteen Years on Vatican Hill*. New York: G. P. Putnam's Sons, 1944.

Mosse, George L. *Confronting History: A Memoir*. Madison: University of Wisconsin Press, 2000.

Mourret, Fernand. *Le Concile du Vatican d'apres des Documents inedits*. Paris: Bloud and Gay, 1919.

Mussolini, Benito. *Gli Accordi del Laterano*. Rome: Libreria del Littorio, 1929.

———. *Opera Omnia di Benito Mussolini*. Ed. Edoardo Susmel. 17 vols. Florence: La Fenice, 1958.

Nicholson, Harold. *Peacemaking, 1919*. Boston: Houghton Mifflin, 1933.

Official German Documents Relating to the World War. New York: Oxford University Press, 1923.

O'Connell, William Henry Cardinal. *Recollections of Seventy Years*. Boston, 1935.

O'Gorman, Mother E., ed. *Papal Teachings: The Church*. Boston: Daughters of St. Paul, 1962.

Oncken, Gugliemo. *L'Epoca della Rivoluzione, dell'Impero e delle Guerre D'Indipendenza, 1789–1815*. Milan: Società Editrice Libraria, 1887.

O'Reilly, Bernard. *Life of Leo XIII. From an Authentic Memoir Furnished by his Order*. New York: John Winston Co., 1903.

Orlando, Vittorio Emanuele. *Discorsi per la guerra e per la pace*. Foligno: Campitelli, 1924.

Pacca, Bartolomeo. *Historical Memoirs*. Trans. George Head. London: Longman, 1850.

Pacelli, Eugenio. *Discorsi e Panegirici*. Milan: Società Editrice "Vita e Pensiero," 1939.

Pacelli, Francesco. *Diario della Conciliazione.* Città del Vaticana: Libreria Editrice Vaticana, 1959.

Panciroli, Romeo, ed. *Paolo VI, Pellegrino Apostolico. Discorsi e messagi.* Rome: Studium, 2001.

Papal Teachings: Education. Selected and arranged by the Benedictine Monks of Solesmes. Boston: St. Paul Editions, 1960.

Papal Teachings: Matrimony. Selected and arranged by the Benedictine Monks of Solesmes. Boston: St. Paul Editions, 1963.

Papal Teachings: The Church. Trans. Aldo Rebeschini. Boston: St. Paul Editions, 1960.

Pasolini, Giuseppe. *Memorie, 1815–1876.* Ed. Pietro Desiderio Pasolini. Turin: Bocca, 1887.

Pasztor, Lajos. "Le 'Memorie sul conclave tenuto in Venezia' di Ercole Consalvi." *Archivum Historiae Pontificiae* 3 (1965): 239–308.

Perfetti, Filippo. *Ricordi di Roma.* Florence: G. Barbera, 1861.

Perraud, Cardinal. *Mes relations personelles avec les deux dermiers papes Pie IX et Leon XIII.* Paris: Tequi, 1917.

Pii X Pontificis Maximi Acta or Acta Pio X. 5 vols. Rome: Typographia Vaticana, 1905–14.

Pirri, Pietro, ed. *Pio IX e Vittorio emanuele II dal loro carteggio privato.* Vol. 1, *La laicizzazione dello Stato Sardo, 1848–1856*; vol. 2, *La questione romana, 1856–1864.* Rome: Università Gregoriana, 1944, 1951.

Pistolesi, Erasmo. *Vita del Somo Pontefice Pio VII.* Rome: F. Bourlie, 1824.

Pius XII and Peace, 1939–1940. Washington, D.C.: National Catholic Welfare Conference, 1940.

Proclaiming Justice and Peace: Documents from John XXIII to John Paul II. London: CAFOD, 1984.

Ratti, Achille. *Essays in History.* Freeport, N.Y.: Books for Libraries, 1967.

Ratzinger, Joseph Cardinal, with Vittorio Messori. *Ratzinger Report.* San Francisco: Ignatius Press, 1985.

Records and Documents of the Holy See Relating to the Second World War: The Holy See and the War in Europe, March 1939–August 1940. Washington, D.C.: Corpus Books, 1968.

Remak, Joachim, ed. *The Nazi Years: A Documentary History.* Prospect Heights, Ill.: Waveland Press, 1990.

Rendtorff, Rolf, and Hans Henrix, eds. *Die Kirchen und das Judentum: Dokkumente von 1945 bis 1985.* Paderborn: Bonifotius Press, 1989.

Rinieri, Ilario. *Napoleone e Pio VII, 1803–1813.* Turin: Unione Tipografico Editrice, 1906.

———. ed. *Corrispondenza inedita dei Cardinali Consalvi e Pacca.* Turin: Unione Tipografia Editrice, 1903.

Rivoluzione francese (1787–1799). Repertorio delle fonti archivistiche . . . conservate in Italia e nella città del Vaticano. 4 vols. Rome: Ministero per I beni culturali, 1991.

Roncalli, Angelo. *Scritti e discorsi, 1953–1958.* 4 vols. Rome: Paoline, 1959–62.

Rosmini, Antonio. *Della misssione a Rome.* Turin: Paravia, 1854.

———. *Epistorlario completo.* 13 vols. Casale: Pane, 1887–92.

Roveri, Alessandro, ed. *La missione Consalvi e il Congresso di Vienna*. Rome: Instituto Storico Italiano, 1970–73.

Rudin, A. James. "Reaction of a Jewish Theologian to the Vatican's We Remember Document." In *The Vatican and the Holocaust: The Catholic Church and the Jews during the Nazi Era*, ed. Randolph L. Braham, 89–98. New York: Columbia University Press, 2000.

Salandra, Antonio. *I Discorsi della guerra*. Milan: Treves, 1922.

Salerano, Federico Sclopis di. *Diario Segreto (1859–1878)*. Ed. P. Pietro Pirri. Turin: Deputazione subalpina di storia patria, 1959.

Schaefer, Mary C., ed. *A Papal Peace Mosaic, 1878–1936: Excerpts from the Messages of Popes Leo XIII, Pius X, Benedict XV, and Pius XI*. Washington, D.C.: Catholic Association for International Peace, 1936.

Schneider, Burkhart, ed. *Die Briefe Pius XII an die Deutschen Bischofe, 1939–1946*. Mainz: Grünwald, 1966.

Selected Documents of His Holiness Pope Pius XII: 1939–1958. Washington, D.C.: National Catholic Welfare Conference, n.d.

Selected Papal Encyclicals and Letters, 1928–1931. London: Catholic Truth Society, 1932.

Shire, William L. *Berlin Diary: The Journal of a Foreign Correspondent, 1934–1941*. New York: Knopf, 1941.

Sixteen Encyclicals of His Holiness Pope Pius XI, 1926–1937. Washington, D.C.: National Catholic Welfare Conference, 1938.

Sonnino, Sidney. *Carteggio, 1914–16*. Ed. Pietro Pastorelli. Bari: Laterza, 1974.

———. *Diario*, vol. 1, *1866–1912*, ed. Benjamin F. Brown; vol. 2, *1914–1916*, and 3, *1916–1922*, ed. Pietro Pastorelli. Bari: Laterza, 1972.

———. *Scritti e Discorsi Extraparlamentari, 1870–1920*. 2 vols. Ed. Benjamin F. Brown. Bari: Laterza, 1972.

Spaur, Countess de. *Relations du voyage de Pie IX à Gaete*. Paris: Didlger, 1852.

St. Thomas Aquinas. *St. Thomas Aquinas on Politics and Ethics*. Ed. Paul E. Sigmund. New York: W. W. Norton, 1988.

Shevardnadze, Eduard. *The Future Belongs to Freedom*. New York: Free Press, 1991.

Stock, Leo F., ed. *Consular Relations between the United States and the Papal States: Instructions and Despatches*. Washington, D.C.: Catholic University of America Press, 1945.

Talks of Paul VI, John Paul I, and John Paul II to the Hierarchy of the United States. Boston: St. Paul Editions, 1979.

Tardini, Domenico, ed. *Memories of Pius XII*. Trans. Rosemary Goldie. Westminister, Md.: Newman Press, 1961.

Taylor, Myron C., ed. *Wartime Correspondence between President Roosevelt and Pope Pius XII*. New York: Macmillan, 1947.

Teaching of the Catholic Faith Today: Twentieth-Century Catechetical Documents of the Holy See. Boston: Daughters of St. Paul, 1982.

The Encyclicals and other Messages of John XXIII. Washington, D.C.: The Pope Speaks, 1964.

The Holocaust: Reflections on the Holy See's Document "We Remember." Mahwah, N.J.: Paulist Press, 1986.

The Persecution of the Catholic Church in the Third Reich: Facts and Documents. London: Burns and Oates, 1940.

The Pope and the People: Select Letters and Addresses on Social Questions by Pope Leo XII, Pope Pius X, Pope Benedict XV and Pope Pius XI. London: Catholic Truth Society, 1932.

The Pope Speaks: The Words of Pius XII. New York: Harcourt, Brace, 1940.

The Roman Journals of Ferdinand Gregorovius, 1852–1875. London: George Bell, 1907.

The Teachings of Pope Paul VI. Washington, D.C.: United States Catholic Conference, 1971.

Thomas, Louis, ed. *Journal d'un Conclave*. Paris: Messein, 1913.

Tisserant, Eugene. *L'Église militante*. Paris: Bloud, 1950.

Treaty and Concordat between the Holy See and Italy: Official Documents. Washington, D.C.: National Catholic Welfare Conference, 1929.

United States Department of State. *Papers Relating to the Foreign Relations of the United States: The World War*. Washington, D.C., 1917–18.

Val, Cardinal Merry del. *Memories of Pope Pius X*. Westminster, Md.: Newman Press, 1951.

Veuillot, Pierre. *Notre Sacerdoce. Documents Pontificaux de Pie X à nos jours*. Paris: Fleurus, 1954.

Visconti Venosta, *Giovanni. Memoirs of Youth: Things Seen and Known, 1847–1860*. Trans. William Prall. Boston: Houghton Mifflin, 1914.

Wilk, Stanislaus, ed. *Achille Rtti (1918–1921)*. 5 vols. Rome: Institum Historicum Polonicum Romae, 1995–99.

Wiseman, Cardinal Nicholas Patrick. *Recollections of the Last Four Popes and of Rome in Their Times*. New York: Wagner, 1958.

Wojtyla, Karol. *Person and Community: Selected Essays by Karol Wojtyla*. Trans. Theresa Sandok. New York: Peter Lang, 1993.

Wycislo, Aloysius J. *Vatican II Revisited by One Who Was There*. New York: Alba House, 1987.

Wynne, John J., ed. *The Great Encyclical Letters of Pope Leo XIII*. New York: Benziger Brothers, 1903.

Yzermans, Vincent A., ed. *All Things in Christ: Encyclicals and Selected Documents of Saint Pius X*. New York: Newman Press, 1954.

Zorratini, Pier Cesare Ioly, ed. *Processi del S. Uffizio contro ebrei e guidaizzanti (1642–1681)*. Florence: Oschki Editore, 1993.

Secondary Sources

Abrahams, Israel. *Jewish Life in the Middle Ages*. New York: Meridian Books, 1958.

Adler, Michael. *Jews of Medieval England*. London: Jewish Historical Society of England, 1939.

Allen, John. *All the Pope's Men: The Inside Story of How the Vatican Really Thinks*. New York: Doubleday, 2004.

Alpert, Michael. *Crypto-Judaism and the Spanish Inquisition*. New York: Palgrave, 2001.

Alvarez, David. *Spies in the Vatican: Espionage and Intrigue from Napoleon to the Holocaust*. Lawrence: University Press of Kansas, 2002.

Alvarez, David, and Robert A. Graham, S.J. *Nothing Sacred: Nazi Espionage against the Vatican, 1939–1945.* London: Cass, 1997.

Anderson, Robin. *Between Two Wars: The Story of Pope Pius XI (Achille Ratti) 1922–1939.* Chicago: Franciscan Herald Press, 1977.

Andreotti, Giulio. *La Sciarada di Papa Mastai.* Milan: Rizzoli, 1967.

Angelucci, G. A. *Il grande secretario della Santa Sede. Sunto della vita di Ercole Consalvi.* Rome: Scuola Tipografia, Pio X, 1924.

Aquarone, Alberto. "La restaurazione nello Stato Pontifico ed i suoi indirizzi legislativi." *Archivio della Società Romana di Storia Patria* 78 (1955): 123–63.

Aradi, Zsolt. *Pius XI: The Pope and the Man.* Garden City, N.Y.: Hanover House, 1958.

Arendt, Hannah. *Antisemitism.* New York: Harcourt, Brace and World, 1951.

Aretin, Karl Otmar von. *The Papacy and the Modern World.* Trans. Roland Hill. New York: McGraw-Hill, 1970.

Aron, Robert. *The Jewish Jesus.* Maryknoll, N.Y.: Orbis Books, 1971.

Artaud de Montor, Alexis. *Histoire du Pape Pie VII.* 2 vols. Paris: LeClere, 1836.

Ascoli, Max. "The Roman Church and Political Action." *Foreign Affairs* 13 (April 1935): 441–51.

Aubert, Roger. *Le Pontificat de Pie IX.* Paris: Bloud and Gay, 1952.

———. *The Church in a Secularized Society.* New York: Paulist Press, 1978.

Baeck, Leo. *Judaism and Christianity.* Philadelphia: Jewish Publication Society of America, 1958.

Baer, Yitzhak. *A History of the Jews in Christian Spain.* Trans. Louis Schoffman. Philadelphia: Jewish Publication Society of America, 1961.

Balducci, Ernesto. *John, the Transitional Pope.* New York: McGraw-Hill, 1965.

Balfour, R. E. "The Action Française Movement." *Cambridge Historical Journal* 3, no. 2 (1930): 182–205.

Ballerini, Rafaelle. *Della questione giudaica in Europa.* Prato: Contrucci, 1891.

Balthasar, Hans Urs. von. *Martin Buber and Christianity: A Dialogue between Israel and the Church.* New York: Macmillan, 1962.

Barlas, C. *John XXIII and His Attitude towards the Jews.* Tel Aviv: Davar, 1959.

Barth, Markus. *Israel and the Church: Contribution to Dialogue Vital for Peace.* Richmond: John Knox Press, 1969.

Barthel, Manfred. *The Jesuits: History and Legend of the Society of Jesus.* Trans. Mark Howson. New York: William Morrow and Co., 1984.

Bartlett, J. V. *The Popes: A Papal History.* Scottsdale: Sim Ridge, 1990.

Baum, Gregory. "Essay on Jacques Maritain and the Vatican's Judaism and the Jews." *Newsletter of the Association of Contemporary Church Historians* 8 (Sept. 2002): 1–4.

———. *Is the New Testament Anti-Semitic?* Glenn Rock, N.J.: Paulist Press, 1965.

———. *The Jews and the Gospels.* New York: Newman Press, 1961.

Bea, Augustin Cardinal. *The Church and the Jewish People.* New York: Harper and Row, 1966.

Beaton, Richard. *Isaiah's Christ in Matthew's Gospel.* New York: Cambridge University Press, 2003.

Becker, Adam H. "Anti-Judaism and Care for the Poor in Aphraphat's Demonstration 20." *Journal of Early Christian Studies* 10 (fall 2002): 305–27.

Belloc, Hilaire. *The Jews.* 3d ed. Boston: Houghton Mifflin, 1937.

Bently, Eric. *The Storm over "The Deputy."* New York: Grove Press, 1964.

Berend, Nora. *At the Gate of Christendom: Jews, Muslims, and "Pagans" in Medieval Hungary, c. 1000–c. 1300.* New York: Cambridge University Press, 2001.

Berliner, Abraham. *Storia degeli ebrei di Roma.* Milan: Rusconi, 1992.

Bernardini, Gene. "The Origins and Development of Racial Anti-Semitism in Fascist Italy." *Journal of Modern History* 49, no. 3 (1977): 431–53.

Binchey, D. A. *Church and State in Fascist Italy.* New York: Oxford University Press, 1941.

Bird, Thomas E., ed. *Modern Theologians, Christians and Jews.* New York: Association Press, 1967.

Blakiston, Noel, ed. *The Roman Question: Extracts from the Despatches of Odo Russell from Rome, 1815–1870.* London: Chapman and Hall, 1962.

Blanshard, Paul. *Paul Blanshard on Vatican II.* Boston: Beacon Press, 1966.

Blet, Pierre, S.J. *Pius XII and the Second World War According to the Archives of the Vatican.* Trans. L. J. Johnson. New York: Paulist Press, 1999.

Blustein, Giacomo. *Storia degi Ebrei in Roma.* Milan: Maglione e Strani, 1921.

Bodian, Miriam. "In the Cross-Currrents of the Reformation: Crypto-Jewish Martyrs of the Inquisition, 1570–1670." *Past and Present* 176 (August 2002): 66–104.

Bolkosky, Sidney M. *Searching for Meaning in the Holocaust.* Westport, Conn.: Praeger, 2002.

Bori, Pier Cesare. *Il Vitello d'Oro. Le radici della controversia antigiudaica.* Turin: Boringhieri, 1893.

Borowitz, Judai Eugene, et al. *Image of the Jews: Teacher's Guide to Jews and Their Religion.* New York: Anti-Defamation League of B'nai B'rith, 1970.

Bottum, Joseph, and David G. Dalin, eds., *The Pius Wars: Responses to the Critics of Pius XII.* Lanham, Md.: Lexington Books, 2004.

Bourgeois, Emile, and E. A. Clermont. *Rome et Napoleon III (1849–1870).* Paris: Librarie Armand Colen, 1907.

Braham, Randolph L. *The Destruction of Hungarian Jewry.* New York: Pro Arte, 1963.

———. *The Politics of Genocide.* 2 vols. New York: Columbia University Press, 1981.

———, ed. *The Vatican and the Holocaust: The Catholic Church and the Jews during the Nazi Era.* New York: Columbia University Press, 2000.

Brandon, Samuel George F. *The Fall of Jerusalem and the Christian Church: A Study of the Effects of the Jewish Overthrow of 70 A.D. on Christianity.* New York: Macmillan, 1971.

Branscomb, Bennett Harvie. *Jesus and the Law of Moses.* London: Hodder and Stoughton, 1930.

Brattan, Carl E., and Robert Jensen. *Jews and Christians: People of God.* Grand Rapids: Eerdmans, 2003.

Bratton, Fred Gladstone. *The Crime of Christendom: The Theological Sources of Christian Anti-Semitism.* Boston: Beacon Press, 1969.

Braun, Robert. "The Holocaust and Problems of Historical Representation." *History and Theory* 33 (May 1994): 172–97.

Brechenmacher, Thomas, and Hardy Ostry. *Rom und Jerusalem. Konzil, Pilgerfahrt, Dialog der Religionen.* Trier: Paulinus Verlag, 2000.

Breger, Marshall J., ed. *The Vatican-Israel Accords.* Notre Dame: University of Notre Dame Press, 2004.

Brennan, Anthony. *Pope Benedict XV and the War.* London: King, 1917.

Brennan, James F. *The Reflection of the Dreyfus Affair in the European Press, 1897–1899.* New York: Peter Lang, 1998.

Brennan, Richard. *A Popular Life of Our Holy Father Pope Pius IX.* New York: Benziger Brothers, 1877.

Bressan, Edoardo. "*L'Osservatore Romano* e le relazioni interazionali della Santa Sede (1917–1922)." In *Benedetto XV e la Pace—1918,* ed. Giorgio Rumi, 233–53. Brescia: Morcelliana, 1990.

Brezzi, Paolo. *Stato e Chiesa nell'ottocento.* Turin: Edizioni RAI, 1964.

Brown, M. L. T. *Eugenio: True Hero of the Holocaust.* McKees Rocks, Pa.: St. Andrew's Productions, 2000.

Buber, Martin. *Two Types of Faith: The Interpenetration of Judaism and Christianity.* Trans. Norman Goldhawk. New York: Harper and Row, 1961.

Burton, Katherine. *Leo the Thirteenth: The First Modern Pope.* New York: David McKay Co., 1962.

———. *The Great Mantle: The Life of Giuseppe Melchiore Sarto, Pope Pius X.* Dublin: Clonmore and Reynolds, 1950.

Buttiglione, Rocco. *Karol Wojtyla: The Thought of the Man Who Became Pope John Paul II.* Grand Rapids: Eerdmans, 1997.

Cadbury, Henry J. *The Peril of Modernizing Jesus.* New York: Macmillan, 1937.

Caffiero, M. *La nuova era. Miti e profezie dell'Italia in Rivoluzione.* Genoa: Marietti, 1991.

Canepa, Andrew M. "L'Atteggiamento degli ebrei italiani davanti alla loro seconda emancipazione. Premesse e analisi." *Rassegna Mensile di Israel* (September 1977): 419–36.

———. "Pius X and the Jews: A Reappraisal." *Church History* 61, no. 3 (1992): 362–72.

———. "Reflections on Antisemitism in Liberal Italy." *Wiener Library Bulletin* 31, nos. 47–48 (1978): 104–11.

Capuzzo, Ester. "Gli ebrei e la Repubblica Romana." *Rassegna Storica del Risorgimento* 86, no. 4 (1999): 267–86.

Carmichael, Joel. *The Satanizing of the Jews: Origin and Development of Mystical Anti-Semitism.* New York: Fromm Publishing, 1992.

Carpi, Daniel. "The Catholic Church and Italian Jewry under the Fascists." In *Yad Washem Studies on the European Jewish Catastrophe and Resistance,* ed. Shaul Esh, 43–56. New York: KATV Publishing, 1975.

Carr, William. "Nazi Policy against the Jews." In *Life in the Third Reich,* ed. Richard Bessel, 69–82. New York: Oxford University Press, 1987.

Carroll, James. *Constantine's Sword: The Church and the Jews.* Boston: Houghton Mifflin, 2001.

Casella, Mario. "Chiesa e fascismi nei primi anni del pontificato. Il conflictto su *L'Osservatore Romano.*" *Riviista di Storia della Chiesa in Italia* 55 (January–June 2001): 109–74.

Cessi, Gellio. *Il Cardinale Consalvi ed I primi anni della restaurazione pontificia.* Milan: Soc. Dante Alighieri, 1931.

Chadwick, Owen. *Britain and the Vatican during the Second World War.* Cambridge: Cambridge University Press, 1986

————. *A History of the Popes, 1830–1914.* Oxford: Clarendon Press, 1998.

————. "The Papacy and World War II." *Journal of Ecclesiastical History* 18 (April 1967): 71–79.

————. *The Popes and European Revolution.* Oxford: Clarendon Press, 1981.

Chargueraud, Marc-Andre. *Les Papes et la Shoah, 1932–1945.* Paris: Labor et Fides, 2002.

Chinnici, Joseph P. "Reception of Vatican II in the United States." *Theological Studies* 64 (September 2003): 461–94.

Christianity and Judaism: Papers Read at the 1991 Summer Meeting and the 1992 Winter Meeting of the Ecclesiastical History Society. Cambridge, Mass.: Blackwell, 1992.

Cicognani, Amleto Giovanni. *A Symposium on the Life and Work of Pope Pius X.* Washington, D.C.: Confraternity of Christian Doctrine, 1946.

Clark, Martin. *Modern Italy, 1871–1982.* London: Longman, 1984.

Clonmore, Lord. *Pope Pius XI and World Peace.* London: Robert Hale, 1937.

Cohen, Arthur A. *The Myth of the Judeo-Christian Tradition.* New York: Harper and Row, 1970.

Cohen, Jeremy. *Living Letters of the Law: Ideas of the Jew in Medieval Christianity.* Berkeley and Los Angeles: University of California Press, 1999.

————. *The Friars and the Jews: The Evolution of Medieval Antijudaism.* Ithaca: Cornell University Press, 1982.

Cohen, Marlin A., ed. *The Jewish Experience in Latin America.* 2 vols. New York: KATV, 1971.

Cohen, Roger. "French Church Issues Apology to Jews on War." *New York Times,* 1 Oct. 1997, A8.

Cohn, Haim. *The Trial and Death of Jesus.* New York: Harper and Row, 1971.

Cohn, Norman. *Warrant for Genocide: The Myth of the Jewish World-Conspiracy and the Protocols of the Elders of Zion.* New York: Harper and Row, 1967.

Colapietra, Raffaele. *La Chiesa tra Lamennais e Metternich: Il pontificate di Leone XII.* Brescia: Morcellina, 1963.

————. "Il Diario Brunelli del Conclave del 1823." *Archivio Storico Italiano* 120 (1962): 76–146.

————. *La formazione diplomatica di Leone XII.* Rome: Instituto per la storia del Risorgimento, 1966.

Collinge, William J. *Historical Dictionary of Catholicism.* Lanham, Md.: Scarecrow Press, 1997.

Connelly, Owen. *French Revolution/Napoleonic Era.* New York: Holt, Rinehart and Winston, 1979.

Conway, John S. "The Meeting between Pope Pius XII and Ribbentrop." *Historical Papers of the Canadian Historical Association* (1968): 215–27.

————. *The Nazi Persecution of the Churches, 1933–1945.* London: Weidenfeld and Nicolson, 1968.

————. "The Silence of Pope Pius XII." *Review of Politics* 27 (January 1965): 105–31.

————. "The Vatican and the Holocaust: A Reappraisal." *Miscellanea Historiae Ecclesiasticae* 9 (1984): 475–89.

Conzelmann, Hans. *Gentiles, Jews, Christians: Polemics and Apologetics in the Greco-Roman Era.* Trans. M. Eugene Boring. Minneapolis: Fortress Press, 1992.

Cook, Michael. "The New Testament: Confronting Its Impact on Jewish-Christian Relations." In *Introduction to Jewish-Christian Relations,* ed. Michael Shermis and Arthur E. Zannoni. New York: Paulist Press, 1991.

Coppa, Frank J. "Between Anti-Judaism and Anti-Semitism, Pius XI's Response to the Nazi Persecution of the Jews: Precursor to Pius XII's 'Silence'?" *Journal of Church and State* 47 (winter 2005): 63–89.

———. "Cardinal Antonelli, the Papal States and the Counter-Risorgimento." *Journal of Church and State* 16 (autumn 1974): 453–71.

———. "Cardinal Giacomo Antonelli: An Accommodating Personality in the Politics of Confrontation." *Biography* 2 (fall 1979): 283–302.

———. *Cardinal Giacomo Antonelli and Papal Politics in European Affairs.* Albany: State University of New York Press, 1990.

———. "Giolitti and the Gentiloni Pact between Myth and Reality." *Catholic Historical Review* 53 (July 1967): 217–28.

———. "The Hidden Encyclical of Pius XI against Racism and Anti-Semitism Uncovered—Once Again!" *Catholic Historical Review* 84 (January 1998): 63–72.

———. "Pessimism and Traditionalism in the Personality and Policies of Pio Nono." *Journal of Italian History* 2 (autumn 1979): 209–17.

———. "Pio Nono and the Jews: From 'Reform' to 'Reaction,' 1846–1878." *Catholic Historical Review* 89 (October 2003): 671–95.

———. "Pope Pius XI's 'Encyclical' Humani Generis Unitas against Racism and Anti-Semitism and the 'Silence' of Pope Pius XII." *Journal of Church and State* 40 (autumn 1998): 775–95.

———. "*Realpolitik* and Conviction in the Conflict between Piedmont and the Papacy during the *Risorgimento.*" *Catholic Historical Review* 54 (January 1969): 579–612.

———. *Pope Pius IX: Crusader in a Secular Age.* Boston: Twayne, 1979.

———. *The Modern Papacy since 1789.* London: Longman, 1998.

———. *The Papacy Confronts the Modern World.* Malabar, Fla.: Krieger Publishing, 2003.

———, ed. *Controversial Concordats: The Vatican's Relations with Napoleon, Mussolini, and Hitler.* Washington, D.C.: Catholic University of America Press, 1999.

———. *Encyclopedia of the Vatican and Papacy.* Westport, Conn.: Greenwood Press, 1999.

———. *The Great Popes through History: An Encyclopedia.* 2 vols. Westport, Conn.: Greenwood Press, 2002.

Cornwell, John. *Breaking Faith: The Pope, the People and the Fate of Catholicism.* New York: Viking Press, 2001.

———. *Hitler's Pope: The Secret History of Pius XII.* New York: Viking, 1999.

———. *The Pontiff in Winter: Triumph and Conflict in the Reign of John Paul II.* New York: Doubleday, 2004.

Corrigan, Raymond. *The Church and the Nineteenth Century.* Milwaukee: Bruce Publishing, 1938.

Corrin, Jay P. *Catholic Intellectuals and the Challenge of Democracy.* Notre Dame: University of Notre Dame Press, 2002.

————. *Chesterton and Hilaire Belloc: The Battle against Modernity.* Athens: Ohio University Press, 1981.

Cournos, John. *An Open Letter to Jews and Christians.* New York: Oxford University Press, 1938.

Curran, Charles E., ed. *Change in Official Catholic Moral Teaching.* New York: Paulist Press, 2003.

Curtis, Michael, ed. *Antisemitism in the Contemporary World.* London: Westview, 1986.

D'Agnel, G. Anaud. *Benoit XV et le conflit Europeen.* Paris: Lethielleux, 1916.

Dagobert D. *The Jew and the Cross.* New York: Philosophical Library, 1965.

Dalmon, Gustaf. *Jesus-Jeshua: Studies in the Gospels.* Trans. Paul P. Levertaff. New York: KTAV Publishing, 1971.

Danby, Herbert. *The Jews and Christianity: Some Phases, Ancient and Modern, of the Jewish Attitude towards Christianity.* New York: Macmillan, 1927.

Danielou, Jean, J. S. *Dialogue with Israel, with a Response by Rabbi Jacob B. Agus.* Baltimore: Helicon Press, 1968.

Daniel-Rops, Henri. *The Church in an Age of Revolution, 1789–1870,* vol. 1. Trans. John Warrington. Garden City, N.Y.: Image Books, 1967.

Daube, David. *The New Testament and Rabbinic Judaism.* London: University of London, 1956.

David, Abraham. "The Expulsion from the Papal States in Light of Hebrew Sources." In *The Most Ancient of Minorities: The Jews of Italy,* ed. Stanislao G. Pugliese. Westport, Conn.: Greenwood Press, 2002.

Davies, Alan T. *Anti-Semitism and the Christian Mind: The Crisis of Conscience after Auschwitz.* New York: Herder and Herder, 1969.

Davies, Alan T. "Religion and Racism: The Case of French Anti-Semitism." *Journal of Church and State* 20 (spring 1978): 273–86.

Davies, William David. *Christian Origins and Judaism.* Philadelphia: Westminster Press, 1962.

Davis, Moshe, ed. *Israel: Its Role in Civilization.* New York: Harper and Brothers, 1956.

De Cesare, R. *The Last Days of Papal Rome, 1850–1870.* Trans. Helen Zimmern. London: Constable, 1909.

De Felice, Renzo. *Storia degli ebrei sotto il fascismo.* Turin: Einaudi, 1962.

Delzell, Charles F., ed. *The Papacy and Totalitarianism between the Two World Wars.* New York: John Wiley and Sons, 1974.

Demarco, Domenico. *Pio IX e la rivoluzione del 1848. Saggio di storia economica-sociale.* Modena: Società Tipografia Modenese, 1947.

Denzler, Georg. *Winderstand ist nicht das rightige Wort. Katholische Priester, Bischoefe under Theologen im Dritten Reich.* Zurich: Pendo Verlag, 2003.

Dietrich, Donald J. "Catholic Resistance in the Third Reich." *Holocaust and Genocide Studies* 3, no. 2 (1988): 171–86.

————. "Catholic Theologians in Hitler's Reich: Adaptation and Critique." *Journal of Church and State* 29 (winter 1987): 19–45.

————, ed. *Christian Responses to the Holocaust: Moral and Ethical Issues.* Syracuse: Syracuse University Press, 2003.

Di Nolfo, Ennio. *Vaticano e Stati Uniti, 1939–1952.* Milan: Angeli, 1978.

Duffy, Eamon. *Saints and Sinners: A History of the Popes.* New Haven: Yale University Press, 1997.

Dulles, Cardinal Avery, and Rabbi Leon Klenicki. *The Holocaust, Never to Be Forgotten: Reflections on the Holy See's Document, "We Remember."* Mahwah, N.J.: Paulist Press, 2001.

Eckardt, A. Roy. "The Nemesis of Christian Antisemitism." *Journal of Church and State* 13 (spring 1971): 227–44.

———, ed. *Brothers in Hope.* New York: Herder and Herder, 1970.

———. *Christianity and the Children of Israel.* New York: King's Crown Press, 1948.

———. "Towards an Authentic Jewish-Christian Relationship." *Journal of Church and State* 13 (spring 1971): 271–82.

Eller, Meredith Freeman. *The Beginnings of the Christian Religion: A Guide to the History and Literature of Judaism and Christianity.* New York: Bookman Associates, 1958.

Elliott, Lawrence. *"I Will Be Called John": A Biography of Pope John XXIII.* New York: Readers Digest Press, 1973.

Ellis, John Tracy. *Cardinal Consalvi and Anglo-Papal Relations, 1814–1824.* Washington, D.C.: Catholic University of America Press, 1942.

Ellsberg, Patricia Marx. "An Interview with Rolf Hochhuth." In *The Papacy and Totalitarianism between the Two World Wars,* ed. Charles Delzell. New York: John Wiley, 1974.

Elon, Amor. *The Pity of It All: A History of Jews in Germany, 1743–1933.* New York: Metropolitan Books, 2002.

Enslin, Morton Scott. *Christian Beginnings.* New York: Harper and Row, 1938.

Falconi, Carlo. *Il giovane Mastai.* Milan: Rusconi, 1981.

———. *The Popes in the Twentieth Century: From Pius X to John XXIII.* Trans. Muriel Grindrod. Boston: Little, Brown, 1967.

———. *The Silence of Pius XII.* Trans. Bernard Wall. Boston: Little, Brown, 1970.

Fattorini, Emma. *Germania e Santa Sede. La Nunziature di Pacelli tra la Grande Guerra e la Repubblica di Weimar.* Annali dell'Istituto storico italo-germanico. Milan: Il Mulino, 1992.

Feldkamp, Michael. *Goldhagens unwillige Kirche.* Munich: Olzog, 2003.

———. *Pius XII. und Deutschland.* Göttingen: Vandenhoeck and Ruprecht, 2000.

Feldman, Egal. *Catholics and Jews in Twentieth-Century America.* Urbana: University of Illinois Press, 2001.

Felice, Renzo de. *Storia degli ebrei sotto il fascismo.* Turin: Einaudi, 1961.

Ferari, Silvio. "La S. Sede e la questione di Gerusalemme (1943–1948)." *Storia Contemporanea* 16 (February 1985).

Fernessole, Pierre. *Pie IX Pape.* Paris: Lethielleux, 1960–63.

Fesquet, Henri. *The Drama of Vatican II: The Ecumenical Council, June 1962–December 1965.* Trans. Bernard Murchland. New York: Random House, 1967.

Finkelstein, Norman G., and Ruth Bettina Birn. *A Nation on Trial: The Goldhagen Thesis and Historical Truth.* New York: Henry Holt, 1998.

Fisher, Eugene J., and Leon Klenicki, eds. *In Our Time: The Flowering of Jewish-Catholic Dialogue.* Mahwah, N.J.: Paulist Press, 1990.

———. *Pope John Paul II on Jews and Judaism.* Washington, D.C.: United States Catholic Conference, 1987.

Flannery, Edward H. *The Anguish of the Jews: Twenty-Three Centuries of Anti-Semitism.* New York: Macmillan, 1934.

Foa, Anna. *Ebrei in Europa.* Rome: Laterza, 1997.

Foerster, Frederick Wilhelm. *The Jews.* New York: Farrar, Straus, 1961.

Fogarty, Gerald P. *The Vatican and the Americanist Crisis: Denis J. O'Connell, American Agent in Rome, 1885–1903.* Rome: Università Gregoriana Editrice, 1974.

Forbes, F. A. *Life of Pius X.* London: Burns, Oates and Westminster, 1918.

Fox, Gresham George. *Jesus, Pilate and Paul: An Amazingly New Interpretation of the Trial of Jesus under Pontius Pilate.* Chicago: Isaacs, 1955.

Franciscis, Maria Elisabetta de. *Italy and the Vatican: The 1984 Concordat between Church and State.* New York: Peter Lang, 1989.

Frankel, Jonathan. *The Damascus Affair.* New York: Cambridge University Press, 1979.

Frassetto, Michael. "Heretics and Jews in the Writings of Ademar of Chabannes and the Origins of Medieval Anti-Semitism." *Church History* 71 (March 2002): 1–15.

Friedlander, Gerald. *The Jewish Sources of the Sermon on the Mount.* New York: KTAV Publishing, 1969.

Friedlander, Saul. *Pius XII and the Third Reich: A Documentation.* New York: Knopf, 1966.

———. *Nazi Germany and the Jews.* New York: HarperCollins, 1997.

Friedman, Philip. *Roads to Extinction: Essays on the Holocaust.* New York: Jewish Publication Society of America, 1980.

———. *Their Brothers' Keepers.* New York: Crow Publishers, 1957.

Frymer-Kensky, Tivka. *Christianity in Jewish Terms.* New York: Westview Press, 2000.

Fubini, Guido. *La condizione giuridica dell'ebraismo Italiano. Dal periodo Napoleonico alla Repubblica.* Florence: Nuova Italia, 1974.

Fumagalli, Pier Francesco. "Nostra Aetate: A Milestone." www.vatican.va/jubilee_2000.

Gager, John G. *The Origins of Anti-Semitism: Attitudes toward Judaism in Pagan and Christian Antiquity.* New York: Oxford University Press, 1985.

Gajani, Guglielmo. *The Roman Exile.* Boston: John P. Jewett, 1856.

Garzia, Italo. *Pio XII e l'Italia nella seconda guerra mondiale.* Brescia: Morcelliana, 1988.

Gavin, F. *The Jewish Antecedents of the Christian Sacraments.* New York: KTAV Publishing, 1928.

Gay, Peter. *The Party of Humanity: Essays in the French Enlightenment.* New York: W. W. Norton, 1971.

Gentile, Emilio. *Le religioni della politica.* Bari: Laterza, 2001.

Giano, Galeazzo. *Ciano's Hidden Diaries, 1937–1938.* New York: E. P. Dutton, 1953.

Gibson, E. Leigh. "Jewish Antagonism or Christian Polemic: The Case of the Martyrdom of Pionius." *Journal of Early Christian Studies* 9 (fall 2001): 339–58.

Gilbert, Arthur. *A Jew in Christian America.* New York: Sheed and Ward, 1966.

———. *The Vatican Council and the Jews.* Cleveland: World Publishing Co., 1968.

Gilbert, Martin. *The Righteous: The Unsung Heroes of the Holocaust.* New York: Henry Holt, 2003.

Gillet, Lev, ed. *Judaism and Christianity.* London: J. B. Shears and Son, 1939.

Giordani, Igino. *Pius X: A Country Priest.* Trans. Thomas J. Tobin. Milwaukee: Bruce Publishing, 1954.

Giovanetti, Alberto. *El Vaticano y la guerra 1939–1940.* Trans. Felice Ximenez de Sanoval. Madrid: Sposa-Calpe, S.A., 1961.

———. *L'action du Vatican pour la paix.* Paris: Fleurus, 1963.

Giuntella, Maria Cristina. "Circoli Cattolici e organizzazioni Giovanili fasciste in Umbria." In *Cattolici e Fascisti in Umbria (1922–1945),* ed. Albertino Monticone, 31–92. Bologna: Il Mulino, 1978.

Giuntella, Vittorio E. "Cristianesimo e democrazia in Italia al tramonto del Settecento." *Rassegna Storica del Risorgimento* 42 (1955).

Glock, Charles Y., and Rodney Stark. *Christian Beliefs and Anti Semitism.* New York: Harper and Row, 1966.

Glueckert, Leopold G. *Between Two Amnesties: Former Political Prisoners and Exiles in the Roman Revolution of 1848.* New York: Garland, 1991.

Godman, Peter. *Hitler and the Vatican: Inside the Secret Archives That Reveal the New Story of the Nazis and the Church.* New York: Free Press, 2004.

Goldhagen, Daniel Jonah. *A Moral Reckoning: The Catholic Church during the Holocaust and Today.* New York: Knopf, 2002.

———. *Hitler's Willing Executioners: Ordinary Germans and the Holocaust.* New York: Knopf, 1996.

———. "What Would Jesus Have Done? Pope Pius XII, the Catholic Church, and the Holocaust." *New Republic,* 21 January 2002, 21–45.

Goldstein, Morris. *Jesus in the Jewish Tradition.* New York: Macmillan, 1950.

Goni, Uki. *The Real Odessa: Smuggling the Nazis to Perón's Argentina.* New York: Granta Books, 2002.

Goodich, Michael, ed. *Other Middle Ages: Witnesses at the Margins of Medieval Society.* Philadelphia: University of Pennsylvania Press, 1998.

Goodman, Paul. *The Synagogue and the Church: A Contribution to the Apologetics of Judaism.* New York: E. P. Dutton Sons, 1908.

Goppelt, Leonhard. *Jesus, Paul and Judaism: An Introduction to New Testament Theology.* New York: Thomas Nelson and Sons, 1964.

Gordis, Robert. *Judaism in a Christian World.* New York: McGraw-Hill, 1966.

Gorresio, Vittorio. *The New Mission of Pope John XXIII.* Trans. Charles Lam Markmann. New York: Funk and Wagnalls, 1969.

Graeber, Isacque, and S. H. Brit, eds. *Jews in the Gentile World: The Problem of Anti-Semitism.* New York: Macmillan, 1942.

Graham, Robert A. *Pius XII and the Holocaust: A Reader.* Milwaukee: Catholic League, 1988.

———. "The 'Right to Kill' in the Third Reich: Prelude to Genocide." *Catholic Historical Review* 62 (January 1976): 56–76.

Granfield, Patrick. "John XXIII (1958–63): The Father of the Second Vatican Council." In *The Great Popes through History: An Encyclopedia,* ed. Frank J. Coppa, 511–18. Westport, Conn.: Greenwood Press, 2002.

Grant, Frederick C. *Ancient Judaism and the New Testament.* New York: Macmillan, 1959.

Grayzel, Solomon. *The Church and the Jews in the Thirteenth Century.* Rev. ed. Philadelphia: Herman Press, 1966.

Greene, Meg. *Pope John Paul II: A Biography.* Westport, Conn.: Greenwood Press, 2003.

Groppi, Ugo, and Julius Lombardi. *Above All a Shepherd.* New York: Kenedy and Sons, 1959.

Guignebert, C. A. H. *The Jewish World in the Time of Jesus.* London: Kegan Paul, Trench, Trubner, 1939.

Guilding, Aileen. *The Fourth Gospel and Jewish Worship: A Study of the Relation of St. John's Gospel to the Ancient Jewish Lectionary System.* Oxford: Clarendon Press, 1960.

Gurian, Waldemar. "Hitler's Undeclared War on the Catholic Church." *Foreign Affairs* 6 (January 1938): 260–71.

Haber, Georges. *Pilgrim of Peace.* Montreal: Palm Publishers, 1967.

Halecki, Oscar. *Eugenio Pacelli: Pope of Peace.* New York: Farrar, Straus and Young, 1951.

––––––. "The Holy See and the Religious Situation in Central Europe, 1939–1945." *Catholic Historical Review* 53 (October 1967): 393–410.

Hales, E. E. Y. *Pio Nono: A Study in European Politics and Religion in the Nineteenth Century.* Garden City, N.Y.: Doubleday, 1962.

––––––. *Revolution and Papacy, 1769–1846.* Notre Dame: University of Notre Dame Press, 1966.

––––––. *The Catholic Chuch in the Modern World.* Garden City, N.Y.: Hanover House, 1958.

Hanson, Eric O. *The Catholic Church in World Politics.* Princeton: Princeton University Press, 1987.

Harrigan, William M. "Pius XII's Efforts to Effect a Détente in German Vatican Relations, 1939–1940." *Catholic Historical Review* 49 (July 1963): 173–91.

Harshbarger, Luther H., and John A. Maurant. *Judaism and Christianity: Perspectives and Traditions.* Boston: Allyn and Bacon, 1968.

Hauer, Christian E., Jr. *Crisis and Conscience in the Middle East.* Chicago: Quadrangle Books, 1970.

Hay, Malcom. *Foot of Pride: The Pressure of Christendom on the People of Israel for 1900 Years.* Boston: Beacon Press, 1950.

Haynes, Stephen R. "Who Needs Enemies: Jews and Judaism in Anti-Nazi Religious Discourse." *Church History* 71 (June 2002): 341–67.

Hearly, John. *Pope or Mussolini.* New York: Macaulay Co., 1929.

Hebblethewaite, Peter. *Pope John XXIII: Shepherd of the Modern World.* New York: Doubleday, 1985.

––––––. *Paul VI: The First Modern Pope.* New York: Paulist Press, 1993.

––––––. *The Year of Three Popes.* New York: Collins, 1979.

Hecht, Robert A. *An Unordinary Man: A Life of Father John La Farge, S.J.* Lanham, Md.: Scarecrow Press, 1996.

Hedenquist, Gote, ed. *The Church and the Jewish People.* London: Edinburgh House Press, 1954.

Heer, Friedrich. *God's First Love: Christians and Jews over Two Thousand Years.* Trans. Geoffrey Skelton. New York: Weybright and Talley, 1970.

Hehir, J. Bryan. "Papal Foreign Policy." *Foreign Policy* (spring 1990): 26–48.

Herber, Charles J. "Eugenio Pacelli's Mission to Germany and the Peace Proposal of 1917." *Catholic Historical Review* 65 (January 1979): 20–48.

Herberg, Will. *Protestant, Catholic, Jew: An Essay in American Religious Sociology.* Rev. ed. Garden City, N.Y.: Doubleday, 1960.

Hergenrother, Giuseppe. *Storia Universale della Chiesa.* Ed. G. P. Kirsch, trans. P. Enrico Rosa. Vol. 7. Florence: Libreria Editrice Fiorentina, 1911.

Hertzberg, Arthur. *The French Enlightenment and the Jews.* New York: Columbia University Press, 1968.

Herzer, Ivo, ed. *The Italian Refuge: Rescue of Jews during the Holocaust.* Washington, D.C.: Catholic University of America Press, 1989.

Hilberg, Raul. *The Destruction of the European Jews.* 3 vols. New York: Holmes and Meier, 1985.

Hill, Leonidas E., III. "The Vatican Embassy of Ernst von Weizsacker, 1943–1945." *Journal of Modern History* 39 (March 1967): 138–59.

Hilldderbrand, Hans. "Martin Luther and the Jews." In *Jews and Christians: Exploring the Past, Present, and Future*, ed. James Charlesworth, 133–43. New York: Crossroad Press, 1990.

Hitchcock, James. *Catholicism and Modernity: Confrontation or Capitulation.* New York: Seabury Press, 1979.

Hoffmann, Peter. "Roncalli in the Second World War: Peace Initiatives, the Greek Famine, and the Persecution of the Jews." *Journal of Ecclesiastical History* 40 (January 1989): 74–99.

Hofmann, Paul. *O Vatican! A Slightly Wicked View of the Holy See.* New York: Congdon and Weed, 1984.

Holborn, Hajo. *A History of Modern Germany, 1648–1840.* New York: Knopf, 1967.

Holmes, J. Derek. *The Papacy in the Modern World, 1914–1978.* New York: Crossroad, 1981.

———. *The Triumph of the Holy See: A Short History of the Papacy in the Nineteenth Century.* London: Burns and Oates, 1978.

Homza, Lu Ann. *Religious Authority in the Spanish Renaissance.* Baltimore: Johns Hopkins University Press, 2000.

Hood, John Y. B. *Aquinas and the Jews.* Philadelphia: University of Pennsylvania Press, 1995.

Huber, George. *Pilgrim of Peace.* Montreal: Palm Publishers, 1967.

Hughes, John Jay. "The Pope's Pact with Hitler: Betrayal or Self-Defense?" *Journal of Church and State* 17 (winter 1975): 63–80.

———. "Review of Thomas Brechenmacher and Hardy Ostry, Rom und Jerusalem." *Catholic Historical Review* 88 (October 2002): 799–800.

Hurtado, L. W. "Pre–70 CE Jewish Opposition to Christ-Devotion." *Journal of Theological Studies* 50 (April 1999): 35–58.

Irani, George Emile. *The Papacy and the Middle East: The Role of the Holy See in the Arab-Israeli Conflict, 1962–1984.* Notre Dame: University of Notre Dame Press, 1986.

Isaac, Jules. *Has Anti-Semitism Roots in Christianity?* New York: National Council of Christian and Jews, 1961.

———. *Jesus and Israel.* New York: Holt, Rinehart and Winston, 1971.

—. *The Teaching of Contempt: Christian Roots of Anti-Semitism.* Trans. H. Weaver. New York: Holt, Rinehart and Winston, 1964.

Jabalot, Ferdinando. *Degli ebrei nei loro rapport colle nazioni cristiane.* Rome: Poggioli, 1925.

Jocz, Jakob. *Christians and Jews: Encounter and Mission.* London: S.P.C.K., 1966.

Johnson, Paul. *Pope John XXIII.* Boston: Little, Brown, 1974.

Kagan, Henry Enoch. *Changing the Attitude of Christian toward Jew.* New York: Columbia University Press, 1952.

Kaiser, Robert Blair. *Pope, Council and the World: The Story of Vatican II.* New York: Macmillan, 1963.

Katz, Jacob. *Exclusiveness and Tolerance: Studies in Jewish-Gentile Relations in Medieval and Modern Times.* Oxford: Oxford University Press, 1961.

—. *From Prejudice to Destruction: Anti-Semitism, 1700–1933.* Cambridge: Harvard University Press, 1980.

Katz, Robert. *Death in Rome.* Cambridge: Harvard University Press, 1967.

—. "Pius XII Protests the Holocaust: Could the Wartime Pope Have Prevented the Final Solution?" In *What If? Eminent Historians Imagine What Might Have Been,* ed. Robert Cowley. New York: Berkley Books, 2003.

—. *The Battle for Rome: The Germans, the Allies, the Partisans, and the Pope, September 1943–June 1944.* New York: Simon and Schuster, 2003.

Keefe, Patricia M. "Popes Pius XI and Pius XII, the Catholic Church, and the Nazi Persecution of the Jews." *British Journal of Holocaust Education* 2 (summer 1993): 26–47.

Kent, George O. "Pope Pius XII and Germany: Some Aspects of German-Vatican Relations, 1933–1943." *American Historical Review* 70 (October 1964): 59–78.

Kent, Peter C., and John F. Pollard, eds. *Papal Diplomacy in the Modern Age.* Westport, Conn.: Praeger, 1994.

—. *The Pope and the Duce.* New York: St. Martin's Press, 1981.

Kertzer, David I. *The Kidnapping of Edgardo Montara.* New York: Knopf, 1997.

—. "The Montrel Affair: Vatican Jewish Policy and French Diplomacy under the July Monarchy." *French Historical Studies* 25 (spring 2002): 265–93.

—. *The Popes against the Jews: The Vatican's Role in the Rise of Modern Anti-Semitism.* New York: Knopf, 2001.

Kisch, Guido. *The Jews in Medieval Germany.* Chicago: University of Chicago Press, 1949.

—. "The Yellow Badge in History." *Historia Judaica* 19 (1957): 89–146.

Klausner, Joseph. *From Jesus to Paul.* Trans. W. F. Stinespring. New York: Macmillan, 1943. Boston: Beacon Press, 1960.

Kleinlerer, Edward D. "Scholars at the Vatican." *Commonweal* 37 (4 Dec. 4 1942): 187–88.

Knight, George A. F., ed. *Jews and Christians: Preparation for Dialogue.* Philadelphia: Westminster Press, 1965.

Kosmala, Hans, and Robert Smith. *The Jew in the Christian World.* London: Student Christian Movement Press, 1942.

Krausnick, Helmut. "The Persecution of the Jews." In *Anatomy of the SS State,* ed. Helmut Krausnick et al. New York: Walker and Co., 1968.

Kreutz, Andrej. *Vatican Policy on the Palestinian-Israeli Conflict: The Struggle for the Holy Land.* Westport, Conn.: Greenwood Press, 1990.

Krieg, Robert A. "The Vatican Concordat with Hitler's Reich." *America* 189 (1 September 2003): 14–17.

Kubovy, Aryeh Leon. "The Silence of Pope Pius XII and the Beginnings of the 'Jewish Document.'" In *Yad Vashem Studies of the European Jewish Catastrophe and Resistance,* ed. Nathan Eck and Aryeh Leon. Jerusalem: Yad Vashem, 1967.

Küng, Hans. "Introduction: From Anti-Semitism to Theological Dialogue," in *Christians and Jews,* ed. Hans Küng and Walter Kasper and trans. John Maxwell. New York: Seabury Press, 1975.

La Farge, John. *Interracial Justice: A Study of the Catholic Doctrine of Race Relations.* New York: America Press, 1937.

———. *The Manner Is Ordinary.* New York: Harcourt, Brace, 1954.

Lamberts, Emiel, ed. *The Black International, 1870–1878: The Holy See and Militant Catholicism in Europe.* Leuven: Leuven University Press, 2002.

Langmuir, G. I. *History, Religion, and Antisemitism.* Berkeley and Los Angeles: University of California Press, 1990.

Lapide, Pinchas E. *Three Popes and the Jews.* New York: Hawthorn Books, 1967.

Lapomarda, Vincent A. "The Jesuits and the Holocaust." *Journal of Church and State* 23 (spring 1981): 241–58.

———. *The Jesuits and the Third Reich.* Lewison: Edwin Mellen Press, 1989.

Lavi, Theodore. "The Vatican's Endeavors on Behalf of Rumanian Jewry during World War II." *Yad Vashem Studies* 5 (1963): 405–18.

Lawler, Justus George. "Deconstructing Deceit: Garry Wills's Papal Sin." *Downside Review* 119 (July 2001): 191–216.

———. *Popes and Politics: Reform, Resentment and the Holocaust.* New York: Continuum, 2002.

Lay, Thomas, S.J., ed. *Jewish-Christian Relations.* St. Mary's, Kans.: St. Mary's College, 1965.

Lease, Gary. "Denunciation as a Tool of Ecclesiastical Control: The Case of Roman Catholic Modernism." *Journal of Modern History* 68 (December 1996): 819–30.

Lederer, Thomas G. "2000 Years: Relations between Catholics and Jews before and after Vatican II." www.Arthurstreet.com/2000 YEARS, 1–24, accessed 18 Oct. 2002.

Leflon, Jean. *Pie VII. Des Abboyes benedictines a la Papaute.* Paris: Plon, 1958.

Levai, Jeno. *Hungarian Jewry and the Papacy.* London: Sands and Co., 1967.

Levy, Richard S., ed. *Antisemitism in the Modern World.* Lexington, Mass.: D. C. Heath, 1991.

Lewis, Bernard. *Semites and Anti-Semites: An Inquiry into Conflict and Prejudice.* New York: W. W. Norton, 1987.

Lewy, Guenter. "Pius XII, the Jews, and the German Catholic Church." *Commentary* 37 (February 1964): 23–33.

———. *The Catholic Church and Nazi Germany.* New York: McGraw-Hill, 1965.

Linafelt, Tod, ed. *A Shadow of Glory: Reading the New Testament after the Holocaust.* New York: Routledge, 2002.

Lindemann, Albert S. *Esau's Tears: Modern Anti-Semitism and the Rise of the Jews.* New York: Cambridge University Press, 1996.

Littell, Franklin Hamlin. "Have Jews and Christians a Common Future?" *Journal of Church and State* 13 (spring 1971): 303–15.

———. "Inventing the Holocaust: A Christian Retrospect," *Holocaust and Genocide Studies* 9 (fall 1995).

———. "Kirchenkampf and Holocaust: The German Church Struggle and Nazi Anti-Semitism in Retrospect." *Journal of Church and State* 13 (winter 1971): 209–26.

———. "Uprooting Antisemitism: A Call to Christians." *Journal of Church and State* 17 (winter 1975): 15–24.

Loewenstein, Rudolph M. *Christians and Jews: A Psychoanalytic Study.* Trans. Vera Damman. New York: Dell Publishing, 1963.

Long, J. Bruce, ed. *Judaism and the Christian Seminary Curriculum.* Chicago: Loyola University Press, 1966.

Lovsky, F. M., ed. *L'Antisemitisme chretienne.* Paris: Cerf, 1970.

Lowenthal, Martin. *The Jews of Germany.* New York: Longmans, Green, 1936.

Lukacs, John. "The Diplomacy of the Holy See during World War II." *Catholic Historical Review* 60 (July 1974): 271–78.

Luzzatti, Michele. "Florence against the Jews or the Jews against Florence?" In *The Most Ancient of Minorities: The Jews of Italy,* ed. Stanislao G. Pugliese. Westport, Conn.: Greenwood Press, 2002.

Maccoby, Hyam. *The Mythmaker: Paul and the Invention of Christianity.* New York: Harper Collins, 1987.

———. "Origins of Anti-Semitism." *Midstream* (December 1998): 38–39.

Madigan, Kevin. "What the Vatican Knew about the Holocaust, and When." *Commentary* (October 2001): 43–52.

Magister, Sandro. *La politica vaticana e l'Italia, 1943–1978.* Rome: Reuniti, 1979.

Malinski, Mieczyslaw. *Pope John Paul II: The Life of Karol Wojtyla.* Trans. P. S. Fall. New York: Seabury Press, 1979.

Marchione, Sister Margherita. *Consensus and Controversy: Defending Pope Pius XII.* Mahwah, N.J.: Paulist Press, 2002.

———. *Pope Pius XII: Architect for Peace.* New York: Paulist Press, 2000.

———. *Shepherd of Souls: A Pictorial Life of Pope Pius XII.* New York: Paulist Press, 2002.

———. *Yours Is a Precious Witness: Memories of Jews and Catholics in Wartime Italy.* New York: Paulist Press, 1997.

Marcus, Jacob Rader. *The Jew in the Medieval World: A Source Book, 315–1791.* New York: Temple Books, 1969.

Marinelli, Luigi. *Via col vento in Vaticano.* 1999.

Maritain, Jacques. *A Christian Looks at the Jewish Question.* New York: Longmans, 1939.

Marrus, Michael R. *The Holocaust in History.* Hanover: University Press of New England, 1987.

Marrus, Michael R., and Robert O. Paxton. *Vichy France and the Jews.* New York: Basic Books, 1981.

Martin, Malachi. *The Encounter.* New York: Farrar, Straus and Giroux, 1969.

———. *The Keys of This Blood: The Struggle for World Dominion between Pope John*

Paul II, Mikail Gorbachev, and the Capitalist West. New York: Simon and Schuster, 1990.

Martina, Giacomo. *Il problema ebraico nella storia della Chiesa.* Rome: Pontificia Università Gregoriana, 1996.

———. "L'ecclesiologia prevalente nel pontificato di Pio XI." In *Cattolici e fascisti in Umbria (1922–1945),* ed. Alberto Monticone, 221–44. Bologna: Il Mulino, 1978.

———. *La Chiesa nell'età del liberalismo.* Brescia: Morcelliana, 1978.

———. *Pio IX (1846–1850).* Rome: Università Gregoriana Editrice, 1974.

———. *Pio IX (1851–1866).* Rome: Editrice Pontificia Università Gregoriana, 1986.

———. *Pio IX (1867–1878).* Rome: Editrice Pontificia Università Gregoriana, 1990.

———. *Pio IX. Chiesa e mondo moderno.* Rome: Edizioni Studium, 1976.

———. *Pio IX e Leopold II.* Miscellanea Historiae Pontificiae. Rome: Pontificia Università Gregoriana, 1967.

Martini, Angelo. "Il Cardinale Faulhaber e L'Enciclica 'Mit Brennender Sorge.'" *Archivum Historiae Pontificiae* 2 (1964): 303–20.

———. "L'Ultima battaglia di Pio XI." In *Studi sulla questione romana e la conciliazione,* ed. Angelo Martini, 175–230. Rome: Cinque Lune, 1963.

Martini, Luciani. "Chiesa Cattolica ed Ebrei." *Il Ponte* 34 (1978): 1454–63.

Massing, P. *Rehearsal for Destruction: A Study of Political Antisemitism in Imperial Germany.* New York: Harper, 1949.

Mattioli, V. *Gli ebrei e la Chiesa, 1933–1945.* Milan: Mursia, 1997.

Maxwell-Stuart, P. G. *Chronicle of the Popes: A Reign-by-Reign Record of the Papacy from St. Peter to the Present.* London: Thames & Hudson, 1997.

McAfee Brown, Robert. *The Ecumenical Revolution.* New York: Doubleday, 1969.

McBrien, Richard P. *Lives of the Popes: The Pontiffs from St. Peter to John Paul II* San Francisco: Harper and Row, 1997.

McDonnell, Kilian. "Pope Pius XII and the Holocaust: Fear of Reprisal and Generic Diplomacy." *Gregorianum* 83 (2002): 313–34.

McGarry, Michael B. "The Holocaust: Tragedy of Christian History." In *Introduction to Jewish-Christian Relations,* ed. Michael Shermis and Arthur E. Zannoni. New York: Paulist Press, 1991.

McInerny, Ralph. *The Defamation of Pius XII.* South Bend, Ind.: St. Augustine Press, 2001.

———. *What Went Wrong with Vatican II?* Manchester, N.H.: Sophia Institute Press, 1998.

McIntire, C. T. *England against the Papacy, 1858–1861: Tories, Liberals and the Overthrow of Papal Temporal Power during the Italian Risorgimento.* New York: Cambridge University Press, 1983.

McManners, John. *The French Revolution and the Church.* New York: Harper and Row, 1970.

Melloni, Alberto. *Fra Instanbul, Atene e la guerra. La missione di A. G. Roncalli, 1934–1944.* Genoa: Marietti, 1992.

Meltzer, Milton. *Rescue: The Story of How Gentiles Saved Jews in the Holocaust.* New York: Harper and Row, 1988.

Merlo, Grado Giovanni. "Memorie e riconciliazione. La Chiesa di fronte alla storia." *Gli Argomenti Umani* 1 (May 2000): 100–106.

Miccoli, Giovanni. *I dilemmi e I silenzi di Pio XII.* Milan: Rizzoli, 2000.

———. "L'enciclica mancata di Pio XI sul razzismo e l'antisemitismo." *Passato e Presente* 15 (1997): 35–54.

———. "Santa Sede e Chiesa Italiana di Fronte alle Leggi Antiebriache del 1938." *Studi Storici* 29 (October–December 1988): 821–902.

Michaelis, Meir. "The Attitude of the Fascist Regime to the Jews in Italy." In *Yad Washem Studies on the European Jewish Catastrophe and Resistance,* ed. Shaul Esh, 4:7–41. New York: KTAV Publishing, 1975.

———. "Fascism, Totalitarianism and the Holocaust: Reflections on Current Interpretations of National Socialist Anti-Semitism." *European History Quarterly* 19, no. 1 (1989): 85–103.

———. *Mussolini and the Jews: German-Italian Relations and the Jewish Question in Italy, 1922–1945.* Oxford: Clarendon Press, 1978.

Micklem, Nathaniel. *National Socialism and the Roman Catholic Church.* London: Oxford University Press, 1939.

Minerbi, Sergio. *The Vatican and Zionism: Conflict in the Holy Land, 1895–1925.* Trans. A. Schwarz. New York: Oxford University Press, 1992.

Modras, Ronald. "Father Coughlin and Anti-Semitism: Fifty Years Later." *Journal of Church and State* 31 (spring 1989): 231–47.

Montefiore, C. G. *Rabbinic Literature and Gospel Teachings.* New York: KTAV Publishing, 1970.

Moore, George Foot. *Judaism in the First Centuries of the Christian Era.* 3 vols. Cambridge: Harvard University Press, 1927–30.

Morley, John F. "Reaction of a Catholic Theologian to the Vatican's We Remember Document." In *The Vatican and the Holocaust: The Catholic Church and the Jews during the Nazi Era,* ed. Randolph L. Braham, 47–67. New York: Columbia University Press, 2000.

———. *Vatican Diplomacy and the Jews during the Holocaust, 1939–1943.* New York: KTAV Publishing, 1980.

Moro, Renato. *La Chiesa e lo sterminio degli ebrei.* Bologna: Mulino, 2002.

———. "Le premesse dell'atteggiamento cattolico di fronte alla legislazione razziale fascista. Cattolici ed ebrei nell' Italia degli anni venti (1919–1932)." *Storia Contemporanea* 19 (December 1988): 1013–1119.

Mosse, G. L. *Toward the Final Solution: A History of European Racism.* New York: Fertig, 1978.

Muchnik, Natalia. "Du Judaisme au Catholicisme: les aleas de la foi au XVIIe siecle." *Revue Historique* 126 (July–September 2002): 571–76.

Murphy, Paul I., with René Arlington. *La popessa.* New York: Warner Books, 1983.

Nederman, Cary J. *Worlds of Difference: European Toleration, c. 1100–c. 1550.* University Park: Pennsylvania State University Press, 2000.

Nicholls, William. *Christian Antisemitism: A History of Hate.* Northvale, N.J.: Jason Aronson, 1997.

Nirenberg, David. "Convesion, Sex and Segregation: Jews and Christians in Medieval Spain." *American Historical Review* 107 (October 2002): 1065–93.

Novick, Peter. *The Holocaust in American Life.* Boston: Houghton Mifflin, 1999.

O'Brien, Darcy. *The Hidden Pope: The Untold Story of a Lifelong Friendship That Is Changing the Relationship between Catholics and Jews; The Personal Journey of John Paul II and Jerzy Kluger.* New York: Daybreak Books, 1998.

O'Dwyer, Margaret M. *The Papacy in the Age of Napoleon and the Restoration.* Lanham, Md.: University Press of America, 1985.

Oesterreicher, John M. *The New Encounter between Christians and Jews.* New York: Philosophical Library, 1985.

———, ed. *The Bridge: Judaeo-Christian Studies.* 5 vols. New York: Pantheon Books, 1955–70.

O'Grady, Desmond. *Beyond the Empire: Rome and the Church from Constantinople to Charlemagne.* New York: Crossroad, 2001.

Olson, Bernhard E. *Faiths and Prejudice: Intergroup Problems Protestant Curricula.* New Haven: Yale University Press, 1963.

Ostry, Hardy, and Thomas Brechenmacher. *Rom und Jerusalem.* Trier: Verlag, 2000.

Pagano, Sergio. "Pius V (1566–72)." In *Great Popes through History: An Encyclopedia,* ed. Frank J. Coppa, 2:333–42. Westport, Conn.: Greenwood Press, 2002.

Palmer, Robert R. *Catholics and Unbelievers in Eighteenth-Century France.* Princeton: Princeton University Press, 1967.

Papeleux, Léon. *Les silences de Pie XII.* Brussels: Vokaer, 1980.

Parkes, James William. *An Enemy of the People: Anti-Semitism.* New York: Penguin Books, 1946.

———. *Antisemitism: A Concise World-History.* Chicago: Quadrangle Books, 1969.

———. *Prelude to Dialogue: Jewish-Christian Relationships.* New York: Schocken Books, 1969.

———. *The Conflict of the Church and Synagogue: A Study in the Origins of Anti-Semitism.* New York: Meridian Books, 1961.

———. *The Foundations of Judaism and Christianity.* Chicago: Quadrangle Books, 1960.

———. *The Jewish Problem in the Modern World.* Oxford: Oxford University Press, 1946.

Parsons, Wilfrid. *The Pope and Italy.* New York: America Press, 1929.

Passelecq, Georges, and Bernard Suchecky. *The Hidden Encyclical of Pius XI,* Trans. Steven Rendall. New York: Harcourt, Brace, 1997. This is the English translation of *L'encyclique cachée de Pie XI. Une occasion manquée de l'Eglise face a l'antisémitisme* (Paris: Éditions La Découverte, 1995).

Pastor, Ludwig Freiherr von. *The History of the Popes.* Trans. E. F. Peeler. St. Louis: B. Herder, 1953.

Patai, Raphael. *Israel between East and West: A Study in Human Relations.* Philadelphia: Jewish Publication Society of America, 1953.

Pawlikowski, John T. "The Papacy of Pius XII: The Known and the Unknown." In *Pope Pius XII and the Holocaust,* ed. Carol Rittner and John K. Roth, 56–69. London: Leicester University Press, 2002.

Paxton, Robert O. "France: The Church, the Republic, and the Fascist Temptation, 1922–1945." In In *Catholics, the State, and the European Radical Right, 1919–1945,* ed. Richard J. Wolff and Jorg K. Hoensch, 67–91. Boulder: Social Science Monographs, 1987.

Payne, Stanley G. "Spain: The Church, the Second Republic, and the Franco Regime." In *Catholics, the State, and the European Radical Right, 1919–1945,* ed. Richard J. Wolff and Jorg K. Hoensch. Boulder: Social Science Monographs, 1987.

Pellicani, Antonio. *Il Papa di tutti. La Chiesa Cattolica, il fascismo, e il razzismo, 1929–1945.* Milan: Sugar Editore, 1964.

Peters, Walter H. *The Life of Benedict XV.* St. Paul, Minn.: Bruce Publishing, 1959.

Phayer, Michael. *The Catholic Church and the Holocaust, 1930–1965.* Bloomington: Indiana University Press, 2000.

Pichon, Charles. *The Vatican and Its Role in World Affairs.* Trans. Jean Misrahi. New York: E. P. Dutton, 1950.

Pichon, Françoise. "La vision des juifs chez Jean Lemaire de Belges." *Revue d'histoire ecclesiastique* 96 (July–December 2001): 333–71.

Pinson, Koppel, ed. *Essays on Antisemitism.* 2d ed., rev. New York: Conference on Jewish Relations, 1946.

Poliakov, Leon. *The History of Anti-Semitism.* Trans. Richard Howard. New York: Vanguard Press, 1965.

Pollard, John F. *The Unknown Pope: Benedict XV (1914–1922) and the Persuit of Peace.* London: Geoffrey Chapman, 1999.

———. *The Vatican and Italian Fascism, 1929–1932: A Study in Conflict.* Cambridge: Cambridge University Press, 1985.

Poncins, Leon de. *Judaism and the Vatican: An Attempt at Spiritual Subversion.* Trans. Timothy Tindal-Robertson. London: Britons, 1967.

Portier, William L. *Isaac Hecker and the First Vatican Council.* New York: Edwin Mellen Press, 1985.

Prinz, Joachim. *Popes from the Ghetto: A View of Medieval Christendom.* New York: Horizon Press, 1966.

Pugliese, Stanislao G., ed. *The Most Ancient of Minorities: The Jews of Italy.* Westport, Conn.: Greenwood Press, 2002.

Pulzer, P. G. *The Rise of Political Antisemitism in Germany and Austria.* New York: Wiley, 1964.

Purdy, W. A. *The Church on the Move: The Character and Policies of Pius XII and John XXIII.* New York: John Day Co., 1966.

Randall, A. W. G. *The Pope, the Jews, and the Nazis.* London: Catholic Truth Society, 1963.

Reese, Thomas J., S.J. *Inside the Vatican: The Politics and Organization of the Catholic Church.* Cambridge: Harvard University Press, 1996.

Reinerman, Alan J. *Austria and the Papacy in the Age of Meternich,* vol. 1, *Between Conflict and Cooperation, 1809–1830,* vol. 2, *Revolution and Reaction, 1830–1838.* Washington, D.C.: Catholic University of America Press, 1979, 1989.

Repken, Konrad. "Connecting the Church and the Shoah." *Catholic Historical Review* 88 (July 2002): 546–53.

Rhonheimer, Martin. "The Holocaust: What Was Not Said." *First Things* 137 (November 2003): 18–27.

Rhodes, Anthony. *The Vatican in the Age of Dictators, 1922–1945.* New York: Holt, Rinehart and Winston, 1973.

Riccardi, A. M. *Roma, "Città Sacra?"* Milan: Vita e Pensiero, 1979.

Richardson, Peter. *Israel in the Apostolic Church.* Cambridge: Cambridge University Press, 1969.

Rittner, Carol, and John K. Roth, eds. *Pope Pius XII and the Holocaust.* London: Leicester University Press, 2002.

Rodelli, Luigi. *La Repubblica Romana del 1849.* Pisa: Domus Mazzininiana, 1955.

Rondet, Henri. *Vatican I, le Concile de Pie IX. La preparation, les methodes de travail, les schemas reste en suspens.* Paris: P. Lethielleux, 1962.

Rosenberg, Stuart. *Bridge to Judaism's Dialogue with Christianity.* New York: Abelard-Schuman, 1961.

Rosenstock-Huessy, Eugen, ed. *Judaism Despite Christianity.* Tuscaloosa: University of Alabama Press, 1969.

Rosenzweig, Franz. *The Star of Redemption.* Trans. William H. Hallo. New York: Holt, Rinehart and Winston, 1971.

Rossi, Ernesto. *Il Managnello e l'aspersorio.* Florence: Parenti, 1958.

Rossini, G. *Il movimento cattolico nel periodo fascista.* Rome: Cinque Lune, 1966.

Rotenstreich, Nathan. *The Recurring Pattern: Studies in Anti-Judaism in Modern Thought.* New York: Horizon Press, 1964.

Roth, Cecil. *The History of the Jews of Italy.* Philadelphia: Jewish Publication Society of America, 1946.

———. *The Jews in the Renaissance.* Philadelphia: Jewish Publication Society of America, 1959.

Roth, Norman. "Bishops and Jews in the Middle Ages." *Catholic Historical Review* 80 (January 1994): 1–17.

Rousmaniere, John. *A Bridge to Dialogue: The Story of Christian-Jewish Relations.* Ed. James A. Carpenter and Leon Klenicki. New York: Paulist Press, 1991.

Roveri, Alessandro. *La Santa Sede tra rivoluzione francese e restaurazione: Il Cardinale Consalvi 1813–1815.* Florence: Nuova Italia, 1974.

Rowley, Harold Henry. *The Servant of the Lord, and Other Essays on the Old Testament.* Oxford: Blackwell, 1965.

Royal, Robert, ed. *Jacques Maritain and the Jews.* Notre Dame: University of Notre Dame Press, 1994.

Rubenstein, William D. *The Myth of Rescue: Why the Democracies Could Not Have Saved More Jews from the Nazis.* New York: Routledge, 1997.

Rubin, Miri. *Gentile Tales: The Narrative Assault on Late Medieval Jews.* New York: Yale University Press, 1999.

Ruether, Rosemary. *Faith and Fratricide: The Theological Roots of Anti-Semitism.* New York: Seabury Press, 1974.

Ryan, Edwin. "Papal Concordats in Modern Times." *Catholic Historical Review* 16 (October 1930): 302–10.

Rychlak, Ronald J. "Goldhagen v. Pius XII." *First Things* (June–July 2002): 37–54.

———. *Hitler, the War and the Pope.* Columbus, Mo.: Genesis Press, 2000.

Saldarini, Anthony J. *Jesus and Passover.* Ramsey, N.J.: Paulist Press, 1984.

———. *Matthew's Christian-Jewish Community.* Chicago: University of Chicago Press, 1994.

Sanchez, José M. *Pius XII and the Holocaust: Understanding the Controversy.* Washington, D.C.: Catholic University of America Press, 2002.

Sanders, E. P. *Paul and Palestinian Judaism.* Philadelphia: Fortress Press, 1977.

Sandmel, Samuel. *The First Christian Century in Judaism and Christianity: Certainties and Uncertainties.* New York: Oxford University Press, 1969.

Scharper, Philip, ed. *Torah and Gospel: Jewish and Catholic Theology in Dialogue.* New York: Sheed and Ward, 1966.

Schmid, Johanna. "Pius XII und die Juden." *Stimmen der Zeit* 220 (June 2002): 397–409.

Schmidlin, Joseph. *Histoire des papes de l'epoque contemporaines,* vol. 1.Trans. L. Marchal, Paris: E. Vitte, 1938.

Schmidt, Stjepan. *Augustin Bea, the Cardinal of Unity.* New Rochelle, N.Y.: New City Press, 1992.

Schneider, Burkhart. *Pius XII.* Mainz: Grünwald, 1968.

Schneider, Peter. *The Dialogue of Christians and Jews.* New York: Seabury Press, 1966.

Schoeps, Hans-Joachim. *The Jewish-Christian Argument: A History of Theologies in Conflict.* New York: Holt, Rinehart and Winston, 1963.

Scholder, Klaus. *The Churches and the Third Reich.* 2 vols. Philadelphia: Fortress Press, 1988.

Schutte, Anne Jacobson. "Palazzo del Sant'Uffizio: The Opening of the Roman Inquisition's Central Archive." *Perspectives* (May 1999): 25–28.

Schweitzer, Frederick M. *A History of the Jews since the First Century A.D.* New York: Macmillan, 1971.

Seiferth, Wolfgang S. *Synagogue and Church in the Middle Ages: Two Symbols in Art and Literature.* Trans. Lee Chadeayne and Paul Gottwald. New York: Frederick Ungar, 1970.

Selznick, Gertrude J., and Stephen Steinberg. *The Tenacity of Prejudice: Anti-Semitism in Contemporary America.* New York: Harper and Row, 1969.

Semeraro, Cosimo. *Restaurazione chiesa e società: La "seconda ricupera" e la rinascità degli ordini religiosi nello Stato pontificio (Marche e Legazioni, 1815–23).* Rome: Salesiano, 1982.

Seymour, David. "Adorno and Horkheimer: Enlightenment and Antisemitism." *Journal of Jewish Studies* 51 (autumn 2000): 297–312.

Shea, John Gilmary. *The Life of Pope Pius IX and the Great Events in the History of the Church during his Pontificate.* New York: Thomas Kelly, 1878.

Shermis, Michael, and Arthur E. Zannoni, eds. *Introduction to Jewish-Christian Relations.* New York: Paulist Press, 1991.

Sidorsky, David, ed. *The Liberal Tradition in European Thought.* New York: Capricorn Books, 1971.

Signer, Michael A., ed. *Humanity at the Limit: The Impact of the Holocaust Experience on Jews and Christians.* Bloomington: Indiana University Press, 2000.

Silver, A. H. *Where Judaism Differed: An Inquiry into the Distinctiveness of Judaism.* Philadelphia: Jewish Publication Society, 1957.

Smit, Jan Olav. *Angelic Shepherd: The Life of Pope Pius XII.* New York: Dodd, Mead, 1950.

Smith, H. W. *The Butcher's Tale: Murder and Anti-Semitism in a German Town.* New York: W. W. Norton, 2002.

Soderini, Eduardo. *Leo III, Italy and France.* London: Burns, Oates and Washbourne, 1935.

Sorani, S. *L'assistenza ai profughi ebrei in Italia (1933–1947).* Rome: Carucci, 1983.

Spicer, Kevin. *Resisting the Third Reich: Catholic Clergy in Hitler's Berlin.* DeKalb: Northern Illinois University Press, 2004.

Stark, Rodney. *One True God: Historical Consequences of Monotheism.* Princeton: Princeton University Press, 2001.

Stehlin, Stewart A. *Weimar and the Vatican 1919–1933: German-Vatican Diplomatic Relations in the Interwar Years.* Princeton: Princeton University Press, 1983.

Stehle, Hansjakob. *Eastern Politics of the Vatican.* Trans. Sandra Smith. Athens: Ohio University Press, 1981.

Steigmann-Gall, Richard. *The Holy Reich: Nazi Conceptions of Christianity, 1919–1945.* Cambridge: Cambridge University Press, 2003.

Steinfels, Peter. *A People Adrift: The Crisis of the Roman Catholic Church in America.* New York: Simon and Schuster, 2003.

Steele, Michael R. *Christianity, The Other, and The Holocaust.* Westport, Conn.: Praeger, 2003.

Stendahl, Krister, ed. *The Scrolls and the New Testament.* New York: Stoughton, 1930.

Stow, Kenneth. *Catholic Thought and Papal Jewish Policy, 1555–1593.* New York: Jewish Theological Seminary of America, 1977.

———. "Conversion, Apostasy, and Apprehension: Emicho of Flonheim and the Fear of Jews in the Twelfth Century." *Speculum: A Journal of Medieval Studies* 76 (October 2001): 911–33.

———. *Taxation, Community and State: The Jews and the Fiscal Foundations of the Early Modern Papal State.* Stuttgart: A. Hiersemann, 1982.

Sullivan, Maureen. *101 Questions and Answers on Vatican II.* New York: Paulist Press, 2003.

Synan, Edward A. *The Popes and the Jews in the Middle Ages.* New York: Macmillan, 1965.

Tal, Uriel. *Christians and Jews in Germany: Religion, Politics, and Ideology in the Second Reich, 1870–1914.* Ithaca: Cornell University Press, 1975.

Tannenbaum, Edward R. *The Fascist Experience: Italian Society and Culture, 1922–1945.* New York: Basic Books, 1972.

Taradel, Ruggero, and Barbara Raggi. *La segregazione amichele. "La Civiltà Cattolica" e la questione ebraica, 1850–1945.* Rome: Einaudi, 2000.

Tavard, George H. "American Contributions to Vatican II's Documents on Ecumenism and Religious Liberty." *Chicago Studies* 42 (spring 2003): 17–30.

Taylor, Miriam S. *Anti-Judaism and Early Christian Identity.* Leiden: Brill, 1995.

Tec, Nechama. *When Light Pierced the Darkness: Christian Rescue of Jews in Nazi-Occupied Poland.* New York: Oxford University Press, 1986.

Tedeschi, Mario. *Francia e Ingiltterra di fronte alla questione romana, 1859–1860.* Milan: Giufrè, 1978.

Thomas, Gordon, and Max Morgan-Witts. *Pontiff.* Garden City, N.Y.: Doubleday, 1983.

Tierney, Brian, ed., *The Middle Ages,* vol. 1, *Sources of Medieval History.* 2d ed. New York: Knopf, 1970.

Tinnemann, Ethel Mary, S.N.J.M. "The Silence of Pope Pius XII." *Journal of Church and State* 21 (spring 1979): 265–85.

Toaff, Elio. *Perfidi Giudei, Fratelli Maggiori.* Milan: Mondadori, 1987.

Touw, H. C. "The Resistance of the Netherlands Churches." *Annals of the American Academy of Political and Social Science* 245 (May 1946): 149–61.

Toynbee, Arnold, ed. *The Crucible of Christianity: Judaic Hellenism, and the Historical Background of the Christ Faith.* New York: World Publishing Co., 1969.

Tozzini, Sandra. "Legal Discrimination against Italian Jews: From the Romans to the

Unification of Italy." In *The Most Ancient of Minorities: The Jews of Italy,* ed. Stanislao G. Pugliese. Westport, Conn.: Greenwood Press, 2002.

Tractenberg, Joshua. *The Devil and the Jews: The Medieval Conception of the Jew and Its Relation to Modern Anti-Semitism.* New Haven: Yale University Press, 1943.

Trattner, Ernest R. *As a Jew Sees Jesus.* New York: Charles Scribner's Sons, 1931.

Trepp, L. *Eternal Faith, Eternal People: A Journey into Judaism.* Englewood Cliffs, N.J.: Prentice-Hall, 1962.

Tripodi, Nino. *Patti lateranese e il fascismo.* Bologna: Capelli, 1960.

Troki, Isaac ben Abraham. *Faith Strengthened (Chizzuk Emunah).* Trans. Moss Mocatta. New York: KTAV Publishing, 1970.

Tumen, Melvin M. *An Inventory and Appraisal of Research on American Anti-Semitism.* New York: Anti-Defamation League of B'nai B'rith, 1961.

Valentin, H. *Antisemitism Historically and Critically Examined.* Trans. A. G. Chater. New York: Viking Press, 1936.

Vecchio, G. *La "Shoah," l'Italia, la Chiesa.* Milan: Ancora, 1988.

Vercesi, Ernesto. *Il movimento catolico in Italia (1870–1922).* Florence: La Voce, 1923.

Verucci, Guido. *Il movimento cattolico italiano. Dalla Restaurazione al primo dopoguerra.* Florence: Casa Editrice d'Anna, 1977.

Vian, Giovanni. "La Santa Sede e I Crimini nazisti. Note e osservazione su i dilemmi e i silenzi di Pio XII." *Rivista di Storia e Lettaratura Religiosa* 37, no. 3 (2001): 505–39.

Vogelstein, Hermann. *The Jews of Rome.* Trans. Moses Hadas. Philadelphia: Jewish Publication Society of America, 1940.

Waagenaar, Sam. *The Pope's Jews.* La Salle, Ill.: Open Court, 1974.

Walker, Lawrence D. "Young Priests as Opponents: Factors Associated with Clerical Opposition to the Nazis in Bavaria." *Catholic Historical Review* 65 (July 1979): 402–13.

Wallace, Lillian Parker. *Leo XIII and the Rise of Socialism.* Durham: Duke University Press, 1966.

Wasserstein, Bernard. *Britain and the Jews of Europe, 1939–1945.* London: Clarendeon Press, 1979.

Webster, Richard A. *The Cross and the Fasces.* Stanford: Stanford University Press, 1960.

Werner, Eric. *The Sacred Bridge: The Interdependence of Liturgy and Music in Synagogue and Church during the First Millennium.* New York: Columbia University Press, 1959.

Wilde, Robert. *The Treatment of the Jews in the Greek Christian Writers of the First Three Centuries.* Washington, D.C.: Catholic University of America Press, 1949.

Wilken, Robert L. *Judaism and the Early Christian Mind: A Study of Cyril of Alexandria's Exegesis and Theology.* New Haven: Yale University Press, 1971.

Williams, Arthur L. *Talmudic Judaism and Christianity.* New York: Macmillan, 1933.

Williams, Paul L. *The Vatican Exposed: Money, Murder and the Mafia.* New York: Prometheus Books, 2003.

Wills, Garry. *Papal Sin: Structures of Deceit.* New York: Doubleday, 2000.

———. *Why I Am a Catholic.* Boston: Houghton Mifflin, 2002.

Winter, Paul. *On the Trial of Jesus.* Berlin: Walter D. E. Gruyter, 1961.

Wistrich, Robert S. *Antisemitism: The Longest Hatred*. New York: Schocken Books, 1991.

Wolff, Richard J. *Between Pope and Duce: Catholic Students in Fascist Italy*. New York: Peter Lang, 1990.

———. "The Catholic Church and the Dictatorships in Slovakia and Croatia, 1939–1945." *Records of the American Catholic Historical Society of Philadelphia* (1978).

———. "Giovanni Battista Montini and Italian Politics, 1897–1933." *Catholic Historical Review* 81 (April 1985): 228–47.

Wolff, Richard J., and Jorg K. Hoensch, eds. *Catholics, the State, and the European Radical Right, 1919–1945*. Boulder: Social Science Monographs, 1987.

Wolfson, H. A. *Philo: Foundations of Religious Philosophy in Judaism, Christianity, and Islam*. 2 vols. Cambridge: Harvard University Press, 1947.

Wood, James E. "Editorial: Jewish-Christian Relations in Historical Perspective." *Journal of Church and State* 13 (spring 1971): 193–208.

———. "A Selected and Annotated Bibliography of Jewish-Christian Relations." *Journal of Church and State* 13 (spring 1971): 317–40.

Woolner, D. B., and R. G. Kurial. *FDR, the Vatican, and the Roman Catholic Church in America, 1933–1945*. New York: Palgrave Macmillan, 2003.

Wynn, Wilton. *Keepers of the Keys: John XXIII, Paul VI, and John Paul II: Three Who Changed the Church*. New York: Random House, 1988.

Yahil, Leni. *The Holocaust: The Fate of European Jewry*. New York: Oxford University Press, 1991.

Yallop, David. *In God's Name: An Investigation into the Murder of Pope John Paul I*. New York: Bentham Books, 1984.

Yates, George A., ed. *In Spirit and in Truth: Aspects of Judaism and Christianity*. London: Hodder and Stoughton, 1934.

Zahn, Gordan C. "Catholic Opposition to Hitler: The Perils of Ambiguity." *Journal of Church and State* 13 (autumn 1971): 413–25.

———. "Catholic Responses to the Holocaust." *Thought* 56 (June 1981): 153–62.

———. *German Catholics and Hitler's War*. New York: E. P. Dutton, 1969.

———. "The Unpublished Encyclical: An Opportunity Missed." *National Catholic Reporter*, 15 December 1972.

Zeender, John K. "Germany: The Catholic Church and the Nazi Regime, 1933–1945." In *Catholics, the State, and the European Radical Right, 1919–1945*, ed. Richard J. Wolff and Jorg K. Hoensch, 92–118. Boulder: Social Science Monographs, 1987.

Zeitlin, S. *Who Crucified Jesus?* New York: Block Publishing, 1964.

Zorattini, Pier Cesare Ioly, ed. *L'Identità dissimulata. Giudaizzanti iberici nell'Europa cristiana dell'età moderna*. Florence: Olschki, 2000.

Zuccotti, Susan. *The Italians and the Holocaust: Persecution, Rescue, and Survival*. New York: Basic Books, 1987.

———. *Under His Very Windows: The Vatican and the Holocaust in Italy*. New Haven: Yale University Press, 2000.

INDEX

The Papacy, the Jews, and the Holocaust was designed and composed in Minion by Kachergis Book Design of Pittsboro, North Carolina. It was printed on 50-pound Natures Natural and bound by Thomson-Shore, Dexter, Michigan.